AF361341

WRITING AND REWRITING THE REICH

# GERMAN AND EUROPEAN STUDIES

General Editor: Jennifer L. Jenkins

# Writing and Rewriting the Reich

*Women Journalists in the Nazi and Post-War Press*

DEBORAH BARTON

UNIVERSITY OF TORONTO PRESS
Toronto  Buffalo  London

ISBN 978-1-4875-4721-9 (cloth)
ISBN 978-1-4875-4722-6 (EPUB)
ISBN 978-1-4875-4736-3 (PDF)

---

**Library and Archives Canada Cataloguing in Publication**

Title: Writing and rewriting the Reich : women journalists in the Nazi and
    post-war press / Deborah Barton.
Names: Barton, Deborah (Editor), author. Series: German and European
    studies ; 48.
Description: Series statement: German and European studies ; 48 |
    Includes bibliographical references and index.
Identifiers: Canadiana (print) 20220442843 | Canadiana (ebook)
    20220442983 | ISBN 9781487547219 (cloth) | ISBN 9781487547363 (PDF) |
    ISBN 9781487547226 (EPUB)
Subjects: LCSH: Women journalists – Germany – History – 20th century. |
    LCSH: Journalism – Germany – History – 20th century. | LCSH: Press –
    Germany – History – 20th century. | LCSH: World War, 1939–1945 – Press
    coverage – Germany. | LCSH: Nazi propaganda. | LCSH: Germany –
    History – 1933–1945.
Classification: LCC PN5214.W58 B37 2023 | DDC 070.082 – dc23

---

The German and European Studies series is funded by the DAAD with
funds from the German Federal Foreign Office

University of Toronto Press acknowledges the financial assistance to its
publishing program of the Canada Council for the Arts and the Ontario
Arts Council, an agency of the Government of Ontario.

*For Graham*

# Contents

# Illustrations

# Acknowledgments

Historians (and journalists) are trained to bring stories and the past to life through words. Yet I find that words are insufficient to express my gratitude to the many brilliant and generous people who helped me publish this book. At the University of Toronto, I benefited enormously from the knowledge and encouragement of Doris Bergen. Her advice and insights have shaped this work and my academic trajectory more than I could ever express. I am also grateful for the time, support, and counsel that Lynne Viola and Jennifer Jenkins provided. Keir Waddington, James Ryan, Jasmine Kilburn-Toppin, and Bronach Kane made my time at Cardiff University fulfilling and productive, and I thank them for their support and their friendship. My experience at the University of Glasgow was equally important to the development of this project thanks to Mathilde von Bülow and Peter Jackson. I am especially grateful to Alex Marshall, who read several chapters of this manuscript and provided invaluable suggestions throughout the process. Thank you to Jamie Doherty for your friendship, humour, and unrivalled ability to turn a good phrase. At the Université de Montréal, I have had the pleasure of working with wonderful colleagues and friends who have listened, advised, and provided unwavering moral support. A special thank you to Susan Dalton, Laurence Monnais, Helen Dewar, David Merren, and Thomas Wien. You've helped make the Université de Montréal home.

Many dear friends and colleagues have enriched this project. Fabien Theofilakis has been a staunch cheerleader, a partner in several academic ventures, and a mentor and friend for many years. His feedback on the structure of the book solved several problems in one shot. Lilia Topouzova's moral support and friendship have sustained me from the time we first met at the University of Toronto. Her scholarship and commitment to effect positive change through history and teaching are an inspiration. Erin Hochmann has been a constant source of counsel and friendship. Her suggestions related to the introduction of the book were invaluable. My deep gratitude to Julie Ault, Jennifer Lynn, Willeke Sandler, Lauren Stokes, and Kira Thurman, who read and commented on several chapters of this book. Your astute questions and perceptive insights were indispensable; your encouragement priceless. Throughout the process of researching and writing, I have benefited from the friendship and support of Rebecca Carter-Chand, Alex Reisenbichler, Tom Haakenson, Jacob Eder, and Colin Lang. Thank you to Anne Zetsche for your enthusiasm for the project and for making Berlin special.

My research was possible only through the generous assistance of many archivists and librarians. Thanks are due to the staff of the Bundesarchiv Berlin, Koblenz and Freiburg; the Archiv der Akademie der Künste, the Landesarchiv, the Deutsches Historisches Museum, the Staatsbibliothek, and the Archiv des Auswärtigen Amtes, in Berlin; the Institut für Zeitgeschichte in Munich; the Deutsches Literaturarchiv in Marbach; the Staatsarchiv Bremen; and the Staatsarchiv Ludwigsburg. Thanks also to the archivists at Yad Vashem, Israel; the Jagiellonian University Archives and the Biblioteka Jagiellońska, Kraków, Poland; the British National Archives, London; the Central State Archives, Ukraine; the Library of Congress and the United States Holocaust Memorial Museum, in Washington, DC.

Generous support for my research and writing came from the Berlin Program for Advanced German and European Studies at the Freie Universität, the Deutscher Akademischer Austauschdienst (DAAD), the Social Sciences and Humanities Research Council, Canada (SSHRC), the Joint Initiative in German and European Studies (JIGES), and the history departments at the University of Toronto, the University of Glasgow, and the Université de Montréal. The suggestions and feedback I received at various conferences greatly improved this book. Thanks in particular to the Centre for Gender Studies, Glasgow, the American Historical Association, the German History Society, Uppsala University, the Universität Trier, the Freie Universität Berlin, the John F. Kennedy Institute for North American Studies, the Russian Academy of Sciences, and Women in German. I am grateful for the outstanding work of the team at the University of Toronto Press and, in particular, my brilliant editor Stephen Shapiro, whose feedback and direction made the publishing process a pleasure. I have been fortunate to work with incredible students at Cardiff University, the University of Glasgow, and the Université de Montréal. Their curiosity and thoughtful questions reinforced to me why the study of journalism is so important, past and present.

Thank you to my parents; my sister, Janell; and my in-laws, Joan, Tony, and Chris Barton. You believed in and supported me throughout the entire process, and I could not ask for a more caring family. Finally, my deepest, ongoing love and gratitude go to my late husband, Graham Barton. He encouraged me from the start, picked me up when I wanted to give up, made me laugh even at the worst of times, and inspired me with his strength, dignity, and kindness. Graham made me promise that I would finish what I started in the archives several years ago. I dedicate this book to him.

# Abbreviations

| | |
|---|---|
| BDM | Bund Deutscher Mädel (League of German Girls) |
| *BT* | *Berliner Tageblatt* |
| DAI | Deutsches Ausland-Institut (German Institute Abroad) |
| *DAZ* | *Deutsche Allgemeine Zeitung* |
| DNB | Deutsches Nachrichtenbüro (German News Agency) |
| DVP | Deutsche Volkspartei (German People's Party) |
| DEFA | Deutsche Film Aktiengesellschaft (East German Film Company) |
| *FAZ* | *Frankfurter Allgemeine Zeitung* |
| FDJ | Freie Deutsche Jugend (Free German Youth) |
| FRG | Federal Republic of Germany |
| *FZ* | *Frankfurter Zeitung* |
| GDR | German Democratic Republic |
| ICD | Information Control Division |
| IDO | Institute für Deutsche Ostarbeit (Institute for German Eastern Studies) |
| KLV | Kinderlandverschickung |
| KPD | Kommunistische Partei Deutschlands (Communist Party of Germany) |
| *KZ* | *Krakauer Zeitung* |
| NSDAP | Nationalsozialistische Deutsche Arbeiterpartei (National Socialist German Workers' Party) |
| NSF | Nationalsozialistische Frauenschaft (National Socialist Women's League) |
| RDP | Reichsverband der Deutschen Presse (German Press Association) |
| RKK | Reichskulturkammer (Reich Culture Chamber) |
| RMVP | Reichsministerium für Volksaufklärung und Propaganda (Reich Ministry for Public Enlightenment and Propaganda) |
| SA | Sturmabteilung (Storm Troopers) |
| SBZ | Sowjetische Besatzungszone (Soviet Occupation Zone) |

SED    Sozialistische Einheitspartei Deutschlands (Socialist Unity Party of Germany)
SPD    Sozialdemokratische Partei Deutschlands (Social Democratic Party of Germany)
SS     Schutzstaffel
VAP    Verein der Ausländischen Presse in Deutschland (Association of the Foreign Press in Germany)
VDA    Volksbund für das Deutschtum im Ausland (People's League of Germandon Abroad)
VDP    Verband der Deutschen Presse (German Press Association)

WRITING AND REWRITING THE REICH

# Introduction

In 1937, journalistic hopeful Ursula von Kardorff landed her first internship at the Nazi Party paper *Der Angriff*. By 1939, she was a permanent staff member on the prominent paper the *Deutsche Allgemeine Zeitung*, where she wrote for the features and "women's" sections. Kardorff described her position on the paper as one that brought her tremendous pleasure and gratification. She prized her career, in spite of the limitations that women faced in the male-dominated field and the controlled nature of the Nazi press, which demanded that journalists act as the regime's mouthpiece. Through her writing, Kardorff fulfilled important press and propaganda goals for the Nazi regime. Prior to and during the war, she published soft news articles that provided humour, entertainment, and morale building for Germany's population, in particular its women. After the war, Kardorff justified her activity in service to the Nazi state by offering a contorted version of her journalistic work within the National Socialist system. In an effort to clean up her past and downplay her contribution to Nazi propaganda, she added the following passage in her diary: "So this is the end of six years' work. I hope that during those years I never sold out to the Promi [Propaganda Ministry] and that I never wrote anything opposed to my convictions. Anyhow, I had the good fortune to be working in features, which saved me from having to do a lot of unpleasant things."[1] By signalling that she did not have to write about "unpleasant things," Kardorff implied that her journalistic work within features was apolitical and far removed from Nazi ideology.

Kardorff was able to continue her successful career after the collapse of the Third Reich, writing for the features section of the US-licensed, democratic paper the *Süddeutsche Zeitung*. In addition to being a prominent journalist, she became well known both inside and outside of Germany thanks to the publication of her book *Diary of a Nightmare: Berlin,*

*1942–1945* (*Berliner Aufzeichnungen, 1942–1945*), published in German in 1962 and English in 1966.[2] The book recounted her experiences during the war and was widely celebrated as an authentic portrayal of everyday life in the last years of the Third Reich. As Kardorff intended, the book served as an effective tool to distance herself from Nazi propaganda, improve Germany's post-war reputation, and contribute to a positive self-identity among the German population.

This book covers the period from the beginning of the Third Reich through the emergence of the Cold War and division of Germany to the end of the Allied military occupation in 1955. By addressing the long-term impact of women journalists' diaries and memoirs on the memory culture of Germany, it moves into the present day. It tells the story of Kardorff and a cohort of female journalists and photojournalists, who, like her, established a career in the Nazi press, enjoyed the benefits that came with the status of "journalist," and then refashioned those experiences in the post-war period to their own and Germany's benefit. I argue that women journalists were important to Nazi press and propaganda goals, despite being severely underrepresented in the field. Press officials valued female journalists, based on the belief that they could write in a more emotional, colourful, and amusing manner than men. They viewed women's journalism as way to influence the public, specifically German women, through charm and subtlety, rather than through the militant language that dominated much of the press. Accordingly, press authorities sought to relegate women to such soft-news domains as features, local news, travel, and, most commonly, the women's sections of newspapers, which were typically composed of fashion, domestic news, self-help articles, and serial novels. Although not prestigious, these soft-news sections were among the most popular parts of the newspaper for women and men alike and formed a central component of the Nazi propaganda platform: such material presented a *gemütliche* version of Nazism and helped to insulate Germans from its terror and destruction. In this way, the work of women journalists afforded them a form of soft power far more significant than their limited numbers would suggest.

At the same time, due to the deep sexism inherent within, although not specific to, the Nazi system, women journalists faced many obstacles in their chosen field and rarely obtained a position of authority or prominence within the press. The notion of women's importance and their simultaneous marginalization influenced women's careers throughout the Nazi period. But, as I argue, it was precisely the ambiguous position of women journalists as both insiders and outsiders within the field during the Third Reich that helped facilitate their transition to the post-war press and influenced their ability to obtain new positions and become spokespersons on behalf of the new Germany(s).

After the Second World War, many women journalists adopted a line similar to Kardorff's and claimed that their focus on "soft" news and/or their status as women meant that their work had been apolitical. For the few women who had reported in more overt political and other hard-news domains, evoking gender still proved an exculpatory strategy. They could emphasize their own subordination within the male-dominated press and could argue that they were victims of a misogynistic regime. Presenting themselves as an important part of the press, but also as outsiders, allowed women journalists to emphasize their professional success and skills, but claim that they were not closely connected to Nazi propaganda. Nazi rhetoric, which maintained that women functioned outside of the political realm, aided them in this claim, and the western Allies largely accepted the notion that many women journalists were less compromised than most men by Nazism. After all, women journalists in the United States, Britain, and France were also clustered in the lower-prestige areas of soft news and typically wrote about seemingly harmless topics related to everyday life and the private sphere. Assumptions about the apolitical nature of women's writing opened up professional opportunities for German women immediately after the war and helped ensure that the Allies and the German public viewed female journalists as legitimate voices when it came to fashioning and promoting a particular memory of Nazism and its repercussions that suited the now divided country's contemporary needs. This, in turn, gave women journalists an ongoing but ambiguous influence in the construction of German post-war identity.

*Writing and Rewriting the Reich* centres on the contention that the convergence of need and opportunity in the critical domain of the media meant that those on the margins of power became complicit in the very exercise of that power. Women journalists occupied a position under the Nazi dictatorship that embodies what Michael Rothberg has termed "implicated subjects." While not "direct agents of harm," they inhabited, contributed to, and benefited from a repressive regime to different extents, even if they did not occupy positions of power or control within that regime.[3] While there is no female equivalent to Nazi press chief Otto Dietrich, the prominent publisher and vicious antisemite Julius Streicher, or the famous war correspondent Hans Schwarz van Berk, women journalists, as this book reveals, were entangled in the hegemonies of power and oppression in Nazi Germany as both actors and objects. Situated on the peripheries of the journalistic profession yet important to it, such women disrupt the binary categories traditionally used to describe individuals living under repressive regimes – victim and perpetrator, bystander and beneficiary. Women in the press could find themselves in more than one category simultaneously or move between them at any given point, depending on where and with whom they worked. Female journalists contributed to Nazi news and propaganda via a variety of genres and to varying extents. Some affirmed the aggressive policies of the regime in a more direct and malevolent fashion than others. Regardless of the nature of their journalism, however, they all experienced the duality of professional subjugation and possibility. While they faced numerous roadblocks in their career progression, were often dependent on male patrons, and endured hostility from male authorities, editors, and colleagues, they also enjoyed a range of opportunities that both diverged from and overlapped with the experiences of men, especially during the war.

This dissonance makes the study of women journalists important to our understanding of the complex relationship between power and gender in Germany and helps us reassess some of the most salient issues in the field: the functioning of press in the Third Reich and a post-war divided Germany; the diversity of Nazi propaganda and the malleability of what constituted the "political" in the Third Reich; the scope for agency under repressive, patriarchal regimes; continuity and ruptures of gender roles across the 1945 divide; and historical memory. The book also contributes to a broader understanding of gender and journalism in the twentieth century and helps shed light on how women expanded the notion of what constituted news, how and why their careers took a particular shape and direction, and the nature of their contributions to the profession under authoritarian and democratic systems.

Based on data collected on 1,500 women – some prominent but most unknown – in over a dozen German and other European archives, this book recovers the individual stories, careers, and activities of female journalists across three political systems and shows the diversity of their experiences and of their contributions to the Nazi press. I utilize a range of archival sources, such as press-school exams, press membership records, personnel files, editorial proceedings, and personal correspondence, as well as newspapers, photographs, and unpublished and published diaries and memoirs. Layering personal accounts and public writing by female journalists with government records about them allows me to demonstrate the full extent of women's involvement in the press, one that was not acknowledged at the time or in subsequent scholarship. Press association records point to the desexualized or masculinized pseudonyms that some women employed in their reporting and render their work visible despite the fact that it was hidden behind a gender screen. Personal accounts, including memoirs and edited diaries, are, of course, subject to the intentions and biases of the writer, as well as the failings of memory, whether intentional or unintentional. I analyse the ways in which an individual's personal presentation would benefit them at the time of publication, compare and contrast various personal accounts to tease out their veracity, and align personal narratives with official documents to obtain an accurate picture of the role of women journalists in Nazi Germany and the first post-war decade.

Although this book focuses on female journalists and photojournalists who worked in print, it is important to note that women contributed in various ways to all forms of media in Nazi Germany. Cinema was an especially vital propaganda tool for the government. As a cheap form of entertainment, movies allowed the regime to connect with the population on a broad scale. Through a range of genres, films provided indoctrination, escapism, cultural diversity, and news, all of which was intended to promote and uphold National Socialism.[4] While women worked in the film industry as actresses, editors, or in behind-the-scenes positions, they rarely worked as directors, a role that arguably is most closely connected with the production of Nazi propaganda. The notable exception is, of course, Leni Riefenstahl, the regime's most famous propagandist. The case of Riefenstahl highlights how, in unique cases, women could manoeuvre into powerful positions and find success in the public domain while promoting the hyper-masculine image on which the Nazi movement prided itself. Hitler admired Riefenstahl's work and selected her to be his director for such prominent films as *Triumph of the Will* (1935), which showcased the 1934 Party Congress in Nuremberg, an overwhelming male gathering, and *Olympia* (1938), Riefenstahl's vision of the 1936 Berlin Olympics. As Susan Tegel argues, Riefenstahl's films "showed the Nazis as they wished to be seen" and, in return, she enjoyed a prominent position in the industry, the likes of which women in other fields could rarely obtain.[5] No woman working in print journalism in Germany, for instance, reached the height of power and influence that Riefenstahl held, although in many ways they too described life in the Third Reich as the regime wished it to be seen.

Radio came of age in the early 1920s and hit its stride in the 1930s. Like film, the medium proved an important propaganda tool for the Nazi regime. Radio offered light entertainment, cultural, and scientific programs, as well as news and current affairs. And, of course, it broadcast music, which constituted 69 per cent of programming by the mid-1930s, a proportion that increased during the war.[6] In Nazi Germany, radio, like the press and cinema, was centralized, and policy decisions were made by the Ministry of Propaganda. Housewives were a particular target of radio propaganda, and the Nazi *Frauenfunk* (women's radio programming) focused most of its attention on practical advice programs for the wife and mother at the expense of cultural affairs programs or those aimed at working women.[7] A typical weekly schedule for women's radio programming in 1937 included programs with titles such as "Caring for Your Lawn and Flowers"; "Make Your Life Easier: Practical Household Tips"; "People Make the Clothes and Clothes Make the People"; and "This Week's Shopping List."[8] Like the press, the importance of radio and cinema increased during the war, as both provided news from the front, as well as morale-building and escapist material.

Despite some crossover between the function of cinema, radio, and the press, and those who worked within these media, this book centres on print journalism, since it offered different roles and, arguably, a greater range of opportunities for women than did radio or film. For example, while women did write screenplays, doing so did not necessarily provide them with a consistent voice in the public realm, or with opportunities for travel and to interact with prominent individuals in the political, social, and/or cultural arena, to the same degree that some women in the press enjoyed. Likewise, a few women journalists toggled between work in print and radio, but evidence suggests that in radio they had little scope to work outside of daytime programs targeting women and children.[9] While communicating with Germany's women was what press authorities envisioned as the primary task of female journalists, this book demonstrates that the press afforded women more diversity in their reporting and some flexibility to move outside of the areas traditionally deemed a woman's realm.

## The Intersection of Journalism and Gender

A rich body of scholarship has helped us understand how the Nazi regime restructured the press, the controls it implemented to harness it for its own purposes, and the opportunities such steps opened up for politically and "racially" acceptable journalists.[10] The regime viewed the press as the main arm through which to influence the population and garner support for its increasingly violent social and political goals. This book uncovers women's place within these processes and the function of their work in National Socialist Germany. It demonstrates that the regime was not only concerned with control and repression of the press, but equally focused on building a loyal cohort of journalists that included women. While there is a small body of work that examines

German women journalists – generally, biographies of high-profile figures – such scholarship has focused primarily on the limitations they faced or cast them as an anomaly within the Nazi state.[11] The historiographical concentration on the under-representation of women in the field and the gendered roadblocks they faced downplays the soft power that women held in the Nazi press, veils the complexity of their roles, and underestimates the privileges the profession granted. The 1920s and 1930s marked the birth of a new mass media culture on a global scale, which advanced states sought to appropriate and employ as a form of soft power to pursue their political goals. Germany was at the very centre of this growth, and the Third Reich represented one of the most modern mass media societies of its time.[12] The interwar years marked a period when journalists, men and women alike, obtained an ever-increasing social and cultural capital.[13]

In many ways, the career trajectories of women journalists in Nazi Germany mirrored those of their counterparts in other western countries. The newspaper industry's desire to attract female readers from the late nineteenth century onwards provided an avenue for women to enter the profession on both sides of the Atlantic, but employers and colleagues viewed them primarily through the lens of gender. I use Joan Scott's analysis of gender as a relational category "based on perceived differences between the sexes." Gender, as Scott determines, is a cultural construct centred on dichotomous stereotypes of what is considered masculine and feminine and constitutes a "primary way of signifying relationships of power."[14] *Writing and Rewriting the Reich* underscores the importance that gender plays in affirming and defending a "natural" hierarchy within the press. It highlights the ways in which the institution itself and the roles of those within it were driven largely by long-standing practices and ideas pertaining to masculinity and femininity, rather than simply Nazi gender ideology.

While the field positioned male journalists as rational, detached, and bold, characteristics that aligned with hard-hitting political news, women were associated with the private sphere and assumed to embody such "feminine" attributes as emotionality, softness, and intuitiveness. As media scholars and historians such as Deborah Chambers, Linda Steiner, Carole Fleming, and Kay Mills have demonstrated, the patriarchal framework of the profession in the West ensured that women journalists were valued specifically as women and expected to write on soft-news issues pertaining to everyday life in the private sphere.[15] If gender functioned as a primary marker of difference in the Nazi press, it did so in democratic systems as well.

But the experiences, role, and perceived utility of German women journalists are more complex than they appear on the surface. Opportunities open to journalists were not based entirely on a static and binary gender formulation. Unlike other professions, such as academia, there were no official constraints on women in journalism throughout the course of the Third Reich. Based on desire and need, Nazi press authorities created pathways for women to enter the profession from 1933 onward. Press authorities encouraged women to pursue journalism, and, beginning with their earliest training, strove to ensure that they felt a valued part of the institution. Although they remained firmly in the minority, women constituted a larger percentage of the press under the Nazi regime than they had during the Weimar Republic, and their presence in the field continued to grow.[16] In 1935, they accounted for only 5 per cent of working journalists; by 1939, they represented close to 9 per cent. During the war, their proportion grew to 11 per cent, as male journalists were called up for military duty.[17] Yet, it was not just increasing possibilities that attracted women to the field.

The status of journalist gave Ursula von Kardorff and her female colleagues a sense of empowerment and of being socially and politically relevant in an overtly misogynistic state. In addition, the profession offered women benefits such as mobility, flexibility, intellectual stimulation, contact with prominent individuals, and access to material goods throughout the 1930s. During the war, these perks became ever more appealing, as women stepped into positions vacated by male colleagues departing for the frontlines. Whether on the home front or in German-occupied Europe, female journalists were in a position to avoid some of the hardships of the war to a greater degree than other segments of the population. Permits, for instance, allowed those working within Germany to travel to regions less affected by bombings or wartime privations to pursue stories. Like German soldiers, women working in occupied Europe enjoyed the benefits of German plunder and obtained luxuries unavailable to much of the home-front population. Some women later described this period as one of professional inclusion, emancipation, and accomplishment. As Thea Fischer recalled of her wartime experiences, "Despite everything, it was a beautiful time."[18]

The experiences of women journalists help us better understand the efficacy and appeal of Nazism and highlight why some Germans continued to think fondly of the Third Reich, despite its crimes, long after its collapse.[19] Nazism was based on inclusion and exclusion: the persecution of certain segments of the population converged with increased privileges for others. Although they were challenged by its inherent sexism, women journalists still benefited from the Nazi system. Historians have shown us that Germans aspired to the sense of belonging and collective identity embodied by the *Volksgemeinschaft* (people's community) and demonstrated how this desire for community founded on racial inclusion and exclusion helped facilitate mass persecution and murder.[20] Their inclusion into the elite body of the press, the esteemed identity of journalist, and anticipated career advantages helped pull women journalists into political service to the state.

The role and importance of female journalists also highlight the malleability of Nazi gender policy, which afforded women some capacity to negotiate the system to their own benefit and helps us see how male and female experiences diverged and overlapped in Nazi Germany. Over the past several decades, historians of gender and Nazism have looked at the different ways in which women participated in the Third Reich and have discounted the long-standing notion that they were restricted primarily to the private sphere, as Nazi ideology insisted.[21] The German state required women's inclusion in various sectors of the labour market, particularly as it increased its efforts to orient the economy toward the preparation for war with the 1936 four-year-plan. And, as this book contends, the gap between gender rhetoric and reality in Nazi Germany was – for a privileged few – even wider than scholars have realized. Nazi ideology allowed some space for young, single women to contribute to the workforce before marriage, primarily in the domains of factory and office work. Yet as press authorities emphasized, journalism offered both married and single women the chance not simply to obtain a job, but to build a career in this most important public domain.

While women's writing largely upheld traditional gender roles, there was a tension between this aspect of their work and the lifestyles some led. As they photographed and wrote about German woman fulfilling such "feminine" tasks as caring for children, keeping a proper home, or working in appropriate jobs, they themselves enjoyed a cosmopolitan lifestyle and level of independence that most women did not. Press authorities positioned journalism as a political profession and used a masculine and militarized language to describe the role of those working with in the field. Journalists were, for instance, "fighters for the new state."[22] During the war, they were "soldiers at their posts," whose job was to "build the Westwall of the [population's] soul."[23] The German Press Association told journalism candidates that they must have characteristics traditionally coded as masculine, including physical and mental vigor, broad shoulders on which to carry their responsibility toward the state, unflappable nerves, and resilience.[24] Paradoxically, authorities also counselled that it was precisely women's supposed feminine traits – compassion, sensitivity, curiosity, and malleability –

that would lead to success in the field.[25] As a result, women journalists had to negotiate the complicated identity of being women and being good journalists.

## Power and Propaganda

*Writing and Rewriting the Reich* asks what gender tells us about the production of Nazi propaganda. While women were subordinated in the press, journalism still afforded them a form of soft power and greater responsibility in the public domain than did most fields. Soft power in journalism relates to material that is persuasive specifically because it appears to be non-coercive.[26] In the Third Reich, this meant the production of news that did not seem to speak with the voice of the regime. Women were tasked primarily with shaping public opinion through appeal and attraction rather than through coercion.

Due to the efforts of various scholars, we know that the regime placed importance on the contentment of the German population within their everyday lives and that it created spaces for private pleasures.[27] Media content seemingly free of Nazi ideology played a significant role in these processes. This book enriches our understanding of this phenomenon by examining *who* the regime tasked with creating the lived experience of normality for the population and how they did so. Throughout the Third Reich, the German language became more aggressive and militaristic, with metaphors for battle in all areas of life as the regime mobilized language for war. By writing feel-good stories focused on private pleasures, the work of women journalists such as Kardorff helped provide Germans with a sense of continuity and normality despite the repressiveness of the dictatorship and, later, the deprivations of war.

Nazi policy and practice that channelled most female journalists into soft-news fields were not unique. During the Weimar Republic, women had been able to make gains in journalism. Although some did write for political papers, most were confined to women's news and human-interest stories, as were their female colleagues in North America and Europe. Scholars such as Alice Fahs, Deborah Chambers, and Carole Fleming have noted that women helped expand the notion of what was considered newsworthy by their focus on the everyday and their concentration on human-interest stories.[28] While women in Nazi Germany worked in these same areas, the function of their work differed. Specific to journalism in the Third Reich was the regime's intent to maintain a sense of pleasure and normality in the everyday, to give the impression that there was a private sphere not entirely dominated by the state, and to act as a counterbalance to the repressive nature of the regime. Yet by writing about the seemingly banal, women journalists also had a role to play in supporting the regime's more overt political ambitions. By acting as the regime's conduit to the female population, they were to educate German women in Nazi ideals and school them on how to shop, save, cook, keep house, and work, all in support of Hitler's regime and its military ambitions.[29] Moreover, articles on relationships, the family, or even fashion underscored the concept of a *Volksgemeinschaft* founded on the exclusion and eventual persecution of those the regime labelled racial, social, or political degenerates.[30] Such pieces were political in their effects, if not in their designation. In this manner, press authorities strove to utilize women journalists for a role that was political in nature but was most often depicted as outside the realm of traditional politics.

In spite of the desire of press officials and editors to restrict women journalists to soft-news realms, German women had some latitude to cross gender demarcations and establish careers in the typically male domain of hard news and foreign politics, just as they did in other countries. In these genres, their experiences and writing mirrored more closely the traditional, masculinized image of what constituted journalism and a journalist. Press authorities privileged talent and perceived utility to the needs of the state above gender. Julie Edwards has demonstrated that female journalists in the United States obtained overseas jobs by arguing that they could deliver more sensitive reports than those of male journalists and provide a woman's point of view.[31] In Nazi Germany, the role of foreign correspondent drew women more directly – or allowed them to push their way – into advocacy of Nazi expansionism and racial persecution. Scholars have shown that Germans were receptive to Hitler's foreign policy successes in the 1930s, which went a long way to build loyalty toward the regime. This book integrates women's contributions into our understanding of these processes.[32] Women journalists worked as foreign correspondents and covered all manner of geopolitical affairs for the Nazi press in a way that helped promote the regime's foreign policy goals and *Weltanschauung*. From articles criticizing alleged British dominance in the League of Nations to pieces designed to align neutral countries with Germany in the event of war, a small group of women contributed to the intellectual framework for Nazi ideas of *Lebensraum* and a new world order. These women are important, but neglected, figures in the study of the press's promotion of Nazi imperialist goals.

Just as they contributed to news about international affairs, some women journalists produced racial propaganda for the regime, which helped promote the categories of internal and external racial enemies and friends – a discourse that would have grave repercussions after 1939. Scholars have pointed to the importance the regime placed on antisemitic and anti-Soviet propaganda and to its efficacy, which built on long-standing stereotypes.[33] Far from being removed from such vitriol, women journalists contributed to it in a particular manner: they blended hard, soft, and tabloidesque news that functioned to demonstrate the purported Jewish and Bolshevik threat to the German population and justify Nazi aggression toward these adversaries. They did so in a way that editors hoped would attract a readership that, while perhaps not inclined toward the vicious headlines produced by the likes of *Der Stürmer*, was still open to Nazi racial thinking. Such material helped lay the groundwork for the violence that the regime would perpetrate throughout the Second World War.

A fruitful and growing body of scholarship examines how women contributed to National Socialist violence.[34] By building on such studies, this book deepens and complicates our understanding of women's complicity in processes of persecution. Although not perpetrating or advocating violence themselves, women, through their journalism, both veiled and beautified processes of violence within and outside the borders of Germany. Since military authorities often denied them access to the frontlines, women journalists in the West pioneered a more human-centric approach to war reporting. They developed new angles that focused less on military developments and more on civilian suffering.[35] While German women journalists rarely reported on military actions, they did write material that supported and justified German hegemony in occupied Europe. By capitalizing on career possibilities within Germany and occupied Europe, women journalists became agents and beneficiaries of the systematic violence their writing both downplayed and praised.

**Gender and the Post-War Press**

Despite the ways in which women journalists helped to buttress the Nazi state, the experiences they acquired within the Nazi press, together with the ambiguity of their roles – situated on the margins of the field but nevertheless important to it – bore fruit in the post-war years. Scholars have discussed how gender ideology and the expectations placed on women acted as a marker of differentiation between the two regions of Germany, the democratic West and the socialist East.[36] Immediately after the war, the Western Zones, and then Federal Republic of Germany (FRG), led a concerted effort to re-establish the traditional family at the heart of society. Women's primary role was envisaged to be in the home, as a wife and mother. Although, in reality, women worked outside the home, they were generally clustered in lower-skilled and lower-paid positions. In contrast, the Eastern Zone, and, after 1949, the German Democratic Republic (GDR), encouraged and expected women's participation in the workforce. Socialist theory considered full-time labor as a precondition for women's economic autonomy, integration into the economy and society, and thus their ultimate emancipation. Like their counterparts in the FRG, however, women in East Germany worked largely in lower-skilled and lower-paid positions.[37]

Tracing the careers of women journalists from 1933 to 1955, and eschewing the typical 1945 temporal divide, brings to light not only the similarities and differences in gender relations between East and West Germany but also demonstrates that gender continuities between pre- and post-1945 Germany were deeply entrenched in the field of journalism. Even with early opportunities open to women, journalism in all four zones of Germany remained male-dominated, especially after the Allies abandoned their denazification efforts and male journalists returned to the field in increasing numbers. Female journalists in both East and West Germany found themselves once again largely restricted to culture and the women's pages. Much like the Nazi regime, western press authorities labelled these areas apolitical, while the East tied them explicitly to politics. But women journalists in both regions became actors in promoting the political agendas of two competing systems and ideologies, each seeking to position itself as the legitimate postwar German state. Their writing functioned to critique the polices of the "other" Germany, most notably with regard to its handling of the repercussions of the war. Women journalists' visibility in the public realm meant that they became entangled in political affairs, regardless of whether the Allies or they themselves deemed their work political. Some found themselves vulnerable to the risks – surveillance, control, arrest – that characterized the Cold War environment their very writing helped to create.

## Historical Memory and the Legacies of Nazism

Individuals, institutions, and societies establish identities and an understanding of themselves through the narratives they create about both the present and the past. Such discourses evolve to suit contemporary needs. After 1945, a small group of women journalists who settled in what would become West Germany successfully employed their gender, profession, and experiences under the Third Reich to refashion the

Nazi past to suit not only their own personal and professional rehabilitation but also that of the young Federal Republic itself.

For West Germans, an important part of rebuilding involved constructing what Robert Moeller has termed "a usable past" – a narrative about the war and its associated crimes that allowed the population to repress memories of German atrocities and privilege its own suffering.[38] A diverse body of scholarship emerged in the West German public sphere after the war on both the narrative of victimization and the jagged process the country took to "come to terms with its past."[39] This book uncovers the important role that a small group of female journalists played in the process of providing a positive post-war identity for the FRG and, later, a reunified Germany.

Thanks to their best-selling diaries and memoirs, four women had a particularly powerful voice in the fashioning and durability of West Germany's post-war image, which was founded on the dual notions of decency and victimhood. As female journalists, they could claim either that they had not contributed to Nazi political discourse or that they had been victims of the regime due to their gender. As journalists, they had the contacts necessary to publish their work and the skills to write in a manner that audiences viewed largely as objective and authentic. They provided a feel-good narrative that evoked the notion of a "good" Germany that had suffered under the Nazi regime and yet had heroically sought to aid the persecuted. Such a discourse suited the needs of the German population as well as their new (Western) allies, in particular the United States, in the midst of rising Cold War tensions. The women accurately viewed their work as testimony that would, as journalist Ruth Andreas-Friedrich wrote, "help to raise the German people a hairsbreadth from its present low degree."[40] Their writing was lauded inside and outside of the country as reflecting a respectable Germany, and it helped create and maintain the country's "usable" past.

This discourse, however, was relevant only to West Germany. While, in the FRG, the Western allies gradually ceded control of the post-war press to the Germans, in the GDR, the media became an arm of the state and was tightly controlled. Women journalists living West Germany were able to publish personal narratives that served to distance themselves and the population from Nazism and offer tales of suffering at the hands of the Nazi regime and, later, the Allied occupation force, especially the Soviets. These two elements were central to the narrative that emerged in West Germany about the Nazi past and its repercussions. Women who had continued their journalism careers in East Germany did not have access to such narratives. The GDR characterized the war as an anti-fascist struggle whose main victims were communists, a discourse that left no room for the narratives of resistance and suffering among the general population that dominated the West German public domain.

## Chapter Overview

Structured both chronologically and thematically, this book addresses several interrelated themes: chapters 1–5 tackle the fluid nature of what the population and the regime considered political and apolitical during the Third Reich; the varied nature of propaganda in the press; the relationship between gender, agency, privilege, and complicity in processes of persecution and violence; and the appeal of National Socialism. Chapters 6 and 7 address continuity and rupture within the journalistic profession and gender politics, the processes of denazification, and the memory of Nazism in the public sphere.

Chapter 1 looks at how Nazi press authorities created a class of professional women, from their training onward, to suit the state's needs and analyses how women's experiences both resembled and differed from those of their male colleagues. Chapter 2 examines the nature of women's roles and writing in the soft-news domains prior to the Second World War and the type of soft power this afforded. It highlights women journalists' contribution to sustaining the regime through a focus on everyday life that positioned it as separate from the racial and police state. With an emphasis on foreign correspondents, chapter 3 also focuses largely on the pre-war years and concentrates on women who worked outside of the traditional realm that press authorities dictated as appropriate for women. Such women reported on a variety of geopolitical events and/or produced articles that underscored Nazi thinking about "race" and space. The convergence between the needs of the state and professional ambition and capacity allowed a small group of women to cover international news in a manner that helped support and promote Hitler's geopolitical and ideological goals. Chapter 4 analyses the influence of women journalists on the home front during the war, while chapter 5 concentrates on their work in occupied Europe. Together, they demonstrate how the writing of female journalists engaged with military actions, wartime atrocities, and violence. Their work buttressed the Nazi state and helped legitimate the German occupation of several European countries. As they engaged in such reporting, female journalists enjoyed autonomy, travel, and professional fulfilment. Chapters 6 and 7 concentrate on the post-war period. Chapter 6 covers these women's transition to the post-war press and analyses how they were affected by, and contributed to, the developing Cold War relationship between the two Germanys. Chapter 7 examines how the autobiographical writing of a small group of women journalists helped shape and sustain a distorted memory of the Third Reich that served the West German state in the decades after the war.

Ursula von Kardorff's career spanned five decades. Her claim that she had not been entangled with Nazi propaganda helped propel her from a journalist whose writing, by default or intention, contributed to the support of the Nazi regime to a respected post-war figure working on one of the most esteemed liberal newspapers founded after 1945. She was not alone. In the Nazi and post-war decades, German women journalists such as Kardorff played a disproportionate role in the maintenance of the state. They served as professional functionaries who helped preserve the National Socialist dictatorship and then refashioned their experiences to help post-war Germany find its footing after 1945. Their writing became a vehicle for the dissemination of politics in various forms – sometimes masquerading as entertainment or personal histories – and for different purposes: maintaining a totalitarian regime and, later, supporting the building of a democratic and socialist state. Located on the outskirts of power, these women became important agents in the exercise of that power.

# PART I

# The Pre-War Years, 1933–1939

## Chapter One

# On the Peripheries of Power:
# Women Journalists in the Nazi Press

In November 1933, as the National Socialist regime expelled Jewish and politically left-leaning journalists from the press, the *Münchner Neueste Nachrichten* published an article titled "Women as Journalists." It told the story of the late British newspaper magnate Lord Northcliffe, who believed that women made ideal journalists. According to Northcliff, since women were tenacious, observant, and possessed an abundance of compassion, their writing could easily appeal to a reader's emotions.[1] The article went on to imply that Northcliffe soon learned an unfortunate but important lesson: women were not suitable for all aspects of journalism. A paper that he had founded, and on which he employed primarily female journalists, had failed miserably. Women, he discovered, were competent to handle the "lighter side of news," but roles with more responsibilities "simply exceed their capabilities. Their sex has its limits," he concluded.[2] For Northcliff, and ostensibly the editor of the *Münchner Neueste Nachrichten*, the lesson was clear: women were an important part of the press, but only in roles "appropriate" for their gender and certainly not in such high-profile positions as editors.

The article, published just months after the Nazi regime came to power, provides insight into the complex experiences of women journalists in Nazi Germany and their position as both insiders and outsiders. Press authorities needed and wanted women in the field. From 1933 onward, they encouraged women to view journalism as a viable profession. Official communication assured women that they represented a vital part of the comradeship (*Kameradschaft*) of the press. In turn, women enjoyed the opportunities, benefits, and status the profession offered. There were no official policies against women's inclusion and progression in the field, but long-standing cultural and professional norms, gendered ideas about the capabilities and roles of men and women, together with the wishes of Nazi press authorities, largely restricted women to particular genres: culture, local news, features, and especially the so-called women's pages. The more prestigious and well-paid positions in politics or foreign affairs remained primarily in the hands of men. Such contradictions provided a useful ambiguity to Nazi press authorities' policy toward female journalists: they could mobilize women in the interest of the regime while also appearing to adhere to Nazi ideology's misogynist view of women's roles within society. This inconsistency in turn afforded women some capacity to negotiate the Nazi system to the benefit of their own careers.

Several studies have examined the character of the Nazi press, the restructuring of the field after January 1933, and the expulsion of those the regime deemed undesirable.[3] These policies worked to the advantage of journalists who were willing to serve the regime for the sake of their careers. By examining Nazi policy and practice with respect to women journalists, their training trajectory, the types of positions they held, and the patronage networks that both aided and limited their careers, this chapter adds to our understanding of these processes and uncovers women's (often opaque) place within the new Nazified press.

The fact that women were under-represented and discriminated against within the journalistic profession was not specific to Nazi Germany. Women also struggled professionally in Germany prior to the Third Reich, just as they did throughout Europe and North America. Media scholars have identified how, throughout the 1930s, women journalists on both sides of the Atlantic were marginalized in the same "feminine beats" as those who worked in Nazi Germany.[4] They grappled with masculine workplaces and encountered colleagues and editors who resented their presence or viewed them only through the lens of gender. Yet as Tracy Lucht and Kelsey Batschelet have pointed out, despite various barriers to their involvement, women found ways to exercise agency and build careers within the media.[5] This dance between discrimination and possibility applied to women journalists working under the National Socialist regime, just as it did to those working in France, Britain, and the United States. However, unique to journalism in the Third Reich was its racial framework and the regime's determination that journalists conduct themselves in a manner that supported the Nazi state and its ideological and political goals.[6] If they were willing to do so, women journalists, like their male counterparts, could benefit from Nazi practices of exclusion and inclusion as the regime expelled from the field those it considered "racially" or politically undesirable and utilized a new cohort of journalists to popularize its message.

Studies concerned with gender in Nazi Germany have rightfully emphasized 1936 as marking a shift in the regime's policy toward women, as it began to actively recruit them for the workforce in order to prepare for war.[7] Yet, despite steps to remove women from certain domains and a plethora of pro-natal incentives, the case of women journalists shows that the regime did not always work against professional women prior to 1936, nor did it view women simply as wartime labour. Nazi press authorities actively created pathways for women in the press beginning in 1933, although opportunities certainly increased after 1936, and even more so during the war. Most Germans aspired to the sense of belonging and collective identity embodied by the *Volksgemeinschaft*, and invoking such sentiments was an important part of the regime's strategy for consolidating and controlling the press.[8] Under the direction of Wilhelm Weiß, the German Press Association (Reichsverband der Deutschen Presse – RDP) sought to appeal to, and ensure the loyalty of, journalists by creating a sense of professional possibility, responsibility, solidarity, and elitism, and some women were included as a part of this privileged clique.[9] At the same time, long-standing obstacles in the field left women on the margins and in the minority. For the select group of women seeking to enter the profession, however, or for those already established within it, the importance with which the regime viewed journalism gave women a sense of belonging and status in an important public domain and helped pull them into political service to the state. As subsequent chapters will show, they became professional functionaries working in various ways on behalf of the Nazi system.

## Purges and Possibilities

By the early twentieth century, the press in Germany was well established, respected, and influential. As the leading source of information and entertainment, the press enjoyed a wide readership, particularly in cities. For most Germans, newspapers had become a necessity of everyday life: "I couldn't even imagine breakfast without a newspaper," confessed one reader in Berlin.[10] By 1932, there were 4,703 newspapers in Germany.[11] During the Weimar Republic, the press was relatively free and decentralized, although very much politicized thanks to the proliferation of party papers in this period.[12] No mandatory guidelines or compulsory journalistic training program existed, although universities did begin to develop programs on newspaper and communication studies.[13] Economist and journalist Karl Bucher had founded the Leipziger Institut für Zeitungskunde (Institute for Newspaper Studies) in 1916. In 1928, the journal *Zeitungswissenschaft* (Newspaper studies) was established by Karl d'Ester and Walther Heide.[14] By the mid-1920s, journalism studies programs were added to the curriculum of a handful of German universities, including Berlin and later Munich. The academic study of journalism was conceived of as interdisciplinary science, closely connected to sociology, that examined the social function of the newspaper (as well as the newer media of film and radio) and its relationship to, and effect on, society.[15]

The coming of the Third Reich meant a semiotic break in the practice of journalism and in its study. Hitler and Goebbels capitalized on the chaotic and overcrowded state of the field to implement measures designed to control and monitor the press and those within it. Prior to coming to power, and consistently thereafter, the Nazi Party made it clear that the media would be instrumental in state building and social control. As Hitler wrote in *Mein Kampf*, "By far the greatest bulk of the political 'education,' which in this case one may rightly define with the word 'propaganda,' is the work of the press. It is the press above all else that carries out this 'work of enlightenment,' thus forming a sort of school for adults."[16] Although such language regarding the didactic responsibility of the press had long roots in Germany, the Nazi Party publicly positioned itself as a force determined to rebuild the press. The field of *Zeitungswissenschaft* too was standardized throughout Germany and no longer viewed as a "politically neutral" subject of research; instead, it was closely tied to Nazi ideology and harnessed to serve the needs of the state. The curriculum focused largely on the nature, implementation, and efficacy of propaganda, with theory taking a back seat to "practical" training.[17]

Hitler's ascent to power in January 1933 opened up opportunities in journalism for those included in the *Volksgemeinschaft*, as journalists targeted by the regime for political or "racial" reasons quickly lost their positions. Although the Nazi government hurriedly enacted laws to remove Jewish Germans from all aspects of professional and civil life, it viewed the purging of the press and its reincarnation as a vehicle for the Nazi message as particularly important. The press was a highly visible and symbolic target for the regime, which charged that Jews controlled the media and dominated German public discourse as a result.[18] Even before it enacted its first official anti-Jewish measures, the regime shut down "oppositional" papers belonging to the Social Democratic and Communist Parties and began to remove those considered politically unreliable, together with Jewish journalists, from the field.[19] Hilde Walter, a left-leaning journalist who published in several well-known dailies, fit into both persecuted categories and was forced out of the profession in November 1933. She recalled that the removal of Jewish journalists ran "on two parallel tracks," with politically contentious

Jews removed even before formal measures were taken to ban all Jewish Germans from the field.[20]

The Editors Law (*Schriftleitergesetz*), promulgated on 4 October 1933 and effective 1 January 1934, legally barred all Jews and individuals with a Jewish spouse from working as journalists or editors and helped facilitate the consolidation (*Gleichschaltung*) of the press. From that point forward, all journalists and journalistic candidates would have to prove their so-called Aryan ancestry and that of their spouse.[21] Wilhelm Weiß devoted much energy during the final months of 1933 and throughout 1934 to removing any remaining Jews from the profession. In November 1934, Weiß asked the head of each regional press association to provide statistics on how many Jews were still working at daily papers.[22] Later, he announced that, over the course of 1934, the regime had removed at least 1,300 "undesirable" journalists – close to 10 per cent of the entire press – from their positions.[23] By comparison with other professions, such as law and medicine, the legislation targeting Jewish journalists was far-reaching: only a handful retained their positions after the *Schriftleitergesetz* was enacted. Weiß summed up the state of the industry in 1937: "We have freed the journalism profession from Jews and Marxists," he boasted. "We have removed all unsuitable elements and constantly work to free the press from those individuals who do not possess the inner discipline to join, unconditionally and without question, a united front in building the National Socialist state."[24]

Due to a combination of apathy, long-standing antisemitism, and above all, opportunism, the industry offered little protest against the expulsion of German Jews. In journalism, a high unemployment rate had caused tensions and anxieties among professionals during the Weimar years.[25] As in other domains, the purging of the press cleared away unwanted competition and opened employment opportunities for "acceptable" Germans. As journalism became a key site of both the Nazification and "de-judaization" of society, female journalists whom the regime deemed acceptable could benefit from these processes in ways that women in other fields could not. Women faced no explicit restrictions in journalism, unlike in the legal or civil service domains, where the regime regulated the number of women who could enter. Professions requiring extensive and expensive training, like medicine, remained difficult for many women to access. And, of course, positions in such fields as the military or clergy remained closed to women.

In his 1936 study *Die Frau im Journalismus* (The woman in journalism), Dr Adolf Dresler, a respected professor at the Institute of Newspaper Science (Institut für Zeitungswissenschaft) at the University of Munich, provided a history of women's journalistic activities. Although Dresler did not attribute the growth in the number of women working in the field solely to Nazism, he did emphasize the increase in the number of women entering the profession since the regime gained power. According to Dresler, a survey conducted by the German Institute for Newspaper Studies (Deutsches Institut für Zeitungskunde) in Berlin revealed that only 222 women were members of the German Press Association in 1932. By January 1935, this number had increased to 687.[26] In other words, Dresler argued that the number of women working in the field had tripled between 1932 and 1935. It is not possible to evaluate the methodological approach and quality of Dresler's work. What is noteworthy is the study's primary message: women had become an increasing part of the press since the turn of the century and even more so during the Third Reich. The study was undertaken and shared in a likely effort to demonstrate that the regime had opened up opportunities for women in the field. Yet it also shows how prominent individuals in the press marked women as "the other," separate and different from male colleagues – afterall, no study was necessary to demonstrate that journalism was a viable profession for men. Such discourse could encourage women to enter the field but could also create barriers to progression and success. Male journalists were treated as "gender neutral" and inherently professional, while women were defined and judged by their femininity.[27] As will be discussed in the next chapters, this meant that editors paid more attention to the areas in which a woman wrote and often raised concerns if she sought to work in a genre especially associated with men, such as political news or as a foreign correspondent.

Discussion that paralleled Nazi aggression against women in other fields also took place within the journalistic profession. Such discourse was particularly pervasive between 1933 and 1935, when unemployment was still high. Male editors and journalists argued that "double-earners" – married women with husbands who were employed – should be removed from the field.[28] In 1934, journalist Rolf Cunz wrote an article for the trade journal *Zeitungs-Verlag* in which he declared that a woman "could not cope with the duties of a full-time journalist [in a manner] that would allow her to focus on raising her children, her domestic duties etc."[29] Still, several women belonged to a group of journalistic hopefuls that helped fill the gaps left by those forced out of the profession. Prominent journalists such as Margret Boveri, Lily Abegg, and Petra Vermehren got their start between 1933 and 1934, as did lesser-known reporters such as Thea Fischer, Gertraude Uhlhorn, and Helma Huffschmid. In 1934, the twenty-year-old Huffschmid began working as a volunteer at the Nazi Party's official paper, the *Völkischer Beobachter*, during a semester break from university. She enjoyed her first journalistic experience despite the fact that, at that stage, she "did not have any journalistic ambition."[30] Others, who had begun their careers in the Weimar years, accommodated themselves to the regime, regardless of whether they were disposed to Nazism: Ruth Andreas-Friedrich, Heddy Neumeister, Else Frobenius, and Ilse Urbach had varying relationships with Nazism. While Friedrich was appalled by the regime and Neumeister appeared apathetic, Frobenius and Urbach joined the party and embraced Nazi ideology. They all continued their careers across the 1933 divide.

While some women gained their start or continued on with ease in the profession, others were losing their once prominent careers and fleeing Germany for their own safety.[31] Jewish journalist Lucy von Jacobi, for instance, lost her coveted position at the newspaper *Tempo*. She immigrated to Switzerland, where she died in poverty in 1956.[32] Others became victims of Nazi violence. Martha Wertheimer was fired from her position at the *Offenbacher Zeitung* in 1933. She devoted herself to aiding the Jewish community and died in June 1942 while on transport to a killing centre in the east.[33] One of the hallmarks of the Nazi period was how the persecution of certain groups in the population dovetailed with others' perceptions of increased freedom and privilege. Some women journalists were beneficiaries of these processes.

In the early days of the Third Reich, women photojournalists had particular advantages in accessing the field. The development of photojournalism as a profession during the 1920s went hand in hand with the plethora of illustrated papers that emerged during the same period. Even before 1933, the press was in desperate need of photojournalists; the Nazis' purging of the field reinforced the niche for women trained in the profession. Although they remained in the minority, female photojournalists had decent prospects to establish a career, given the lack of skilled photographers and the regime's growing demand for image-based propaganda.[34] *Die Schriftleiterin* (Guide for women journalists), first published in 1936 by the Academic Information Office (Akademisches Auskunftsamt) in conjunction with the German Labour Front (Deutsche Arbeitsfront), noted that women were indeed "finding success" in this genre of journalism.[35]

Charlotte Rohrbach, Karoline Krieger, and Margot Schuenbach all got their start shortly after the passing of the Editors Law. Erika Groth-Schmachtenberger too built her prominent career during the Third Reich. Shortly after graduating from the Bavarian State School of Photography in 1932, she received her first commission in early 1933, when a contact at the press office of a radio station suggested she try publishing in illustrated radio magazines, a genre that was growing in popularity.

"For me it was the best of luck," she later recalled, "because at the time there were hardly any trained press photographers."[36] The editor of *Die Illustrierte Rundfunk*, Dr Ernst Heimeran, offered Schmachtenberger her first assignment, and with a generous fee. Yet as she acknowledged in her memoirs, Heimeran "did not have it easy back then." Schmachtenberger witnessed his arrest by the Gestapo sometime between 1933 and 1934 and never saw him at the magazine again. "I guess he wasn't politically 'reliable,'" she surmised.[37]

With the purging of the press moving ahead rapidly in 1933 and 1934, officials shifted their focus to journalistic training to ensure that those making up the new press cohort would not only be racially acceptable but also ideologically apt. The German Press Association outlined the steps necessary to become an accredited journalist: a nine- to ten-month internship at a German newspaper, magazine, periodical, or news bureau; an entrance exam to the Reich Press School (Reichspresse-schule); and graduation from the school's training program. The school, which was founded in January 1935, was the jewel in the Nazi's training program. After it closed in 1939, due to the war, candidates were required to take a final exam.

Just as the regime sought to create a *Volksgemeinschaft* founded on its notion of supposed "Aryan" superiority, authorities presented the press as a particularly elite and privileged institution and encouraged all journalistic hopefuls to view themselves as leaders and influencers with bright futures. The regime stressed inclusion, camaraderie, and success, in order to encourage a trainee's adherence to Nazi ideology and build a sense of loyalty toward the regime.[38] Of course, with these opportunities came stipulations. The party made clear to all within the field that, going forward, a journalist's primary task was to communicate National Socialist ideals and strengthen the *Volksgemeinschaft*.[39] The professional guide *Der Schriftleiter* (The journalist) echoed this message, noting that journalists' roles in the Third Reich were markedly different from what they had been prior to 1933: They now had "a higher calling" in service to the Nazi state.[40]

Press authorities particularly valued those who were starting out in the field, since they would presumably be easier to mould. The regime presented measures to control the media as an opportunity for a new generation to gain a foothold and succeed in the profession. In a 1934 article in the trade journal *Deutsche Presse*, Dr Wolf Meyer-Christian, the future head of the Reich Press School, stated that the current journalist cohort could not always be relied on to communicate the National Socialist message. Despite the fact that many older journalists had "dedicated themselves honestly and earnestly to the National Socialist idea," they had been shaped by earlier professional norms. "Where is the guarantee that this press would not fail when put to the first psychological or moral test?" Meyer-Christian asked. More reliable was "the up-and-coming generation of journalists."[41] There could be no illusions about a journalist's mission under Nazism. Yet if one were willing to play by Nazi rules, one could be rewarded with stature and privilege. Journalists often had access to important cultural and political events and forged connections with prominent individuals. For women, the profession allowed them some freedom to break out of prescribed gender roles.

From early on, press authorities took pains to assure women journalists that they too were an important part of this elite institution. The Editors Law racialized the field, but it made no distinction with regard to gender, class, education, or even party membership.[42] In this respect, the press (officially) remained an accessible, flexible, and open profession and was presented as such. Press authorities assured women that they would play an important role in the field and encouraged them to view journalism as a challenging career choice requiring interest, capability, stamina, and, commitment.[43] In a 1936 speech to a group of female journalists in Berlin, Wilhelm Weiß declared that women must be firmly established in the profession: "If the journalistic profession is to receive the necessary prestige in the National Socialist state, it must represent a cohesive unit. Women who are a part of it will be doing a service not only for their own career, but also for the German press as a whole."[44] As will be discussed in the following chapter, the Nazi regime sought to use women journalists to normalize the dictatorship as well as to act as a conduit to the female population.

From 1935 to 1939, promotional material, newspaper articles, and personal communication to and from the RDP recognized and spoke of the specific challenges women faced as they attempted to establish a foothold in the field.[45] The organization also offered women support. In 1934, press authorities founded the Committee of German Women Journalists (Reichsausschuss der Schriftleiterinnen), a sub-department of the German Press Association, chaired by Annie Juliane Richert. Among the standard components of membership meetings were talks concerning the professional situation for female journalists.[46] The 1936 *Schriftleiterin* encouraged women to enter the field and drew attention to the pathways open to them. Although the guide acknowledged the difficulties women faced, it advised that "anyone who trusts enough in her talent and enthusiasm and possesses the will to meet such challenges head on will progress in her career."[47] Weiß maintained that "those who have an instinct for topicality and psychology will always be successful in journalism. Even women."[48]

The Press-Propaganda Department of the National Socialist Women's League (Nationalsozialistische Frauenschaft – NSF) also showed an interest in the career path of female journalists and involved itself in their professional lives, beginning with their training. Part of the task of the NSF was to further expand women's presence in the field and foster young female talent, albeit primarily as a mouthpiece for the NSF itself. Among other activities, the NSF held professional days focusing on the viability of women having a career in journalism.[49] A typical course agenda included sections such as "Is Journalism a Women's Profession?"; "What Behavior Do We Expect from a Journalist?"; and "The Career Path for Journalists in the Women's League."[50] The NSF's Press-Propaganda Department also helped journalistic hopefuls find internships in order to begin their training – a task that was much harder for women than men. In May 1939, the head of the department, Erika Kirmsse, contacted the editor of the *Kölnische Zeitung* to thank the paper for accepting Herta Müller as an intern. Following success as an intern, Müller was attending the Reich Press School and preparing to take her final examinations, Kirmsse noted. She asked if the editor would train another female intern: "You are probably aware that some time ago a new section for young, female journalists was established within the framework of our Press-Propaganda Department," she explained. "Its mission is to help talented girls to enter the profession. We thank you in advance."[51] Such advocacy indicates that the regime not only accepted women journalists, but also needed them to support Nazi press and propaganda goals. At the same time, professional communications targeted to women reveal that press authorities both saw and desired a distinction between the roles of male and female journalists. They sought to channel women primarily to soft-news beats. This combination of inclusion and separation began with a journalist's professional training.

### Camaraderie, Status, and Sexism: Training a New Cohort of Nazified Journalists

In theory, there was little distinction on the basis of gender in the journalistic training program that the regime implemented. Professor Adolf Dresler praised the program, noting that "women would receive the same education as men."[52] In reality, education and training for prospective male and female journalists converged and diverged at various points. Sexism – which was not limited to the National Socialist state – meant that gender significantly influenced a woman's internship experience. Finding a paper willing to take on a female intern was the most difficult task. In 1937, the official at Helene Rahms's local press office purportedly laughed when she inquired about securing an internship and training as a journalist.[53] Candidates often had to rely on men for assistance – an experience they shared with their counterparts in democratic systems.

In post-war reconstructions of their careers, some women emphasized how they obtained their positions due only to their own initiative, tenacity, and inventiveness, and not the entreaties of the Nazi state. There was some truth to the women's claims. *Die Schriftleiterin* implied that, to become successful in the field, women were required to assert agency, find a way to work the system, adapt to situations as necessary, and be strategic.[54] In other words, Nazi press material subtly advised women that they should move beyond prescribed gender norms and use the gaps between ideology and the needs of the state to manoeuvre their way into the field. The need for such self-empowerment was not unique to women in the field in Nazi Germany. The French foreign correspondent Andreé Viollis, for instance, declared that a woman primarily needed "patience and tenacity" to work in journalism.[55] German journalist Elisabeth Noelle-Neumann too credited her professional start to her tenacity as well as her ambition. After completing her *Abitur* (a high-school diploma that qualified an individual for university) in 1935, Noelle-Neumann attended a lecture being given by the well-known professor of journalism studies Dr Emil Dovifat. She claimed that she made a spur-of-the-moment decision to approach the famous academic and express her desire to complete her doctoral work and become a journalist. She sent him material to review, and a few days later Dovifat replied that he thought her prospects were good.[56] Noelle-Neumann began to study journalism and history at the University of Königsberg and later in Munich. Twenty-year-old Gertraude Uhlhorn began her apprenticeship at the *Badischer Residenz-Anzeiger*, a small paper in Karlsruhe in 1934.[57] She strategically avoided a large daily, where she figured she would not be on the editor's radar. At a small paper, she rightly assumed that she would have a better chance of more intensive training.[58] She shared an office with the paper's three employees, all former reporters on the *Frankfurter Zeitung* (FZ), one of most respected papers in Germany at the time. As a result, Uhlhorn received training in all aspects of journalism.

Certainly, as the war progressed, more possibilities opened for female journalistic hopefuls as men left for the front and women stepped into the vacated positions. Yet, even prior to 1939, women landed internships at almost every type of paper, including party papers. Ursula von Kardorff, for example, began her volunteer internship in 1937 on the party paper *Der Angriff*, founded by Joseph Goebbels in 1927. Ursula Roeh began her journalism career in 1935 as a journalist-in-training at the *NS-Kurier* in Stuttgart. After she attended the Reich Press School from January to March 1937, Roeh freelanced for both party and non-party papers.[59] In 1936, the Nazi paper the *NSZ Westmark* trained at least three female journalistic hopefuls, and it trained several more over the course of the war. By 1944, female interns working on the paper outnumbered men three to one.[60]

When a male or female candidate did find an internship, the German Press Association attempted to ensure that they were correctly trained as journalists. Both Ilse Hannak and Rothraut Vrtel received poor evaluations on the final examination that followed their internships. According to the RDP, the young women were not to blame. The official noted that the editors of the two newspapers where the women had worked had not fulfilled their duty to train them properly. In one case, the RDP concluded that the young woman in question had been used as a cheap, temporary worker in the editorial department and that the editor had paid scant attention to her training. The RDP allowed both women to retake their exam in six months and directed the papers to improve their training practices.[61] The press association attempted to ensure that, although far fewer in number than the male cohort, women journalists were trained to the same standards within the areas in which they would work.

The experiences of female interns were, of course, not monolithic. Some women maintained that they had enjoyed responsibility during their training, while others had to struggle to gain professional experience. Kardorff hoped to establish a career as a cultural journalist. At *Der Angriff*, however, she started out writing what she referred to as "fashion reports and kitschy articles with political undertones."[62] In 1938, Helene Rahms was disillusioned by the meagre experience she initially received as a trainee at the *Saale-Zeitung* in Halle. Her primary task was sorting, rewriting, and organizing the local segment, which consisted of trivialities in "broken" German submitted by postmen, café owners, and other locals: "The goal to write about art, theatre, and literature seemed so distant and so unreachable," she observed.[63]

Rahms followed the advice of her one female colleague and grabbed the first opportunity to land a scoop in the hope of propelling herself into more challenging waters. She took a daring approach. Her editor wanted to secure an exclusive interview with a trio of tightrope acrobats who had arrived in town, and he ordered someone to contact the group. Rahms quickly spoke up with the suggestion that whoever took on the assignment should ask to be carried across the tightrope and then describe their experience.[64] The editor loved the idea and assigned her the story. Rahms had landed her first solo reportage by employing a strategy that women had used since the late nineteenth century to break into the field. Women journalists resorted to dramatic or daring moves in order to land a compelling story – a practice known as "stunt" journalism.[65] One of the first and best-known "stunt girls" was Elizabeth Cochrane, reporting under the name Nellie Bly, who had had herself committed to a mental asylum in New York in 1885 in order to expose its deplorable conditions.[66] Often perceived as sensationalist, such acts nevertheless allowed women access to a form of investigative reporting. Thanks to her "stunt," Rahms gained experience during her internship, although most of it centred on local news: "I had to learn from the ground up," she recalled. "They sent me to a zoo, a chicken farm, a children's hospital, a lost property office, a mask rental [place], and a champagne breakfast at a travelling circus."[67]

Elisabeth Noelle-Neumann was well aware of gender roadblocks in the profession and, in her memoir, maintained that she had had to go above and beyond to establish the type of career she desired. Scholarship on women in journalism and the autobiographical writing of well-known female journalists outside of Germany, such as Martha Gellhorn, demonstrate that women had to find ways to prove themselves within the patriarchal institution of the press, whether via "stunts" or attempting to assimilate as "one of the boys."[68] Noelle-Neumann, however, used gender limitations to explain her involvement in Nazi organizations. In 1937, she joined the Nazi Student Association, which she contended was the only way to obtain a spot on a study-abroad program. She became a cell leader in the association and founded a female-only journalism study group. Noelle-Neumann eventually entered a writing competition; her impressive submission secured her a spot in the German Academic Exchange Program to the University of Missouri, one of the top journalism schools in the United States.[69] Despite the fact that Noelle-Neumann published a number of articles about her experiences abroad in two esteemed papers, the *Deutsche Allgemeine Zeitung* (*DAZ*) and the *Berliner Zeitung*, when she decided to seek a newspaper internship and begin the formal steps toward establishing a career, the editor of the *DAZ*, Karl Silex, advised her to first complete her doctorate. As a woman, he counselled, she would have a much better chance at a successful career if she had a title.[70]

Despite this advice, the field did not formally require prospective journalists to complete a university degree or even an *Abitur*, which meant that journalism was a viable profession for women who were traditionally disadvantaged when it came to the ability to complete high school or pursue postsecondary education. Despite rhetoric that suggested that innate talent was more important than formal scholarly training, the Press Association preferred and encouraged candidates, male or female, to obtain as extensive an education as possible. Weiß maintained that, "in the interests of the profession's prestige … a high level of education must be required." Still, he confirmed, "it is not possible from the outset to reject someone because he does not have an *Abitur*."[71] Although incomplete archival records on the education levels of journalists make definitive conclusions difficult, documentation on forty-two female journalists working in Germany between 1933 and 1939 indicates that 43 per cent received their *Abitur*.[72] Journalism was open to all, but middle-class women with access to education certainly had a better chance of succeeding in the field, and those with university degrees, including doctorates, fared best.[73] The author of *Die Schriftleiterin*, Dr Else Boger-Eichler, had, for example, received her doctorate in German literature prior to beginning her journalistic career.[74] In this respect, the profession had not changed dramatically from the nineteenth century.[75]

For all journalistic hopefuls with the opportunity and means to attend university, press officials clearly outlined the preferred course of study.[76] Although the RDP counselled men and women on the importance of receiving a broad education, it advised only male students that political science, together with history, law, and philosophy, should form the backbone of their studies, especially if they intended careers as political correspondents.[77] It directed young women toward culture (art, music, dance), history, languages, and German literature. Such an education would give women the cultural, intellectual, and technical requirements for a press career in areas where the regime wanted to mobilize the talent of women.

Press authorities encouraged prospective journalists to combine their academic studies with a practical journalism program. The percentage of female students enrolled in journalism studies grew steadily, from 18.4 per cent in 1929 to 28.2 per cent in 1939.[78] Gertraude Uhlhorn recalled that, when she studied journalism with Professor Emil Dovifat in the mid-1930s, there were already many women in the program, but "later in the war he had almost only women," as "the men were all drafted."[79] The rising numbers of female students can be attributed partly to the fact that press authorities encouraged women to take up this field of study.[80]

The German Press Association offered a surprising level of support for women journalism candidates, from ensuring that their internships were advancing to advising on their education plan. The creation of spaces for women intensified during the war. As men were increasingly conscripted, earlier efforts to recruit women were stepped up as the civilian mobilization of women became more crucial. By 1944, women made up 49.71 per cent of journalists in training.[81] In some regions, including the Sudetenland, Brandenburg, Danzig West Prussia, Westphalia, Saxony, and Silesia, they accounted for over half of, and occasionally almost all, journalists in training.[82]

From the beginning, the regime saw a need for women journalists and took steps to ensure that they would become effective mouthpieces for the Nazi state. From 1935 until its closure at the beginning of the war, the Reich Press School was the primary means through which the regime hoped to build a cohort of Nazified journalists. The training of young journalism candidates at the school revolved around establishing a comradeship based on "race," the notion of elitism, shared physical activities, and ideological indoctrination. In 1935, the school's director emphasized that the pedagogical purpose of the school was to develop a compulsion for "community building" among all participants and "foster a coexistence based on solidarity."[83] While men and women largely followed the same training trajectory, which involved a ten-week course at the school itself, there were distinctions. Prior to attending the school, male candidates spent one to two weeks at a paramilitary training camp; as part of their own ideological indoctrination, female candidates spent eight to ten days in the Press-Propaganda Department of the NSF.[84] This division made clear that women journalists would largely be expected to work within "women's news," whether inside or outside of the NSF. But gender-delineated training was malleable, in order to accommodate the regime's desire not only to unify and politicize a new cohort of journalists, but also to instrumentalize them for different purposes when they graduated and began their careers.

The press school itself functioned like a boarding school. Although the overtly militant aspects of men's initial camp experience were toned down, the school still had a militaristic bent. Both men and women participated in mandatory, early morning, military-oriented exercises, a fact that demonstrates the inclusive nature of the training.[85] Yet photos of the school that were included in an article in the *Deutsche Presse* featured only male trainees participating in such masculine activities as roll-call and team sports.[86] This dichotomy reveals that neither the inclusion nor the exclusion of women journalistic candidates was absolute. At the same time, by, quite literally, leaving women out of the picture, this article, at least, provided no visible discrepancy between the regime's general rhetoric about women's place in society and the nature of their training for a journalism career.

In early 1936, Wilhelm Weiß outlined three categories for young journalists' professional development: journalistic training, character development, and political education.[87] Political education included ensuring that students adhered to the Nazi *Weltanschauung* and understood Nazi press policy. In the winter of 1939, after having completed her training with the NSF, Ursula von Kardorff took part in the course at the Reich Press School. She later described her experience:

> A strange time … We were five girls and around twenty men. We had to participate in early morning sport, which included throwing around hand grenades made out of wood. We were trimmed and trained politically, learned about the profession, of course, took various trips to hear lectures, attend the theatre and so on.

Kardorff wrote to her friend that, by the end of the course, she and others from the "non-party" papers had "built a wonderful clique."[88] Her words demonstrate that the school created a sense of professional unity, even among those not entirely reconciled to Nazism. Although she claimed to be put off by the ideological bent of the training, Kardorff wanted a career in journalism, and she was willing to accept the restrictions and compromises this required.

The school's program was taxing but stimulating. Students attended lectures in the morning, with daily sightseeing trips (*Ausflüge*), including visits to galleries, museums, film screenings, and court proceedings, organized for the afternoon.[89] The school maintained a close relationship with the Reich Ministry of Public Enlightenment and Propaganda (Reichsministerium für Volksaufklärung und Propaganda), and students were given the opportunity to attend the daily press conference.[90] The emphasis on the attendees' cultural experiences and social life pleased candidates: it introduced an element of privilege and fun into the training, despite the ideological saturation, and helped normalize the school for those, such as Kardorff, who may have been resistant to some aspects of Nazi ideology.[91]

Although the school's directors promoted the ideal of a camaraderie that did not distinguish between genders, they acknowledged that women might be hesitant about attending, because of the gender disparity.[92] The large gap between the proportion of female and male students was not based on a quota but, rather, reflected the limited internship opportunities open to female journalistic hopefuls. Still, evidence suggests that Nazi communications directed toward women regarding a career in journalism bore fruit. In 1936, women made up approximately 10 per cent of press school attendees.[93] This figure was almost double the percentage of women already active in the press at this point, and the number of women attending the school grew throughout the late thirties. By early 1939, it reached 25 per cent.[94] By comparison, the Columbia Graduate School of Journalism in the United States maintained a 10 per cent quota on women students until 1968.[95] These figures contradict the general perception about the degree of gender restriction in Nazi Germany. In some ways, gender ideology and the act of women stepping outside of prescribed gender roles may have been less important for Nazi press authorities than for those in other countries, if it served the needs of the state.

In 1936, thirty-year-old journalist-in-training Elsie Günther published an article in the trade journal *Deutsche Presse* about her experiences at the Reich Press School: "It was a special joy for those of us who are usually the only female member on staff … to have the opportunity to be together with other women day after day," she wrote.[96] Titled "'Seven to Seventy': Young Female Journalists in the Reich Press School Community" the article was meant to assure potential female journalism candidates that, despite their low numbers at the school – in Günther's cohort seven women to seventy men – they would be an integral part of the close-knit, elite community of journalists-in-training. While "Seven to Seventy" pointed to the gender inequality in the numbers among student attendees, it sought to downplay its impact on female candidates. Instead, Günther emphasized the close and supportive relationship that developed between male and female students. She ended her article by praising her experience at the school: "It was only ten weeks and yet what rich weeks they were for us."[97] Given the controlled nature of the Nazi press, one can assume that Günther had little choice but to put a positive spin on her experience at the school. The fact that she was likely commissioned to write a glowing article about the training program, however, underscores how the regime strove to address and alleviate young women's concerns about the challenges they would face with their training. Male students also published positive accounts of their time at the school, but such articles focused on the importance they felt as members of a future press corps, along with the stimulation and adventure the school provided.[98]

There were no female instructors at the school, but in 1938 the school's leaders created the position of *Kameradschaftsleiterin*, who was to act as an adviser to female students. Twenty-four-year-old Ruth von Kondratowicz was the first to hold this position. Kondratowicz embodied a diversity of experience in areas that the school's leaders deemed appropriate for a female journalist. In 1934, she completed her *Abitur* in home economics and joined the NSF; in 1936, she participated in English- and French-language courses; studied stenography, typing, fashion, gymnastics, and dance; and began her journalistic training; in 1937, she completed her volunteer internship and eventually attended the press school herself. In December 1937, she became an accredited journalist in *Kunstbetrachtung* (art commentary), a field in which press authorities encouraged women's involvement.[99] Both the hiring of a *Kameradschaftsleiterin* and Günther's article demonstrate how press officials viewed professional training through the lens of gender. The fact that they felt the need to emphasize women's inclusion indicates that gender negatively affected women's involvement and acceptance into the *Kameradschaft* of the press; male journalists did not need to stress their inclusion, nor did the regime. At the same time, the school did offer women a support system and networking opportunities.

The position of *Kameradschaftsleiterin* was intended, in part, to ensure the success of female candidates, but another critical element was to observe students' attitude toward National Socialism – an important aspect of training, given that these young women were preparing for a public role in service to the state.[100] This screening took place throughout each journalist's training. Prior to admittance to the press school, candidates were required to take an entry exam. After the school closed in the fall of 1939, students were given an exam at the end of their internship. The exam requirements changed very little prior to and during the war, with the exception of specific war-related questions.[101] Journalistic potential and adherence to the Nazi world view displayed during the exam were the major factors that allowed candidates prior to 1939 to enter the Reich Press School, and, after 1939, to enter the field. Before the war, women made up only a small percentage of those taking the exam, although the surviving documentation does not allow for precise statistical analysis. In 1938, Helene Rahms was the only woman out of fourteen candidates at her press school exam. Only two candidates passed – Rahms and one of her male colleagues. If a woman secured and succeeded at an internship and thereby reached the exam stage, an examination committee did not typically discriminate against her when it came to entering the school or the profession.[102]

Exam committees questioned women in the same manner as they did men. Officially, they had high expectations and specific demands with regard to a candidate's exam performance. While some students described the process as strenuous, others later maintained that they had a hard time taking the exam seriously. Writing to a friend in 1939,

Kardorff deemed the exam a farce in which "journalistic talent did not play a role."[103] According to Kardorff, she had to slog through five hours of abstruse questions, including the need to precisely recite the Führer's historical words. She believed that she impressed the committee with the supposed passion with which she reeled off the names of sixteen men who fell during the November 1923 Beer Hall Putsch. She astutely downplayed her attendance at her aristocratic high school and emphasized her work at *Der Angriff*.[104] Accounts from the time placed a thorough knowledge of Nazi policies and even verbatim quotations from Hitler's speeches and writing as central to the exam process, yet post-war recollections by journalists have conveniently downplayed this requirement. In her memoir, Helene Rahms alleged that she had simply skimmed *Mein Kampf* on the train the morning of the exam: "I mastered the art of speed reading rather perfectly, made note of a few keywords that lent themselves to quotes and glossed over the gaps in [my] knowledge with bluster."[105] By retrospectively invoking the idea of "bluster," Rahms could distance herself from a close knowledge of Nazism.[106]

Regardless of what field an applicant hoped to work in, the German Press Association viewed journalists first and foremost as political employees and, accordingly, wanted all candidates to be conversant in National Socialist politics.[107] For this reason, Weiß decreed that each exam committee must include a political journalist.[108] The political section of the examination addressed such topics as the Anti-Comintern Pact, Nazi social and economic policy, Marxism versus National Socialism, race, and the occupation of the *Ruhrgebiet*. Other sections of the exam included Third Reich history, culture, and the journalism profession itself. Cultural topics were connected to Nazi ideology and included the nature of German art in the "contested" East, questions about Wagner, and the meaning of *Sturm und Drang*. Topics related to the profession included how one should write for the various sections of a newspaper and the importance of photojournalism.[109]

From fragmentary exam reports, it is difficult to conclude how easy it was to pass or fail, although evidence suggests that the majority of candidates passed, at least during the later war years. Due to the war, a much higher proportion of women took the final press exam to enter the field. Out of forty-four candidates who sat the exam between 1942 and 1944, thirty-one (70 per cent) were women; 87 per cent of this group passed. Of the thirteen male candidates, nine (70 per cent) passed.[110] These results suggest that women were at least as likely as men to pass the exam. But, once a woman was an officially credited journalist, she faced gender-related roadblocks in her career.

## The Professional Landscape

Despite the fact that official communications positioned women journalists as an important part of the profession, they were generally regulated to the lower-paying and less prestigious soft news areas. It was particularly difficult for women to find a permanent home on a daily newspaper, and only in rare cases was a woman able to obtain a position in political or international affairs.[111] The fact that women were more tenuously situated in the field than most of their male colleagues may have made them especially compliant and willing to undertake whatever press authorities demanded of them in order to establish or continue on in their career. Moreover, they often needed a male patron to get ahead.

In October 1936, Dorothea Thimme, a recent graduate from the Reich Press School, wrote to Hans Schwarz van Berk, the editor of the party paper *Der Angriff* and a close associate of Joseph Goebbels, pleading for his help to find a job. "Since autumn 1935 I have been working as press advisor with the National Socialist Women's League," Thimme wrote. "However, by December I would like to be out of here because I hardly learn anything new, and I do not get any stimulation. It is very difficult to find a position. I have basically done everything that one can do. Could you give me any advice?" she asked.[112] Thimme went on to note that she had always trusted Schwarz van Berk as a professional comrade and that he had the type of career she hoped to build. Thimme had followed the steps that press authorities outlined for women journalists: she joined the National Socialist Women's League in 1935, completed her internship at a newspaper, and attended the Reich Press School. The NSF's reference for Thimme declared that she was talented and especially suited for a career in journalism.[113] Schwarz van Berk responded that he was happy to advise Thimme and counselled that it was a good idea to leave her position as press advisor within the NSF because, otherwise, she could be stuck there until "she turned grey."[114] Schwarz van Berk noted, though, that he had no position in mind for her at that moment. "As you well know," he wrote, "in our office no female journalists are employed [full-time] and the publisher will probably not deviate from this rule." The best course of action, he advised, was to approach the press office of the NSF for assistance in finding a spot on a daily newspaper. Thimme was not able to secure such a position and instead continued to work in the Press and Propaganda Department of the NSF throughout the war.[115]

Margret Boveri, the most famous foreign correspondent during the Third Reich, credited her eventual success in large part to Paul Scheffer, the editor of the *Berliner Tageblatt*, the first paper for which she worked. Highly educated but unable to secure a full-time position, Boveri worked as a freelance journalist until a personal contact recommended her to Scheffer in August 1934. She soon became Scheffer's protégée. "It was due to Scheffer," recalled Boveri, "that I started to become a name."[116]

Other women took advantage of family connections. Waltraud Fest obtained both her journalist internship and later position at the *Duisburger General-Anzeiger* through her father, who worked for the paper himself.[117] Edit von Coler, a divorcée, was a cousin of Himmler's wife.[118] Although not trained as a journalist, in March 1935, based on Himmler's personal recommendation, von Coler became the foreign press chief for the Reich Office for Food and Agriculture (Reichsnährstand).

Sexism was rampant in the field, and women journalists were both judged by their looks and femininity and called on to use them to further their careers. This situation, of course, was not specific to Nazi Germany or to the period. As Deborah Chambers has noted, "women find that they are not only deliverers but also objects of news – they become part of the spectacle themselves."[119] US war correspondent Marguerite Higgins, for example, witnessed the liberation of Dachau at the end of the Second World War and eventually covered the Nuremberg Trials. Despite her proven skill, she was referred to in the press and among male colleagues as "Marilyn Monroe" and accused of using her sexuality to land important interviews. When searching for an internship in Nazi Germany, Thea Fischer recalled an editor's suggestion to try her luck with the editor of the paper the *Heimat am Mittag*. His advice: "Go there and introduce yourself. Make yourself chic, he appreciates well-dressed women."[120] Elisabeth Noelle-Neumann described how she had approached the *Königsberger Zeitung* in an effort to get her work published. The male editor treated her as simply "an attraction" (*Sehenswürdigkeit*) rather than a journalist there for a serious discussion.[121]

Helene Rahms's boss Bernd Olaf took her under his wing due not only to her journalistic potential but also to his attraction to her. He demanded high professional standards and rigorously critiqued her work. At the same time, he called her "cookie" and presented her with professional opportunities linked to his personal desires. After a particularly harsh critique of her writing, he proclaimed, "You'll never be a journalist!" Noticing Rahms's distress, he allegedly laid his hand on her shoulder and said "'Now, now, it'll all work out.' The hand lay there for a few moments too long." Rahms recalled.[122] Knowing her desire to write about culture, Olaf suggested a joint trip to Prague, which would ostensibly expand her horizons and allow her to report on German art and life in the region. His intentions were clear to Rahms before the trip, although he allegedly stated that "nothing would happen … that she did not want."[123] The two began a sexual relationship. Rahms described their first liaison as consensual, yet her writing also suggests that she felt some pressure to become intimate with him. She had felt completely out of her depth on her first press trip and diminished by the seasoned male journalists that she and her boss encountered in Prague. Rahms later wrote that she had hesitations about an affair, but, at the time, she said to herself: "He opened the world for you, you should be thankful to him."[124] Such experiences demonstrate the dependence that women often had on men in positions of power and the precarious situations they could face as they struggled to advance their careers.

Rahms's experiences at the *Saale-Zeitung* under the tutalege of Olaf also provide insight into how women journalists felt both included and marginalized within the field. Although only a trainee, Rahms was among the small group of colleagues invited to evenings at her boss's house, where they discussed the paper and, purportedly, their discomfort with Nazism. According to Rahms, she was included because, in the eyes of her older male colleagues, she was an "innocent, somewhat cheeky young thing," there to "pour their tea or serve as decoration."[125] Even so, Rahms felt the evenings were a sign of trust, and she was pleased to have been included, despite the fact that her only female colleague warned her that even if she were the boss's protégée, she would not find much opportunity in the field beyond editing the women's supplements.[126]

If they sometimes showed support for women, men in senior positions could also limit a woman's progress. For instance, the head of the Silesian branch of the Press Association wrote to the Berlin office to complain that the editor of the *Schlesische Sonntagspost* was using the work of too many female photojournalists, while men's requests to be published were not being met.[127] It was not necessarily women's presence in the field that met resistance, but rather the idea that they were usurping male opportunities.

Often with little or no choice, many women journalists worked on a freelance basis. While some may have preferred freelance status due to the flexibility it provided or because of family obligations, editors and press authorities endorsed this practice. Adolf Dresler encouraged women to pursue freelance opportunities since, he counselled, the "consistent, gruelling work in editorial offices would be less to [their] liking" – a discourse intended to dissuade women from competing with men for more stable employment.[128] The high unemployment rate that began during the last years of Weimar ensured that, in the early 1930s, most of the few permanent journalistic positions available went to men.[129] Of 142 women journalists working in the pre-war years, at least 50 per cent were officially documented as freelance – the actual number is likely much higher.[130] The most experienced and esteemed journalists often worked freelance at some stage of their career. Dr Heddy Neumeister was a highly educated, skilled journalist who became a permanent staff member on the *Kölnische Zeitung* in 1930. Neumeister quit the paper in 1932 due to a lack of professional opportunities. She freelanced in Berlin until she eventually found a position on the *Frankfurter Zeitung* in 1936, writing about everyday life, society, and travel.[131]

Freelance work was often precarious and could lead to financial insecurity. Based in Rome, journalist and author Adelheid Dehio had been a steady freelance correspondent for *Der Angriff* since 1932.[132] She wrote on a variety of themes, including industry, business, travel, and local and national news. Dehio's communication with the paper's editorial department throughout 1938 and 1939 demonstrates the vulnerability of even established freelance journalists. She repeatedly had to request remuneration for her work. In early March 1939, she complained to the editor of *Der Angriff*, Kurt Kränzlein: "I have unfortunately heard absolutely nothing about the work that I submitted, which your editorial department commissioned from me … I am unfortunately not in a position to work for free."[133] Dehio also struggled to get the paper to publish her on a regular basis and repeatedly rebuked Kränzlein for not using articles she had submitted. After filing several articles written during travels in Libya, Dehio wrote in June 1937 that she was discouraged by how little exposure her writings had brought for her in the paper:

> It was very painful on my return to find out that not one of my articles was printed in *Der Angriff*. I had written five long articles, always late in the evenings after a packed day, which I sent, as you requested, only to *Der Angriff*. Since no more than eight journalists participated in this very interesting trip, I could have successfully published my work anywhere else in Germany. Now they've all fallen under the table.[134]

Although frustrated, Dehio had no qualms about pushing for increased professional opportunities, which speaks to women's claims that much of their success depended on tenacity, even if the trait was more often associated with men.

Despite her complaints, it was Kränzlein who had arranged and financed Dehio's trip to Libya.[135] He valued women's contributions to the paper and presented journalists like Dehio with freelance opportunities. Yet he also attributed less value to her work than he did to that of her male colleagues. Despite the length of her association with the paper, Dehio remained concerned about the security of her position. She had joined the Association of the Foreign Press in Germany (Verein der Ausländischen Presse in Deutschland – VAP) in her capacity as correspondent for *Der Angriff* in 1932. In January 1938, Dehio discovered that she had been deleted from the association's membership list and instead included on its list of "occasional" journalists. This was the "exact opposite of a promotion," she complained to Kränzlein. Dehio particularly feared that she would be pushed into the background during the upcoming visit of the "Führer" to Rome and that, going forward, a male correspondent for the paper would be given the most important assignments. "This," she complained "despite the fact that I have held this position abroad for the purpose of the NSDAP [Nationalsozialistische Deutsche Arbeiterpartei, the Nazi Party] for so many years."[136] Even though Kränzlein sent the reference that Dehio requested to facilitate her reinclusion in the VAP, her concerns about her position were justified. In April 1938, Dr Waldemar Lentz, who had recently arrived in Rome to assume responsibility for reporting from that city, wrote to the editorial office in Berlin that he had met Dehio, and he requested that Berlin clearly delineate their responsibilities.[137] *Der Angriff*'s answer described Dehio's role as "insignificant," noting that she was an old associate that the paper had helped "by throwing occasional work her way." According to the paper, the arrangement had functioned well and had not affected the work of their "permanent correspondents."[138] Although Kränzlein classified Dehio as insignificant, he continued to publish her work along with freelance material from other female journalists working inside and outside of Germany.[139]

Despite its precarity, freelance work could result in journalists having a more expansive audience than that enjoyed by their male or female counterparts in full-time positions. Although press policy sought to restrict women journalists to a female audience, in reality, their freelance status meant that they often worked for a variety of publications with a diverse readership. Dresler pointed out in his study that "the journalistic work of women has been more broadly based than in-depth."[140] Gertrud Burath, for instance, published work in varied publications, such as popular illustrated tabloids, numerous dailies, women's magazines, and trade publications related to various industries. In 1936, she published almost thirty articles in *Der SA-Mann* – a publication targeted entirely at a male paramilitary audience.[141] Herta Herbst published articles on travel and local news in a range of papers and magazines, including the popular *Berliner Lokal-Anzeiger*, the conservative *Deutsche Allgemeine Zeitung*, the Nazi *Westdeutscher Beobachter*, and the women's magazine *Mode und Heim*. She also wrote for the popular and growing market of magazines related to radio programs, which were widely read by both men and women.[142] Freelance journalists were also dependent on the state-run German News Agency (Deutsches Nachrichtenbüro – DNB), which often gave their work a wide distribution. As the largest central Nazi news agency, the DNB provided much of the content destined for Germany's newspapers, making it a critical tool for the regime.[143] Yet, more often than not, women did not receive credit for their work distributed by the DNB. Regardless of how wide the audience for a particular piece, it was not always clear that a woman had written it. The fact that many women (and some men) did not receive a byline in newspapers, coupled with the relatively popular use of pseudonyms (*Decknamen*), rendered women somewhat invisible in the field, despite the fact that their work received broad exposure.

Names possess social power, and it was not uncommon for women to write under a pseudonym – almost 10 per cent did so.[144] This practice was often, but not always, due to their sex. The use of pseudonyms could help women traverse the boundaries between professional options, acceptance, and perceived legitimacy on the part of readers and even colleagues. An alias could, for instance, desexualize or even masculinize a woman's name. Cultural journalist Katharina Kleikamp wrote under the initials KK, and Gertrud Burath under the name H. Maden. Franziska Bilke used the male name Franz, and Helga Bousten-Schmucker published under Hans Georg. Foreign correspondent Margret Boveri published under the name Dr M. Boveri. As, Boveri herself noted, "the femininity was gone. The readers sometimes asked whether I was the wife of Dr. M."[145] It is worth noting that Boveri began to use a gender-neutral byline only after she started to make a name for herself as a foreign policy expert, a traditional male domain. Nazi press authorities and (male) editors believed that, in the area of hard news, a masculine or gender-neutral name held more legitimacy than a female one. The right name in a byline could help the regime bridge the space between its gender rhetoric and the activities of women journalists.

At the same time, the use of masculine or desexualized aliases was not always tied to the area of reportage or type of paper for which women wrote. Although Boveri was a foreign correspondent when she began to use an alias, other female journalists who used male pseudonyms wrote primarily for women's and family magazines and the women's supplements of daily newspapers.[146] Gertraude Uhlhorn used the name Gert Bub because, that way, "anyone could imagine what they wanted, a man or a woman."[147] Aliases could be used to differentiate a journalist's work if he or she was also an author of books or wrote different types of material for different publications. Out of a compilation of thirty-five female journalists who used *Decknamen*, almost half used a gender-neutral or male name.[148] Men also used pseudonyms but primarily took on other male names.[149] Given women journalists' freelance status, use of pseudonyms, and the fact that they often received no bylines, the scope of their voice echoed far beyond the recognition they received in the field. In spite of the difficulties and their relative invisibility, journalism was an appealing profession for women.

Nazi press authorities sought to portray journalism as a serious and demanding, yet stimulating and accessible, career for women, and in many ways it was. The profession and tasks of women journalists not only conflicted with Nazi rhetoric about motherhood being the primary role for women, but also with policies that created space for women to work in industrial, commercial, or office positions until they married. Despite the discussion about double earners that took place in the early years of the Third Reich, a woman's ability to work in journalism was not typically limited by her marital status. Married women, mothers, and single women worked as journalists. An analysis of 250 female journalists who worked during the Third Reich shows that 53 per cent were, in fact, married.[150] Although sources do not allow for a precise breakdown of the number of journalists who were also mothers, it is clear that several had families. Maria Reese, Petra Vermehren, Edit von Coler, and Ruth Andreas-Friedrich, for instance, were all single mothers.

In 1941, the popular magazine *Die junge Dame* (The young lady) published two reports on the profession, in which an accredited journalist and a journalist-in-training wrote about their experiences in the field. The stated purpose of the article was to help other young women determine whether they might be suited for a career in the press. Full-time journalist Senta Ulitz cautioned that the role was strenuous and required long days and the ability to work at a fast pace. She went on to describe how no day looked the same: each was filled with interviews, local events, and cultural happenings as she ran from a meeting with a well-known actress to an exhibition to a theatre performance, happy to have a chance to grab a quick cup of tea along the way. But the article's primary takeaway was that journalism was a glamourous and stimulating profession. Ulitz encouraged those with talent to pursue such a career "because – told in confidence – it is a wonderful profession!"[151]

The pictures accompanying the article also pointed to the action and exhilaration the profession provided. They depicted a day in the life of a young, chic journalist by the name of Fräulein Gerber as she conducted interviews with artists, interacted with soldiers, discussed her work with her editor, and finally, experienced the thrill of seeing her words in print. Certainly, the timing of the article in the middle of the war was significant, as women were needed to step into roles vacated by men who were on the frontlines. But more striking is the fact that the article implied that women could find fulfilment and purpose beyond marriage and children – a narrative not typically supported by the Nazi regime, whose pro-natal ideology remained in place throughout the war.

In the same issue, trainee Anneliese Schwahl wrote that she "could not imagine a more beautiful profession than that of a journalist, which offers so many interesting and beautiful things every day and broadens one's view on all areas of life."[152] Schwahl described how she felt being at the center of action and able to witness and report on events as they took place. "This is an undreamt-of enrichment for a young person," she enthused. She ended her article by wishing good luck to all women who dreamed of becoming journalists: "May they prove through their capabilities and diligence that a woman can take on a man in this field as well."[153]

Schwahl's and Ulitz's depictions of the profession as fast-paced and action-packed, and one that placed them on equal, if separate, footing with men, were only some of the reasons that women found the profession appealing. Other aspects that drew women to the field included intellectual stimulation, status, freedom and flexibility, travel, and, often, simply a love of writing. Women were drawn not only to these very real benefits, but also to the image and reality of living unconventional and independent lives. For some, their role as a journalist formed an important part of their identity. Given that many, although by no means all, female journalists came from the middle class, they started out with more financial and educational advantages than those from the working and lower-middle classes. They often spoke additional languages, which facilitated professional and personal travel opportunities. Marta Hillers spoke French and some Russian, which she had picked up from her schooling and travels. Born in 1911, Hillers initially trained as a secretary. She travelled extensively from 1931 to 1933, touring countries such as Poland, Georgia, Armenia, Russia, Turkey, Greece, and Italy. Her photographs from her travels appeared in European and American publications. In 1934, she completed two semesters studying history and art history at the Sorbonne and began to work as a freelance journalist in the fall of 1934.[154] Single and independent, Hillers enjoyed opportunities to take on whimsical assignments with her friend and fellow journalist Trude Sand. In December 1934, for instance, the two took an amusing road trip across Germany with long-haul truckers and produced a series of articles based on this experience.[155]

Erika Schmachtenberger's photojournalism career took off so quickly in 1933 that she was soon able to buy her first car – a rarity for a single woman at the time – which allowed her to travel extensively for her profession and take on only those assignments that suited her.[156] Her work took her to Italy, Austria, France, Hungary, Romania, and Yugoslavia. In 1934, the *Münchner Illustrierte* sent Schmachtenberger on a trip to New York aboard the *Bremen* to take photographs of the largest German steamship to date. Schmachtenberger recalled the trip with enthusiasm and extolled the first-class travel accommodations on the ship: "I had a bathtub [that provided] hot water – either saltwater or fresh water – cold water, both salt and fresh. So, four types of water for one bathtub."[157] Schmachtenberger's career soared thanks to such reports. Her photographs appeared on at least 30 per cent of the *Illustrierter Rundfunk*'s front covers between 1933 and 1940. She also published many photo essays in the magazine itself.[158] With a car and a flourishing career, Schmachtenberger fit the stereotype of the much-debated and politicized *neue Frau* (modern woman) that emerged during the Weimar Republic – the type of single, independent woman derided in Nazi propaganda in the 1920s and early 1930s.

Schmachtenberger's own sense of self was certainly tied to the notion that she was a bold and independent journalist who did not subscribe to traditional notions of femininity. She used adjectives generally associated with masculinity, such as "daring" or "competitive," to describe herself. Some women framed their professional identity as "one of the boys" because it allowed them a feeling of self-empowerment within a field shaped by patriarchal assumptions.[159] Schmachtenberger did so under a regime that projected itself as hyper-masculine. She emphasized the quality of her work and her willingness to take on challenging projects for the sake of her career. Schmachtenberger recounted, for instance, how she had received an assignment in 1933 to take photographs aboard a Hindenburg aircraft in flight. Rather than take conventional shots out of the window, she had wanted unrestricted photographs of the view below. One of the pilots showed her a hatch in the floor that opened and asked, "Do you dare to take a picture down there?" "Yes I dared!" she declared in her memoir.[160] She drew attention to the fact that the pilot was a certain Captain Bauer, later the flight captain for Hitler. According to Schmachtenberger, the editors at the magazine the *Illustrierte Rundfunk* knew that she "liked to take dangerous pictures" and made suggestions for photo reportages that might appeal to her sense of adventure.[161]

Elisabeth Noelle-Neumann too described herself as someone who had always been unwilling to conform and who viewed journalism as a profession that would suit her personality.[162] Travel also appealed to Noelle-Neumann. In 1938, she began a trip around the world. Over a six-month period, the *Deutsche Allgemeine Zeitung* published monthly reports from her trip, although she had not yet completed her journalism studies.[163] Margret Boveri also relished her identity as an unconventional woman. She took flying lessons, had her own car, and travelled in regions most Europeans, let alone women, rarely had the opportunity to visit. In 1933, she drove through Morocco, Tunisia, and Algeria; her articles about this trip constituted her first publications.

Helene Rahms viewed journalism as a route to the "Bohemian life" she craved and a profession in which she could indulge her passion for culture and writing.[164] But an identity as a journalist and the sense of importance and community it provided also held appeal. In her memoir, Rahms recalled how she and her colleagues "wrote, edited, ate, drank, danced, and romanced. Hectic gaiety, unleashed by the pressure of daily work."[165] She repeatedly used the term "clique" to describe how she and other journalists viewed themselves during and after the Third Reich: "I fell in with groups, clubs and cliques that existed as islands in the 'national community,' cut off from outside [influences] but in agreement within."[166] Certainly, in her autobiographical writing, Rahms sought to disassociate herself and her colleagues from Nazism. Yet her words also demonstrate that part of Nazism's appeal to elements of the German population, particularly its youth, was that it addressed their hopes for a better life and brighter future.[167]

## Conclusion

In 1938, Ursula von Kardorff wrote to a friend that her trainee position on the *Deutsche Allgemeine Zeitung* provided her with indescribable joy: "I am so happy there that I would even go in on Sundays if I could."[168] She confided that she feared her time at the *DAZ* would come to an end after her internship: "Unfortunately, this paradise will end forever in January because they will not keep me; in principle they take no women. Out of 43 full-time journalists, one other (female) volunteer and me are the only women … Where will I find something like this again?"[169] Kardorff's words point to the appeal journalism held for women as well as the obstacles they faced in the field.

The Nazi regime restructured and co-opted the press for its own purposes, and women journalists such as Erika Schmachtenberger, Helene Rahms, and Ursula von Kardorff were a product of these processes. Press authorities succeeded in ensuring that women largely felt included in the community of the press and found a sense of importance and fulfilment through their work. At the same time, differential treatment, sexist working conditions, and limited opportunities for advancement compounded the complications of entering a field that the Nazi state was ostensibly encouraging women to join. Such inconsistences allowed the regime space to create the politicized media cohort it desired without appearing to compromise its rhetoric on women's place and use in the German community: women would be a critical part of the press but not in a manner in which they would be particularly visible or prominent. Although women found the profession appealing for a number of reasons – not least because it allowed them to step out of prescribed gender roles – their work largely reproduced traditional gender norms and was instrumentalized in service to the Nazi state.

# Prettying Up Politics and Normalizing Nazism, 1933–1939

In her 1938 dissertation on the history of women in the press, Josephine Trampler-Steiner, a young doctoral candidate in journalism studies at the University of Munich, argued that, despite severe obstacles, both past and present, women had "conquered" the press. They now worked as journalists as well as editors, and some even held positions as publishers. As she pointed out, the women's inserts and the features (*Feuilleton*) sections of newspapers, as well as magazines, were open to capable women journalists. Those who attempted to "move into the political pages of a newspaper," however, continued to experience difficulties.[1] Yet Trampler-Steiner contended that most women were not upset by the fact that men held more positions and greater authority in the area of political news because this notion related only to a narrow conception of politics. If one held to a broader definition of what constituted the political – one that included domestic, social, and cultural topics – Trampler-Steiner argued, then women journalists wielded enormous influence, since these areas represented "purely the women's realm."[2] Her argument pinpoints the importance Nazi press authorities placed on women journalists and the goal assigned to them: they were to serve as a bridge to the private realm and function as an intermediary between the state and Germany's women – a role that authorities defined as both political and apolitical, depending on the context.[3]

While the previous chapter looked at what it took for women to enter the journalism profession, this chapter explores the form of soft power that they held within the areas that the regime deemed best suited to their feminine talents: soft-news topics such as travel, entertainment, culture, fashion, and, most importantly, lifestyle and domestic concerns. Soft power in journalism is typically understood as relating to a form of communication that is persuasive but non-coercive.[4] Propaganda on behalf of the state embodies this form of soft power precisely when it does not appear to be propaganda – that is, when it is not aggressive, threatening, or overtly coercive. It is used to attract readers and obtain their compliance toward particular policies, whether political, economic, or cultural, as well as to influence their receptiveness to state ideology.[5] Women journalists functioned in service to the Nazi state by producing a form of positive propaganda about the private realm that helped market the "appeal" of Nazism, and, after 1936, sought to rally Germany's women to prepare for the war that Hitler intended.

Scholars of the National Socialist press have rightly pointed out that women made up only a small percentage of working journalists during the Third Reich. It is true that, prior to the war, this proportion was never more than 9 per cent.[6] But the story is more complex than the numbers would imply. Despite their limited presence, women journalists were significant producers of media that contributed to one of the most important facets of Nazi propaganda: seemingly harmless material that focused on everyday life. Such articles, which reflected a generally cheerful perspective, had a soft-power function that was important to the regime's political and ideological objectives. They were to provide diversion, pleasure, and a façade of normalcy – primarily for German women, but also for men.

Historians have shown how the German government policed the private realm after the First World War, particularly in the areas of sexuality and reproduction.[7] While one cannot draw hard lines between private and public life during the Weimar Republic, the blurring of both spheres became more pronounced in Nazi Germany, a trait typical of authoritarian regimes.[8] Yet as the historiography has also demonstrated, the regime's attempts to create a space for pleasure, a sense of normality, and the illusion of a private realm played an important role in aligning the population more closely with the Nazi movement. The media was instrumental in this mission.[9] This chapter deepens our understanding of this phenomenon by examining who played a critical role in the production of material that created space for happiness and the notion of a private life within a brutal and repressive regime. Such suggestions of normality helped the regime maintain the support of the population and reassure Germans still hesitant about Nazism; it also functioned to keep open a pressure valve that emphasized continuity rather than rupture – at least for those Germans included in the *Volksgemeinschaft*.

Women journalists in Nazi Germany worked within a gendered world that was based not only on the regime's ideology but also on long-held concepts of manhood and femininity and the corresponding behavioural expectations in the professional and private realms. Given beliefs that women were the more sensitive sex, and therefore better able than men to tap into and provoke readers' emotions, Nazi press authorities especially valued women's contributions to the genre of soft news. They deemed women's voices more emotional, amusing, and light-hearted – implicitly more entertaining – than men's.[10] Of course, the association of femininity with the private sphere was not unique to Nazi Germany. Indeed, this belief had allowed women to gain a foothold in journalism throughout Europe and North America. From the late nineteenth century onward, newspapers and magazines sought to engage women readers in a bid to increase circulation and advertising revenue – a process that opened up journalistic opportunities for middle-class, educated women.[11] A female journalist's value was based on the notion that she was better suited than her male counterpart to write on topics related to women. While women journalists in general helped expand what was considered "news" via a focus on the everyday and "women's issues," the work of female journalists in these same areas in Nazi Germany proved useful for the regime's political goals.

The perceived continuity of "normal life" assisted in diverting the population's attention – or helped it look away – from the state's persecution of those fellow Germans whom the regime deemed undesirable. Prior to, but even more so after, the launch of the 1936 Four-Year Plan, which was designed to prepare the country for war, the work of women journalists functioned to school Germany's women in Nazi ideals, foster a sense of unity for those included in the *Volksgemeinschaft*, generate support for the regime's agenda, and achieve a level of readiness for Hitler's war of "race and space."[12] After 1936, such material promoted a "new" normal in which the ordinariness of private everyday life overlapped ever more closely with the regime's nationalistic, expansionist, and violent goals.

Female journalists were to address such topics in a "womanly" way, and their gender afforded them the authority to do so. Nazi rhetoric that all women stood outside of politics validated the notion that women journalists addressed only apolitical topics, despite discourse that emphasized the political importance of journalists – both male and female – in Nazi Germany. As discussed in chapter 1, the 1934 Editors Law defined the journalistic profession as a public mission and bound it legally and intellectually to the state.[13] Accordingly, the German Press Association instructed journalists that "press and politics belong together," and Deputy Reich Press Chief Helmut Sündermann went so far as to declare that "a born journalist is a born politician."[14] In the aftermath of the Second World War, the notion that women worked outside of politics allowed women journalists to argue that they had not been entangled with Nazi propaganda. Despite such claims, these women were important conveyors of material aimed at soliciting the support – or ensuring the apathy – of the population in order to create space for the regime to achieve its political ambitions.

## The Importance of Women Journalists

The regime's conception of journalism as a political profession in support of the state provided women with a sense of professional importance in areas that were public in their reach and impact. Annie Juliane Richert, chair of the women's branch of the German Press Association, declared that the Editors Law had, for the first time, given women journalists a prominence within the state and recognized their work as having political value. Richert used the language of the regime to elevate the status of women journalists and imply that Nazism provided them a position of privilege and a form of emancipation: She characterized them as the "confident leader of the women's world."[15] Still, Richert did not stray too far from Nazi gender rhetoric, repeating the regime's stance that women journalists were to serve primarily as the conduit between the state and the female population.[16]

Via women's magazines and newspaper supplements, female journalists were to connect with women in the areas where they functioned: as wives and mothers, in local and domestic affairs, in social work, education, culture, youth work, and travel.[17] Such areas were important to the regime, as the head of the German Press Association, Wilhelm Weiß, made clear in a 1936 speech to women journalists. Weiß urged women to view coverage of these "traditionally undervalued" domains as critical and not simply as "the sections of the newspapers which male journalists did not deem their responsibility."[18] Moreover, press authorities believed that female journalists held more legitimacy when it came to writing content that related to a woman's private or public world given their supposed inherent understanding of women's lives.[19] *Die Schriftleiterin* (The guide for women journalists) counselled that only women had "expertise in the special, female life spheres."[20] In his 1936 study on women in journalism, Dr Adolf Dresler concluded that "the journalistic work of women will be limited mainly to entertainment, literature, fashion, education, the family, and related topics because the female nature corresponds to these areas. The woman will always write more with her heart than the man." He also noted that, in "her selected areas, a woman journalist's work was sometimes even better than a man's."[21] Weiß too declared that "women have the gift of seeing things more colourfully, more amusingly than men."[22]

To describe journalists' responsibilities, authorities employed a masculinized language of camaraderie and battle that cast journalists as "fighters for the new state" and "comrades on guard" in service to National Socialism.[23] An 1934 article in the party paper the *Völkischer Beobachter* declared, "the struggle with the pen is no less important for the future of the nation than the struggle with the fist."[24] Journalism guides also counselled that, to succeed in journalism, both men and women required traits traditionally associated with concepts of masculinity: strong nerves, speed, resilience, physical and mental robustness, and a willingness to take on a journalist's significant responsibility to the state and to the public.[25] At the same time, women were encouraged to rely on their "feminine characteristics" to achieve professional success. They should employ a woman's supposedly unique imagination, curiosity, compassion, and eye for detail in the everyday.[26] Such a dichotomy reveals how, even in Nazi Germany, gender was a malleable formulation, and gender expectations were framed depending on the situation. Thus, women journalists were asked to employ characteristics that were typically associated with both sexes in order to fulfil their professional obligations, even when engaging with the so-called private sphere.

Some female journalists echoed claims that women connected more emotionally with readers and believed that such qualities made them good, if not better, journalists than men. The use of such gender stereotypes allowed them to argue for more authority and legitimacy. When reflecting on her career during and after the Third Reich, Gertraude Uhlhorn stated that "journalism is actually a decidedly female profession," since "the nature of men is such that they cannot empathize with other people as they should."[27] Annie Juliane Richert maintained that most women, journalists and readers alike, believed that the women's pages of daily newspapers should be edited exclusively by women. "After all, it would be too much to ask even the smartest man to be prepared for all of the colourful diversity of women's lives."[28] Press authorities did seek to channel women into the areas Richert described, and they did so successfully: throughout the Third Reich, at least 68 per cent of women journalists worked primarily in "women's" or soft news.[29]

Male journalists too worked in these areas, although this was not a role most desired. Some women also resented being shunted into these domains. Many years after she began her career working on the local news pages of the Nazi Party paper the *Westdeutscher Beobachter*, Felicitas Kapteina maintained that the women's pages of newspapers were a "ghetto."[30] Helene Rahms resented the fact that she was restricted to local news when she began her journalism career.[31] Her primary task was writing about what she described as trivialities: "Farmer R. fell from a ladder and broke three ribs"; "Nazi women's group forms sewing circle"; "Local group leader dedicates the new party flag."[32] Despite that fact that she longed for a position on the *Frankfurter Zeitung*, Margret Boveri turned down the paper's offer to work on its women's section, fearing she would be pigeonholed there throughout her career. At the same time, some women desired to work in "female-appropriate" areas, not because of Nazi instructions to do so, but because they simply found them most interesting or appealing.[33]

The German public also found the areas in which women typically worked the most pleasing.[34] Studies of press reception conducted during the Third Reich demonstrated that readers often ignored the politics section of newspapers, preferring the local, human-interest, sports, and entertainment sections.[35] A 1939 doctoral dissertation by Alfred Schmidt analysed reader response to newspapers in a small Saxon town and concluded that 88 per cent of readers read the local news section, 88 per cent read the classified ads (normally located in the women's supplements), and only 40 per cent read the politics section.[36]

Along with the soft-news sections of newspapers, women's, family, general interest, and illustrated magazines were a major force in Germany's media landscape.[37] The work of women journalists in such publications helped create a feel-good media that provided readers with a seemingly depoliticized realm of blissful domesticity, self-improvement, adventure, travel, and escapism. Millions of Germans, women and men alike, were attracted to such material. Indeed, articles in trade journals advised journalists that men, prior to and during the war, also enjoyed reading "women's news" and reminded their wives, "Don't forget our magazine!"[38] Nonetheless, as a result of their strong position as media consumers, women remained the primary target of such publications. Making material pleasing to consumers was particularly important to Minister of Propaganda Joseph Goebbels, given the conformity and blandness of the news that resulted from the regime's strict control of the press. Much discussion took place in trade journals on the importance of making soft news warm and interesting, lively and fresh, versatile and entertaining.[39] The *Zeitschriften-Dienst*, a weekly newsletter for magazine editors, noted that magazines were "an important and entertaining means of educating people about National Socialism via the small issues of daily life."[40]

Freelance journalist Marta Hillers wrote for various illustrated tabloids, women's magazines, and dailies.[41] Her work for the general-interest magazine *Die neue Gartenlaube* provides an example of the type of cheery and uncomplicated material that focused on private pleasures and concerns. In "Hairstylist Much Sought After," for instance, Hillers bemoaned her hairdresser's recent engagement and recalled how, like most women, she looked forward to her bi-weekly hair appointments. "And then it happens: One day we look in the mirror and see a ring on Miss Müller's hand," Hillers wrote.[42] The article went on to point out how women rarely achieved the status of "master stylist" because, inevitably, they left the profession once married. Yet Hillers also described the opportunities open for women within the field before they settled into marriage. With talent and hard work, she assured, one could certainly "get ahead." Hillers's article was free of National Socialist rhetoric, although her work corresponded to Nazi gender expectations in two ways: she highlighted women's (and the regime's) alleged preference for a marriage and family over a career; and, at the same time, she underscored the reality of life in Nazi Germany that allowed space for a single woman to work in an appropriate field.

Hillers also published regularly in the *Berliner Lokal-Anzeiger*, a popular daily newspaper with one of the highest national circulations at the time. Like many dailies, it included a weekly women's supplement called *Die Welt der Frau* (The world of women). The supplement was emblematic of women's news in general and included sections on fashion, recipes, lifestyle advice, culture, and child-rearing, as well as housekeeping and shopping tips.

Similar to most women's magazines, the material published in the women's supplements of newspapers did not change significantly after 1933. As Jennifer Lynn shows, there was much continuity between the Weimar Republic and the Third Reich with regard to the content of women's and illustrated magazines, as the regime sought to cater to the reading interests of the female population.[43] This continuity contributed to the illusion that a semblance of normality remained within the private realm. Rather than project the Nazi vision of natural beauty and health, Annaliese Reese, who wrote about fashion for the *Berliner Lokal-Anzeiger*, focused on elegant, modern clothing and promoted the latest cosmetics and accessories. In a 1934 article entitled "One Piece Does Not Suit All" she discussed how women could cleverly mask physical imperfections by making the latest fashion trends work for them: "Who has not bemoaned a small flaw," she wrote. "No one's appearance is perfect." Reese advised that, "while the season's waist-length capes and flared collars were particularly flattering for tall figures, petite women should stick with streamlined looks" and "one could never go wrong with black and white."[44] Topics such as how to make the most of one's appearance or combat the signs of aging were timeless and subtle propaganda that life continued as usual under the Nazi dictatorship.

In contrast to the fashion and lifestyle sections, the weekly column "Women's Professional Life" conformed more closely to Nazi ideals for women. It provided advice on finding positions in social work, education, and other fields assumed to suit the characteristics of women. Occasionally an article would address opportunities for women in a field outside of traditional domains, but these too served to promote a limited view of women's professional opportunities. A 1934 article on women's place in the legal profession noted that, while women were (officially) still able to study law, it was a "man's responsibility to uphold the law."[45] A woman was not suited to a career within the judiciary, as a public prosecutor, or as a practising lawyer. In other words, obtaining a degree in law would not lead to career opportunities within the field itself. Rather, the article advised, women could expect to work in a lawyer's office, "where the line between secretary and [legal] colleague is fluid," or as a legal adviser in the personnel department of private companies. Yet studying law, the article declared, could also lead to a successful journalistic career. Along with publicizing the Nazi view that women had no place as professional lawyers in the Third Reich, the article underscored that the regime viewed journalism as a suitable career choice for women.

While most articles in the supplements of the *Berliner-Anzeiger* were aimed at women, some targeted men directly, indicating that they too read such material. In December 1934, for example, Carola Ihlenberg wrote several articles that advised men on how to shop for their wives and children. According to Ihlenberg, it was equally easy to buy gifts for women and children, since their needs were simple: "The most important thing was to make the gifts personal," she advised.[46] While "a small bottle of perfume [could] change the whole world for a woman at a stroke," expensive but less thoughtful presents were not always as well-received: "I knew a rather well-off man who gave his wife an onion grater, a new kitchen lamp, an illustrated recipe book and a vacuum cleaner," she wrote. Yet his wife was most overjoyed with a cheap and cheerful necklace because it was a bobble she would not buy for herself. "Just consider the passion with which women do their shopping – aren't they captivated by every other window display … So it can't be difficult to find something suitable," Ihlenberg concluded.[47] Like the work of Hillers and Reese, Ihlenberg's articles on shopping and domestic life fit into a genre that was important to the regime: her writing evoked personal pleasure and harmonious, and complimentary, relationships. Moreover, such pieces served to spur consumption, which not only encouraged Germans to fulfil individual desires, but also had national consequences: during the first two years of the Third Reich, individual consumption acted as a stimulant to the economy.[48]

Illustrated magazines, with their emphasis on photography, also attracted the population as a whole and were the primary medium that conveyed a depoliticized image of the Third Reich.[49] Press authorities viewed photographs as a particularly effective form of propaganda because they easily captured a reader's attention and (at least to their viewers) reflected an "objective" form of reality.[50] Here, too, press authorities valued the contribution of women photographers because of the supposedly feminine skills they brought to the task. As one photo critic wrote, "many women practise the profession of photojournalist with enthusiasm and skill. Mostly they turn to cultural themes: from travel and theatre to topics that showcase women's social work. In the creation [of their work], the distinctly feminine way of seeing and interpreting is always critical."[51]

Unabashedly sensationalized, illustrated magazines were an undemanding read that gave their audience a glimpse into the lives of the wealthy and famous, visions of idyllic travel destinations, and international and domestic events. Reporting for such magazines could prove pleasurable for journalists as well. Photojournalist Erika Groth-Schmachtenberger focused on warm-hearted and whimsical topics for her reportage in the *Münchner Illustrierte* and the *Illustrierter Rundfunk*: "School's Out," "An Elite Class of Figure Skating" (figure 2.1), "Germany's Highest Chimney Sweep," and "Fashionable Hats for Sicilian Horses."

In 1937, Schmachtenberger published "On the Lido of Rome," which included shots of elegant Italian women swimming and sunbathing in the "most daring bathing suits" (figure 2.2): "The beautiful, proud women of southern blood sunbathe on the fine-grain sand of the beach," Schmachtenberger wrote. "In the coolness of the hotel lobbies, people dance to modern jazz music … This is the beach outside of Rome, where Roman emperors and the rich patricians of ancient times spent their hot summer days."[52] Schmachtenberger's pictures conjured up images of glamour and *la dolce vita* in the capital of fascist Italy and functioned to transport German readers, most of whom could only dream of such a holiday destination, to a world of sophistication and relaxation. Her pictures not only evoked visual pleasure, but the images of women in skimpy swimming costumes were intended to attract and titillate male readers. Her text and photographs also exuded warmth and humour. Next to a photo of a group of toddlers playing in the sand, Schmachtenberger wrote, "On the beach, black-eyed children gather like cherubs.

2.1  German world ice-skating champions Maxie Herber and Ernst Baier, by Erika Groth-Schmachtenberger, 1938

Photo credit: bpk Bildagentur / Erika Groth-Schmachtenberger / Art Resource, NY

Small brown arms and legs have to work energetically to secure a place [on the bench]."

Schmachtenberger specialized in photographing seemingly apolitical motifs associated with a traditional, everyday German lifestyle, particularly in a rural setting. Her work captured peaceful landscapes, quaint folk festivals, farmers working the fields (figure 2.3), and families in traditional clothing (*Trachten*) (figure 2.4). Such images of an idyllic, rural Germany echoed Nazi blood-and-soil ideology. Historians and media scholars have termed such photos "Heimat photography" and have shown how positive depictions of rural life satisfied the longing of broad sections of the population for a sense of security, nostalgia,

2.2 *Illustrierter Rundfunk* photo reportage, "On the Lido of Rome," by Erika Groth-Schmachtenberger, 1937

Photo credit: Institute für Zeitungsforschung Dortmund / Erika Groth-Schmachtenberger

2.3  Farmers ploughing on the Hirschberg near Weilheim in upper Bavaria, by Erika Groth-Schmachtenberger, 1937

Photo credit: Bezirk Oberbayern, Archiv Freilichtmuseum Glentleiten / Erika Groth-Schmachtenberger

2.4  Dancing couple in traditional costume (*Trachten*) at a wedding in St Gilgen, Austria, by Erika Groth-Schmachtenberger, 1936

Photo credit: Salzburger Landesinstitute für Volkskunde/ Erika Groth-Schmachtenberger

and escapism, especially during periods of uncertainty or instability, whether social, political, or economic.[53]

Schmachtenberger's photographs typically presented Germans in traditional gender roles. In "Girls in Land Service," she photographed young female volunteers who had travelled to the countryside to help a farmer's wife during the harvest. Her photographs captured the girls caring for children, doing the laundry, and, in their leisure time, riding horses. In her text, Schmachtenberger emphasized the "joyful camaraderie" among the girls and wrote that, despite the many tasks to be done, "the farm maids go to work with courage and cheerfulness."[54] While the photos and texts appeared free from Nazi ideology, the *Landdienst* program was designed not only to combat unemployment and help rural families, but also to indoctrinate German youth in the National Socialist worldview.

Reportages on exotic travel destinations or articles on shopping destinations read as apolitical and de-Nazified and in no way coercive. Yet they served the soft-power role of distracting Germans from the repressive elements of Nazism. Articles that focused on household management, however, had an even more overt political function because Nazism closely linked domesticity to its political agenda.

## Politicizing the Private Sphere

In 1936, Hermann Göring's Four-Year Plan was launched in a bid to increase Germany's preparations for war. The regime directed resources away from consumer goods and toward the production of war materials. Wives and mothers were responsible for family purchases and thus an economic force that the government recognized. Convincing women to alter how they kept house, cooked, shopped, and sewed in order to support German war preparation became an important propaganda goal. In fact, housewives were among the first to feel the impact of Germany's rearmament.[55] Accordingly, the importance of women journalists also increased.[56] Women became an increasingly significant target of Nazi propaganda disseminated through the press. And, from articles that included recipes for one-pot dinners to those that provided tips for growing one's own vegetables and suggestions on how to freshen up an old winter coat, women journalists were the conveyors of such material.

After 1936, female journalists continued to write primarily about motherhood, family, culture, and women's roles in the *Volksgemeinschaft*, but the end goal of such writing expanded. Wilhelm Weiß stressed that female journalists must connect with Germany's women in both the public and private realms in a manner that would have the most impact on the state's survival and would not simply focus on the *gemütliche* aspects of the field. In this way, women journalists were to help "fight the hard fight."[57] Weiß's words reflect both continuity and rupture with regard to the role of female journalists before and after 1936. They were now tasked not only with providing material that normalized the Third Reich, but also with creating content that spoke to women's growing importance, whether on the factory floor or in the kitchen, with respect to physical and psychological preparations for war. The publications of the National Socialist Women's League (Nationalsozialistische Frauenschaft – NSF) and its auxiliaries best exemplify how women journalists fulfilled these goals.

A position within the Press-Propaganda Department of the NSF or on one of its publications corresponded most closely to press authorities' beliefs about the ideal role for women journalists in the Nazi state: to communicate the Nazi way of life and world view through a party publication targeted entirely at Germany's women. Even before 1936, the Press-Propaganda Department focused its message on the importance of women to the Nazi state, not only as wives and mothers, but also as agents in the social and cultural fields, and as conveyors and maintainers of racial purity and the *Volksgemeinschaft*. *Frauenkultur*, the monthly magazine of the German Women's Bureau (Deutsches Frauenwerk, DFW), and the official party paper the *NS Frauen-Warte* mainly served such propaganda purposes and provided a form of self-promotion for the Nazi movement, the NSF, and its subsidiaries.[58] The *NS Frauen-Warte*, which was published bi-weekly, enjoyed a particularly wide distribution. Recipients included party members as well as women who were not connected to any National Socialist organization. In fact, the NSF deemed it more important to target women who were not politically organized, connecting the league – and the party – to those who continued to distance themselves from Nazism. For this reason, the price of the publication was kept low enough for most women to afford.[59]

In the fall of 1937, in the midst of the Four-Year Plan, the NSF undertook a massive advertising campaign to further increase the paper's circulation. The head of the league, Gertrud Scholtz-Klink, announced that the organization had to increase the paper's distribution in order to justify their work and entice women to the Nazi cause.[60] The campaign was a success: at the end of 1937, the *NS Frauen-Warte*'s circulation was 700,000; by the beginning of the Second World War, it had increased to 1,500,000, making it the leading women's publication in Germany.[61] The paper's circulation numbers gave those who wrote for it a particularly large audience. Moreover, the NSF's Press-Propaganda Department actively sought to place its articles in larger daily papers, which further increased the journalists' reach.

Early on, the NSF positioned the paper as an important medium in encouraging women to support the National Socialist struggle. A memo to the organization's district leaders declared that "the goal of our movement is not only to gain followers, but to make convinced and exemplary National Socialists out of them. And in this work the main task falls to the woman."[62] But women also had to assert their importance in relation to the paper and safeguard their role in its production, and in the NSF itself. In October 1933, the paper's publisher, Lydia Gottschewski, wrote that the NSF and its publications must temper male control: "If male leaders are involved in too many places, there is a very serious danger that male ideas and male values will be carried over into the women's movement."[63] Certainly male journalists and experts in various fields regularly contributed to the *Frauen-Warte*. Women journalists typically wrote only 36 per cent of the articles published in the paper; men were responsible for approximately 21 per cent (42 per cent were produced by authors whose sex was indiscernible either due to an alias or the absence of a byline).[64] Still, women did find full-time work at, or steady freelance assignments from, the paper. The most prominent journalists associated with *Frauen-Warte* tended to be party members of long standing. Gottschewski joined the Nazi Party in 1929, and editor Ellen Schwarz-Semmelroth joined in September 1930.[65] Renate von Stieda, Irmgard von Maltzahn, and Alice Rilke, all regular contributors to the paper, had joined the party by 1930.

*NS Frauen-Warte* covered a range of topics, the predominance of which changed according to the goals of the regime and, later, the events of the war. Each issue was composed of articles pertaining to general news, fashion, recipes, *Feuilleton*, and household tips. The features section included book reviews, poems, short stories, serial novels, and various cultural offerings. Semmelroth wrote a short column called "Politische Rückblick" (Political retrospective), which provided an overview of current events on the domestic and international front. Not surprisingly, more than two-thirds of the articles related to the National Socialist construction of womanhood – that is to say, women's roles as housewives and mothers.[66] In this way, the paper modelled the ideal National Socialist lifestyle for a woman and her family.

Journalists at the *NS Frauen-Warte* focused much attention on producing material that instructed women on how best to run the household and advised them of their responsibility as consumers. Such pieces had a two-fold political function. The first was to aid in the Nazi regime's goal of achieving autarky. In this vein, articles such as "Our Participation in the Work of the Führer," "German Women Use German Eggs," and "A Beautiful Home through Proper Care," instructed housewives how to shop, save, and preserve in a manner that reduced their consumption of certain products and allowed the regime to channel resources into preparing for and fighting the war.[67] Second, as Nancy Reagin has argued, the paper linked particular idea of "German" domesticity and housekeeping to German nationalism. This was to have violent repercussions after 1939, with the occupation of Polish and Soviet territories.[68]

Even seemingly benign decorating tips had anti-foreign or racist undertones. The article "Our Apartment Becomes a Home," for instance, featured photos of two bedroom sets. It described the "fancy" art deco–inspired set as "how the bedroom should not look": "This bombastic form, using foreign wood … does not correspond to the lifestyle of the German people."[69] Another photo displayed an appropriate bedroom suite, one with a simple form, constructed from beech wood, without any decoration that "attracted dust." Such articles demonstrate the subtler and less overtly political ways in which Nazi racial policy developed and took hold. Dust and dirt, for instance, were key words used to refer to housekeeping but also to the "nature" of "inferior" peoples such as the Soviets and Poles, who stood in contrast to notions of German order and cleanliness.

Fashion articles too were political in their effect, if not in their designation. Journalist and photographer Gertrud Villforth published in the housekeeping and fashion sections of the *Frauen-Warte*. She joined the NSF in 1934 and the party itself in 1939.[70] Prior to and after the 1936 announcement of the Four-Year Plan, Villforth's articles lauded German-made goods both for their quality and the ways in which they embodied the "taste and character" of the German woman.[71] Individual consumption had an important place in the "new Germany" – as long as consumers chose German goods and retailers for economic and ideological reasons.[72] Villforth's suggestions that women should purchase inexpensive "handmade jewelry crafted from precious metals with beautiful, genuine German stones" helped in this goal. In a subtle manner, her writing supported the party's desire to purge any foreign or "non-Aryan" influences from the fashion industry.[73]

Villforth's work also functioned to help the regime in its goal of diverting material for consumer goods to the war effort. From September 1939 onward, she adhered to press directives to emphasize that readers should stick to the motto "From Old to New."[74] She recommended, for instance, that German women select clothing made of durable fabric to last several seasons and urged readers to reject the international trend toward long skirts because they used too much material. Decisions about how to spend and when to save had highly political ramifications for the Nazi regime, and women journalists were an important medium to help influence and educate the female population to make the right choices and necessary sacrifices.

The writing and associated imagery in articles about motherhood and family typically depicted tranquility and a sense of personal fulfilment,

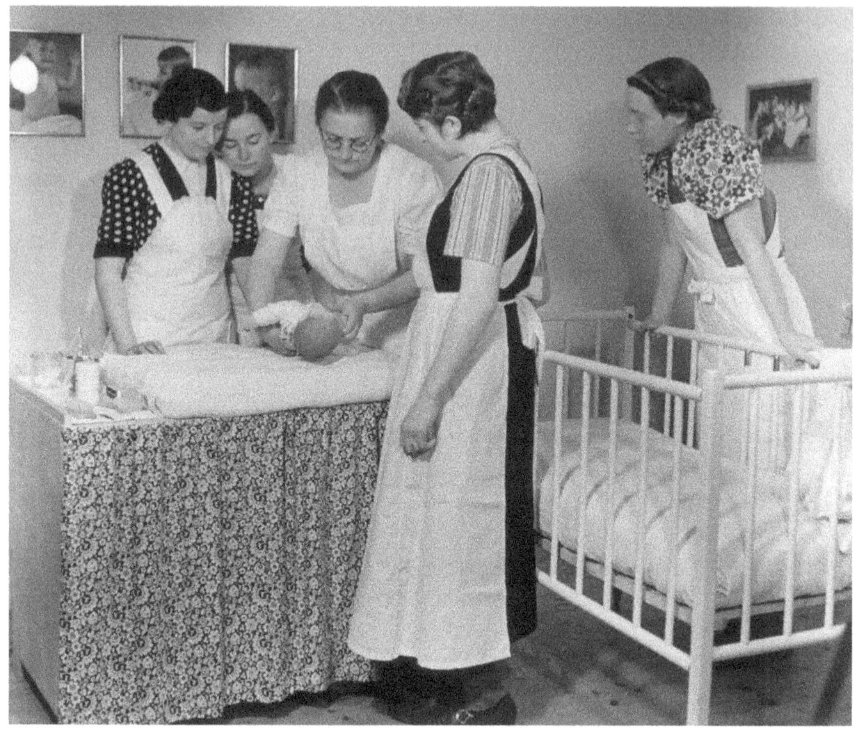

2.5  Women being trained in baby care at the maternity school (*Mütterschule*) in Oberbach/Röhn Germany, by Liselotte Purper, 1937

Photo credit: bpk Bildagentur/Liselotte Purper / Art Resource, NY

despite their political implications. Photojournalist Liselotte Purper's reportages in both *Frauenkultur* and *NS Frauen-Warte* contributed to this image of women, content within their "natural" roles as prescribed by the regime. In January 1937, Purper published an article titled "The Maternity School in Berlin-Wedding: A Place of Feminine Culture and Womanly Support" in *Frauenkultur*. Purper often photographed *Mütterschule* courses, which were held throughout Germany to teach new mothers how to care for their infants, and her work presented the regime's pro-natalist agenda and its related programs as an aid and support to women in this most important role (figure 2.5). Social-service organizations, such as the Mother and Child Relief Agency (Hilfswerk Mutter und Kind) and the Reich Mother's Service (Reichsmütterdienst des Deutschen Frauenwerke), that offered courses for women on how to prepare for, and care for, their family drew on Nazi ideals. The programs were designed to intervene directly in family life and politicize the private sphere, as the regime sought to implement increasing controls over women's bodies and determine who could, and could not, reproduce.[75] Purper's other reportage for the magazine in 1937 included "The House of a German Woman" and "A Day at the National Socialist Women's League Camp for Regional Youth Group Leaders." Purper would continue to photograph an idealized woman's world in regions annexed by Germany or under German occupation, including the Sudetenland in October 1938, and Poland from 1939 onward – a task connected with processes of extreme violence.

The *NS Frauen-Warte* provided female journalists with a platform to disseminate material more blatantly aligned with Nazi rhetoric. Journalists writing for the paper addressed the regime's "race and space" ideology through women-centric topics, specifically motherhood, domesticity, and culture. Articles such as "Preserving and Strengthening the Family: A *kinderreiche Mutter* Shares Her Experiences" encouraged women to contribute to the *Volksgemeinschaft* by having a large family, therefore becoming the mothers of future soldiers.[76] Such material also made clear that German Jews were not members of the people's community, but were, instead, a threat to its unity and survival. An August 1933 issue of the paper centred entirely around the "Jewish question." Articles included "A German Girl among Jews" by Lisa Goedel, who wrote of the harmful influence of Jews and their supposed unsavoury interest in "Aryan" girls. The paper did not shy away from material that echoed the well-trodden Nazi claim that Jewish men represented sexual threats to "Aryan" girls.

Twenty-five-year-old Renate von Stieda began her career as a journalist at the *NS Frauen-Warte* in May 1933.[77] A dedicated National Socialist, Stieda often addressed culture in her writing, embracing Nazi rhetoric about the alleged degeneracy and decline that took place in the cultural and social realms during the Weimar Republic. She lauded not only the regeneration of a "pure" German culture that had rid itself of Jewish influence, but also the unity of the *Volksgemeinschaft* under Nazism as a counterpoint to the division and conflict of the Weimar system. In the September 1933 issue of *Frauen-Warte*, she praised Nazism for making art accessible to the masses and repeated the Nazi line that, throughout the Weimar years, German art was controlled by foreigners and Jews, which had led to its increasing depravity and elitism.[78]

In some articles, Stieda wrote about Germany's alleged enemies in a direct fashion and warned women that, despite the regime's victory over the Jewish-Bolshevik threat that existed throughout the Weimar republic, they would need to stand on guard for Germany in order to prevent a return to chaos.[79] Stieda advocated vigilance and sacrifice to ensure the security of the Reich against the forces that sought its destruction. Such language was designed to help prepare Germans psychologically for future Nazi aggression and the war that Hitler desired against his perceived racial enemies. In her coverage of the 1937 Party Congress in Nuremberg, Stieda glorified the masculine nature of the Nazi movement. For the first time, she wrote, the rally would include sporting competitions (*Kampfspiele*) organized by the Storm Troopers (Sturmabteilung – SA) to showcase the physical ability and endurance of Germany's boys and young men. But, as Stieda pointed out, sports were "only a means to an end." The goal was to improve Germany's military strength. Stieda praised the efforts of the SA in this realm and noted that its paramilitary training was necessary in order to "defeat our internal enemy," meaning Jews and political opponents to the regime.[80] Sports would build comradery and unity within the *Volksgemeinschaft* and were important to the ideological indoctrination of the youth. In other words, sports were an inherent part of the training of future soldiers and, as Stieda wrote, would allow Germany "to eradicate the last traces of the creeping Jewish-Bolshevik poison from our national body."[81]

Stieda's writing underscored an important element of Nazi racial propaganda: the myth of internal and external enemies whose threat to Germany needed to be eradicated via policies of persecution and, later, a war of defence. The other side of this narrative focused on racial comrades outside the borders of the Reich, whose support Hitler deemed necessary for his colonial ambitions. As historians have shown, much of Hitler's thinking was influenced by ideas of empire, whether through annexation of countries like Austria or conquest of territory in Europe and beyond. Promoting *Lebensraum* and the uniting of ethnic German communities topped the list of Nazi press directives.[82] Accordingly, the *NS Frauen-Warte*'s most frequent theme prior to the war was the East as a colonial space, a discourse that addressed both Germany's racial enemies and friends.[83] Articles about and for the *Volksdeutsche* (ethnic German communities) in regions east of Germany served both to justify Hitler's claim that these territories were inherently German and should become part of the Nazi empire and to promote the so-called civilizing influence of German culture within these areas. The Nazi government defined *Volksdeutsche* as those whose language and culture had German roots but who did not hold German citizenship. The term also had connotations of blood and race.[84] This discourse had violent ramifications during the Second World War, as the regime expelled Poles in the region of Poland it annexed to Germany and massacred millions of Jews as part of the scheme to "Germanize" the region.[85] These actions also connected to Hitler's popular message to overturn the 1919 Treaty of Versailles and allow Germany to regain territory lost to Poland.

The July 1935 issue of *NS Frauen-Warte* centred on the importance of Silesia, a large portion of which had been ceded to Poland after the First World War. In "Silesia as a Border Country," Hanna Koblick described how German women were working to create "proper Germans" out of *Volksdeutsche* living in the border regions. Although Koblick focused on women's work in such Germanization efforts and put a soft spin on Nazi imperialist ideology, she also utilized a discourse of survival and struggle: "We are fighting for our Silesian homeland not only for the sake of Silesia – but ... for the sake of our whole German Reich and Fatherland."[86] Her words repeated the Nazi trope that ethnic Germans were victims of Polish persecution and violence. The very notion that communities of ethnic Germans existed outside of Germany's borders and were persecuted by foreign governments provided a pretext for Hitler's eventual war, which resulted in the displacement and murder of millions.[87] Thus, as Doris Bergen points out "if the *Volksdeutsche* had not existed, the Nazis might have invented them."[88]

Koblick went on to claim that, despite the hardships faced by Germans living in Poland, "the German culture flourished and the German spirit, which holds fast to its goal, will ensure that in a few decades only the German language and German customs will be valid in this region."[89] The goal to which Koblick referred was the regime's desire not only to reclaim German territory lost after the First World War, but also to claim Polish regions as a whole. Articles such as those by Koblick illustrate ways in which women journalists helped encourage and report on the work of female activism in Nazi colonial ambitions. "I hope that [this article] will help ensure that Silesia receives the recognition it deserves in the Empire," Koblick concluded, issuing an understated call to all German women to support Nazi imperialist ambitions.[90]

The following month, the paper published Erika Meyer's article "Danzig in Need." Meyer described the charms of the city in which "every stone ... knows the German language and the industrious German hand."[91] But, she informed her readers, this old German Danzig had disappeared. Due to its status as a free city and its separation from Germany, the region had become impoverished, and housewives struggled to feed their families. German culture, according to Meyer, was slowly being eradicated due to Polish intransigence. Meyer ended her article with the plea "Don't forget Danzig, which stands alone on guard and fights and waits for us up in the east."[92]

Both Koblick's and Meyer's articles came after the January 1935 Saarland plebiscite, in which the region voted to reunite with Germany. Both women contributed to propaganda that agitated for a further renunciation of the Treaty of Versailles and for regions in the East to be returned to Germany.

Stieda too wrote several articles about the East as German space, including her 1933 article "Trip over the Border" about her travels in Poland, as well as the 1937 book *Krieg über der Kindheit* (War over childhood). The book, which was aimed at German youth, described Germany's First World War experience on the Eastern front from Stieda's viewpoint. Born in Riga, Latvia, in 1918, Stieda fled to Germany at the age of ten with her mother and siblings. Her father died near Riga in 1920.[93] Given her family background, Stieda was attracted to Nazism, its claim that *Volksdeutsche* communities in the East were a part of the *Volksgemeinschaft*, and Hitler's calls for *Lebensraum*. In a letter written much later in life, she recalled her excitement when German soldiers had entered Riga in 1917:

> I stood by the roadside, and, as a nine-year-old child, I learned for the first time that you can cry for joy. In 1919, however, I stood with my mother as a refugee in front of the train station in Königsberg and suddenly realized that I had arrived in Germany … These decisive childhood experiences led straight to the path to National Socialism.[94]

Like Stieda, Else Frobenius had a connection to the East that informed her work on behalf of the Nazi regime as she travelled throughout Europe with the goal of connecting to, and writing about, ethnic German communities. A fervent nationalist, Frobenius enjoyed a long and prominent career prior to and during the Third Reich, writing primarily about women's issues. Her political beliefs, the status of ethnic Germans, colonialism, and Germany's First World War defeat featured in much of her writing. Born in 1878 to a family of German origin, Frobenius grew up in Estonia, then part of the Russian Empire. In March 1908, after experiencing the upheaval of the Russian Revolution in 1905 and her husband's bankruptcy in 1907, Frobenius moved to Berlin.[95] There she became politically active in the areas of women's rights, colonialism, and German nationalism. She joined the nationalistic German People's Party (Deutsche Volkspartei – DVP) in 1919 and the National Socialist Party in May 1933. On behalf of the NSF, Frobenius travelled throughout the country, lecturing about German colonialism.[96] She had also travelled in the Saar region prior to the plebiscite, lobbying the population to vote to join the Reich.[97]

The move to Berlin had allowed Frobenius to launch a fulfilling career. She published her first article in May 1909 in the *Neue Preußische Zeitung*. In the fall of 1920, she received a letter from Hugo Stinnes, founding member of the DVP and by then publisher of the conservative daily the *Deutsche Allgemeine Zeitung (DAZ)*. Stinnes invited Frobenius to take on the management of the publication's women's supplement.[98] The paper's first issue with the inclusion of the supplement *Frau und Welt* appeared in January 1921 under Frobenius's tenure.[99] Due to economic difficulties, the *DAZ* stopped printing this supplement in 1922, but Frobenius continued to work for the paper as a reporter on behalf of women's associations. She also wrote for the women's supplements of other newspapers and took over the direction of the women's pages for the publication *Auslandswarte, die Zeitschrift des Bundes der Auslandsdeutschen* (Journal of the association of Germans abroad).

Frobenius joined the German Press Association in 1923 and remained a member throughout the Third Reich. The type of journalism Frobenius practised did not change significantly from the Weimar Republic to the Third Reich, except with regard to its political end. She wrote consistently about women's issues for the *DAZ*, *Blatt der Hausfrau*, and the *NS Frauen-Warte*.[100]

During the Third Reich, Frobenius often undertook press trips for the People's League of Germandon Abroad (Volksbund für das Deutschtum im Ausland – VDA). She wrote articles about festivals, landscapes, art, and literature – most with a *völkisch* bent. Given her nationalistic outlook and her own background, her work celebrated the lifestyle and culture of *Volksdeutsche* communities in regions east of Germany. On a trip to Latvia, for instance, she visited a German folk festival and an exhibition "promoting the agricultural riches of the region," later writing about both.[101] In 1936, she purchased a small journal called *Verkehrspresse*, which she initially published in conjunction with the VDA. The publication was distributed in the border regions of Germany and to ethnic German communities outside of the Reich in a bid to stimulate the communities' imagination about pan-Germanism and "cultivate their love for Germany."[102]

Frobenius's career directly aligned with what press authorities maintained was suitable for women journalists, particularly her press work with the NSF and the National People's Welfare (Nationalsozialistische Volkswohlfahrt), and her focus on German *völkische* culture. Under the veneer of travel and entertainment, her articles carried political messages concerning Nazi views about colonizing the East and bringing all ethnic Germans in those regions together under Nazism. She cherished her career precisely because it allowed her to "express my love for Germany through my articles about my 'Heimat,'" she noted.[103] Articles about the East by women journalists, whether published in the *NS Frauen-Warte* or mainstream dailies, were primarily intended to create a sense of German ownership for such regions and raise support for Hitler's later plans to colonize Eastern territories.

Both *Frauenkultur* and *NS Frauen-Warte* included articles about women's work outside of the home, but only in fields the regime deemed appropriate for women and only in relation to women's service to the Nazi state and its domestic and foreign policy goals. In 1935, Hitler officially announced German rearmament and the reintroduction of conscription. Like their male counterparts, working-class women toiled in metal and armament factories. The *Frauen-Warte* spoke of the need to protect the health of these important female workers. In November 1935, Alice Rilke wrote an article praising new measures put in place to protect women in factories and advocated for further accommodations. Her recommendations included better air quality and a limitation on heavy lifting for women workers: "In the metal industry," Rilke noted, "a woman should not be responsible for arduous labour because it could harm her body."[104]

The health of female workers was important to the regime in two respects. First, women in factories contributed to production targets associated with economic recovery and the plan for war. Second, women's bodies also had to remain healthy for childbearing. Rilke made clear that protective measures were important "not only from the point of view of labour law, but also to protect motherhood."[105] In the same vein, photojournalist Barbara Lüdecke published a photo series aimed at providing working women with tips on hygiene and health, as well as exercises to improve their fitness. The first article in the series was targeted to women working in factories. According to Lüdecke, such women age more quickly because they have limited opportunities to unwind, especially as they often have responsibilities at home.[106] The reportage demonstrated the types of daily exercise women should do in order to remain healthy on and off the job.

Although Nazi rhetoric about women's place in the home continued after 1936, there was also a concerted effort to direct women into the workforce, both in blue-collar jobs and such typically female professions as secretarial or social work. The January 1936 issue of the *NS Frauen-Warte* was devoted to women at work, and included articles with titles such as "A Bit about the Nursing Profession" and "Happy and Healthy Teachers."[107] The articles in this issue advised women to consider professions in domestic science, social work, and nursing.[108] In the same issue, "New Ways of Educating Girls: *Abitur* to Career" decried the state of girls' education in Germany and argued that, rather than receiving the same education as boys, girls should be trained in the areas that adhered to their talents and where their skills would be most valuable. An *Abitur* was not useful for women, the article maintained, because "only a minority of young girls possess purely intellectual ability."[109] As a result, girls were leaving school "unaware of their real value, intellectually overfed but their minds malnourished." The article advocated a female-oriented education that would impart the practical skills girls needed to prepare for careers in appropriate areas such as nursing as well as to "participate meaningfully in shaping the destiny of their people." For a young girl's future professional or personal life, "practical skills, human warmth and a willingness to serve are more important than school knowledge."[110]

Although the writing of women journalists in the party papers echoed the language of the Nazi regime most closely, the content of women's supplements to newspapers and of general women's magazines also supported the regime's political goals and helped politicize women's private and working lives. The value of such material centred on the fact that it was less Nazified, and its connection to the regime's ideology and aggressive policies was less perceptible than in the hard news published in daily and party papers. While women's writing in such arenas constituted an important part of Nazi propaganda, we cannot assume that it always appeared that way to the journalists themselves. For those women not disposed toward Nazism, writing about the everyday may have seemed a way in which they could pursue their career in a manner that they felt did not entangle them as closely with the regime compared to colleagues who wrote for the party papers or those who reported directly on domestic and international politics. Articles on decorating or fashion, in other words, served a political purpose for the regime but one that may not have been entirely clear to the journalist herself. At the same time, women accepted the constraints that came with writing for a state-controlled press because it offered them professional and personal advantages.

Despite the fact that not all women wanted to work in the women's realm, doing so could provide an avenue for those typically on the sidelines of the profession to gain some measure of responsibility. Liselotte Purper's career took off in 1936, when her work came to the attention of Hanna Holzwart, the editor of *Frauenkultur*. Purper's connection with Holzwart provided her with contacts within the Press-Propaganda Department of the NSF, and she published prolifically in the organization's various journals.[111] Thanks largely to her work for the NSF, depicting an idyllic feminine lifestyle centred on the needs of the

Nazi state, Purper was able to build a successful freelance career and achieve a level of wealth and independence not open to most women prior to or during the Third Reich. Ilse Urbach was nineteen years old when she began her career as an intern on the *Berliner Lokal-Anzeiger* in 1931. She joined the popular and respected *Berliner Tageblatt* in June 1933 and the weekly women's and entertainment supplement provided her a vehicle for advancement: seven months later, she was the editor of this section.[112]

General interest and women's publications could provide a seeming refuge from the oppressiveness of the Reich Ministry for Public Enlightenment and Propaganda (Reichsministerium für Volksaufklärung und Propaganda – RMVP) for readers and journalists alike. Although they were subject to their own press conferences and directives, prior to the war the regime did not subject magazines to the same rigorous control it applied to daily newspapers.[113] This meant that both men and women who worked on magazines enjoyed marginally more creativity and intellectual freedom. Katharina Kleikamp built a successful freelance career writing about art and home economics for the popular *Kölnische Illustrierte Zeitung*, as well as various fashion and household magazines, despite the fact that the party had "serious doubts" about "her attitude to the Nazi state."[114] Evidence also suggests that the regime did not control the women's supplements in newspapers quite as vigorously as it did other sections. In 1938, for instance, the leaders of the Reich Press School decided that fashion journalists did not have to attend the school at the end of their internship year: they simply did not require the same level of ideological training as journalists working in other fields.[115]

Writing for women's, family, and general interest magazines gave women a broad public platform. Ruth Andreas-Friedrich began her career in 1925 as a journalist reporting for a range of women's publications. When Hitler came to power in 1933, she continued along the same professional track. Her work included reportage about topics ranging from culture and cosmetics to advice about interpersonal issues, addressed in articles with titles such as "Problems within the Marriage: The First Few Months."[116] Andreas-Friedrich published in some of Germany's most popular magazines, including the *Frankfurter Illustrierte Blatt* and the beloved magazine for young single women, *Die junge Dame* (The young lady).[117] Along with general reporting, Ilse Thien focused on serialized novels for well-known women's and general interest magazines, including *Blatt der Hausfrau* (Housewife's journal), one of Germany's most popular magazines, with a circulation of close to 600,000.[118] Based on her research, Trampler-Steiner argued that the serialized novel was the part of the paper that women readers most loved.[119] Serialized novels themselves seemed harmless, as they veered away from overt political issues and instead engaged people's imaginations through tales of romance, adventure, or scandal. Yet, by default or intention, the writing of women journalists in the realm of "soft news" conformed to and supported the needs of the Nazi state, often in a widespread manner. Given that they wrote in the very areas that were the most popular with the German public, women journalists had a larger voice than their limited numbers would suggest.

**Conclusion**

Minister of Propaganda Joseph Goebbels wrote that "the best propaganda is that which works invisibly, penetrates the whole of life without [audiences] having any knowledge of the propagandistic initiative."[120] Goebbels's words point to the regime's desire to create the illusion that everyday life continued in an ordinary fashion after 1933. News, culture, and entertainment seemingly devoid of ideology were important components of the regime's "invisible" propaganda. They connected to areas with which the population could personally identify and supported a lived experience of normality. Such material also created a sense of insularity and security in the face of larger events; the banality of the everyday provided a refuge for Germans from the brutality of the regime. Even articles that appeared seemingly insignificant to the broader socio-political narrative served an important political function. By contrast, the front pages of a newspaper focused on national and world events spoke more explicitly with the voice of the Nazi regime.[121] Yet articles about family and motherhood, although in line with traditional German and European gender norms, also corresponded with Nazi racist and expansionist ideology, particularly those by journalists publishing in the *NS Frauen-Warte*.

After 1936, women journalists' writing helped prepare the country for Hitler's intended war as they provided advice to German women on how to shop, save, and work in a manner that would contribute to the regime's political ambitions. The regime strove to utilize women journalists for a role that was political in nature but most often depicted as outside the realm of traditional politics. Yet some women managed to forge careers in hard-news areas typically reserved for men and, by doing so, participated in and engaged with Nazi aggression in a more direct manner than those who worked in the "women's realm."

## Chapter Three

# Traversing Borders, Pushing Boundaries: Female Foreign Correspondents and the Lead-Up to War

After the [First World] war, hatred and blindness divided the world in two: the victors and the vanquished. The victors assumed that they were entitled, albeit peacefully, to eliminate the vanquished. Over the past twenty years we have seen the ramifications of this faulty calculation. The result has been financial turmoil and economic disaster … Thanks to an ideology that has harnessed all of the force and reserves of its peoples, Germany and Italy have gotten their economies back on track … A country of 80 million people has saved itself without outside assistance, for the welfare and progress of all nations.

Edit von Coler, Curentul, 23 February 1939

Journalist Edit von Coler wrote these words in an article that critiqued the balance of power in Europe after the First World War and praised fascism for setting Germany on the path to prosperity and prominence. Her words reflect not only her own view that Germany had been treated unjustly in world affairs, but also echoed Nazi propaganda that claimed the country was a victim of a post-war order orchestrated to ensure that it remained a weakened and vanquished nation. Born in Berlin in 1895, von Coler lived a wealthy and privileged life. She joined the Nazi Party in 1931 and had friends and acquaintances high within the regime. She worked as a freelance foreign correspondent for various newspapers in Germany and abroad, including the Berlin-based *Deutsche Allgemeine Zeitung* (*DAZ*) and the Romanian *Curentul*. The subjects of her work ranged from culture and travel to agriculture and contemporary politics. Von Coler eventually used her journalism as a vehicle for political influence and created a role for herself as a non-official diplomat working on behalf of Nazi Germany. In particular, she sought to foster a closer economic relationship between Germany and Romania and thereby draw that country into Germany's orbit. This goal was an element of German foreign policy that was particularly important in the lead-up to the Second World War.

Gaps between Nazi gender policy and practice presented a small measure of flexibility and opportunity for some female journalists to navigate a career as foreign correspondents, a role far outside of the soft-news arena to which women were typically relegated. In this role, the work of women journalists garnered support for the regime's political agenda, foreign policy goals, and ideological platform. Their writing promoted Germany's alliances and spoke to the ostensible threat posed by its enemies. Although the archives do not allow for a precise statistic on the number of female correspondents working in the Third Reich, it is possible to discern that they worked on all types of papers, both inside and outside of Germany. Among their ranks were prominent journalists, including Margret Boveri and Lily Abegg, who wrote for national dailies,[1] Others, such as Edit von Coler, Gisela Döhrn, and Mia Passini, wrote for a range of national, regional, and/or party papers. Irene Seligo, for instance, wrote for the *Frankfurter Zeitung* (FZ) and the Nazi paper the *Völkischer Beobachter* in her position as a foreign correspondent based in Portugal.

Scholars have begun to examine the work of female correspondents in Britain, France, and the United States and have pointed to the various strategies that women employed to succeed in this almost all-male corner of journalism. Some utilized their gender to achieve foreign correspondent positions by offering to provide a "woman's point of view" on international politics. Others focused on the humanitarian repercussions of war and conflict.[2] Yet little work has been done on their counterparts working under authoritarian regimes. Despite the attention paid in both historiography and popular culture to famed American female correspondents such as Martha Gellhorn and Dorothy Thompson, reporting on the political landscape of Europe in the years leading up to the Second World War is still viewed as having been generated primarily by men.

This chapter helps to bridge a gap by writing German women into the history of foreign correspondents working within the Nazi-controlled press, as well as into the larger history of female journalists who forged international careers in the fraught interwar period.[3] There are commonalities between the experiences of women correspondents who worked on behalf of Nazi Germany and those who reported for democratic systems. Their shared status as outsiders in this domain meant that they were often subjected to more ridicule, rejection, and hostility from their male colleagues than were women working in soft news. Most were prohibited from covering war or conflict – the bread and butter for foreign correspondents – and those that did were generally refused access to the frontlines, regardless of their willingness to accept the danger that came with such work. However, while their female colleagues reporting for American, British, and French newspapers concentrated largely on the human and social dimensions of interwar conflict, correspondents reporting for Nazi Germany were tasked with legitimating Hitler's foreign policy and ideological goals, as well as those of his allies. Such writings helped justify Nazi aggression toward its principal adversaries: Bolshevism and international Jewry.

Female foreign correspondents in Nazi Germany offer an important case study on the interrelation between fascism, gender politics, and geopolitical affairs. Nazism prided itself on being a hyper-masculine movement. Yet the fact that some women pursued and succeeded in atypical roles, just as they did in less militaristic and nationalistic countries, points to the malleability of Nazi press and gender policy. If a female journalist secured an opportunity outside of the "women's realm" and proved herself an asset to Nazi press and propaganda goals, there was scope for success: privilege, talent, tenacity, and perceived utility trumped sex. A rich body of research on gender and Nazi Germany has shown the gap between ideology and the reality of women's (and men's) lived experiences.[4] The professional trajectory and work of female foreign correspondents deepen our understanding of this phenomenon – not only of the limitations women encountered in an authoritarian, patriarchal state, but also the opportunities and scope for individual agency open to them in the very genre of journalism most associated with masculinity.

From the mid-nineteenth century onward, international news provided by foreign correspondents became *the* component that determined a paper's prestige. By the turn of the century, the role became associated with romantic images of intrepid (male) reporters, travelling the world in search of distant cultures or bravely covering wars and revolutions.[5] Foreign correspondents consequently represented the pinnacle of professional success within the journalistic field, and their role was never more valued or prominent than during the interwar years. This period of heightened international anxiety, when news became ever-more critical and the consequences of events ever-more significant, resulted in what John Maxwell Hamilton has termed "the golden age of foreign correspondents."[6]

By the mid-to-late 1930s, international politics centred around general rearmament and the quest for raw materials in the event of war, changing power dynamics in Europe, and the scramble for alliances, with Germany, Italy, and Japan pursuing expansionist agendas. In this context, German female correspondents played a role as non-state actors or unofficial diplomats. Their writing encouraged the German population to support the regime's foreign and racial policy as they expounded aspects of the Nazi world view that the population came to admire most: military strength, national pride, a rejection of the terms of the Treaty of Versailles, the desire for expanding geopolitical power, and the curtailment of perceived communist aggression. By presenting an appealing, even scintillating, face for Nazi foreign policy and its depiction of friends and enemies, these women became a part of the phenomenon that helped to foster passive support for the regime's geopolitical goals and contributed to its growing popularity throughout the 1930s. In return for their service, they were able to establish prominent and stimulating careers.

## Covering International News for the Dailies

In Europe and North America, a position as a foreign correspondent for a quality paper attracted some of the best talent in the profession, and Germany was no exception to this trend.[7] Such a post offered many advantages, including foreign travel, the excitement of being an eyewitness to dramatic events, status, and, in some cases, even fame. The role could also be extremely demanding. Foreign correspondents had to contend with issues that those working in their home country did not, including navigating the local language, culture, and social system. While domestic reporters typically had a narrow beat, such as the arts or economics, a foreign correspondent had to be a jack of all trades, capable of writing appealing travel stories as well as hard-hitting political pieces.[8] The challenges were even more significant for women, whose presence in the field was often unwelcome among male colleagues and editors.

Although the war and the conquest of territories expanded opportunities for German women journalists to work abroad, a handful had already obtained positions as foreign correspondents prior to September 1939. Famed foreign correspondent Margret Boveri wrote of the hurdles she and other women had to overcome in order to secure a position on a prominent daily. "The first women that the *Frankfurter Zeitung* employed as full-time staff before the outbreak of the Second World War had to earn this honour through hard physical labour," Boveri recalled. "Lily Abegg travelled by military truck through inhospitable terrain deep in China, and I had to repair my own car on the muddy roads of Anatolia."[9] The opportunities and setbacks Boveri encountered on her quest to become a foreign correspondent with the *FZ* provide one example of how gender could inhibit and, occasionally, aid in the realm of hard-news reporting prior to the Second World War.

Born in 1900 to a German father and American mother, Margret Boveri developed an interest in foreign cultures and politics early in her life after time spent working with people from various countries at a zoology station in Naples. Because there was no university program in foreign policy in Germany, Boveri studied German, history, philosophy, and English at the University of Würzburg. She completed her doctorate in 1932 in Berlin, with a thesis on British foreign policy.[10] Boveri presented a negative view of Britain's international relations in her dissertation and held to that view throughout her journalistic career. Although she had planned to pursue a career in diplomacy or politics, Boveri claimed that she decided against that route after Hitler came to power in January 1933; she did not want to work closely with the Nazi regime. Instead she chose journalism. That same year, Boveri set her sights on working for the esteemed *FZ*, but her efforts were met with rejections and claims that "women do not belong in politics" and "we cannot use women here."[11] It took more than five years to achieve her goal of working full-time for the paper.

Boveri secured a full-time internship on the *Berliner Tageblatt* (*BT*) in the summer of 1934.[12] Despite the fact that the *BT* had a long history as one of Germany's most liberal dailies, little of the paper's left-leaning stance remained by the time Boveri arrived in August 1934. As Norbert Frei has shown, the Nazi regime subjected the large democratic papers to particularly strict monitoring and controls.[13] In an attempt to ensure its profitability and standing, the new editor, Paul Scheffer, sought to reinvigorate the paper's appeal by hiring new talent. Scheffer attached particular importance to the foreign policy and features (*Feuilleton*) sections of the paper. In addition to Boveri, he hired three interns, Petra Vermehren, Hans Gerth, and Karl Korn, to work on them; all three interns launched successful careers at the paper. Under Scheffer's stewardship, the paper remained one of the most renowned in Germany.[14]

Scheffer was initially reluctant to allow Boveri to write about foreign policy; instead, he encouraged her to work on the literature and *Geistiges Leben* (intellectual life) sections of the paper.[15] In this respect, he conformed to Nazi policy that viewed women as particularly suited to working on the cultural sections of a newspaper. Yet, as their correspondence shows, shortly after her arrival at the paper, Boveri began to report on foreign affairs, both past and present. Already in August 1934, she published her first editorial on the Anglo-Japanese alliance of 1902, followed shortly thereafter with an article on the Balkan Entente.[16] Although she soon realized that her hope to snag a high-profile position as the paper's London correspondent was a pipe dream, Boveri's career progressed rapidly at the *BT*, and her opinion pieces appeared regularly on the front page. As she recalled enthusiastically, "nobody had heard of me before, … and suddenly [the name] Margret Boveri was everywhere, on the front page [and] in the literary section."[17] As her biographer, Heike B. Görtemaker, has shown, Boveri was both prominent and prolific during her time at the paper.[18]

Boveri attributed her growing success not only to her own persistence and ambition, but also to Paul Scheffer's willingness to act as her mentor. Scheffer opened doors for Boveri, introduced her to useful contacts, including diplomats and foreign journalists, and took her to various meetings and conferences held by the Foreign Office and State Department. He gave her prominent assignments inside and outside of Germany and allowed her to act as his representative at important meetings and functions. In light of the hostility she faced from her own male colleagues, as well as those at other papers, Scheffer's support became so critical that Boveri feared her career would be over without it.[19] While female journalists working in all areas of news often had to rely on a male advocate, this practice was especially critical for foreign correspondents, who had dared to venture into this male-dominated arena.[20]

In the summer of 1935, at the invitation of the Greek government, the Reich Ministry for Public Enlightenment and Propaganda organized a press trip to Greece and selected a small group of journalists to take part. The ministry allowed Boveri, the only woman among fifteen men, to replace Scheffer, who was too busy to undertake the trip. In Athens, Boveri and her colleagues had to attend daily press conferences where they were given instructions on what they could and could not write. Boveri conveyed her disappointment to Scheffer that "political discussions" were off the table.[21] While all journalists had to deal with the restrictions of the Propaganda Ministry, Boveri had additional frustrations. Her male colleagues, in particular the representative from the RMVP, Wilfried Bade, made clear their resentment that a woman was along for the trip. Boveri maintained that she retired to her quarters early each evening so that the "male clique could continue on undisturbed" by the presence of a woman.[22] In a letter to Scheffer, Boveri complained about the attitude of her colleagues. Her mentor advised Boveri that, if she felt "some coldness" due to what he termed "her peculiarity," she should "fight it with extra kindness" and never show her upset.[23] In other words, Scheffer suggested that Boveri would be better off if she adhered to, and performed, traditional expectations with regard to her gender.

In line with the instructions from the Propaganda Ministry, Boveri produced a series of articles that addressed the harmony in German-Greek relations and showcased the beauty of the country and its people.[24] Boveri's success in Greece and the fact that she had not ruffled any feathers at the RMVP led to the more politically oriented assignments she desired. In the fall of 1935, as Mussolini prepared to invade Abyssinia, Scheffer sent Boveri to Malta to report on events as they unfolded. Boveri's proven talent, along with her language abilities and knowledge of Italy, made her the natural choice. It was this assignment, she believed, that consolidated her status in the field as a capable foreign news reporter.[25] Colonialism was an important topic for the Nazi regime in the leadup to the Second World War.[26] Press authorities especially demanded material critiquing British colonial policy, and Boveri's editor trusted her with the task.

While based in Malta, Boveri reported on Italy's reason for invading Abyssinia: the desire to acquire colonial territories, just as the British had done for centuries. In "Flight to the Mediterranean," for instance, she wrote that Italians viewed British (and the League of Nation's) criticism of Italy's actions and its stance on the importance of Abyssinia's sovereignty as blatant hypocrisy. Boveri quoted Italian citizens who supported Mussolini's aggression. "The English have so many colonies," one complained, "Why won't they grant us the slightest favour?"[27] Another asked, "And what are these philanthropic British doing to Afghanistan at the moment? And all the Indians who are killed, their villages bombed?"[28] By focusing on the Italian population's perspective on the conflict and their anti-British sentiments, Boveri sidestepped the fact that Italy was waging an aggressive and violent war that the League of Nations condemned. Her article invoked sympathy for an expansionist foreign policy and suggested that Italy was simply standing up for its rights – or at least pursuing the same rights that Britain enjoyed, given its vast empire. Boveri's time in the Mediterranean, and particularly her critique of the British, as desired by Nazi press authorities, was advantageous to her career. She used her experiences as the basis for her book *Das Weltgeschehen am Mittelmeer* (World events in the Mediterranean), which brought her international acclaim and recognition as an expert on the region.

Despite her talent and growing prominence, or perhaps because of it, Boveri's gender began to play an even bigger role in the development of her career. At times it was an asset; more often, a hinderance. She attributed part of her success in Malta to the fact that, as a woman, she was able to travel incognito: "I think part of my effectiveness as a journalist when I was on the road was based on the fact that I got through quite unnoticed. I did not look like a special correspondent for an international newspaper."[29] Boveri's gender and outsider status may have meant that witnesses and officials were less guarded with regard to the information they shared. While some female correspondents claimed to have employed their "feminine attributes" to gain advantages within a male-dominated field, Deborah Chambers reminds us that this worked only if a woman was young, extremely attractive, and confident about her sexual allure.[30] The thirty-five-year-old Boveri found that the ability not to draw attention to herself was a better tactic in her quest for stories.

Scheffer told Boveri that she had proven herself in the field and that he would happily give her responsibility for the international news section of the paper, if only he could find a way to do so. Unfortunately, he feared a "palace revolution" if he took this step.[31] Boveri's talent and ambition also worked against her: her male cohort considered her serious competition.[32] In her memoir, Boveri described her struggles with difficult co-workers and the "jealousies, rivalries [and] intrigues" that were endemic at the *BT*. She attributed her feelings of inferiority and susceptibility to imposter syndrome to the toxic atmosphere.[33] While we only have Boveri's word that she endured such hostility, the testimonies of many female correspondents point to similar discrimination and rejection. During the same period, British correspondent Shiela Grant Duff, who, like Boveri, infringed on what was assumed to be a male space, repeatedly found herself ostracized by male colleagues and subjected to salacious rumours about her personal life, which affected her physically and mentally. Sarah Lonsdale has noted that such practices "reveal how protective the masculine hegemony was of its privilege."[34]

Although Boveri had not been permitted to travel to Abyssinia as a proper war correspondent, Scheffer did give her opportunities to travel to the Middle East and North Africa. He eventually offered her a position as interim foreign correspondent in Rome, an important assignment in 1936. Boveri's arrival in Rome coincided with the recent signing of a treaty of cooperation between Germany and Italy. The agreement formed the basis for the Berlin-Rome Axis and bound Italy and Germany as allies in the case of war. Despite her proven talent, Boveri was not considered for a permanent position. Instead, she was to fill in for a period while the male reporter selected by the paper was trained in foreign politics in Berlin. In 1936, at the *Berliner Tageblatt*, "the anti-feminism had become so strong," Boveri recalled, "that only with the utmost effort was Scheffer able to secure my dispatch. He had to take full responsibility for everything I was to write."[35] Scheffer advised Boveri not to take anything personally. Any objections that had been raised were not about her journalism, but rather her gender. "The decision of nature works against you," Scheffer observed.[36]

Forewarned by Scheffer not to write anything that would destabilize Germany's relationship with Italy, Boveri's first article covered what she termed "Mussolini's Great Speech." By recounting the fascist leader's words and the crowd's "rapturous" response, Boveri provided Mussolini with a public platform within Germany to promote and defend his aggressive foreign policy. He warned that Italy would have to quit the League of Nations in order to "pursue a policy of peace."[37] His words echoed those of Hitler, who talked peace throughout the 1930s, despite flouting the Treaty of Versailles and remilitarizing the Saarland in March 1936. Mussolini's threat to quit the League of Nations suggested that Hitler had been right to do so in 1933.[38] By giving voice to Mussolini, Boveri's article helped discredit the efficacy of the League of Nations. She recounted Mussolini's praise of Germany and his enthusiasm for the Berlin-Rome agreement that had "produced understanding between the two countries" on important issues facing Europe, particularly the need to prevent the spread of Bolshevism. By quoting Mussolini, Boveri found a more detached and sedate way of discussing foreign politics and the demonization of the Soviet Union than could be found in much of the Nazi press. She blamed France and Britain's supposed inefficacy in geopolitical affairs for the Spanish Civil War that began in July 1936 and the division of Europe into two opposing ideologies.

The positive spin Boveri put on Italian foreign policy, along with her critique of England, France, and the Soviet Union, corresponded to the importance Italy held within Hitler's political agenda. Her work underscored Nazi anti-Bolshevik propaganda and praised the relationship between Italy and Germany as a bulwark against communist expansion. "Fascism," she wrote, "was a fight against communism. National Socialism had set itself the task of protecting Germany from Bolshevism."[39] The fact that such a well-respected authority as Boveri praised Germany and Italy's newfound partnership, which focused on destabilizing the European order, functioned to support Hitler's foreign policy, which would only grow more aggressive from 1936 onward.

Scheffer left the *Berliner Tageblatt* in January 1937, and Boveri was not far behind, citing her dislike for the new editor-in-chief, SS member Erich Schwarzer. Despite quitting the *BT*, Boveri had not fallen out of favour with Nazi press authorities. She began to write a monthly article about German foreign policy for the *Europäische Revue* and published regular pieces on various topics for the *Deutsche Rundschau*. The publications received funding from the Ministry of Propaganda and the Wehrmacht, respectively, and both were supported by the Foreign Office (Auswärtiges Amt). In the fall of 1937, Boveri began to work as deputy editor-in-chief for the magazine *Atlantis*, where she remained for over a year.[40] At the same time, she again tried to secure a position with the *Frankfurter Zeitung*. Despite her stellar reputation and the respect that she had garnered in the field, the paper's managing director, Wendelin Hecht, felt that "it was not possible for a newspaper of such standing as the *FZ* to be represented by a woman in important posts, such as Washington."[41] According to Boveri, the head of political reporting, Benno Reifenberg, showed her the room where the daily news conference was held and explained that the room was the heart of the paper. Here decisions were made, and a sense of camaraderie prevailed – a camaraderie that did not include women. Purportedly, Reifenberg told Boveri that he intended to ensure that this state of affairs remained.[42]

Boveri instead proposed a freelance trip to the Middle East, and the *FZ* agreed to publish her work from her travels.[43] Once again, Boveri was able to enjoy the adventure, flexibility, and freedom her career offered, even if she had not yet achieved a permanent post as a foreign correspondent. Her articles from the trip offered a mix of history, current affairs, and travel. Upon her return in early 1939, Boveri finally became a permanent staff member at the *Frankfurter Zeitung*. It had taken six years of hard work and struggle. While one cannot make a definitive claim regarding the timing of the newspaper's offer of a full-time position to Boveri, the fact that it came only months before the launch of the Second World War suggests that the industry had begun to hire more women in critical positions in order to be prepared for the conscription of male journalists in the event of war. The Propaganda Ministry supported Hecht's decision to give Boveri a position as the paper's Swedish correspondent. Boveri, however, was unsatisfied with her new posting, which she felt placed her on the sidelines of important European events. Still, she managed to use her position in Stockholm as a vehicle to continue her critique of Britain and France and their alleged mistreatment of Germany. In an article published on 20 August 1939, five months after Hitler had occupied what remained of Czechoslovakia after the September 1938 Munich Agreement allowed Germany to annex the Sudetenland, Boveri critiqued the *Times* in Britain for publishing what she characterized as falsities about Germany and its oppression of the Czech population.[44] By writing that the German occupation had not, in fact, stripped the Czechs of their independence, Boveri justified Hitler's dissolution of Czechoslovakia, an act that was an important step in the regime's plan for war.

In the post-war years, Boveri claimed that she had been an opponent of Nazism. Yet she clearly respected Hitler's foreign policy, which sought to undermine Western democracies and set in motion his primary goal: a war of race and space to eradicate Judeo-Bolshevism and acquire *Lebensraum*. She was especially impressed by the signing of the Molotov-Ribbentrop Pact on 22 August 1939. She wrote to Scheffer that, so much did she approve of "this coup with Moscow," she was "almost ready to join the [Nazi] Party."[45]

Margret Boveri launched her career under the Nazi regime, and by the mid-1930s her star was on the rise. She eventually obtained her loftiest goal, to work as a permanent correspondent for the *Frankfurter Zeitung*. Her reportage with respect to the expansionist policy of Germany and its Italian ally boosted her professional profile and afforded her the opportunity to publish on issues that had staggering implications for much of Europe. Her reporting consistently supported the regime's notion of an unjust hegemony in world affairs that only fascism could counter. Such articles were part of the process that helped create support for the regime's policies, even among non-Nazis. In her post-war memoir, Boveri emphasized the discrimination she faced as a woman working in the realm of hard news and downplayed the advantages she had gained under the Nazis. By doing so, she used the very real gender inequality with which women journalists contended to her advantage in a bid to ensure a positive post-war – and posthumous – legacy, despite her service to a violent system.

Boveri may have become the most prominent female foreign correspondent working on the *FZ*, but she was not the first. That honour went to Lily Abegg. Born in Hamburg and raised partly in Switzerland, Abegg spent much of the first fifteen years of her life in Japan. After the family returned to Europe, she studied economics and political science in Geneva and Hamburg and eventually became an assistant at the University of Heidelberg's Institute of Newspaper Studies (Institut für Zeitungswissenschaft). From 1930 to 1933, she worked as a freelance journalist in Berlin. Aided by her knowledge of the country and language, Abegg began her career as a freelance foreign correspondent in Japan in 1934 at the age of thirty-five.[46] She reported for various German and Swiss papers, and her work also appeared in the British and Dutch press.

Abegg quickly became known as an expert on Japanese politics. From the beginning, she covered developments in Japan's foreign policy that had far-reaching geo-political implications. In an article from April 1934, she discussed rumours about whether Japan intended to terminate the Washington Naval Treaty, highlighting the tense relationship between the two countries that existed throughout the 1930s.[47] In December 1934, Japan repealed the treaty, an act that drew approval from the Nazi regime, since it positioned Japan as strong power, capable of standing firm against the United States. In 1936, Abegg published a book about the Japanese mindset, echoing the route taken by Bovari.[48] In the same year, the *Frankfurter Zeitung* hired her as its first, and at that point only, female foreign correspondent. She reported on the Far East, holding this position throughout the war.

A posting in Japan for an esteemed paper had important political implications in the 1930s and 1940s. As Ricky Law has shown, the Nazi regime felt a natural affinity to Japan, as a power that, like Germany, was in the process of rejuvenation and required colonial territories for *Lebensraum*. Hitler respected Japan's military prowess and successful expansionist agenda and viewed the country as a natural ally.[49] In November 1936, the two countries signed the Anti-Comintern Pact, aimed at containing the Soviet Union. In the leadup to the pact, Japan was featured regularly in the German press as a great power that would be capable of rendering help when necessary.[50]

Although not a member of the party, Abegg was intrigued by, and sympathetic to, Nazism. In June 1932, as the party was on the rise, she wrote to a friend that she was interested in politics and had begun to read the *Nationalsozialistische Monatshefte* and *Der Angriff*.[51] In 1936, a Japanese paper quoted her as having said "there is nothing to criticize about Hitler."[52] In February 1939, she ended a letter to a contact in Germany's Foreign Office with "Many greetings to 'Proteus' (*Heil und Sieg!*)" – a take on the Nazi salute "Sieg Heil."[53] Margret Boveri recalled a conversation with Abegg early in the war in which she stated that she hoped to see Japan enter on the side of Nazi Germany.[54]

Abegg's position in Asia gave her a higher degree of autonomy and freedom than Boveri enjoyed in Europe, but it also exposed her to physical danger. While Boveri felt that she was on the sidelines of major events during her posting in Stockholm, Abegg was on the frontlines of the Sino-Japanese war, which began in July 1937. She travelled as a war correspondent to China in the fall of 1937 to cover military developments. Her articles appeared regularly on the front page of the *FZ*. Like Boveri, whose articles appeared under the byline MB, Abegg often used the pseudonym AB rather than her full name. She had earned her position as a war correspondent and was well respected at the *Frankfurter Zeitung*, but her work was degendered nonetheless.

Abegg had high-ranking contacts in the Chinese and Japanese governments and military, including the deputy prime minister of China. In her articles, she speculated on Japanese military strategy – a discourse far removed from German press authorities' contention that women should write on soft-news topics – and theorized that, "given the movement of the Japanese troops to date, one can assume that the Japanese are not marching directly to Nanking but that they will first advance on Wuhu," a strategy "that would place the Chinese troops stationed near Nanking in danger of encirclement."[55] In an article published in December 1937, she wrote of Japanese military daring and the tactical shortcomings of China's provincial armies: "Military experts report that the Chinese ... are very successful when on the defensive, but find it difficult to attack. The Japanese have always understood how to take advantage of the Chinese stance and have often gambled on operations that would have been impossible with another opponent."[56] Abegg's articles echoed the Nazi regime's admiration for Japan's military endeavours; in contrast, her female counterparts reporting for French or American newspapers wrote about the ramifications of Japanese militarism on the Chinese civilian population.[57]

Abegg's articles were more measured than those published in the party press, since she touched on the Sino-Japanese war from the perspectives of both sides, while papers like the *Völkischer Beobachter* presented it as an ideological conflict in which Japan simply sought to curb the spread of communism.[58] Abegg's seemingly more balanced reporting contributed to a particular aspect of Nazi press goals. The regime allowed the *Frankfurter Zeitung* a modicum of flexibility with regard to its foreign news reporting as a sign to the international community that, even under Nazism, the German press remained objective and distinguished.[59] Whatever her personal sentiments about the war, Abegg did not include much overt pro-Japanese sentiment in her articles, and her sober and straightforward approach added credibility to her words. She acknowledged that Japan was the belligerent in the conflict, albeit in an indirect fashion, by quoting the Chinese government's statement "which branded the new [Japanese-installed] government in Peiping as unlawful."[60]

In December 1937, Abegg witnessed Japanese attacks on the Chinese city of Nanking. Her reporting alluded to the suffering of the Chinese population but did not reference the mass violence perpetrated by Japanese troops. At the same time, her words implied that the Chinese were unable or unwilling to care for the victims:

A train arrived at Nanking station with 2,000 wounded; no one cared for them, no military personnel were present. After two days they were unloaded and laid on the platforms, together with the people who had died in between. The dead polluted the air. Refugees from the city ran and jumped over the wounded, hitting them with their luggage ... The Chinese public stood by indifferently.[61]

Regardless of whether or not Abegg empathized with the Chinese, the language she used to describe the country and its leaders implied a backward and uncivilized nation – a discourse that matched more overt Nazi propaganda aimed at China.

Like Margret Boveri, Lily Abegg established a prominent career and published many distinguished front-page articles by writing about geopolitics as a matter of importance to the "new Germany." Yet she did not write solely for German newspapers. She received many requests from Japanese papers to provide them with articles about China and Germany. More important, Abegg also sent reports on her impressions of the political climate in the Far East and Japan's relationship to National Socialism to the Foreign Office in Berlin.[62] Given that the Foreign Office and the German embassy in Japan viewed these topics as important with regard to navigating Germany's East Asian foreign policy, it seems likely that Abegg received a directive to do so. Her knowledge and impressions of the region thus reached the German public as well as Nazi officials. Such roles were not uncommon for journalists in the interwar period.[63] As John Maxwell Hamilton notes, "by being a bridge between the people they cover and the people for whom they report, correspondents are envoys. But at times they go beyond reporting to become moving parts in the machinery of diplomacy."[64] Such was the case for Edit von Coler.

## Winning Friends and Influencing People

Edit von Coler dedicated her professional life largely to forging a closer relationship between Germany and Romania. Bringing the traditionally francophile country into German's orbit would become especially important during the Second World War. Her skills as a journalist enabled her in this role, as did the support she received from various offices and ministries, including the Foreign Office, the Ministry of Agriculture, and the Ministry of Propaganda. Von Coler's professional and personal activities during the Third Reich provide perhaps the clearest and most exceptional case of a woman journalist who used her role, and in turn was utilized by various officials, to engage in political machinations on behalf of her country.

While Margret Boveri largely felt restricted within the field due to her gender, von Coler employed her femininity to advance not only her journalism career, but also the political, economic, and rearmament interests of the Nazi regime. She soon became not only a producer of news, but also an object – an experience she shared with other female correspondents who were viewed as special or "peculiar" due to their presence in a so-called man's world.[65] As a member of the German aristocracy, von Coler was well known in the salon culture of Weimar and the Third Reich, where she entertained and socialized with the German political and cultural elite. She acquired a reputation as elegant, charming, and able to step into a man's world without renouncing her femininity. Various newspapers wrote about von Coler and her love of adventure and sailing. An article from November 1932 described her as "the dashing Edit von Coler" and "the first woman to take the exam for her helmsman's licence."[66] Another piece, which focused on her various voyages, noted that von Coler had "as much navigational practice as any man."[67]

Although not trained as a journalist, von Coler became the foreign press chief for the Office for Food and Agriculture (Reichsnährstand) in March 1935, based on Heinrich Himmler's personal recommendation. There she worked under Richard Walther Darré, the Reich farm leader, Reich minister of nutrition and agriculture, and the first chief of Himmler's Race and Resettlement Office (Leiter des Rasse- und Siedlungshauptamts).[68] The Reichsnährstand regulated all aspects of agriculture, including the production, distribution, and prices of agricultural products – an important office, as Hitler prepared for war and needed to ensure access to food stores. Via Germany's "new agricultural policy," the office sought to increase agricultural production and achieve self-sufficiency.

As von Coler spoke English and French fluently, part of her role was to review articles concerning agriculture published in French and British newspapers. More important, she wrote pieces about Germany's new agricultural policy. Her work functioned in two ways: first, to highlight the critical role of farmers in Nazi Germany and help stem the ongoing exodus of agricultural workers who sought more lucrative jobs in the city; and, second, to placate the German population, which had begun to experience significant price increases as a result of the regime's drive for food independence.[69] Von Coler began a 1937 article on the Reichsnährstand's annual exhibition by reminding her readers of Hitler's words: "'There is no advancement, whether national, local, or economic, that does not being with the farmer.'"[70] According to von Coler, the exhibition educated visitors about the importance of Germany's ongoing "battle for food autonomy" and noted that success meant making sacrifices for the "good of their fellow countrymen." She praised the progress German farmers had made in increasing food production and described the enthusiastic crowds visiting the exhibition, which gave "all visitors rich insight into the progress of National Socialist agricultural policy."[71]

Von Coler connected her articles for the Reichsnährstand both to Germany's domestic situation and to Nazi ideology and geopolitics. The April 1936 election of the leftist Popular Front government in Spain had led to increasing tensions over land reform and the possibility of collective farming, as well as violence associated with the peasants' appropriation of land owned by the wealthy. In May 1936, von Coler wrote that the "Spanish people, drunk on the beautiful words of communist agitators, have elected a government that is sailing in the wake of the Comintern."[72] Collectivization had failed horribly in the Soviet Union, she continued, and led to corruption, poverty, and starvation, as well as to long workdays and the breakdown of the family. Von Coler lamented that the Spanish had not learned from the Russian example. She concluded with a message for Germans: "The events in Spain repeatedly remind us of the danger Germany had faced."[73] She encouraged German farmers to be grateful for the "advantages" they enjoyed, despite the controls implemented by the Nazi regime, and reminded the general population that the country was no longer at risk of a communist takeover, all thanks to Hitler. The regime directed much of its propaganda initiatives to stoking the fear of communism traditionally prevalent among the rural and middle-class population. Articles like von Coler's sought to garner the population's support for Germany's eventual military intervention on the side of Franco's fascists after the outbreak of the Spanish Civil War in July 1936.

In her role as a journalist, von Coler continued to catch the eye of the press. In a piece from June 1935 titled "Germany Is Rising," a Danish journalist discussed a new farming settlement established by the Reichsnährstand. What struck the journalist most was not the new village and adjoining farms, but rather the woman who "stood out in the male crowd." The journalist claimed that Edit von Coler, who had the responsibility to maintain contacts with the foreign press representatives in Berlin, "sits in a position of trust within the Reich." At the same time, he emphasized her femininity: "In every respect Frau von Coler is living proof that Nazism does not force them [women] to ... renounce all aids such as modern clothes, jewelry and other things that help enhance and increase the female 'charm.'" The journalist praised von Coler as an "elegant little woman" and admired how she "smoked her cigarette with the same comfort as the male participants on this trip."[74] Von Coler's overt femininity juxtaposed with her visible position in a traditionally male role made her an anomaly but also enabled her to serve as an unofficial diplomat on behalf of the Nazi regime.

Von Coler sought to make her mark within the realm of Germany's preparation for war and the *Drang nach Osten* (a goal that later became part of the regime's more aggressive "General Plan for the East"). Her initiatives sometimes, but not always, connected to orders from Nazi government officials, all related to the goal of tying Romania to Germany economically, politically, and culturally. In the wake of the Four-Year Plan, Romania's importance to the German government increased, as the regime endeavoured to secure access to the country's abundant raw materials. By the summer of 1938, Romanian oil become a principal interest of German diplomacy. The country also occupied a strategic location for Germany's eventual invasion of the Soviet Union.

With the support of the Reichsnährstand and the Foreign Office, von Coler travelled to Romania in 1938, ostensibly in her role as a press representative for Nazi Germany's agricultural offices. Once there, thanks to her oft-cited charm and talent for mediation, she parlayed her status as a journalist into that as an unofficial diplomat. Von Coler sent reports back to various German ministries, including the Reich Chancellery and the Foreign Office, on the mood of the country vis-à-vis Germany, the state of Romania's agriculture and economy, her discussions with key figures about the Romanian press, developments within Romania's *Volksdeutsche* communities, and the connections she sought to build with influential individuals.[75] A report dated 11 June 1938 described the discussions she had had with the Romanian assistant director general for press and propaganda and the deputy director of the press in Bucharest about the media and its perspective on Germany. "Our intention," she wrote, "was to free the Romanian press of its capitalist influence and interest it in the German experiences in this arena."[76] Von Coler's words suggest an intention to exploit antisemitic sentiment within Romanian society, which manifested itself in resentment toward Jews as alleged representatives of capitalism.[77]

Von Coler wrote articles for readers in Germany and Romania that were designed to highlight how both countries could benefit from a closer economic relationship and to dispel, for both populations, existing stereotypes about the backwardness of the Romanians and the aggressiveness of the Germans. She succeeded in securing an interview with the Romanian minister of agriculture, Gheorghe Ionescu-Sisesti, for the Nazi paper the *Landpost*.[78] The article painted a positive picture of Romanian agriculture and industry and its reliance on German trade. The minister stressed how Romania valued its economic relationship with Germany and would continue to buy German machinery.[79] With titles such as "Romania's Farmers Can Be Comrades for Germany," von Coler's writings sought to convince the German population that Romania was an industrially progressive country.[80] In 1938, she published an article about her travels throughout the country titled "Romania under Reconstruction." She praised the beauty of the country and its people, the fertile land, the construction of modern buildings and factories, and the involvement of young, bright Romanians in the processes of modernization.[81] The ongoing industrialization of Romanian agriculture would benefit Germany with regard to trade and its quest to acquire raw materials, von Coler assured her readers. She also linked Romania to Nazi blood-and-soil ideology by writing that, despite its rapid modernization, Romania would "remain a peasant country, if only to preserve its tranquility and its art," which was supposedly rooted in its land.[82] Von Coler's dialogue cut both ways, as she also sought to convince Romania that Germany would make a good partner. In November 1938, she reported to Berlin that she had successfully placed an article about German agricultural policy in the Romanian newspaper *Universal*. This development, she hoped, would "pave the way for further cooperation, which will have an impact in the near future. Documents about this are in the Foreign Ministry."[83]

Von Coler's actions in Romania also contributed to the regime's effort to create a larger European National Socialist movement by connecting with ethnic Germans outside of the Reich. Together with Fritz Fabritius, chair of the German People's Community in Romania (Deutsche Volksgemeinschaft in Rumänien), von Coler worked to create a sense of unity among the approximately 800,000 Romanian *Volksdeutsche* – an important step toward ensuring the group's loyalty to Hitler.[84] In November 1938, she reported: "After several negotiations I was able to reach an agreement among the ethnic German groups, which had hitherto threatened to destroy each other in bitter fratricidal strife."[85] A 1936 report on ethnic Germans in Romania had described how the community was indeed internally fragmented but particularly susceptible to National Socialism.[86]

Edit von Coler acted in conjunction with official German diplomacy that sought to align ethnic Germans with National Socialism. Her actions and success suggest that a woman could play an important role in soft diplomacy, while men worked in a more formal capacity. Von Coler was keen to promote her efficacy to prominent individuals in Germany and Romania, but she did so in a manner that appeared humble and did not stray too far from Nazi gender rhetoric. In a letter to the wealthy industrialist Nicolae Malaxa (a close friend of the Romanian king), for instance, she noted that she had done all she could to clear up any misunderstandings among various groups of ethnic Germans – as far as "simply a weak woman" was capable.[87] Despite von Coler's self-deprecation, Fabritius attested to her success in this area.[88]

Reporting on developments with regard to Romania's Jewish citizens, von Coler noted that actions to purge Jews from official offices and new laws targeting Jews, including forbidding ownership of pharmacies and agricultural land, were forthcoming. She maintained that Jews in Bucharest were beginning to sell their property, and she accused the Jewish community of trying to disrupt Germany's relationship with Romania.[89] Antisemitic legislation in Romania benefited the country's ethnic Germans. Due to the government's expropriation of Jewish property in 1940, ethnic Germans were able to take over Jewish businesses and expand their role in the Romanian economy.[90] The country became a German ally in November 1940, and its relationship with Germany had devastating repercussions for its Jewish population. Local actions, together with German policies, resulted in the massacre of between 380,000 and 400,000 Jews in Romanian-controlled areas during the Second World War.[91]

While several factors contributed to Romania's decision to ally itself with Nazi Germany during the war, not the least of which included German diplomatic pressure and Romanian internal politics, von Coler also held some sway with important Romanians prior to the outbreak of the war. In an October 1938 letter to the German Foreign Office, diplomat and head of the German Embassy in Romania, Wilhelm Fabricius, discussed von Coler's efficacy in Bucharest: "With great skill, she has established relations in Romania with the most diverse circles, especially with the press … She has made a lasting impression on all of the Romanian authorities with whom she has been in contact."[92] Such individuals included Romanian industrialists, the foreign minister, the state secretary for press and propaganda, and the commissioner for minority rights. Based on the wishes of her Romanian contacts, von Coler moved to Romania in January 1939 for what was initially to be a twelve-month period. Her primary purpose was to function as the silent editor-in-chief of a new Romanian newspaper founded by Nicolae Malaxa.[93] Malaxa conceived of the paper as a vehicle to improve relations between Germany and Romania. Through the German Embassy in Bucharest, Fabricius reported to the Foreign Office in Berlin that Malaxa had specifically requested von Coler's assistance because she was the only one who "seems to have the ability to give this newspaper the desired orientation." Fabricius described von Coler's role as both advisory and hands-on, since she would have to give the paper the "right shape and direction."[94] Von Coler reported that Malaxa was a sincere advocate for Germany and claimed that he viewed her work as important for Romania and its "rapprochement with Germany."[95]

Von Coler was no doubt eager to promote her success and may have exaggerated her influence in her own reports. Still, the Foreign

Office, the Reichsnährstand, and the German Embassy in Bucharest approved of her move to Romania, and she was given a sabbatical from her work with Reich minister Darré. According to von Coler, the Romanian press was taking a noticeable interest in the on-going trade negotiations between the two countries. The Nazi government exerted pressure on Romania to cooperate with German industry and form an alliance that would assist Germany in its preparation for Hitler's intended war; von Coler worked in conjunction with this goal. Ultimately, Romania signed a "trade peace agreement" with Germany in March 1939. A British paper attributed success in securing this agreement to Edit von Coler, with an article headline claiming "Pretty Young Fraulein Edith von Kohle [sic], Hitler's Roving Envoy in the Balkans, Played a Leading Part Last Night in Securing King Carol's Signature to a Treaty of Trade Peace with Germany."[96] According to the author, after months of discussion with the German delegation, Romanian ministers were still hesitant to sign, fearing it was more of an "economic ultimatum" than a mutually beneficial trade pact. The article claimed that "Fräulein von Kohle was called in from a cocktail party at Bucharest's most luxurious hotel ... Quickly she summed up the anxious Romanians. 'If you sign,' she said smilingly, 'I will ring up Berlin at once and tell them to be good.'" The journalist quoted Romanian foreign minister Grigore Gafencu, who allegedly stated that "Fraulein von Kohle has served the cause of peace in Central Europe."[97] The German Foreign Office had the article translated into German for its files.

Under Nazism, women who were able to make connections in a "womanly" way held a form of political power. Those who knew von Coler in Romania, including the German-American journalist Rosie Goldschmidt Waldeck, attributed her effectiveness to her "feminine" charms and beauty. In other words, contemporaries believed that von Coler's gender allowed her to play her role in German political posturing. According to Waldeck, von Coler was "blood and soil alright, but streamlined by Elizabeth Arden and dressed by Molyneux."[98] More important, she believed her to be a woman who "had done more than the German legation and the Gestapo combined to wean Romanian statesmen and society away from the French and [make] Nazi Germany palatable to them."[99] Waldeck conceded that von Coler was "quite a good journalist" but maintained that her most important role was in the "Nazi fifth column" in Romania: Von Coler employed soft-power techniques to charm the country into Germany's sphere.[100] According to Waldeck, von Coler's particular strength was assuaging Romanian fears and convincing its governmental and business leaders that stories of German atrocities were untrue:

> In the case of Romania, the task of Nazi propaganda practically achieved at that time had been to sell Romanians of wealth and influence – key men of industry, banking and assorted intellectual and artistic professions – on the idea of collaboration with Nazi Germany. It had not been an easy task. Aside from being pro-French, these Romanians had been frankly frightened: the wealthy had been unfavorably impressed with stories of the Nazis doing away with wealth; the women had been unfavourably impressed with stories of the Nazis doing away with lipsticks and rouge; the intellectuals had been unfavourably impressed with stories of anyone who opened his mouth going straight into a concentration camp.[101]

Von Coler helped to refashion this unattractive picture of the Third Reich.[102] Much like the women journalists who wrote on "lighter" topics for the German population, she sought to convince influential Romanians that, under Hitler, Germans continued to lead a normal and pleasant life.

It was not only her fellow journalists who viewed von Coler as an important actor on behalf of Nazi Germany. Foreign intelligence officials, especially the French, followed her activities with concern, including her work on *Curentul*, which published many pro-Nazi articles. France had traditionally enjoyed close relations with Romania and hoped to maintain them. In March 1939, the French Central Intelligence Service in Bucharest noted:

> Frau von Coler's personality is very interesting and deserves our full attention. She is Himmler's cousin and is considered the most dangerous of all of his spies in the service of Germany. Since her arrival in Bucharest, she exerts all kinds of activities and operates in all areas. The Romanian police strictly monitor her. She will probably stay for a long period in Romania.[103]

While the French belief that von Coler was a spy cannot be confirmed, the fact that she was viewed as such points to her prominence as an unofficial diplomat working on behalf of Nazi Germany. What tasks and responsibility the Foreign Office assigned to von Coler and what work she undertook of her own initiative is also difficult to ascertain. What is clear is that at least several officials in the Foreign Office, Reichsnährstand, and Chancellery were not only aware of but actively supported and encouraged her efforts in Romania – at least for a period.

By the outbreak of the Second World War, however, von Coler had become a divisive figure in Nazi governmental circles and was being monitored by the Gestapo.[104] She was not afraid to send urgent reports to the chief of the Reich Chancellery, Dr Lammers, criticizing Nazi foreign policy. In October 1939, she argued that the regime's acceptance of the Soviet demand to take over Bessarabia would mean "a huge loss of prestige for Germany" in Romania's eyes.[105] In July 1940, she was officially summoned back to Germany at the request of Foreign Minister von Ribbentrop, who felt that she was "no longer suited to the Foreign Office in its activities in Romania."[106] Throughout the summer and early fall of 1940, King Carol II's power declined as Romania was forced to cede Northern Transylvania to Hungary and South Dobruja to Bulgaria. The king abdicated in September 1940 and the fascist Iron Guard took power under Ion Antonescu. His dictatorship officially allied with Germany and the Axis powers in November 1940. By that time, the German Foreign Ministry no longer considered the soft diplomacy that von Coler practised necessary; rather, Germany employed strong-arm tactics to force Romania's hand.

Nevertheless, Edit von Coler's activities in Romania point to some of the ways in which the Nazi government used the German and foreign press as a political tool and how exceptional figures such as von Coler could play a soft-power role in politics precisely because they were women. Numerous reports refer to her charm, beauty, and social skills, and these attributes, along with the idea that (most) German women were apolitical, helped von Coler to penetrate important circles in Romania and work informally toward achieving Nazi Germany's political goals.

## Scintillating and Scandalous: Reporting on Germany's Political and Racial Enemies

While Edit von Coler sought to forge an alliance between Nazi Germany and Romania by way of her journalism, Gisela Döhrn's work as a foreign correspondent in Moscow from 1936 to 1941 contributed to the demonization of Germany's ideological enemy, the Soviet Union. In her articles and her 1941 book about her four years as a foreign correspondent in the USSR, Döhrn covered a mixture of politics, economics, local events, and the goings-on of Soviet leaders, foreign diplomats, and fellow journalists. She also wrote about the lives of Soviet women. Her writing reframed and underscored long-existing stereotypes in Germany about the inferiority of the Soviet state and population in a manner that traversed the boundaries between hard and soft news. The

Nazi propaganda machine employed an array of journalistic genres and styles in order to reach a part of the German public that did not always connect with the front-page political headlines. Historians have long discussed the importance of anti-communist propaganda for the Nazi regime. Ian Kershaw has shown that Nazi propaganda was particularly successful at building on pre-existing, anti-Russian and anti-Bolshevik sentiment among the German population and was able to reinforce negative and derogatory stereotypes about the Soviet state.[107]

Born in 1909 in the Rhineland city of Elberfeld, Döhrn studied musicology, philosophy, and literature. She received her doctorate in 1936 with a dissertation on Brahms. By 1934, she had already begun to publish film critiques for the *General-Anzeiger Wuppertal* and the women's magazine *Moderne Welt* (Modern world). Although she did not join the Nazi party, Döhrn was a member of the NS Frauenschaft, and the nature of her writing suggests that she was a supporter of Nazism.[108] An author and poet, Döhrn turned to journalism full time in 1936 after her marriage to Herman Pörzgen, a reporter on the *Frankfurter Zeitung*. The couple briefly lived in Warsaw before relocating to Moscow in July 1937, when Pörzgen became the Moscow-based correspondent for the *FZ*. In Moscow, Döhrn worked as a radio correspondent and a freelance journalist for various papers, including the *Münchner Neueste Nachrichten* and the *Hamburger Fremdenblatt*.[109] By the late 1930s, Döhrn and her husband were the only two remaining German correspondents based in the Soviet capital. Numerous papers, including the official party paper, the *Völkischer Beobachter*, were therefore dependent on their reporting. This gave Döhrn a more extensive audience for her work than most foreign correspondents enjoyed. The couple remained in Moscow until the German invasion of the Soviet Union on 22 June 1941.

Döhrn's reporting from Moscow ranged from relatively benign, soft-news articles on local events to the coverage of politicized topics, such as Soviet foreign minister Vyacheslav Mikhailovich Molotov's trade mission to Berlin. She also wrote on more inflammatory issues, such as the Soviet state's persecution of its own citizens.[110] In 1937, Döhrn reported on the mass purges taking place under Stalin, drawing attention to Soviet violence toward alleged traitors. In "Mass Arrests of Academics," she described how the Soviet leadership portrayed the Moscow Academy of Sciences as a "nest of enemies of the state, high traitors, and terrorists" under the influence of Nikolai Bukharin, who had fallen into the Soviet regime's disfavour.[111] The purges and show trials underway in the Soviet Union in the mid-1930s garnered much attention in Germany and abroad. They bolstered Nazi propaganda about the vicissitudes of Soviet policy and the cruel nature of the regime that repressed millions of its own citizens. Döhrn's reporting of these events contributed to this discourse and helped sow fear of communism among the German population. Still, her articles published while she was living in Moscow were relatively restrained compared to the virulent, anti-Bolshevik propaganda typical of the party papers. This reserve was likely due to fear of retribution by the Soviet secret police.

Once she was back in Germany, Döhrn's writing underscored Nazi rhetoric about the dangers and failures of communism in a tabloidesque manner that introduced German readers to the ostensible underbelly of Soviet society. Sensationalist items or tabloid journalism had been a component of the western press since the late nineteenth century and was intended to attract readers by encouraging an appetite for scandal. In Germany and other countries, female journalists were appreciated for their ability to attract readers through this style of writing, which was designed to stir public emotion, whether amusement, excitement, or outrage.[112] In an article published shortly after she returned to Germany, Döhrn portrayed the Soviet state as one that was so corrupt and impoverished that its citizens pillaged churches and crematoriums to acquire basic goods.[113] In this and other pieces, Döhrn included anecdote after anecdote about the depravity of the Soviet state. She cast Soviet citizens as drunkards who lived in crowded and filthy conditions and were unable or unwilling to care for their children. In one article, Döhrn told the story of a worker who lived with his wife and four children in a small hovel. "To forget his miserable life," she wrote, "he drank a bottle of vodka every evening," instead of feeding his family.[114]

Döhrn published her book *Das war Moskau: Vier Jahre als Berichterstatterin in der Sowjetunion* (That was Moscow: four years as a reporter in the Soviet Union) in 1941, shortly after she returned to Germany. In it, Döhrn recounted her alleged experiences at various events, balls, receptions, and press briefings, which made for captivating reading. She wrote of the political intrigues, rivalries, flirtations, and fashion she encountered at various receptions held for foreign diplomats and the press corps. Döhrn described the wives of Bolshevik functionaries as lacking in feminine charm and beauty, certainly in comparison to the style of the European women, whom they watched with jealousy.[115] The "dourness" of Soviet women was a favourite theme in Nazi anti-Soviet propaganda. When writing about such topics, Gisela Döhrn could rely on her gender and "feminine instinct" to give her voice authority.

Döhrn covered other topics, such as the challenges of reporting from Moscow, in the manner of a spy drama, serving up entertainment, tension, and intrigue for her readers when writing about the dangers she and her husband faced as they dodged various schemes the Soviets hatched to instigate their deportation or even arrest. She described numerous attempts by Soviet authorities to thwart her ability to report the news, from their supposed unwillingness to connect her to Berlin in time for the morning press conference, to alleged messages from her editors stating that they did not wish to speak with her.[116] Döhrn wrote that such actions were emblematic of the Soviets' attempts to destroy the Reich, even after the Molotov-Ribbentrop agreement of 23 August 1939. The Soviets continued in the private sphere what they could no longer do publicly: "Despite promises and assurances to the contrary … they harassed, they provoked, they spied, and they sabotaged," she wrote.[117] The narrative of Soviet paranoia ran throughout Döhrn's work.

Much of her book outlined supposed Soviet plans for war against Germany – a discourse that sought to retroactively justify Germany's invasion as a defensive measure to confront the Bolshevik threat. This narrative was mirrored in Nazi pre-war and wartime propaganda published in both the large dailies and the party papers. Döhrn wrote of conversations that ostensibly took place between Stalin and Molotov, where Stalin made it clear that, although he desired war against Germany, he preferred to wait until the Soviet industrial machine was more prepared. In such a telling, the Soviets themselves were responsible for the German invasion of their territory. According to Döhrn, "the Bolsheviks let a great opportunity pass by unused: The German Reich was ready to come to a permanent détente in the East. It had offered the Soviets an honestly meant peace."[118] Döhrn wrote that Stalin invaded Lithuania, Estonia, Latvia, Bessarabia, and northern Bucovina in "cold-blood" and "in violation of all the solemn agreements with Germany," and she informed readers that Soviet foreign policy was directed against Germany "in every gesture."[119] Her narrative was a clear falsehood, given what historians now know about the secret protocol in the Molotov-Ribbentrop pact that divided eastern Europe and the Baltic states between Germany and the Soviet Union. Yet for German readers, Döhrn's work echoed Hitler's pre-war discourse that stressed the Nazi state's desire for peace, even while he prepared for war.

No matter how unlikely it was that Döhrn would have been privy to the types of conversations between Soviet leaders that she described in her book, as a journalist she did have access to the upper echelons of power in Moscow. This proximity to high-level politicians was a privilege shared by the likes of Margret Boveri, Lily Abegg, and Edit von Coler. Also a qualified photojournalist, Döhrn had the opportunity to photograph Stalin in close conversation with Soviet officials, along with the daily activities of foreign diplomats in Moscow. Her access to the Soviet leader lent authenticity to what she presented as her recollections. Döhrn's position as journalist and an eyewitness to life in the Soviet Union legitimized Nazi stereotypes about the Bolshevik threat. At the same time, Döhrn benefited from the pathways the regime and its foreign policy goals opened for a select group of female journalists that allowed them access to those in power.

Despite the political – if tabloidesque – nature of her writing, a review of her book by the *Düsseldorfer Nachrichten* claimed that Döhrn "treated such difficult, gloomy material with a charm and grace that sometimes seemed to border on playfulness, yet [she] knew how to do justice to the factual." Döhrn, the review continued, "as a representative of some of the major German daily newspapers has shown not only political understanding, but more than that, political feeling."[120] Her (male) colleague thus drew attention to what press authorities valued in women journalists – their alleged ability to write in an emotional and colourful fashion. According to the review, Döhrn reported on "heavy" topics in a feminine manner; the reviewer thus pointed to similarities and differences between her work and that of male correspondents while alluding to traditional assumptions about the nature of male and female journalism.

Female foreign correspondents not only covered geopolitical affairs and Nazi foreign policy; they also contributed to Nazi racial propaganda that sought to justify Nazi Germany's aggression toward Judaism and Bolshevism. The regime's antisemitic and anti-Bolshevik ideologies ran parallel to each other and were mutually reinforcing beliefs that converged into the myth of a Judeo-Bolshevist world conspiracy aimed at the destruction of Germany. Nowhere was such propaganda presented with more vitriol than in the party press. In the most rabid Nazi party papers, including the *Völkischer Beobachter* and *Der Angriff*, some of the articles that cast Judaism and communism as dangerous and degenerate were written by women.

Founded by Joseph Goebbels in 1927, *Der Angriff* played an important role in the rise of National Socialism in Berlin. Goebbels paid particular attention to the paper's content and strove to create an aggressive tone that appealed to his constituents. Adept at playing on the atmosphere created by Germany's depression following the First World War – particularly widespread unemployment, misery, and frustration with the Weimar Republic – *Der Angriff*'s propaganda was mostly negative in character. The paper became important in Berlin's political life and soon began to rival other political newspapers.[121] Virulently antisemitic, *Der Angriff*'s central claim was that Germany's Jews were responsible for the failings of the Weimar Republic. After January 1933, the party press was preoccupied with growing its readership beyond the narrow circle of party members, in order to influence a larger segment of the population. The paper's antisemitic and combative language were to remain, but *Der Angriff*'s editorial team was also aware of the need to expand the paper's repertoire and improve its quality in order to engage a wider circle of readers. For Nazi party papers in general, the tension between their image as the movement's "fighting" press and the need to broaden their readership by including engaging, titillating, and entertaining stories created room for journalists who could toggle between overt and more subtly Nazified articles.[122]

In 1938, the editor-in-chief, Kurt Kränzlein, requested more soft-news material as a counter to the screaming Nazified headlines that dominated much of the paper. In a memo to all foreign correspondents, Kränzlein asked for a short article about New Year's celebrations around the world: "The Report Should Be Short and Funny; No Politics," he stressed.[123] To counter competition from the illustrated papers, in 1939 Kränzlein requested that all articles be submitted in active voice, which he felt many readers preferred. Such writing, he believed, would give *Der Angriff* an edge: "Reports in such a style have a stronger impact and are truer to life. On the whole [they] help to loosen up … the newspaper." He requested that, going forward, all journalists "work in this more relaxed style for us."[124] Just as they did in the women's supplements for daily papers, women journalists contributed to this aspect of soft news for *Der Angriff*.[125] Kränzlein actively encouraged women to write for the paper, though only as freelancers.[126]

In a letter to journalist Frau von Scheele-Willich, Kränzlein expressed concern that his criticism of her work had upset her to the point that she no longer believed that *Der Angriff* would publish her articles. Such an idea, he assured her, was "completely false"; his criticism was based only on a stylistic issue. "Due to the corrections, you perhaps are reluctant even to reapproach the piece," he wrote. "But that doesn't hold water for me." Kränzlein's concern was that von Scheele-Willich had attempted to write in a style that was not her own and had not succeeded. But, he assured, her work was important to the paper – so much so that he had based the rest of the page around it. "Simply write in a style that is natural," he advised her. "Only write soon and send me your piece quickly, so that I can see what you've written and know what else I must obtain. But please do it."[127]

Kränzlein's predecessor, Hans Schwarz van Berk, had also commissioned work from women journalists. Among others, Ursula von Kardorff began her training at the paper under the direction of Schwarz van Berk in 1937. A year earlier, Schwarz van Berk sent a rejection letter to Paris-based Cecilie Ihlenfeld for an article on fashion. He thanked her for her piece but noted that they would not publish it because it did not adhere to the paper's overriding purpose of critiquing its enemies via any means possible: "Even though we agree with you on many points, we [will] refrain from publishing it. Most of all, because at this paper we also criticize or ridicule the fashion of other countries, in particular that of extravagant America."[128] *Der Angriff* considered even fashion articles important enough that they had to suit the image and purpose of the paper – the condemnation of Germany's purported adversaries. The paper blamed these enemies for all of the country's ills and critiques levelled at the Nazi state.

Despite Kränzlein's desire to "loosen" up and even soften *Der Angriff*'s style, it largely adhered to the hyper-masculinity, political aggression, and lurid antisemitism and anti-communism inherent in Nazi ideology. Foreign correspondents, men as well as women, were especially important contributors to such propaganda, as Kurt Kränzlein expressed to his London correspondent in February 1938: "In connection with our goal to fight against lies from abroad … *Der Angriff* will include a daily column: 'The daily lies from abroad.' But I cannot achieve this goal without the keen collaboration of our foreign correspondents. This action is of paramount importance."[129]

The case of foreign correspondent Mia Passini shows us that women journalists had a role to play in the dissemination of racial vitriol and propaganda about the destructive influence of Jewish communities in countries that would ultimately go to war against Germany. Passini's early support for Nazism rendered her an important correspondent for Kränzlein. Born in Austria in 1908, Passini worked as a journalist, press photographer, and author. A reference praised her as a person of importance within the National Socialist realm:

> I have known Mia Passini for many years, and she has worked as my editorial colleague for illustrated publications for five years. She is an important journalist and press photographer. She repeatedly exposed herself politically by smuggling material for Austria's provincial Nazi leaders to Munich. I can warmly recommend her inclusion.[130]

Together with her close friend and former sister-in-law Greta (Margarethe) von Urbanitzky, Passini was politically engaged with the Nazi movement in Austria in the early 1930s. She moved to Berlin in 1933 and freelanced for several magazines and newspapers over the course of the Third Reich. Urbanitzky soon fell out of favour with the Nazi regime, and the two relocated to France in 1936.[131] From her base in Paris, Passini offered *Der Angriff* articles designed to support the Nazi view that its enemies – the French, communists, socialists, democrats, and, most notably "international Jewry" – posed a security threat to Germany.[132] In May 1938, Kränzlein wrote in praise of her work: "I was very pleased to hear from you again and would very much like you to regularly publish things written in the manner of these articles," he noted. "I'd almost say that you could not send me enough."[133] Kränzlein was referring to two of Passini's recent articles, one about violence allegedly perpetrated by the "reds" in the ongoing Spanish Civil War, and another that recounted tales of antisemitism in France. In his correspondence, Kränzlein emphasized how much he valued Passini's contributions to the paper. Her articles were desexualized, signed only with MP, which allowed Passini to contribute to the regime's racial politics and preparation for war in a manner that did not openly conflict with the regime's discourse that women journalists worked only on apolitical material.

During the late 1930s, Passini published front-page articles about one of the most violent events that took place in Europe in the interwar period, the Spanish Civil War. In what was widely thought to be the first European conflict between fascism and socialism, Germany offered military support to General Franco's fascist Falange movement, which sought to overturn the democratically elected Spanish Republic in July 1936. The Soviet Union intervened on behalf of the struggling Republicans. Passini's writing evoked images of Republican and Soviet savagery and accused the French government of subversively supporting the Republicans in spite of its official policy of non-intervention and the Anglo-French arms embargo against Spain. In "Bloodbath at the Border," she wrote that a group of young Spanish men seeking to escape the "red mobilization order" were gunned down at the French border by "red Spanish henchmen."[134] The lurid tone of Passini's writing appealed to Kränzlein, who praised her work. Another article charged that France was illegally smuggling arms to the Republican side by hiding them in shipments of dehydrated vegetables.[135] Her words functioned to justify Germany's continued and active support for Franco's fascists. According to Passini, the mainstream French press did not report on the smuggling activities – a charge that all but accused the French state of muzzling the press and disseminating "fake news."

Through such articles, Passini contributed to the fomentation of a conspiracy culture that alleged that only extreme nationalists tell the "real" truth. As historians have shown, a significant part of Nazi propaganda focused on mythical conspiracies about the danger of Jewish-Bolshevik worldwide hegemony, the desire of Judeo-Bolsheviks to destroy Germany, and the claim that Jews were exploiting Germans both politically and financially and polluting them racially.[136] In August 1938, Passini reported on the visit of Henry Morgenthau, the US secretary of the treasury, to France. In "Morgenthau's Mission," published on *Der Angriff*'s front page, she described the American politician as a "short-sighted Jew with squinty eyes hidden behind thick glasses."[137] The article included cartoon caricatures of Morgenthau. Passini highlighted his privileged background, suggested that he had "purchased himself a significant position within the Democratic Party," and toted out the Nazi myth that the American government was under the thumb of Jews such as Morgenthau. Passini charged that Morgenthau was in Paris on a mission to conduct "highly suspicious, secret negotiations" with the French, British, and Soviet governments to form an alliance aimed at the destruction of Germany. Both the United States and the Soviet Union, Passini wrote, were "ruled by Jews," who would also drag France and England into conflict with Germany. Passini ended her article with an alleged quote from the French minister of colonies and outspoken opponent of Nazism, George Mandel (né Rothschild). "War against Germany?" he purportedly said. "Better today than tomorrow."[138] Part of Hitler's strategy to prepare the German population for his planned war was to claim that, if conflict were to break out, it would be a defensive action on Germany's part, since its main enemies had aligned to destroy the Nazi regime.

The regime used the press to publicize antisemitism in other countries as a way to legitimate and encourage acceptance of its own exclusionary policies. Shortly after Germany annexed Austria in March 1938, Passini published "Metropolitan Ban on Emigrants," in which she drew attention to French antisemitism. Her words suggested that France was loath to admit Jewish refugees fleeing Germany and Austria and was set to implement its own form of segregation and persecution:

> According to a new police regulation that has just come into force, emigrants from Austria who arrived on French soil after the historic days of March will no longer be allowed to live in Paris but will have to find accommodation at least 50km outside of the French capital. According to the Ministry of the Interior, this order is to be carried out ruthlessly.[139]

In response to Kränzlein's enthusiasm for "Ban on Emigrants," Passini proposed further articles on the growth of antisemitism in France and the opinion of the "man on the street" concerning the so-called Jewish question.[140] One successful element of Nazi propaganda was convincing the German population that there was indeed a "Jewish problem" that needed solving in the first place; Passini underscored this narrative.[141] Kränzlein wrote of his enthusiasm regarding her "fruitful" ideas.[142] With one article, Passini enclosed a page of cartoons from the right-wing French newspaper the *Gringoire* and suggested that *Der Angriff* could include a few antisemitic jokes to demonstrate the nature of antisemitism in France.[143] Passini contributed to the regime's desire to grab the population's attention through humour and amusing anecdotes, even on topics that had political and violent repercussions. Humour provided a counterbalance to excessive Nazi solemnity yet could still be used to promote a world view based on racism and exclusion.[144]

In November 1938, shortly after *Kristallnacht*, Kränzlein issued another communication to his foreign correspondents, stating that the paper intended to take on the "Jewish question" much more than it had to date. To do so, he needed current stories from abroad. Kränzlein instructed that articles must not only demonstrate how Jews in other countries took up positions against Germany but should also encourage these countries to treat their Jewish citizens as criminals.[145]

In order to capture readers' attention, Kränzlein suggested that Passini concentrate on titillating pieces like scandals and murders. She responded to this request for lowbrow items with articles such as "The Corpse in Room 13: The Murder Solved," which described an investigation concerning a baker whose body had been discovered in a Parisian hotel.[146] In December 1938, Passini brought together Kränzlein's desire for scandal and his request to produce more antisemitic material in two articles about fraud charges brought against Bernard Natan, a French-Jewish film producer and owner of the studio Pathé-Natan. The studio's 1935 bankruptcy had led to the charges. In her article, Passini referred to Natan by his birth name of Tannenzapf, emphasizing his Jewish heritage and linking it to his alleged criminality: thanks to this "Romanian-born, Jewish specimen," Passini wrote, "there is already talk of 700 million francs flowing into the unfathomable pockets of Jewish criminals."[147] Passini alleged that Natan had also directed and acted in pornographic films.[148] Her focus on this aspect of the discourse surrounding Natan satisfied Kränzlein's request that she "not only discuss political positions, [but] rather address the areas that concern themselves with film and theatre. Also handle the eroticism of the Jews who – due to their domination in this area – sow their wild oats," Kränzlein advised.[149] Passini suggested further articles about the "the eroticism of Jews" and the "Jewish exploitation of women in Parisian film schools."[150] As noted earlier, Nazi propaganda often charged that Jewish males posed a sexual threat to "Aryan" girls, and

Passini readily contributed to narratives that depicted Jews as sexual predators.[151]

Passini's recommendations and Kränzlein's enthusiasm for her work demonstrate a demand among *Der Angriff* readers for a type of scandalous content that merged with the regime's inflammatory antisemitism. Passini met this need by providing material that both titillated readers and instilled a sense of fear and outrage in them. The language she employed in her work – "Jewish gang of crooks" and "the racketeering of these disciples of the tribe of Israel" – contributed to what *Der Angriff* hoped to achieve through its journalists, who acted as a conduit to the population: linguistic violence that helped underscore Nazi categories of race and citizenship and foster hatred among the German population for those excluded from the *Volksgemeinschaft*.[152] As Passini's case highlights, women contributed to public discourse that had genocidal repercussions.

## Conclusion

In 1940, journalist Anneliese Zander-Mika wrote an article entitled "Women and the Press," which claimed to address practical questions surrounding women's work in the field: "Among the considerable number of German women journalists today, there are scarcely any who write for the political pages," the article noted.[153] Zander-Mika's text pointed to Nazi policy and, to a large degree, reflected the reality of women journalists working in the Third Reich prior to the Second World War. But it did not provide the whole picture. Journalists such as Margret Boveri, Lily Abegg, and Edit von Coler, working in the traditional male realm as foreign correspondents covering such hard-news topics as international relations and conflict, are neglected but important figures in the landscape of the Nazi press.[154] Few professions outside journalism gave women a public platform and allowed them to become active in geopolitics. Female foreign correspondents were on the radar not only of various Nazi ministries but also of foreign information services. The French and British monitored Edit von Coler's work in Romania in the late 1930s. During the war, the British and Americans observed the activities and work of both Abegg and Boveri, fearing that they were spies for the Nazi state. Regardless of the unsubstantiated accusations of spying, the interest of foreign secret service departments demonstrates that these women were viewed as an arm of the Nazi state.

Boveri, Abegg, and von Coler had different relationships to Nazism and different paths to professional success, but they also share commonalities. Their success in atypical roles shows that class and connections mattered in determining whether a woman could break out of the soft-news domain. All three were well educated and had had the opportunity to travel and live abroad before they began their careers. Boveri spoke English and Italian, Abegg was fluent in Japanese, and von Coler spoke French and English and had a working knowledge of Romanian. All three women had numerous high-level contacts within the countries they worked. Yet differences among these women were also apparent.

Boveri and Abegg reported on the same events – to the extent possible – as their male colleagues, and the nature of their articles did not conform to what was expected of female foreign correspondents at the time, namely, an empathetic or humanitarian approach to world events with a focus on the suffering of women and children. Characteristics typically understood as "feminine" did not correspond to the professional identity and type of journalism that both women projected and practised.[155] Their career success suggests that they generally accepted and strove to emulate the masculine nature of the field and points to some degree of overlap between male and female reporting in the Third Reich. By contrast, Edit von Coler was defined and judged by her femininity, which she used to her advantage. Von Coler's gender performativity allowed her to express extreme positions in a "feminine" manner that aligned with Nazi soft-power goals.

While some women wrote on Nazi foreign policy and became a part of the phenomenon that saw millions of Germans take pride in the regime throughout the 1930s, others contributed to Nazi ideological and racial discourse. Historians have paid much attention to the regime's overt propaganda: the screaming antisemitic headlines and frightening depictions of the "Bolshevik threat" that dominated so many newspapers, particularly the party papers. Women such as Gisela Döhrn and Mia Passini contributed to Nazi racial discourse via a combination of hard and sensationalist news, which garnered a readership that, while perhaps not disposed to vicious political propaganda, was nevertheless open to Nazi racial thinking, certainly when it was laced with scandal and conspiracy theories. Although not direct participants in processes of persecution related to Nazi racial goals, such women became indirect actors in helping to lay the groundwork for the violence that the regime would perpetrate, both before and during the Second World War.

Regardless of the nature of their journalism, all female correspondents shared an ability to navigate the spaces the Third Reich allowed for career progression in the very area of journalism most associated with men and acted as agents for their own interests. As women, they were never fully accepted into the profession, but they nevertheless communicated opinions and beliefs in support of Nazism. The influence of women journalists would only increase after September 1939.

# PART II

## The War Years, 1939–1945

# Opportunity and Influence on the Home Front, 1939–1945

Decades after the Second World War, journalist Christa Rotzoll reflected on her journalism career, which she had begun in 1943 as an intern on the domestic politics and cultural sections of the well-known and respected paper *Das Reich*. "We had to do something, not simply sit at home," she declared. "Many [women] were able to become something they never would have if they had had male competition."[1] Rotzoll's words point to the positive impact that the war had on her career and on the opportunities that had opened for her and other female colleagues. The nature of her wartime writing showcases how assumptions about gender roles and the capabilities of women journalists created space for their contribution to wartime journalism in a manner that put a positive spin on the war for the home front.

In "Eastern Workers in the Camp and in the Factory," for instance, Rotzoll wrote about Soviet and Ukrainian women at work in German armament factories. "The rooms all look like a children's party is taking place. Paper chains hang between the beds with lanterns in between, and handmade paper plants," Rotzoll described. "On the walls there are pictures of saints, family photos from the East, and pictures of bathing suits from German fashion magazines, sparkling birthday cards and pictures of young Frenchmen."[2] Although the article acknowledged the women's hard work, it downplayed the mistreatment and oppression such women, many of whom the Nazi regime had forcibly deported from the Soviet Union, suffered in Germany. Instead, Rotzoll's writing emphasized the leisure that they allegedly enjoyed in their cozy quarters. "Today is a rainy Sunday and they do what one does on such a day," she wrote. "They write postcards, of which they are only allowed a certain number each month, they watch the sky, they flip through a Tolstoy from the library or one of their camp newspapers[,] ... they mend, and one even sews curtains."[3] Rotzoll's article absolved

Germans of any sense of guilt or concern about the millions of foreign forced labourers toiling (often to death) in German fields and factories and softened the nature of the war for her readers.[4]

This chapter examines how the war generated professional possibilities for women journalists, which in turn allowed them to contribute to various forms of Nazi wartime news and propaganda directed at the home front. During the war, the regime's need for women journalists and the professional possibilities open to them converged ever-more closely into a mutually beneficial relationship. With more opportunities for travel, food, access to privileged information, and other perks not easily accessible to the majority of Germans, women journalists were in a position to experience the war more positively than were other segments of the population. A number, in fact, recalled the period as one of professional inclusion and accomplishment, which testifies to the success of the regime's presentation of the field as elite and its efforts to create a sense of camaraderie within the press. Like Rotzoll, some women journalists even defined the war as a conduit for female empowerment.

Throughout the Nazi regime, press officials recognized the need to present a veneer of normality and keep the population entertained. As shown in the preceding chapters, women journalists made an important contribution to this goal throughout the 1930s. During the war, they played a more significant role in the regime's need to connect to, distract, encourage, and bolster the public's mood and determination to hold out. They worked in the very areas that the public most craved: lighter fare such as culture and travel as well as local and "women's news." Such material became particularly important when the tides of war turned against Germany and the population's trust in hard news plummeted.[5]

Scholarship on public opinion, private life, and the appeal of Nazism has shown the importance the regime placed on the contentment of the German population.[6] This chapter deepens our understanding of this phenomena by examining the work of women journalists whom the regime tasked with creating a sense of happiness, community, and private space for the population in the midst of war. Building on the scholarship of historians who have examined National Socialist wartime propaganda, it also analyses women's contribution to a more negative form of propaganda that critiqued Germany's enemies in the political, social, and cultural realm in an effort to justify German war aims. Via various genres, women journalists became agents in managing the wartime relationship between the state and the German public.

Still, the war did not mean that women were able to progress in their careers in a straightforward manner. They faced various restrictions in their professional advancement, due to long-standing constraints as well as new obstacles created by the war itself. Women journalists were important to Nazi press goals and yet remained marginalized within the field, even as their soft-power influence grew.

**Expanding Horizons**

The number of women journalists grew throughout the war, albeit only marginally. By March 1944, they constituted approximately 11 per cent of the press (1,870 women), up from 8.8 per cent in 1939.[7] With many male journalists conscripted into the Wehrmacht or the frontline Propaganda Units (Propagandakompanie), however, by 1944 women likely represented a higher percentage of those actively working within Germany than press association membership numbers suggest. Significantly, by January 1945, 5,252 male journalists, approximately 35 per cent of those entered in the professional registrar of the German Press Association (Reichsverband der Deutschen Presse – RDP), had been drafted into the Wehrmacht, police, or Organisation Todt.[8]

This seemingly modest increase in the number of working female journalists downplays the opportunities that opened up during the war, as well as women's growing importance and influence on the home front. Authoritarian regimes establish and maintain their hegemony in part through manipulation via the press. Daily papers were at the centre of this managerial relationship between the state and the public – and never more so than after 1939, when Germans were far more likely than in the pre-war period to read newspapers. The population eagerly consumed news about military victories in the first years of the war, but the soft-news sections became especially important as wartime deprivation and destruction impacted Germans in ever-larger numbers.[9] During the war, journalists, male as well as female, reached a larger audience than they had during peacetime.[10] From September 1939 onward, possibilities opened for women journalists that made the field more accessible, afforded them increasing responsibility, and in many ways rendered the profession more interesting and appealing to women.

Press authorities, however, initially relied on both men and women to ensure that the profession continued to function as smoothly as possible. From the outset, the RDP anticipated a possible shortage of journalists due to Wehrmacht conscription. It implemented the *Kriegssonderliste* (Special War List), which endeavoured to bring former journalists out of retirement and ease entry requirements into the field where and when necessary. Although women were also listed in the *Kriegssonderliste*, it initially consisted primarily of men.[11] By 1940, however, the RDP announced that the growing number of conscripted journalists had led to difficulties in finding replacements.[12] The regime launched an extensive campaign to recruit journalists, which focused on finding young talent, whether male or female. Beginning in 1941, increasing numbers of job offers appeared in the trade journal *Deutsche Presse*. Women's presence in the press grew as a result. By 1944, women made up 50 per cent of journalists in training and outnumbered men in some of the regional offices, including the Sudetenland, Bohemia and Moravia, Brandenburg, Danzig West Prussia, Westphalia, Saxony, and Silesia. Some of the party papers, including the *NSZ-Westmark*, the *Volksgemeinschaft*, and the *Hakenkreuzbanner*, engaged more female than male interns.[13]

Professional opportunities for women journalists also increased within the Reich Ministry for Public Enlightenment and Propaganda (Reichsministerium für Volksaufklärung und Propaganda – RMVP). By January 1942, as the Wehrmacht stalled before Moscow, it was clear to military and party leaders that Germany would not achieve an easy victory in the East. At the same time, discussions took place in Wannsee on how to coordinate the murder of European Jews. Both processes would require more manpower. It was at this stage that the RMVP endeavoured to use women to fill positions vacated by men, from drivers to office workers to journalists. According to the ministry's dossier titled "Increased Use of Female Employees," at the beginning of the war there were approximately 1,000 employees within the ministry, 70 per cent of whom were men.[14] By April 1942, women made up 59 per cent of the 1,452 persons employed within the RMVP. They typically worked in areas made more important by the war, including wire-tapping analysis, censorship, propaganda, and editorial work.[15]

The Ministry of Propaganda was particularly interested in recruiting female journalists. In January 1942, it requested lists from all regional press associations of women who were capable of standing in for conscripted male colleagues to work within such areas as press, radio, film, theatre, music, and literature.[16] Women journalists were to fill propagandistic roles that dealt particularly with culture, sports, fashion, and Germany's youth. In 1942, the ministry approached Thea Fischer to write travel articles, Helene Rahms to write theatre reviews, and Elisabeth Noelle-Neumann to work personally with Goebbels on public opinion research.[17] All three women maintained that they were able to turn down the ministry's offer without consequences, although Thea Fischer did take on some contract work for the RMVP. Other women, both seasoned journalists such as Else Frobenius and women who were at earlier stages of their careers, chose to accept the ministry's offer of work.[18] An internal memo from February 1942 announced that the ministry's personnel department was pleased with the number of female journalists who had registered to work within the organization.[19]

During the war, press authorities valued foreign-language skills, and women with such competencies were particularly well positioned to transition into journalism from other jobs. This need created more opportunities for middle-class women who had been able to complete their *Abitur* or attend university. The Ministry of Propaganda specifically wanted to recruit for foreign press services female journalists who were fluent in English, French, "a northern language," Spanish, Portuguese, Serbo-Croatian, Romanian, Greek, Dutch, and Russian or Ukrainian.[20] Elisabeth Eisenhardt, who spoke French and English, began the war as a secretary and foreign-language assistant in the "special service" office of the Nazi press chief, Otto Dietrich. There, Eisenhardt compiled and translated material from the English press. Dietrich's office valued her instinct and judgment when it came to selecting important material. She soon became a journalist employed by the Ministry of Propaganda.[21]

Some women found alternative paths to journalism during the war. Prior to 1939, Helma Huffschmid had had no interest in the field, although she had occasionally assisted her journalist husband with his work. Bernd Huffschmid was a freelance correspondent, writing for the business section of the party paper the *Westdeutscher Beobachter* and the *Frankfurter Zeitung* (FZ). In 1940, he was conscripted into the Wehrmacht but endeavoured to continue working. Helma Huffschmid took over part of her husband's work. With a young baby at home, she noted that, "during the day I played the housewife and gardener and during the night, when the child was in bed, I took over the material [my husband sent] with pleasure."[22] She worked anonymously: all articles appeared under her husband's name. Despite not receiving recognition for her work, she loved the job and continued on after the war.

Positive change also came for women already in the field. Gertraude Uhlhorn had completed her studies in journalism in February 1938, hoping to find a full-time position. Prior to the war, she was able to land only a four-month contract on a small regional paper, but, in the fall of 1939, she began to publish regular book and film reviews and articles for the women's supplements of various newspapers.[23] After the death of her husband on the Eastern front in June 1944, Uhlhorn needed more consistent work to support herself and her child. Despite the fact that she had been out of the field for two years after the birth of her son, she obtained a job on the *Pforzheimer Anzeiger*. The editor hired her on the spot, claiming, "Heaven sent her to me! My reporter for local news will be sent to the front tomorrow."[24] In August 1944, Uhlhorn became the paper's first female reporter.

The experiences of female journalists during this period suggest a modest – and temporary – shift in gender relations in the field, as editors came to rely on the work of women. As a result, some enjoyed increasing responsibilities and expanding horizons. Dr Gertrud Hoffmann became the replacement editor of the trade journal *Deutsche Presse* when Hans Henningsen left the role in 1944. Hoffmann was also head of the German Press Association's professional registrar throughout the war and, in January 1945, became the acting head of the association itself.[25] Edith Hamann replaced Ernst Poggo as editor of the women's magazine *Die elegante Welt* (The elegant world), and Grete Ratemann stepped in as the cultural editor of the daily *Donauzeitung*. Some women lobbied for more recognition and responsibility. In January 1945, for instance, Luise Herklotz contacted the RDP, demanding the right to continue political reporting for the party paper the *Heidelberger Beobachter*, despite the fact that she was not officially qualified as a political journalist. Herklotz noted that, since the editor had left the paper, she had been working practically independently on the political section, something, she argued, that no one would have allowed if she had not mastered the area.[26]

In 1940, shortly after she got her start as a trainee on the *Deutsche Allgemeine Zeitung* and with the encouragement of her fiancé, Peter Erich Neumann, Elisabeth Noelle-Neumann joined *Das Reich*, one of the most prominent papers in the Third Reich. With Goebbels's backing, the paper was founded in May 1940 to showcase quality German journalism inside and outside of Germany.[27] Goebbels allowed the paper marginally more intellectual freedom, to give the impression of liberality and candour to domestic and international audiences. *Das Reich* included (comparatively) factual and quality content in the areas of politics, war reporting, business, and features (*Feuilleton*). Due to its sophisticated cultural section and its staff made up of the most accomplished and well-known journalists in Germany, the paper was a huge success from its first issue onward. Circulation grew from 500,000 in the paper's first year to over 1,400,000 by 1944.[28] In 1941, when Peter Neumann left for the Eastern front as a war reporter, the young Elisabeth Noelle-Neumann took over his role as head of the national affairs section of the paper – a hefty responsibility.[29]

After starting out as an intern on a small, provincial paper in 1938, Helene Rahms had, by November 1941, replaced a male colleague as the lone reporter on the party paper the *Mitteldeutsche Nationalzeitung*.[30] In 1943, the ambitious journalist sent a sample of her work to *Das Reich*.

The editor published her piece and hired her shortly thereafter.[31] Rahms recalled, "Now no one was bothered that women filled in the gaps [at the paper]."[32] From the time it was launched until the paper closed down at the end of the war, *Das Reich* employed a number of women journalists, some already prominent in the field, and others just starting out: Ilse Urbach, Petra Vermehren, Christa Rotzoll, and Margret Boveri all wrote for the paper. Other women worked freelance for *Das Reich*.[33] Toward the end of the war, the editor, Rudolph Sparing, gave Christa Rotzoll, who was still only a trainee, and Helene Rahms almost complete responsibility for the cultural pages: "We sat at the desks of the cultural reporters, young, reckless, and fun-loving ladies," Rahms noted.[34] Like Rotzoll, Rahms viewed the war as an opportunity for professional growth.

Margret Boveri had worked in her desired role as a foreign correspondent before September 1939, yet the war also expanded opportunities for her. When she was in discussions with the *Frankfurter Zeitung* in the fall of 1938, the paper informed Boveri that, although they were well aware of her achievements, a woman could not represent a paper of its standing in the United States.[35] By late 1940, however, Boveri had secured a position as the paper's full-time New York correspondent – a significant promotion over her previous position in Stockholm.[36] After Hitler declared war on the United States in December 1941, Boveri was briefly interned as an enemy alien. She was soon sent back to Europe, where she continued to write for the *FZ* as a correspondent in Lisbon. She returned to Berlin in 1944, where she too began to work at *Das Reich*.

**Restrictions and Hostility**

Despite the fact that women progressed more easily to higher-profile positions during the war, Nazi Germany remained a sexist state, and women were still outsiders in the field. The number of male journalists on *Das Reich* still far outweighed the number of women, for example. Despite the professional gains they had made, no woman ascended to the position of editor of a major daily.[37] Conditions were particularly difficult for those who worked in hard news. Boveri felt that the *FZ* did not publish her work often enough, a fact she attributed to her gender. When Noelle-Neumann joined the paper in 1943, she recalled that Boveri and two other female foreign correspondents, Irene Seligo and Lily Abegg, had to sit along the edges of the conference room during meetings, rather than at the table with the male journalists.[38] Editors and male colleagues still marked women as different and separate, regardless of the fact that some reported in the same hard-news fields. In April 1940, Boveri declined to contribute to a book about international affairs because the other authors were mostly women. She feared that her participation would further harden the gender divide between herself and her male colleagues, whom she felt still did not view her as an equal.[39] Boveri attempted to overcome the structural and cultural barriers to her acceptance in the field by assimilating into its masculinized culture.[40]

The obstacles that continued to limit women's progress in the field were long-standing, such as the difficulties of balancing home and career, or the resentment of male colleagues. Erika Hoffmann had a well-established career in journalism that began with her internships at the party papers *Der Angriff* and the *Völkischer Beobachter* in 1933. She subsequently worked freelance for various newspapers and magazines as well as for government agencies, including the Office for Food and Agriculture (Reichsnährstand) and the Foreign Office (Auswärtiges Amt). Hoffmann continued her career after she married in 1940. In 1942, she was offered a position as a reporter in the Ministry of Propaganda's radio broadcasting division. Although Hoffmann valued her career, and her supervisor praised her work, she resigned unwillingly in June 1943 after the birth of her first child. As she wrote to the ministry's personnel department, despite all of her efforts, she was unable to find domestic help and childcare and therefore had to ask to be released from her contract.[41]

Conditions caused by the war brought opportunities, but they also presented disadvantages to both established female journalists and those just starting out. As more women began to enter the field, they faced a greater backlash from male journalists. Melita Maschmann, who became famous after the war for her memoir in which she attempted to acknowledge and understand her commitment to Nazism, began her career as a journalist at the age of eighteen, working for the League of German Girls (Bund Deutscher Mädel – BDM).[42] In addition to producing press and propaganda materials for the BDM, Maschmann worked as a freelance journalist for papers in Berlin and East Prussia. Shortly after the war began, she relocated to the Wartheland, a region of Poland that Germany had recently annexed. There, she completed her formal journalism internship on the German occupation paper the *Ostdeutscher Beobachther*. Maschmann remembered well the hostility she faced from male colleagues:

> Every one of my colleagues there without exception considered that women were out of place on an editorial staff, except as secretaries. From the beginning, I entertained the suspicion that in many cases they upheld

this position because they were afraid of competition from women. My new colleagues were more or less "militant champions for men's rights" and the reception they gave me was correspondingly unfriendly.[43]

Toward the end of 1944, Max Baumann, the editor of the *Hamburger Tageblatt* and the director of the RDP for the region of Hamburg, published an article that spoke to male worries about women in the field. He assured his male colleagues:

> Naturally, they will not leave their jobs immediately after the end of the war because their livelihood is based on their occupation, and moreover, it would not be fair if they had to leave immediately after they had been welcomed as workers during the war years. In the course of a longer period of time will they gradually retire or marry and devote themselves to housewives' and mothers' duties.[44]

Baumann went on to state that, although women made up a larger percentage of journalism students than men at the moment, the profession must not worry that the situation would negatively affect the career prospects of future male students serving on the frontlines. Women, he assured his male colleagues, would leave the field quickly once marriage became a viable prospect.[45] Baumann's text was in keeping with Nazi rhetoric that officially encouraged young women to work until marriage and justified married women's involvement in the workforce as an "exception" of the war and with the assumption that they would leave the field soon after the men returned.

Men's education and careers were certainly delayed or even dashed due to their military duty, and those who had been drafted in the Wehrmacht expressed concern to the German Press Association. Officer J.M. Pirwitz returned from the front in early 1944 after both of his feet were amputated. He approached the RDP to inquire if he would be able to pursue his intended career as a journalist despite his disability. The association advised that, since journalism was physically and emotionally demanding, he would have difficulty in the field.[46] Werner Sack had also been severely injured during the war. In November 1944, he wrote to the Ministry of Propaganda to express his frustration at being unable to find a volunteer position. Sack worried that, due to his military service, he had already "lost a lot of time" with regard to establishing a career.[47] To counteract such concerns, some regional press offices, already disconcerted about the number of women obtaining internships, sought to ensure that spaces were left open for men with war disabilities.

Conscription into the Wehrmacht did not always prevent men from practising journalism, however. Many male journalists acted as war reporters, publishing in newspapers throughout Germany and for military publications. Military newspapers from the frontlines did not fall under the Editors Law, which meant that men who worked for these publications did not have to be on the RDP's professional registrar, but rather were included in the *Kriegssonderliste.* In this way, war opened up opportunities to gain some professional experience for male journalistic hopefuls who had not yet begun their journalistic training.[48]

Not unlike their male counterparts, women journalists could also have their careers interrupted or delayed due to war service, including recruitment into armaments factories or *Flakhelferinnen* (flak gunnery assistant) brigades. In January 1943, the RMVP requested that regional press associations compile a list of all male and female journalists who were fulfilling important tasks related to the war by way of their journalism. Those not listed would become candidates for wartime service.[49] Although unemployed or freelance journalists were more likely than those with full-time positions to be called up for service, journalists with jobs deemed unimportant by the regional press association, or by an editor, could also be conscripted. Both Ursula von Kardorff and Elisabeth Noelle-Neumann feared that they would be designated for factory service. In August 1944, Kardorff noted, "There is a rumour in the office that I and some others are to be dismissed and sent to work in a factory. My name was put on the list by one of the directors who does not like me."[50] Thus, connections and relationships with male superiors continued to influence women's careers throughout the war.

Kardorff managed to avoid wartime service, but others were not so fortunate. In July 1944, journalistic hopeful Rita Münchenberg wrote to the German Press Association asking for details about whether and how one could still train to be a journalist after the war, since she was currently in service at the Ministry of Aviation (*Reichsluftfahrtministerium*) for its duration.[51] In November 1944, journalist Elisabeth Grass wrote to the RDP asking them to forward her mail to her field post number, as she was working as a librarian in a mobile library at the front (Frontbuchhändlerin bei der Wehrmacht), which was designed to keep soldiers entertained.[52] After more than a year working within the RMVP, cultural journalist Charlotte Jossner was assigned to the navy, although records do not show in what capacity.[53]

As the war progressed, the possibilities for both accredited journalists and those in training were negatively affected by material shortages and newspaper closures. These processes, which began in a limited fashion at the start of the war, further restricted women in a field where they already faced roadblocks. In mid-1941, the RDP informed its regional associations that, due to the closing of printing facilities, it would begin shutting down newspapers and magazines, and that other publications would be merged.[54] By 1943, paper shortages affected even the flagship paper of the National Socialist Women's League, the *NS Frauen-Warte*. In November of that year, the paper was reduced from bi-weekly to monthly. Renate von Stieda, a full-time member of the paper's editorial team wrote to the Reich Writing Chamber (Reichsschrifttumskammer) asking for assistance in finding additional work. Stieda noted that, due to conditions brought on by the war, her work on the paper had become so limited that she wanted to turn her energies to another task: "Because I know that the prospects for female journalists overall are not promising, especially with the paper restrictions, I am considering something within a publishing house or something to do with writing."[55] By the end of the war, the number of newspapers published in Nazi Germany had dropped by 28 per cent. Material shortages hit magazines even harder, and by 1944 only one-tenth of the 1939 titles were still being published.[56]

Although an increasing number of women were entering the profession, the overall number of internships was shrinking, with the drafting into military service of many male editors who would have trained these volunteers. In the fall of 1944, women made up the majority of those applying to take the journalism entrance exam. At the same time, the German Press Association confirmed that admissions had shrunk: only 50 per cent of candidates were accepted to take the exam, compared with the previous year. It instructed all regional association heads to use this figure as a guide when admitting new trainees.[57] Still, the RDP assured prospective journalists that the training program had not been completely suspended. Throughout 1944 and the first months of 1945, women were still entering the field and even securing internships. For example, at the end of February 1945, the editor of the *Bodensee-Rundschau* registered his new intern, Rosemarie Fabian, for the next press entrance exam.[58] Magdali Eleonore Bülle, who had succeeded in finding a newspaper in West Prussia to take her on as an intern, wrote to her regional press association in October 1944, hoping to take the exam as soon as possible but concerned that she would have to wait until March 1945 to do so.[59]

The population's longing for news of any kind ensured that newspaper circulation remained at approximately 25 million to the end of 1944.[60] Likewise, the field remained viable for women journalists until the end of the Third Reich. Throughout the war, the German Press Association and various women's publications continued to encourage women to view journalism as a worthwhile and appealing profession. It is no coincidence that articles promoting the field of journalism and photojournalism in publications such as *Die junge Dame* and the German Women's Bureau publication *Frauenkultur* appeared in 1941 and onward – in other words, as the war dragged on and it became clear that there would be no easy victory for Nazi Germany.[61] The RDP's 1936 assurance that journalism was an important, challenging, and exciting career for women became reality for many female journalists after 1939. Moreover, the advantages they acquired – freedom of movement and access to important individuals, privileged information, and material goods – became more valuable during the war than they had been during peacetime.

## Travel, Information, and Privilege

Women journalists whose work afforded them such privileges as the opportunity for travel in and outside of Germany could enjoy benefits much of the female population on the home front had little access to, especially as the war progressed. Of course, many German men travelled as soldiers, and aspects of that travel were also highly enjoyable.[62] In this respect, the wartime experiences of some women journalists more closely resembled those of male soldiers than they did other women. Travel to other countries or to the countryside provided women a respite from wartime bombing and destruction, as well as access to ample food and drink. From 1942 onward, British bombing campaigns against Germany intensified, and the level of destruction rose again in 1943, after the United States joined their Allies in bombing German cities.

Helene Rahms enjoyed travel opportunities throughout the war. On a 1942 press trip to Königsberg, she travelled first class and relished the wine and theatre tickets her hosts provided: "We were spoiled, pampered, warmed up with grog, greeted with champagne, and hosted by the mayor with a solemn speech and a pompous dinner."[63] After having travelled to Vienna for work, Rahms recalled that it felt like a different world, with more food and drink and fewer bombs.[64] In July 1944, Ursula von Kardorff was pleased about her assignment to report on rest homes in Silesia because it offered her a respite from Berlin: "It will be nice to get out of this roundabout of fear, even if for only a short time," she noted in her diary.[65]

Photojournalists Ursula Litzmann, Erika Groth-Schmachtenberger, and Liselotte Purper travelled throughout much of Germany and the rest of Europe during the war. Litzmann began her career in the first year of the war and worked freelance, often for the film industry. She enjoyed, among other trips, a number of weeks in Amsterdam and The Hague in the winter of 1943.[66] In 1940 and 1941, Schmachtenberger relished several assignments in the German and Austrian Alps, where she photographed the Wehrmacht's mountain troops and the signal corps undertaking artillery exercises. Such assignments appealed to her love of the mountains. Schmachtenberger delighted in the praise she received from the troops for her climbing abilities as well as the sense of camaraderie this provided. "In 1941, in the mountains one could still afford to have fun," she fondly recalled after the war.[67]

The year 1941 was an especially pleasurable one for Schmachtenberger. Through the BDM, she arranged an assignment to photograph the group's counterpart in Spain. "I was not at all interested in the Falange girls," she claimed, "but it was the only way to get out of our dark country in the middle of the war. In Spain there were no blackouts and there were still large quantities of whipped cream, butter, and southern fruits."[68] On the one hand, Schmachtenberger's recollections and photographs of the trip acknowledged the despair and poverty that had resulted from the Spanish Civil War. On the other hand, her photography captured a sense of tranquility and tradition that cast the violence and divisiveness of the war that had ended with a fascist victory in April 1939 as all but a distant memory. Schmachtenberger accompanied a group of men and women in traditional Andalusian costumes to a festival and noted: "On the journey from Seville to the festival, one did not notice anything of [the recent war]. Rather, the girls danced and sang their flamenco songs ... A beautiful day," she enthused.[69]

Schmachtenberger's work also took her to Croatia, Romania, and occupied Poland. From 1942 to 1944, fearing that, as a freelance photojournalist, she would be assigned a job that did not suit her, Schmachtenberger accepted a position as a press photographer at the Tobis-Filmgesellschaft, one of the most prominent German film companies of its time.[70] Her new position brought its own set of advantages, to which the photojournalist had grown accustomed, and working on mountain films proved particularly stimulating. Not only did she enjoy meeting and socializing with popular film stars, she was also insulated from the increasing violence of the war. In May to July 1944, Schmachtenberger shot the press and publicity photos for *Vielleicht sehen wir uns wieder* (Perhaps we shall see each other again), which was filmed almost exclusively in the picturesque Heiligenblut am Grossglockner in Austria.[71] She noted that the photographers and actors were happy to be out of the cities and on the mountain. In July 1944, bombers flew over the region on their way to a devastating attack on Munich. From her

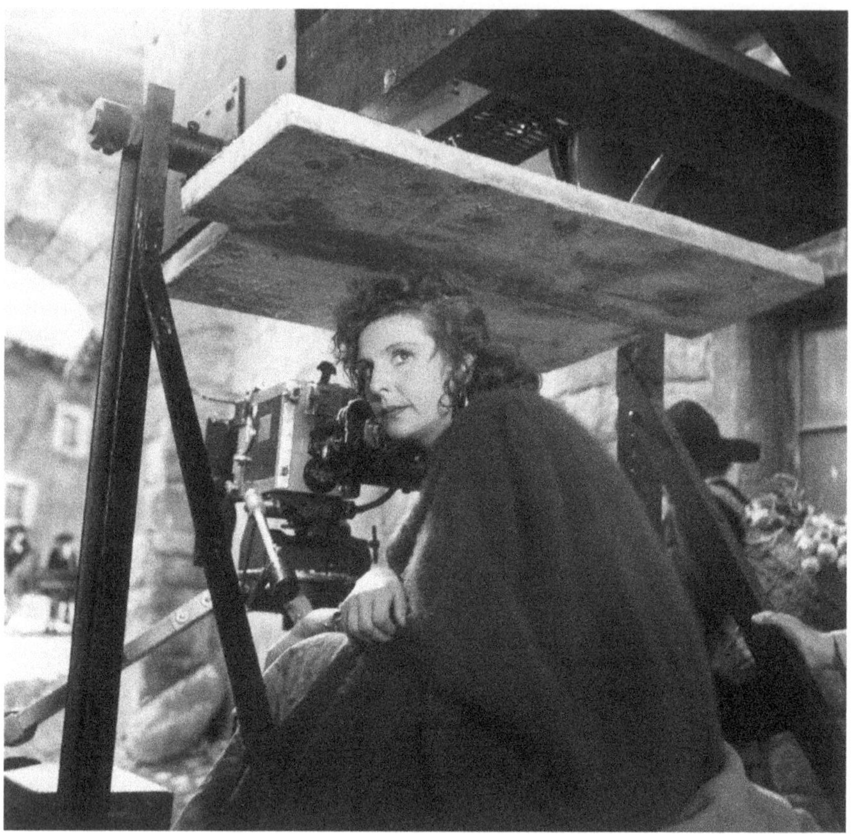

4.1  The director Leni Riefenstahl during the filming of *Tiefland* (Lowlands) in Krün, Bavaria, by Erika Groth-Schmachtenberger, 1940

Photo credit: bpk Bildagentur / Erika Groth-Schmachtenberger / Art Resource, NY

position on the mountain, Schmachtenberger recalled, "We knew what was coming to this city."[72]

Her subjects were not always shielded from wartime atrocities. In the fall of 1941, as a photographer for Tobis, Schmachtenberger travelled to Krün in Bavaria to work on the film *Tiefland* (Lowlands), which Leni Riefenstahl was directing (figure 4.1). The stills that Schmachtenberger took included Sinti and Roma, whom Riefenstahl had taken from the Nazi internment camp Maxglan on the outskirts of Salzburg to work as "extras." When they returned to the camp after the end of filming, the group was deported to Auschwitz, where most perished.[73]

Liselotte Purper's wartime travels took her to France, the Netherlands, Belgium, Denmark, Norway, Poland, Ukraine, Hungary, the Protectorate of Bohemia and Moravia, and Romania. She enjoyed these trips for the professional advantages, adventure, and material benefits they provided. In 1942, she admired the beauty of the Black Sea when visiting Odessa. In the winter of 1943, her work in the General Government region of Poland allowed her to ski in the Tatra mountains. In her downtime, she relaxed in an SS convalescent home in Zakopane, enjoying the local arts and crafts, and social evenings fuelled by Glühwein.[74] In July 1943, when rations were beginning to decline in Germany, Purper participated in a press trip to Denmark and Norway with a group of women journalists from Berlin. In her diary, she described the exquisite meals they enjoyed: "Tea, coffee, hot chocolate – yes please, everything one desires! 'Bread and butter ... yes, we have them.' And what bread and what butter. In silver baskets there is white bread, brown bread, crispbread, and fragrant, light pastries."[75] Purper and her colleagues frequented the best cafés, packed their travel bag with treats, and benefited from German material plunder in occupied territories.[76] In February 1944, after photographing soldiers convalescing in the Austrian Alps, Purper's primary concern was how her healthy and suntanned appearance would be received in Berlin.[77]

Purper's travels did not just lead to opportunities for leisure and material advantages, it also furnished her with occasions to meet and socialize with state leaders. On 26 July 1942, she recorded in her diary her excitement at having been welcomed to the home of the Romanian prime minister Ion Antonescu: "I'm so happy, I'm so happy, I'm so happy! Hada and I were welcomed by Marshal Antonescu! ... The fulfilment of our greatest wish came true: The state leader of Romania and his wife joined us in the garden."[78] Purper had the opportunity to photograph the couple and wrote: "After the photos, the Marshal invited us for a snack ... Mrs Antonescu told us about her country and her respect for all Germans."[79] Under Antonescu's dictatorship, Romania participated in the invasion of the Soviet Union in June 1941 and implemented harsh anti-Jewish policies. Although Antonescu's government ultimately refused to hand over Romanian Jews to the Germans, his own forces brutally killed hundreds of thousands of Jewish citizens, mainly from Bessarabia, Bukovina, and western Ukraine.[80]

For her column "Thea" in the *Heimat am Mittag*, Thea Fischer had the opportunity to travel and try out different wartime jobs, some more glamorous than others. On a contract for the Ministry of Propaganda, she reported on the evacuation of mothers and children to the countryside: "In the beautiful month of May, I was allowed to go to ... the Black

Forest and poke around. I can still see the beautiful blooming meadows with fruit trees that I travelled through."[81] The trauma and upheaval associated with the forced evacuation of mothers with their children contrasted with Fischer's enjoyable experience. When recalling the war, Fischer noted, "I did well for myself and was applauded for it. Despite everything, it was a beautiful time."[82]

Journalism could provide physical safety on the home front. Elisabeth Noelle-Neumann was able to leave Berlin in March 1945 for the relative security of the countryside, despite the regime's policy that the civilian population remain; as a reporter, she had a travel permit. Ursula von Kardorff also fled from Berlin to Bavaria with a female colleague in February 1945.[83] Erika Groth-Schmachtenberger largely worked freelance and could choose her assignments. Toward the end of the war, she elected to leave the threat of bombs in Munich for the picturesque Bavarian town of Ochsenfurt.[84]

Along with travel and material advantages, journalists had access to privileged information that afforded them a deeper understanding about the course of the war and the incontestable knowledge of atrocities perpetrated by Germans in occupied Europe. Newspaper offices received news from the German News Agency (Deutsches Nachrichtenbüro – DNB). The agency coded reports by colour according to their secrecy and what could and could not appear in newspapers. As Noelle-Neumann recalled, journalists could follow the reports and, in this way, learn factual information about the war that was denied to most Germans.[85] Discussions in the editorial department of newspapers also provided journalists with information not available to the general public. Male journalists working as war correspondents on the frontlines brought back information to their colleagues, for instance. Already in the fall of 1941, Erich Peter Neumann from *Das Reich* was transferred to a Propaganda Unit on the Eastern front, where he saw an Einsatzgruppen massacre of Jews. He later described what he had witnessed to his journalist fiancée.[86] In November 1944, Ursula von Kardorff recorded in her diary that, even though she was not writing much, she continued to go to the *Deutsche Allgemeine Zeitung* (*DAZ*) office in order to access information: "What matters to me is the news, the bulletins from the Promi [Propaganda Ministry], and the wireless news, which the paper gets and which Bärchen [the editor's secretary] lets me see. These enable me to get a good idea of the situation."[87]

Those working in the press had easier access than the majority of Germans to foreign newspapers, which offered a more complete understanding of German wartime crimes. As Noelle-Neumann observed, the regime did not even attempt to cut off journalists from information to the degree that they did with the general population.[88] Throughout the war, Margret Boveri continued to keep her archive of various international papers, which she started in the 1930s. In December 1944, Kardorff recorded in her diary that she had read an article in a Swiss newspaper, the *Journal de Genève*, about the genocide of European Jews: "There was a horrifying article by two Czechs who escaped from a concentration camp in the East. They say the Jews there are systematically gassed ... It is said the camp is at a place called Auschwitz."[89] Kardorff was referring to the Vrba-Wetzler report. In April 1944, two Slovak Jews, Rudolf Vrba and Alfréd Wetzler, escaped from Auschwitz and produced one of the most detailed descriptions of the organization and functioning of the camp and killing centre.[90] Millions of Germans were well aware of the deportations of German Jews, but fewer knew specifics about the killing centres in the East. By contrast, journalists such as Kardorff had access to foreign newspapers that published quite detailed, albeit sometimes inaccurate, information about the death camps.[91]

Journalists and editors, particularly at the large dailies such as the *Deutsche Allgemeine Zeitung* and *Das Reich*, often had contacts with state officials high in the government, which provided another avenue of news. Hans Schwarz van Berk, a reporter with the Waffen SS, travelled back and forth between the Eastern front and the home front. He had a close relationship with Goebbels and would report back to colleagues on *Das Reich*, including Helene Rahms, about the "whims and moods" of the propaganda minister, through which one could discern more about the war situation in general.[92] Despite their knowledge of the course of the war and the degree of violence perpetrated by the Germans, women journalists continued to provide news that helped maintain a sense of normality in everyday life among the population, as they had done throughout the 1930s.

### *Alles ist in Ordnung*: Crafting Diversion, Pleasure, and Optimism

At the beginning of the war, coverage of German army successes dominated newspapers, often at the expense of news articles of the kind that women were most likely to write. In December 1939, the *DAZ* informed freelance journalist Ilse Thien that it would not publish her previously commissioned article on fashion in Spain. According to the editor, the focus on the war meant that hundreds of articles that the paper would normally have included would not see the light of day.[93] The regime soon began to call for lighter fare, however, as propaganda efforts increasingly focused on comforting, entertaining, distracting, and bolstering the mood and attitude (*Stimmung und Haltung*) on the home front in order to ensure its continued support for the war. Given Hitler's belief that Germany had lost the First World War due to the collapse of the home front, these efforts only grew in importance to the regime as the country's military losses increased in late 1942 and 1943.

Goebbels too linked the press and its task of preserving morale to actions on the military front. In April 1942, in the midst of the Soviet army's "Winter Campaign" and a few months before what would become the prolonged and bloody battle for Stalingrad, Goebbels made clear the mission of the press: "The preservation of the mood of the German people, especially in the present time and before the biggest military decisions, is of the highest importance."[94] The year 1943 began with the loss of Stalingrad and continued with defeat in North Africa and the Allied landing in Sicily. In February of that year, as the regime was preparing to close or reduce the pages of additional magazines and newspapers due to material shortages, it announced that publications and content geared toward entertainment and the everyday would be less affected by such closures.[95]

A report from the German Press Association acknowledged that entertainment was a proven tool for diversion and relaxation and had a positive emotional impact on the attitude of the population. Yet the regime believed that such content helped support the war beyond providing a distraction for the population: because magazines and newspapers were later shipped to the front, they also helped strengthen the bond between the military and home front.[96] The Reich Culture Chamber (Reichskulturkammer – RKK), a part of Goebbels's Ministry of Propaganda, confirmed that the role of the cultural press – providing stories, serialized novels, humour, and poetry – had become increasingly important as the population's appetite for such material increased. The RKK was clear: it did *not* want cultural or entertainment material focused on military or war themes. On the contrary, the population, and even frontline soldiers, needed content that provided a break from war reportage.[97]

Always aware of the importance of public opinion, the regime worked to monitor and improve propaganda directed toward the German population. In July 1943 – the same month the Allies landed in Sicily and five months after the *Rosenstraße* protest in Berlin – the Central Party Propaganda Office grappled with the following questions: "How could the regime raise the prestige and reception of propaganda among the population? What means could be used to favourably influence the mood and attitude of the population? What propaganda methods were best suited to have a sustained effect on the widest circle of the population?"[98] By 1943, the German population had grown increasingly alienated and frustrated by overt Nazi propaganda, especially its presentation of the war, that did not correspond to what many knew to be the reality of Germany's military situation. Thus, material devoted to diversion became ever-more pivotal to the regime. Women journalists, charged with writing colourful, uplifting, and/or amusing pieces, had an important role to play in this scenario.[99] *Das Reich* provides one example. In line with the Nazi world view, the paper published antisemitic propaganda and vitriol directed at the Allies.[100] Nevertheless, the *Feuilleton* section, which covered literature, art, and science, as well as travel and local news, often constituted almost half of the paper.[101] Witty and intellectually stimulating, *Das Reich* proved a huge success.[102]

During her time with *Das Reich*, Helene Rahms worked in features, covering plays, exhibitions, and occasions such as a poetry evening at the Romanian embassy, as well as the seasonal wine harvest in Austria. Her column in the paper, "Aus den Ländern" (From the provinces), relayed everyday events taking place in idyllic towns, prose about the scenery, and descriptions of cultural festivals. Rahms later described her work as "pretty filler that avoided all political motives" – a self-serving description designed to downplay her connection with Nazi propaganda – but she also noted that it was important to the paper.[103] Rudolph Sparing, the paper's editor, allegedly referred to Rahms as *Das Reich*'s "Spezialistin für Stimmungen" (mood specialist).[104] In an article from April 1944, titled "Berlin by the Lake," Rahms described the beauty and timelessness of a frozen Berlin lake on which children still skated as they had for decades past. The lake's "beauty changed with the light of the morning and the twilight of the evening," Rahms wrote.[105] Such pieces were important in the eyes of the Ministry of Propaganda: they brought to mind bucolic images of stability and peace, and imparted hope by providing a glimpse of what life would return to after the war.

Yet the press could not entirely ignore the bombing of German cities, particularly Berlin. If the press, and by extension the state, failed to recognize the current circumstances in which the population lived, all news would become suspect, even irrelevant, and the relationship between the state and the population would be weakened. In "Berlin by the Lake," Rahms made an indirect and benign reference to the bombing of the capital city. An enemy plane that had taken part in an attack on Berlin the week before had been shot down and had crashed into the lake. "Shards of metal, wood and red rubber shimmered through the ice," Rahms wrote. "Now the pieces lay frozen under a blanket of ice, like fossils. Skaters glided over them."[106] Rahms's mention of the plane read as a reference to the effectiveness of Berlin's anti-aircraft artillery as well as the population's fortitude to carry on and "glide over" the hardships of the war.

Articles by *Das Reich* journalists Ilse Urbach and Christa Rotzoll also put a decidedly upbeat spin on the destruction of Germany's cities and the ramifications faced by the population. In May 1944, Rotzoll published a piece in which she wrote that it had become customary to ponder how cities and citizens were enduring the Allied raids. "Does Berlin Remain Sociable?", the title of the article asked. The piece acknowledged that some Berliners complained about the difficulty of manoeuvring around the city, the loss of transportation infrastructure, and the need to relocate, often more than once. Yet others celebrated Berlin's ongoing vitality and welcomed the opportunities to socialize and form personal connections that one would not necessarily establish in peacetime.

Rotzoll wrote of a painter who spent several "amusing" hours in a cellar with a group of fellow Berliners during a bombing raid, enjoying a bottle of Bordeaux and jaunty banter. More than ever, "city districts and streets are a source of local conviviality," Rotzoll declared.[107] Berliners believed that moments of threat and fear revealed an individual's true character. One young woman, Rotzoll cheekily wrote, used this principle to test out potential suitors: "In order to really get know a man," the young girl quipped, "you have to witness him in two situations: when he is drunk and during a bomb attack."[108] Rotzoll concluded that, despite some understandable grumbling, Berliners loved their city and, whether through humour, hospitality, or material assistance, were supporting each other – friends and strangers alike – and Berlin remained a congenial city. Rotzoll's article was breezy yet thoughtful, amusing yet earnest, direct yet uplifting. It acknowledged and empathized with the hardships faced by the German population. By emphasizing the harmony among residents, it also spoke to the Nazis' well-trodden discourse about the unified *Volksgemeinschaft*. For the German population, "Does Berlin Remain Sociable?" was readable and relatable. It not only provided Germans with an amusing read but reminded them that they were not alone in their difficulties.

In July 1944, Ilse Urbach published an article about the relocation of the Berliner Volksoper to a small town in the Thuringia mountains. Urbach downplayed the bombing of the opera's headquarters in Berlin and instead wrote of the enthusiasm and hospitality of the village and the warm relationships that developed between the locals and the members of the company. Like Rotzoll, Urbach emphasized the unity of the population and described the ways in which the opera's presence in the village swept away class barriers and the typical urban/rural divide: "The forest worker ... enjoys the melodies just as gratefully as the aged baroness, who whispered excitedly to her granddaughter, a BDM girl, during the performance of The Butterfly."[109]

The work of female journalists such as Rahms, Rotzoll, and Urbach in *Das Reich* focused on everyday life during wartime in a manner that drew attention to the unexpected pleasures and sense of community the war had created. Through their writing, they suggested that Germans continued to live bright, contemplative lives supported by friends and strangers alike. Although records do not establish the degree to which such articles bolstered morale in 1944, they did not invoke the population's anger and frustration in the way that blatantly false war-related propaganda did. More likely, they helped soothe Germans' growing dissatisfaction with the regime, the war, and its slanted coverage. Their writing helped assure readers that "Alles ist in Ordnung"!

Less-illustrious papers, including National Socialist papers such as the *Völkischer Beobachter*, *Der Angriff*, and the *Westdeutscher Beobachter*, also wanted lighter fare for their readers. Cultural, travel and local news had always proved important to Germans, and never more so than during the war. These areas connected more easily with what they knew to be reality, helped them feel integrated into their community, and provided a sense of shared experience.[110] To help satisfy this need, the DNB commissioned articles and short stories from journalists to distribute to magazines and newspapers. Topics it requested specifically from female journalists included anniversaries for German (or Austrian) composers and painters, art exhibitions, reviews of theatre performances, and articles about aspects of life abroad such as the Parisian theatre scene.[111] Already in 1940, the agency requested material that was "pretty, amusing, cheerful and life-affirming."[112] In 1943, the head of the DNB in Vienna wrote to his correspondent in Paris, Elfriede Meyn, advising her of the type of material he was seeking: "I think to myself that in Paris there must be a whole range of authors who can provide what I am looking for, lively, witty, funny, even a little cheeky, also erotic in a good sense."[113]

Of course, male journalists also contributed travel, cultural and local news to the German News Agency or to specific newspapers. Many, however, also worked in hard-news sections, such as national and international affairs, that related more directly to the war. Female journalists could discuss events or news related to the war, such as the downing of an enemy plane in softer, indirect ways, or divert attention from the war completely, through coverage of the "women's world." More important, women journalists could connect more directly with the female population. The regime viewed female readers as an important audience. Since women made up approximately half the population and represented the majority of those "manning" the home front, articles aimed at women were especially important during the war. In March 1940, *Der Zeitschriften-Verleger*, a trade magazine for magazine publishers and journalists, published an article on its front page pointing to this fact. The piece, titled "The Importance of Women's Magazines in War," instructed that, regardless of their form, women's publications served a political job: they had to mobilize women psychologically and physically to help them get through difficult times. Women's magazines, it continued, had done such a good job in this area prior to the war that they could now be credited with the willingness of the female population to put up with current circumstances. Such publications, the article continued, might not address politics in relation to domestic and foreign policy, but they did bring a different type of politics to the page: they taught their readers how to think about and deal with aspects of women's lives, which were, the article noted, "made of up many small things that might not seem heroic in the everyday." But a woman was as heroic as a man, the article assured, and "women's magazines during the war must emphasize this."[114]

Although the publication of magazines had dropped dramatically by 1944, standards denoting who could work in "women's issues" remained stringent, pointing to the fact that the regime continued to view these areas as important. When aspiring journalist Ruth Schultze completed her journalism exam in 1944, the examination committee agreed that she made a good overall impression, noting that she was well versed in culture and politics, and her ideological viewpoint was beyond reproach. Though she was designated a full-fledged journalist, she was not yet allowed to write about "women's issues." The committee felt that Schultze did not yet have the necessary know-how for this specialized and important area.[115]

Ruth Andreas-Friedrich became the editor of the wartime women's magazine *Kamerad Frau* in 1943.[116] Due to material shortages, press authorities merged three long-standing women's publications, *Die junge Dame*, *Wir Hausfrauen*, and *Die Hanseatin*, to form *Kamerad Frau*. With its focus on everyday life of women on the home front, *Kamerad Frau* provides one example of how women journalists packaged the war, its ramifications, and its possibilities for Germany's women. The magazine addressed how they could support the war effort on the home front and provided tips on how to shop and save, as well as how to cook, clean, and make household goods and clothing with limited materials. It also acknowledged the difficulties created by the war, including long work hours in factories, separation from loved ones, and the constant fear of death. In contrast to magazines published by the National Socialist Women's League, *Kamerad Frau* appeared to be more or less free of Nazi ideology. The community of women it presented were dealing with the war in a confident and constructive manner, finding happiness in the everyday, and using the war as a vehicle for self-improvement. Along with articles profiling women in various war-related professions, typical pieces included "Tired? No Wonder, If You Still Have to Manage Your Household in Addition to Your Work," "My Love Is War-Disabled," and "Your Health, Your Beauty."[117]

In its inaugural issue, Friedrich and her editorial team introduced the magazine in a personal and witty manner: "Dear readers, dear comrades, I am coming to you today for the first time … I am not shy because I am a very self-confident woman, but I am a woman after all and so I am anxious to find out how you like me."[118] Friedrich's introduction went on to assure readers that the magazine would address all issues and questions related to the demands of the war: "No matter how old the reader, no matter how she serves the war, no matter in which city or region of Germany she lives, [this magazine] comes to her as a good comrade, and what is more valuable in these hard times than a good comrade?"[119] Under Friedrich's direction, the magazine encouraged dialogue with its readers and sought to create a sense of trust and support. It asked readers to write to the editor with their questions and to share their troubles and their pleasures. Friedrich promised openness, a lack of judgment, and frank debate about topics that were normally considered taboo.[120] Through such exchange, the magazine and its journalists offered counsel, consolation, and a sense of community to its female readers. It is possible that such material also provided the Propaganda Ministry with insight into the issues that preoccupied the female population.

Through her advice column "Reden wir doch mal darüber!" (Let's talk about it), Friedrich claimed to address women's most pressing questions and concerns. Despite the publication's declaration to function as a resource for women in the context of war, the column most commonly dealt with such timeless issues as personal relationships or the desire for self-improvement. Friedrich's work allowed readers to focus on and retreat into their private everyday lives. Advice columns like "Reden wir doch mal darüber!" were one of the most popular and well-read sections in newspapers and magazines for this very reason.[121] They also provided female journalists with an accessible genre that aligned with the regime's discourse on gender and the private sphere.[122]

Friedrich's writing was not only amusing, but it also addressed situations with which most adults could easily identify. In June 1944, for instance, she wrote about the fear of aging. While almost everyone wants to live a long life, she noted, very few look forward to the aging process itself. She recounted how various Berliners described the first time they felt old: "The first time a young girl gave up her seat on the tram for me," one man recalled. "The first time men began to court my daughter and not me," another woman responded. Friedrich's column was light-hearted and uplifting. She reminded readers that "people can think as sharply and clearly in their midlife as they do at the age of twenty."[123] The secret to a happy life, Friedrich advised, was a conscious love of it.

Although several of Friedrich's columns sought to provide readers with a smile and a break from topics related to the war, others attempted to help the population cope with the war's ramifications. Her writing contributed to the regime's goal to strengthen the bond between the home and military fronts in an effort to maintain the moral of Germany's soldiers. In an article about the art of letter writing, Friedrich advised women how to write to soldiers at the front and counselled them not to "burden" their men with their own worries and problems: "Even if he wanted to with all his heart, your beloved cannot change the fact that [your child] was naughty once again, that you stood in line for three hours in search of cabbage … He cannot conjure up cabbage from Russia. Letters of this kind are only likely to spoil his mood," Friedrich counselled.[124] Instead, she recommended that women write about their achievements and the ways they were finding happiness as the best approach to help their men through the difficult separation.

Friedrich also addressed an unrelenting aspect of life in wartime Germany: death and grief. In August 1944, in "The Golden Bridge Back to Life," she wrote of how Germans navigated a tightrope between life and death. She acknowledged that, for many on the home front, their farewell to a loved one turned out to be the final goodbye, and she recognized that one short sentence in the newspaper – "died heroically for folk and fatherland" – concealed a world of sorrow, struggle, and resignation.[125] While she echoed the narrative of heroism that dominated Nazi discourse about the war, Friedrich also spoke empathetically to the suffering it caused – an important admission for the bereaved. In contrast, male writers such as Ernst Jünger tended to negate wartime suffering. Jünger's discourse, for instance, aligned more closely with the regime's notion of heroism, which emphasized hardness, discipline, and self-sacrifice.

Friedrich acknowledged the pain of physical separation but encouraged readers to take comfort in the belief that their loved ones lived on in their hearts and memories. She advised readers not to focus on what they might believe to be a bleak future, but rather to honour their loved one by moving forward. Friedrich also offered practical advice for widows about how to care for their family, how to establish a career, and how to find fulfilment in the everyday. By doing so, widows would find the "Golden bridge back to life." Media scholars such as Liesbet van Zoonen have shown that female journalists tend to favour a more human and empathetic approach to journalism, which can appear to be at odds with the professional tenets of objectivity and detachment.[126] Of course, Nazi press authorities did not promote journalistic objectivity. But historians of the German press have focused much attention on the more detached style of reporting practised by, and associated with, male journalists. Friedrich's writing reveals that, under the Nazi system, there was also space for a type of journalism that spoke to readers' needs and emotions.

"The Golden Bridge" is one example of how *Kamerad Frau* tackled, in an uplifting or compassionate manner, the many challenges the war brought to Germany's women. The magazine encouraged readers to live life to the fullest by cultivating positivity, courage, and gratitude. Friedrich herself summarized it best in her introduction to the magazine: "Just as we are prepared to solve difficult problems together, we also want to be happy together, where the war allows for happiness[,] ... and draw new strength from it for a new day."[127] Friedrich was deeply involved in a resistance group that provided aid to Jewish Germans and others targeted by the regime. It is therefore unlikely that she intended her articles to serve Nazi goals in any meaningful way – or that she even considered that they might. On one level, her work simply offered compassion and comfort for human suffering and uncertainty. Regardless of Friedrich's intentions or desires, however, her writing contributed to one of the most important strands of the regime's wartime propaganda – morale building for the female population.

**Feminine Heroes**

In 1944, the German News Agency reminded journalists that women were one of the most critical populations to consider with regard to propaganda.[128] In connecting with Germany's women, a journalist's task was twofold: to provide articles designed to recruit women to wartime service and praise their heroism, and to avoid anything that could deflate women's will to hold out. The work of Ursula von Kardorff provides a telling example of how journalists wrote with such responsibilities in mind. Kardorff's writing recast the regime's public and political aims as ones that offered women growth and fulfilment. Her wartime work ranged from light articles that described the frustration of torn stockings, to pieces lauding the heroism, capability, patriotism, and *joie de vivre* of German women in the midst of hardship.

In two articles published in the *DAZ* in 1944, Kardorff wrote about *Flakhelferinnen* and promoted the fun and fulfilment women enjoyed through such war service, as well as the contribution they made to the defence of their homeland, all the while maintaining their femininity. In both pieces, Kardorff was clear: German women were not soldiers. They were first and foremost women and approached their duty in a "womanly" way.[129] This observation separated women from the overtly military (violent) aspect of the war – a rhetoric they would find beneficial in the post-war period. *Flakhelferinnen* enjoyed an exciting and healthy lifestyle that provided numerous comforts, important this late in the war, including plentiful food, entertainment, visits to the beauty salon, and abundant free time. "The war needed men," wrote Kardorff, "and women were successfully stepping into vacated, sometimes leadership, roles with gusto, bravery, and success."[130] She ended the article "Helper and Not Soldier" with a line about the lasting impact this experience would have on women by quoting a lieutenant who exclaimed that, when peace returned, these women would be able to say, "when it really mattered, I was there too."[131] Kardorff's message that it was important for women to contribute to the war for their own good and for Germany's blended the concept of service for the nation with personal enjoyment and growth. Her text offered a far more appealing message than the increasingly thin calls for more sacrifices.

Encouraging women to register for work within flak gunnery brigades was an important topic for the regime. A memo to all Reich Propaganda Offices stated: "The role of Flak Gunnery Assistant is a Wehrmacht assignment and is therefore fundamentally more important than any civilian position [for women.]"[132] Accordingly, articles from other female journalists on the topic appeared in newspapers and magazines such as the *Völkischer Beobachter*, *Kamerad Frau*, and *NS Frauen-Warte*.[133] Although recruiting women to such positions would suggest that the war was all but lost, Kardorff's article helped veil this dilemma, describing the *Flakhelferinnen* role as one that was not only patriotic and fun, but that also came with perks, downplaying the danger and futility of such a job, and distracting readers from the visibility of Germany's impending loss.

Kardorff also championed women's more general wartime experiences. In "The Women in Berlin: Letter to a Neutral," written in March 1944, she addressed common questions about life for women in Berlin.

Her words acknowledged hardships but placed more emphasis on the heightened intensity, joys, and appreciation of life that came from living in the current circumstances.[134] Kardorff evoked an ideal of a female camaraderie that could not be destroyed by bombs, and she created a sense of pride for women in Berlin to hang onto – a much-needed morale injection in 1944 – and a sense of wonder that the rest of the population could admire: "If I am to be completely honest, please don't feel this is a propagandistic exaggeration ... [I'd] prefer to be here, at the heart of it where the pulse beats stronger than anywhere else," she concluded.[135] Packaged as feminine fortitude, Kardorff's text engaged with the violence of the war and the repercussions of German military actions. Yet its message that living in wartime Berlin was exciting and life-affirming downplayed the danger. Kardorff's request that readers not dismiss her words as propaganda testifies to the population's distaste for such material and may have resulted in a more positive reception for her article.

In "The Thirty-Year-Old Woman," Kardorff used the image of a "magic film" to depict her view of today's woman. The "film" begins in 1929 and describes the experiences of a generation of women born during the First World War and on the brink of adulthood when Hitler assumed power. Kardorff traced the difficult but exciting shared history of this generation, their youth curtailed by the deprivations of the war, the violence and upheaval of the aftermath, and the inflation of the early 1920s. Her words juxtaposed feminine innocence and suffering with strength and capability: "Is this a despairing sex?" she asked. "No, exactly like plants that grow under difficult conditions, they became tough and flexible, and that serves them well today."[136] These women overcame hardships unknown by previous generations and sought opportunities: they pursued professions, travelled, married, and began families. This exciting and formative time coincided with the early years of the Nazi regime. Kardorff presented the mid-1930s as a time of stability and prosperity for women. In 1944, when most of the population was suffering the deprivations of war, Kardorff's words transported her readers back to the days when many women had been enthusiastic about Nazism, once again providing a boost for those on the home front and for the regime.

Kardorff's depiction of women both supported and pushed the boundaries of Nazi gender rhetoric in a way that was useful to the Nazi government. Women were fighters and actors in the public realm, but they were first and foremost women and made their contribution in a "feminine" way. Women were vital and strong in the face of adversity, but always tranquil; family remained their primary responsibility.[137]

This ambiguity allowed Kardorff to support the regime's need for the political mobilization of women without drifting too far from Nazi gender norms.

In an article in April 1945, Christa Rotzoll addressed a topic that Kardorff had only alluded to: were the war and women's contribution to it leading to radical feminism and the militarization and "masculinization" of Germany's women?[138] Rotzoll argued that such a worry was unfounded. While the war had certainly opened up education and career possibilities in areas normally reserved for men, women were most grateful for the fact that these opportunities facilitated better understanding between the sexes. Women, Rotzoll maintained, had made limited use of their emancipation, and, more important, the military was neither intended for nor of interest to them. Women do not learn how to become *Flakhelferinnen* for their own sake, she wrote, but to satisfy the nation's need. "The world of aerial warfare has hardly enticed women, but it needs them: the women will therefore satisfy it but not succumb to it."[139] Some outwardly masculine things such as the *Bubikopf* (bobbed hair cut) are completely harmless, Rotzoll assured her readers. Women were certainly heroic, but they were no threat to men.

Other publications, like the *NS Frauen-Warte*, also published pieces that encouraged women to step into male roles in the name of war duty and sought to boost their morale. But Kardorff and Rotzoll's articles were published in respected dailies, giving their text a more credible tone than could be found in party papers. The fact that the *Deutsche Allgemeine Zeitung* and *Das Reich* dedicated space for this type of material in 1944 and 1945, when the number of pages for newspapers had been significantly reduced, some to only two pages, demonstrates the importance with which press authorities viewed such writing. As late as April 1945, the Reich Press Office demanded that all components of the press and propaganda machine must "exclusively serve the purpose of raising morale and the spirit of resistance."[140]

**Negative Propaganda**

Articles containing buoyant messages and dedicated to diversion, pleasure, and the building of female morale on the home front formed a significant component of women's journalism during the war years. But, just as they had prior to the war, some female journalists also contributed to the regime's racial and political discourse about Germany's proclaimed enemies – the Allies and, above all, "international Jewry." High-ranking officials in the Ministry of Propaganda and the Reich Press Office knew by the fall of 1941 that Germany had begun the mass murder of European Jews. To support this policy, they used the media to provoke hatred toward German Jews and offer justifications for the government's murderous policies and actions. After Germany's loss at Stalingrad in January 1943, Hitler instructed the press to keep up a near constant bombardment of antisemitic headlines and articles.[141]

Female journalists working on publications ranging from women's magazines and dailies to party organs contributed to this line of Nazi rhetoric. As Ursula von Kardorff recorded in her diary in May 1943, "All newspapers have been told to include antisemitic stuff in every possible sort of piece, including feature articles."[142] *Kamerad Frau* was largely free of overt Nazi ideology, but it still included inflammatory articles about Jews under Ruth Andreas-Friedrich's tenure as editor. With little room to sidestep the demands of press authorities, Friedrich fulfilled the requirements of her profession by including antisemitic articles in the paper. She did not, however, write such material herself.

In January 1944, *Kamerad Frau* introduced the series "They Are to Blame," which aimed to show how great thinkers identified the ways in which the "actions of the Jews" had sought to crush the German people and culture throughout history. The February 1944 issue included an article titled "Kosher Art: How Jews Saw Women," which displayed pictures of deformed and overtly sexualized paintings and sculptures of women that the author deemed degenerate.[143] Such texts were designed to make Jews the scapegoat for German frustration over the war and their own suffering and losses.

In early 1943, while working as a foreign correspondent in Lisbon, Margret Boveri received a telegram from the *Frankfurter Zeitung* with instructions to write an article about "the Jewish question" in America. Boveri satisfied her editor's request. The *FZ* published her article "Landscape with a Safety Net: The Influence and Camouflage of Jews in America" on 28 May 1943. Boveri wrote that there was a strong current of antisemitism in America, which was kept quiet since it did not fit with the myth of equality among all Americans.[144] The article was largely a critique of American politics and way of life – a common theme that Boveri took up in her private and public writing without any prompting from her editors.

It did, however, include a particularly antisemitic paragraph, charging that American Jews had led the United States to enter the war against the Reich, since they viewed "Germany as their principal enemy" and sought its "downfall."[145] It had, of course, been Hitler who declared war on the United States, but such inaccuracies were irrelevant in the German press in 1943. The type of language included in Boveri's article helped justfiy physical violence against racialized minorities and connected journalists indirectly to the processes of the Final Solution.[146] Evidence suggests that the paper's editors added this paragraph prior to publication, without Boveri's knowledge.[147] Although she was initially upset with the changes made to her text, Boveri remained with the paper. She justified the modification and accepted the reasoning of her colleague Oskar Stark that the editors had added the paragraph in an attempt to save the paper, which the regime had repeatedly threatened to close.[148] Despite the paper's adherence to orders to publish antisemitic vitriol, the regime shut down the *FZ* in August 1943.

Rather than attacking the Jewish adversary, much of Boveri's wartime writing dealt with the United States itself. Anti-American material was an important component of Nazi propaganda. While based in New York, Boveri had written pieces on American racism, criticizing US hypocrisy in reproving the Nazi state for its antisemitic policies while simultaneoulsy opressing Black Americans. For the Nazi regime, such material helped justify Nazi racial persecution and violence. She also wrote about what she deemed America's inferior culture and capitalist greed and criticized its elections, charging that democracy and equality did not exist in the United States. Claims that the United States was simplistic, that it lacked cultural sophistication and an understanding of Europe, that the Allied "terror" bombing was immoral, and that America stood for nothing but rabid consumerism, proved popular topics in the German press; many of Boveri's articles echoed such discourse.[149]

Press authorities assigned similar tasks to other women journalists. In March 1944, the German News Agency gave Margret Gröblinghoff a few suggestions for articles, including something with the recommended title "Every Anglo-American Bomb only Benefits the Soviets."[150] This article, the agency noted, needed to argue that, without troops on the ground, the most that England and the United States were accomplishing was to weaken the German Eastern front and ensure further Soviet penetration within Europe. The DNB also suggested a piece titled "American War" that would provide a historical overview about how the United States had never before fought real opponents. Rather, it had only conquered "Indians" and, during the First World War, an already asphyxiated Germany. The American army would therefore never be able to defend Europe against the Soviets if Germany were destroyed.

Elisabeth Noelle-Neumann had spent an exchange year in the United States during her university studies. Before the United States had even entered the war, she too published articles that disparaged the country. Her article "The American Image of History," published in *Das Reich* in May 1941, maintained that the United States was a naive country with no understanding of European history and politics.[151] According-ing to Noelle-Neumann, history courses taught at universities focused only on American history, while breezing through hundreds of years of European developments. She further charged that courses at American universities included blatant and misplaced judgments: "The moral enthusiasm exhibited during discussions about foreign politics by every student who had attended the lecture 'European History' was almost touching in its naivety, if it did not cost humanity so much blood and sorrow."[152] She implied that the United States was responsible for condoning and encouraging violence in Europe because its leaders did not understand European politics. In other words, it could not grasp why Germany had had to go to war.

Noelle-Neumann's work brought together discourses about the United States and international Jewry. In "Who Informs America? Journalists, Radio Broadcasts, and Films," she turned to traditional Nazi rhetoric concerning Jewish control of the press, arguing that such was the case in the United States: "Jews write in the papers, own them, have virtually monopolized the advertising agencies and can therefore open and shut the gates of advertising income as they wish."[153] Noelle-Neumann contributed to Nazi tropes about Jewish control of the financial industry but in a more sober tone than could be found in the *Völkischer Beobachter* and its ilk. *Das Reich* was popular in Germany due to its "factual" and restrained tone, which the population viewed as more credible than simple agitation. From women's magazines and papers that the regime marketed as respectable and that the population accepted at face value, to party tabloids, women journalists contributed to a wartime narrative that sought to demonize Germany's supposed enemies and encourage feelings of derision and hatred among the population that would, the regime hoped, ensure continued support of the war.

## Conclusion

In her essay "Truth and Politics," Hannah Arendt wrote, "Images made for domestic consumption, as distinguished from lies directed at a foreign adversary, can become a reality for everybody."[154] Arendt's words provide a useful framework within which to consider the importance of women's wartime journalism in Germany. Female journalists contributed to several stands of propaganda important to the regime's presentation of wartime reality, including antisemitic, anti-Soviet, and anti-American rhetoric that overlapped with the type of reporting undertaken by their male counterparts. Their primary role, however, was to connect with German women on the home front and offer cheerful material that would bolster their morale and provide relief from the everyday stresses of war. After 1942, the German public viewed hard news about the war with growing scepticism. At the same time, the appetite for material devoted to entertainment and diversion increased. Women journalists encouraged readers to retreat into private pleasures, hobbies, and everyday life, which allowed the population to better cope with their wartime reality and thereby helped stabilize the home front. While writing about everyday life and the private sphere, women journalists served the state in a public manner.

Along with their growing public influence, female journalists' importance to the regime increased during the war years. The Nazi government needed such women to support the state; in turn, the state supported them by providing opportunities for career advancement, pleasure, and fulfilment. Many of the most prominent, as well as lesser-known, journalists and photojournalists got their big break in journalism during the war. They acquired advantages that the general population could not access: mobility, material possessions, and a sense of elitism. As Helene Rahms put it, journalists "were included in this illustrious circle and felt high above the clouds of war, as if we were on Parnassus."[155] Female journalists, however, did not only help support the Nazi state on the home front; they also became actors helping to maintain German hegemony in occupied Europe.

## Chapter Five

# The Beautification of Total War and Occupation

On 28 January 1945, one day after the liberation of Auschwitz, German journalist Gerda Pelz wrote a final letter to Hans Frank, the governor general of the General Government region of Poland. Pelz had worked closely with Frank in Krakow for four years but had returned to Germany as the Red Army advanced westward. "Will we ever again experience such a rich and stimulating time in Krakow?" she asked. "Every Wehrmacht report brings great sorrow."[1] In response, Frank thanked Pelz for her years of outstanding work on the General Government's flagship paper the *Krakauer Zeitung* and assured her that "you too have planted German roots in the Eastern soil that, if fortune provides, will once again grow when this fateful Russian winter [that has fallen] over Poland has ended and a new German spring has sprung."[2] Pelz's fond memories of her time in Poland and Frank's praise of her work exemplify how female journalists found opportunity, autonomy, and fulfilment while helping to support German hegemony and acts of extreme violence in occupied Europe.

The previous chapter looked at the advantages enjoyed by women journalists working on the home front and their contribution to propaganda designed to ensure the population's continued support of the regime. Such material was aimed mainly at Germany's women. This chapter examines the various ways in which women journalists based or travelling in German-occupied Europe during the Second World War beautified Nazi expansionism and wartime violence. Writing for German audiences at home and in the occupied regions, women journalists both engaged the population and distanced them from the war. By reporting on issues such as German culture, local events, and themes directed to women and youth, they masked the processes and repercussions of extreme violence and made the war more palatable for German civilians at home and in the occupied regions.

Women journalists fed into an intellectual (and masculine) narrative already present in interwar Germany about the beauty and glory of war and violence, although they did so in a "feminine" manner.[3] At the same time, the possibilities for travel, privilege, prestige, and professional advancement grew for female journalists working in occupied Europe, as it had for those working on the home front. Prior to the war, *Die Schriftleiterin* (Guide for women journalists) emphasized that opportunities existed for women to work abroad if they had the language skills and knowledge of the culture.[4] Throughout the war, however, as press authorities established German-language papers in the regions they conquered, women without language or cultural knowledge also saw their chances of working outside Germany increase.

Historians and media scholars have demonstrated that women journalists in Europe and North American were typically denied access to the frontlines of conflicts, which disqualified them from covering wars in the traditional manner.[5] Of course, there were some exceptions to this rule: US correspondents such as Margaret Bourke-White and Peggy Hull, for example, did manage to access conflict zones. Nonetheless, most women reported on the humanitarian impact of wartime violence – a genre pioneered by female journalists in response to their limited access to military action.[6] While, as we saw in earlier chapters, German women journalists did not engage in a humanitarian approach with respect to interwar conflict or the Second World War itself, they did contribute to expanding the genre of German war reporting by offering their readership a softer and more upbeat form of wartime news and propaganda than their male colleagues typically wrote. During the war, such material provided a counterbalance to the militant language that permeated much of the coverage about, and within, the occupied territories. As Germany's military situation deteriorated, women journalists' writing became an increasingly important vehicle for morale building, giving them a form of soft power that helped to validate, put a peaceful spin on, and later stabilize the German occupation. At the same time, there were possibilities for female journalists to work beyond the "womanly realms" and that allowed them to engage with, and glorify, wartime violence in a more direct manner. By capitalizing on opportunities in occupied regions, women journalists became actors and beneficiaries in the systematic violence their writing both camouflaged and commended.

This chapter contributes to the rich and growing body of scholarship on the ways in which women aided and abetted National Socialist violence. Claudia Koonz has shown how German women maintained the illusion of a softer realm that simultaneously contributed to, and provided refuge from, the public, militant sphere and its associated violence. Elizabeth Harvey has demonstrated that the domestic work of girls and women from Germany proper contributed to the regime's plans to "Germanize" the Wartheland region of occupied Poland. This role connected women to the violent displacement and killing of hundreds of thousands Poles and Jews. Wendy Lower's study on German women in the Soviet territories points to ways in which a small group of women actively perpetrated violence against individual Jews via their professional and personal roles.[7] In contrast to these women, female journalists assisted in the German occupation of Europe in a more widespread fashion, since their work was disseminated to and consumed by a broad audience. Their presence in occupied regions led them into a more complicit relationship with wartime brutality, compared to that of their counterparts on the home front. They not only helped justify Nazi empire-building through their work, but they also witnessed first-hand the acts and ramifications of violence perpetrated by the system that their writing helped to sustain.

## Occupation and Opportunity

As Hitler launched his war of race and space in Poland in September 1939, professional opportunities for German women journalists soon followed: job prospects only increased in tandem with German aggression. In June 1940, the army conquered France. By April 1941, the Wehrmacht had invaded Yugoslavia, and two months later it attacked Soviet territories. Much as it did in Germany, the Nazi government took over the press in these regions and quickly established its own papers. In July 1941, Eva Klempp began her journalistic training at the newly established *Donauzeitung* in Belgrade, the official publication of the German military occupation in Serbia. She then worked in occupied Ukraine as a full-fledged journalist.[8] Lilo Zingler too began her career working on the business pages of the Belgrade-based paper, in January 1942. By July 1944, she was fully responsible for the paper's important Balkan section.[9]

Career advancement was one motivation for women to travel to the occupied territories. This was the case for Hella von Einsiedel. Born in 1915 in Dresden, Einsiedel worked as a secretary prior to the war. Sometime after June 1941, she secured a secretarial position on the *Deutsche Ukraine-Zeitung* and quickly turned this into an opportunity to train as a journalist in the paper's local news section. In July 1943, she began to work as a journalist in the Einsatzstab Rosenberg, in Ukraine. The Einsatzstab was the organization responsible for the cultural plunder of occupied Europe – a violent process in and of itself. In her application letter, Einsiedel specified that she hoped to eventually take her final journalism exam and that a position in the Einsatzstab would allow her to further build her skills and educate her in Ukrainian affairs.[10] As officials pointed out, Einsiedel's experience in Ukraine made her a desirable addition to Rosenberg's staff.[11]

Women's journalistic opportunities outside of Germany were not limited to the East; women worked in occupied Western and Northern Europe, as well as neutral countries and territories aligned with Germany, including Slovakia, Bulgaria, Romania, Hungary, Sweden, Spain, Portugal, and Iraq. Ilse Thien had built her career throughout the 1930s writing for various women's magazines in Berlin. By April 1943, she had relocated to Norway, where she worked for the German-occupation paper the *Deutsche Zeitung* and became acting editor of the *Deutsche Monatshefte in Norwegen*. Just as it was for German soldiers, France was a particularly desirable destination for journalists who wanted to enjoy French culture and the splendour of Paris.[12] Ilse Flach began her career as a secretary in the Ministry for Public Enlightenment and Propaganda (Reichsministerium für Volksaufklärung und Propaganda – RMVP) in March 1939. In July 1940, only one month after the German invasion of France, she requested a transfer to Paris, telling her employer that to work in the French capital would be her "most fervent wish."[13] The RMVP fulfilled Flach's request, and she was transferred, which led to further opportunities. By July 1943, she was a journalist-in-training at the Paris office of the German News Agency (Deutsches Nachrichten-büro – DNB). Elfriede Meyn also worked at the DNB in Paris and was among only five remaining members of the agency in June 1944 – the rest had been called up to military duty.[14] At least two women worked for the Propaganda Ministry's Paris office as fashion journalists, and two others reported for the occupation paper the *Pariser Zeitung*.[15] By January 1942, around twenty German foreign correspondents were based in occupied France, at least two of whom were women; in Vichy France there were four men and one woman.[16] Other female journalists travelled to France throughout the war to report for various papers and magazines.

Most women journalists travelling or working in Europe typically wrote for the women's pages and/or the travel, culture, or local news sections of German-based papers or those established by the regime in the occupied region. Ilse Urbach was no exception. Prior to the war, she had established a successful career writing for some of the most long-standing and high-profile German newspapers and magazines. During the war, she enjoyed opportunities to travel in Western and Eastern Europe for *Das Reich*. In the spring of 1941, Urbach visited occupied France and wrote about her travel experiences.

Her article "Sunday on the Seine" described a stroll she had taken in Paris. Urbach's Paris was a seemingly tranquil city, where German soldiers and Parisian civilians co-existed in harmony. She described the spring weather, the blooming flowers, and the splendour of famous Parisian landmarks such as the Arc de Triomphe and the Jardins du Luxembourg. From the picture Urbach painted, it was almost impossible to discern that a war was taking place. Her depiction of the German soldiers she witnessed on the streets of Paris evoked images of a happy-go-lucky atmosphere in the occupied city. She described how members of the Wehrmacht and the local population enjoyed the Sunday atmosphere as they listened to a concert put on by the German Air Force: "Many women sit on iron chairs, little ones in their arms ... Couples lean arm in arm against the thick tree trunks, a Breton woman crochets in a white bonnet, her husband reads the *Petit Parisien*."[17] While Urbach's article put a serene spin on the German occupation, it also included a reference meant to showcase French antisemitism by describing the purported queue at a Parisian cinema waiting to see the notoriously antisemitic German film *Jud Süss*.[18] Urbach's writing suggested to German audiences that the occupation of France was benign, that the population was resigned or even pleased with the presence of German soldiers, and that Parisians too harboured hatred toward Germany's Jewish enemy.

While Urbach's writing represented the type of material women journalists typically produced during the war, some female journalists found important roles outside of soft news. They worked for publications and on topics that more directly connected them to military events, but that still beautified the processes of war. Although women did not typically work as war correspondents, Lily Abegg was a notable exception. Abegg, who had worked as the *Frankfurter Zeitung*'s Far Eastern correspondent from 1936 onward, was the only woman out of eight German journalists who followed closely behind the Wehrmacht as it advanced into Paris.

She began her report from Dunkirk and described the rubble of this and other French towns along the route to the capital; she laid the blame for the destruction firmly at the feet of the British. English incendiary bombs had burned the city of Amiens, Abegg wrote, because "that is how the English are."[19] In Abegg's depiction, the English wreaked havoc in France, while the Wehrmacht sought to preserve the country's cultural beauty. Abegg praised the army for taking the capital without a fight, thereby avoiding the destruction that battle would undoubtedly have brought. From now on, she wrote, the Arc de Triomphe – constructed to honour the glory of the French army – would represent German victory and "war booty." Abegg described the thrill of seeing the swastika "fluttering above" Versailles. Although propaganda had "poisoned" the local population against Germany with false stories of German atrocities, she noted, the French were learning that the "German army does not consist of wild barbarians." Rather, she claimed, civilians often approached her to describe how the French government had lied to them about the nature of Germans and that "they would have starved to death long ago without the bread the German soldiers gave them."[20] In Abegg's depiction, the German army was altruistic and peaceful.

The article appeared in the *Frankfurter Zeitung* on 20 June 1940, just a few days after German troops occupied Paris. Like Urbach, Abegg beautified the invasion of France. She too downplayed the fear and displacement experienced by the French and replaced it with the image of a grateful population enjoying – or at least at peace with – the German occupation of their country. Yet Abegg did so as a war correspondent. In Nazi-occupied Europe, German women journalists had some opportunity to work in areas outside of the typical women's realm. Still, as with her coverage of the Second Sino-Japanese war during the late 1930s, Abegg signed her articles with "LA" rather than her full name, a practice that degendered her work. Although press authorities and editors in Nazi Germany were prepared to allow a limited number of women to operate in typically male arenas, they were reluctant to publicly acknowledge women's contribution to news from the frontlines.

Hildegard Faber also worked for a publication whose content did not correspond to the soft-news topics on which women journalists typically wrote. Born in 1914, Faber studied philosophy, German, theatre, and dance at the University of Cologne. She became a fully accredited journalist in December 1940 and began her career working on the typically feminine beats of culture and entertainment for a German newspaper in Karlsbad – a city in the Sudetenland that Germany had annexed in September 1938. At the beginning of 1943, Faber landed a position in her "beloved Paris," writing for Organisation Todt's illustrated magazine, the *Frontarbeiter*. This position moved her work beyond the feelgood area of travel and culture and directly connected her writing to the masculinized world of Germany's war production and defence activities and the violence inherent within these processes.[21] For Farber, the position was ideal, since it allowed her the opportunity to travel and to live in the city she most desired.

Organisation Todt was founded in 1938 for the construction of large-scale engineering projects in Germany.[22] During the war, it was restructured into a paramilitary organization under the authority of the Minister for Armaments and Munitions. It also incorporated the construction units of the Wehrmacht. The group became responsible for projects within Germany as well as in the occupied territories of Eastern and Western Europe.

The organization employed conscripted Germans and local volunteers, though, as the war continued, it relied increasingly on slave labourers, prisoners of war, and concentration camp inmates. Forced to work under the grimmest conditions, many workers did not survive.

The *Frontarbeiter* reported on Organisation Todt's work on different fronts and covered topics such as the construction of buildings, visits from Nazi officials, the life of the construction workers, news from the frontlines, and articles about the landscape, politics, and history of particular regions in which the organization was active. Accompanied by photographs, typical pieces included "German U-boats in the Caribbean Sea" and "Economic Efficiency through Standardization." Since articles in the paper rarely included bylines, it is impossible to attribute specific pieces to individual journalists. Nevertheless, as a full-time staff member, Faber contributed to the *Frontarbeiter*'s discourse that depicted workers as soldiers and heroes, and equated labour with virility, strength, and discipline. Such reporting connected Organisation Todt and its activities to the very attributes that would (supposedly) lead Germany to victory.

In France, the organization's projects included the construction of the Atlantic Wall. As the war on the Eastern front began, Hitler decided to fortify the Atlantic coast in the occupied Western territories. The organization worked to reinforce ports and anti-aircraft batteries and constructed large bunkers that the regime intended as production sites. Propaganda over such projects aimed to highlight the invincibility of Nazi Germany. After losses at Stalingrad and North Africa in early 1943, the importance of such reportage increased for the Nazi government, even if its credibility eroded. Hitler strove to boost the morale of the German population by attempting to convince them that an Allied invasion was all but impossible.[23]

The war presented some female journalists the opportunity to toggle between positions in a traditional (and acceptable) area for their gender, and work that connected them more directly to militarized organizations, wartime defence, and, as in the case of Organisation Todt, Germany's perpetration of war crimes. Faber was not the only journalist to write for publications connected to various aspects of the military. The writing and photography of women journalists appeared in publications like *Das Schwarze Korps*, the official newspaper of the SS (Schutzstaffel); the *Luftwaffenkurier*, the frontline magazine for the air force; and the illustrated magazine *Signal*, which was a propaganda tool of the Wehrmacht for audiences in neutral countries and in the regions occupied by Germany.[24]

Women journalists sanitized practices of violence associated with Germany's invasion and occupation of France. Through their writing, they cast the relations between the Wehrmacht and the local population as serene, if not altogether pleasant. At the same time, they contributed to the glorification of German military might. For German readers, such writing helped create a sense of pride, not only in the strength of the German army, but also in the purportedly gallant and benevolent way it wielded its power. While the German occupation force wrought much destruction and violence in Western Europe, the Nazi assumption that Western culture and society had some value meant that countries like France generally experienced a lesser degree of destruction and brutality in comparison to what was taking place in the occupied East. Women journalists travelling and working in the East contributed to a narrative about the occupation and its repercussions in a manner that was ultimately more destructive and that implicated them in the masking and extolling of violence as well as the maintenance of a repressive occupation.

### Resettling the *Volksdeutsche* in the East

Poland held a particularly important place in Germany's war efforts. It was an essential region in Hitler's pursuit of *Lebensraum* and a site of mass brutality and displacement associated with the regime's processes of Germanization. The Nazi regime viewed Poles as inferior occupants of territory that alleged was inherently German. During the war, Hitler sought to erase any form of Polish culture and enslave its citizens. Moreover, the killing centres established to murder European Jews and other victims of Nazi violence were located on Polish territory. Together these factors led to a degree of repression and bloodshed that far exceeded what took place in Western Europe. Women journalists travelling or working in this region were well-informed of the degree of violence perpetrated in their midst.

The Nazi regime divided Poland into two regions. The Western region, the Wartheland, was annexed to Germany proper. The central and eastern regions of Poland were referred to as the General Government and were placed under German occupation. A number of female journalists found reporting from both regions of Poland an appealing prospect.[25] Elizabeth Harvey has identified a variety of reasons why German women were attracted to work in Poland. While some believed in Nazism, others sought travel and adventure or the opportunity to progress professionally in ways that were not open to them prior to the war or in Germany proper.[26] The same holds true for journalists.

During the war, the writing of women journalists became a means to underscore the so-called benefits of German expansionism, stimulate the

German population's imagination about the beauty of the East, and emphasize the personal and professional opportunities that it offered to women. The typical female journalist's beat covering local, travel, and domestic or household news converged with material that addressed the resettlement of the *Volksdeutsche* (ethnic Germans). Under the aegis of its *Heim ins Reich* (Home to the Reich) program, the Nazi regime began to resettle communities of ethnic Germans from the Baltic States and the Volhynian region of eastern Poland and Ukraine to the Wartheland shortly after the war began. *Heim ins Reich* was the first step in Hitler's long-term goal to colonize and Germanize Eastern Europe.[27] To Germanize the annexed territory and accommodate ethnic German settlers, Nazi authorities planned the expulsion of Poles and Jews.[28] By the end of 1941, the Germans had expelled close to half a million people and appropriated their property.[29]

Ignoring the inherent brutality of these processes, women travelling and based in the East reported on various ways in which German women were helping "resettled" *Volksdeutsche* communities become "proper" Germans. On 29 December 1940, for example, *Das Reich* published an article by Ilse Urbach titled "Female Help in the Wartheland."[30] In glowing terms, Urbach's article described her visit to a group of young German women who worked with resettled communities of ethnic Germans. From her lyrical descriptions of the Polish landscape – "endless meadows with no border between sky and earth" – to lauding the brave and industrious work of the young women caring for the new settlers, Urbach's article put an industrious and *gemütlichen* spin on processes dependent on extreme violence. She enthused that "Posen had joyfully returned to a German life."[31] Her text implied that Germany had a right to this former Polish region because the land was German in its very essence. Urbach visited Lodz (renamed Litzmannstadt), where the Germans had established a Jewish ghetto in February 1940. She wrote of the improvements the Germans had brought to the region and contrasted German progressiveness, order, and cleanliness with Polish slovenliness.

Above all, Urbach focused on the domestic support young German women provided in these areas, caring for children, sewing, cleaning, and guiding the ethnic Germans, both the new settlers as well as the local community, toward a so-called German way of life. Yet under the Nazi regime, domestic practices became part of racism and persecution in occupied Poland, since German women working in the region applied a particular notion of German domesticity to gauge the "Germanness" of a family or individual.[32] Those whose houses were considered slovenly were often categorized as Polish and denied the advantages given to the *Volksdeutsche*. Such practices led to further violence. The Nazi government defined *Volksdeutsche* as those whose language and culture had German roots but who did not hold German citizenship.[33] In reality, it was not so easy to distinguish them from their Slavic neighbours.[34] The *Volksdeutsche* were the intended recipients of Polish and Jewish property, but the ambiguity and malleability of the term meant that their "Germanness" was often in doubt. Those who attempted to prove their "Germanness" often found that the easiest way to do so was to demonstrate their adherence to Nazism, which, in turn, meant perpetrating violence against Jews.[35]

While Urbach's article offered a mostly cheerful portrait of the war in Poland, it also included antisemitic rhetoric. She described Wielun as "the city of the Jews," where "they still run around here freely." "Shuddering," her article continued, "we turned away from the swarm of yellow stars of David on backs and chests."[36] Urbach's text alluded to the ghettoization of Jews that was taking place throughout Poland. Through the use of language such as "swarm" and "shuddering," she adopted Nazi vitriol that equated Jews with pestilence and dirt and thus implied the necessity of actions to contain and expel them. Such discourses served to create repulsion toward Jews and Poles among German readers. Urbach ended her article with the words, "this land will bloom." In reality, it became soaked with the blood of millions. But Urbach's version of the war was brought home to readers in the Reich. Her article was published in a major daily newspaper with a circulation of 1.4 million at its peak and appeared at a time of military successes, when the German population was particularly receptive to war news and propaganda. During the first two years of the war, as the Wehrmacht appeared to go from victory to victory, Germans were much more inclined to read newspapers than they had been prior to 1939.[37]

The Ministry of Propaganda especially valued the contribution of Hitler Youth leaders to its press and propaganda efforts in occupied Poland and sought to position them as the next generation of the Nazi press.[38] Melita Maschmann was among this cohort. She travelled to the Wartheland to take charge of the Hitler Youth and its regional press office only two months after the German invasion. A true believer in Nazism, Maschmann was enthusiastic about her opportunity to work in Poland. It provided her not only with a sense of being a part of something significant on behalf of Nazi Germany, but also a degree of responsibility not open to her in the so-called *Altreich*.[39] Her work as a press officer for the Hitler Youth consisted of writing reports for newspapers and youth magazines in Germany about the role of German youth in the ethnic struggle against the Poles. Maschmann also covered local events and film screenings for the *Ostdeutscher Beobachter*, the official party paper for the Wartheland.[40] With a daily circulation of almost 250,0000, the paper was popular among Reich and ethnic Germans living in the region, as well as those on the home front.[41]

Maschmann's work functioned to create a sense of community and comradery between ethnic and Reich Germans and encouraged the German population to view the new settlers as part of the *Volksgemeinschaft* (people's community). Like other women journalists, Maschmann promoted the responsibility of the League of German Girls (Bund Deutscher Mädel – BDM) in the care and education of the new settlers. In a July 1941 article, she described a camp for ethnic German girls where the leaders of the BDM schooled them in National Socialist ideology and the German language and history.[42] Those with potential, Maschmann explained, were training to become BDM leaders themselves. Such articles sought to instil a sense of loyalty to the Nazi regime among communities of ethnic Germans, as well as to assure the "Altreich" population that these new Germans would integrate, and that the region would indeed be Germanized.

One of the resettlement camps' primary goals was to provide vocational training for ethnic German girls in the field of agriculture or social work. In her articles, Maschmann described how young women had been placed in apprenticeships that set them on the path to a rewarding future. The Nazi world view envisioned the Wartheland and regions further East as the future breadbasket of the German empire, and ethnic Germans were to cultivate the territory to feed future soldiers. While Hitler Youth leaders sought to ensure that ethnic German girls had the proper domestic and agricultural training to support this future "utopia," women journalists endorsed and promoted this vision.

Although, like Urbach, Maschmann's articles did not address the war directly, she did write about the honour and the duty of Germany's young women behind the frontlines: "The fate of the German people lies in the land of the East," she wrote. "Every German must have the honour of having worked here, at least for a period of time. Above all, the youth must fulfil this duty and honour while their comrades do their service with weapons." Maschmann equated women's work in the East with military service and insisted that those who returned to Germany after serving in the Wartheland "must report enthusiastically about the East in order to attract new volunteers to the service."[43] Her article served a public relations role, encouraging young women to take part in Germanization processes in the region. She painted an appealing picture of the vital service women would undertake and the independence and fulfilment that came with making a difference. Career ambition, the longing for travel, and the desire to do something different were not simply male desires or experiences during the war. Maschmann was personally and professionally fulfilled by the type of work she undertook in occupied Poland, and her articles encouraged others to join her by making life seem attractive in a region rife with bloodshed.

Male reporters covering the war and occupation also wrote about the *Volksdeutsche*, but in a markedly different manner than the articles women journalists usually published. For instance, in an undated piece titled "Under Moscow's Stranglehold, German Colonists in the Caucasus," war correspondent Karl Bayer wrote of the "toughness and resourceful nature" of the *Volksdeutsche*, despite the atrocities perpetrated toward this group by the "Jewish Bolsheviks." In graphic language, Bayer went on to describe this alleged violence, employing explicit antisemitic and anti-Bolshevist vitriol.[44] In contrast, women tended to write emotional and inspiring pieces about the resettlement of the *Volksdeutsche* that focused on mothering, youth, domesticity, and local affairs. Such articles presented as soft news, despite their political implications, and were not restricted to the women's supplements or magazines. Rather they appeared in large and small, mainstream and Nazi publications, reaching a broad audience inside and outside the borders of Germany. The war in the East afforded women journalists spaces for advancement and positions of authority. But, within these opportunities, they most often had to write in a manner that underscored traditional gendered tropes about women's roles in German society. Through this feminized narrative, they helped legitimate Nazi racial policies and beautify wartime programs that the regime hoped would lead to its ideal of a Germanized East.

**The Visual Beautification of the War**

Women journalists communicated a version of the war to the German public not only through their texts, but also through their images. The regime relied heavily on photojournalism as a tool in its propaganda arsenal. Willy Stiewe, a Nazi specialist in the use of photography as propaganda, argued that photojournalism provided the most influential and powerful reportage because even the most sceptical readers trusted what they saw "with their own eyes."[45] Stiewe attributed the efficacy of photographs to the fact that they made the reader an "eyewitness" to events, presented a topic in a seemingly unambiguous manner, and were memorable to readers.[46] The Ministry of Propaganda's "urgent need" for photojournalists in the East, together with the importance it placed on photography, led to increased but distinct possibilities for men and women alike during the war. As discussed in chapter 1, however, women had already begun to experience marked success in photojournalism by the mid-1930s.[47]

Male photojournalists were often employed by German-occupation papers or were members of the armed forces' own Propaganda Units (Propagandakompanie) and engaged directly with the violence of the war. The RMVP directed these men to present a heroic vision of German soldiers in action. By contrast, they were to provide negative, dehumanizing pictures of Germany's enemies and ensure that they did not portray the enemy as "people" or in a manner that could evoke compassion or respect among the German population.[48] Women photojournalists often worked freelance and published their work in papers within Germany and the occupied territories. They typically contributed to a genre of feel-good propaganda that presented the occupation in a positive manner. Such photographs included portraits, shots of local events or objects of history, pictures of the bucolic landscape or charming villages and towns, instructive images on how to make a recipe or fashion a hat, and depictions of Germans enjoying leisure activities. Their photography helped make Germans "eye-witnesses" to a carefree version of the war and offered the German population a view of an idyllic life in the East that was theirs for the taking. Miriam Y. Arani has described such photographs as "mood" pictures, and Elizabeth Harvey has referred them as providing "visual pleasure" associated with Nazi expansionism.[49] Despite the *gemütliche* nature of women's photojournalism, their work still functioned to illustrate German superiority, justify Germany's claim to the East, and build the morale of the German population as it became increasingly clear that Germany would lose the war.[50]

Female photojournalists concentrated much attention on the resettling of communities of *Volksdeutsche*. Such coverage offered visual evidence of the ethnic Germans' ostensible joy and gratitude at coming "home to the Reich" and the processes by which they became "proper" Germans. Through their depiction of the ethnic German communities themselves or through a focus on German women and girls helping these new "settlers," female photojournalists helped promote and legitimate German empire-building.

Photojournalist Ebba Feldweg was born in Saxony in 1901 but spent her early years in Lithuania and was herself considered an ethnic German. In 1939, she moved to Poznan, in the Wartheland, and began to take press photos of everyday life in the region for the Nazi Party paper *Der Angriff* and German-occupation papers in Poland.[51] Feldweg's work for the *Ostdeutscher Beobachter* highlighted the ways in which the National Socialist Women's League helped Germanize settlers by providing everything from courses on the German language and instruction on how to properly care for their children to advice on how to organize and decorate their homes. An image from New Year 1941 showed a table laden with toys for ethnic German children gifted from Germans in the *Altreich*, which ostensibly depicted the generosity of the German population and created the perception of their acceptance and welcoming of the ethnic Germans as part of the *Volksgemeinschaft*.[52] In March of that same year, Feldweg photographed how a "truly German home" should appear: "natural, unaffected and harmonious," with a cozy, simply furnished dining room set up for an idyllic family life.[53] The visual message was clear: clutter and dirt were un-German.

Feldweg photographed a young ethnic German from the Baltic for a special supplement of the *Ostdeutscher Beobachter* titled "We Live in the German East."[54] The reportage was designed to showcase and normalize everyday life among communities of ethnic Germans. Feldweg's photo was included among others depicting ethnic Germans from the Wartheland, Baltic States, and Volhynian and Galicia – communities that had become part of the *Volksgemeinschaft* thanks to German military victories and Nazi governance. The report underscored discourse that the Wartheland was attracting new settlers that would help "shape the German essence of this land."[55] Through Feldweg's photographs, life in the region appeared peaceful, harmonious, and, above all, German. At the same time, such images presented ethnic Germans as strange and foreign creatures who would be transformed into suitable members of the Germanic community only through the hard work of German women.

Liselotte Purper was the most prominent female photojournalist in the Third Reich, and the war propelled her to the height of her success. In 1940, her revenues reached 3000–4000RM per month, compared to the 300–500RM earned by most of her female freelance peers. By 1942, she had two full-fledged photojournalists and two interns working for her.[56] Owing to her connections with the Press-Propaganda Department of the NSF, she became the organization's main photographer and travelled extensively in this capacity. The photos Purper took on such trips were distributed throughout Europe, which delighted her. In a letter to her fiancé Kurt Orgel, she exclaimed, "Just imagine, we have sold photos via the Reich government to Spain, Italy, Romany, and Norway. Did I tell you that in a tiny hovel in that godforsaken 'village' Rogowo in the expanses of former Poland there was a photo of mine hanging on the wall? Isn't that fun?"[57]

Purper's wartime success was directly tied to Nazi expansionism. In 1941, she was featured in an NSF exhibit titled "Women's Work in Germany," in which she was classified as the epitome of a successful female photojournalist. The exhibit included several of her photographs from the annexed Wartheland.[58] The German Institute Abroad (Deutsches Ausland-Institut) purchased Purper's photograph of a Volhynian German resettled in a formerly Polish household in 1940 and another of members of the National Socialist Women's League distributing food to the newly arrived *Volksdeutsche*.[59] Purper herself did not fit the Nazi

5.1   German women in the women's auxiliary service treating wounded German soldiers at the military airport of Lemberg, Poland (today Lviv, Ukraine), by Liselotte Purper, 1943

Photo credit: bpk Bildagentur / Liselotte Purper/Art Resource, NY

stereotype of the ideal German woman. Rather, she was promoted as an example of success because the nature of her work benefited the regime, which needed professional, adventurous women to travel to the East and depict an idealized German space.

Much of Purper's commissioned work focused on scenes of pastoral beauty and tranquility, an especially important visual as the war came home to Germany and the population craved diversion and a sense of comfort in the midst of increasing destruction. She was even more prolific, however, when it came to photographing German women contributing to the war in traditionally feminine ways.[60] Her photographs erased the violence that had taken place in war-torn areas and put a heroic spin on the regime's expansionism and the work of German women in this regard (figures 5.1 and 5.2).

5.2  German women in the women's auxiliary service caring for children near Kyiv, Ukraine, by Liselotte Purper, October 1942

Photo credit: bpk Bildagentur / Liselotte Purper / Art Resource, NY

In October 1940, in connection with the National Socialist Women's League, Purper travelled to Belgrade to report on the resettlement of *Volksdeutsche* from Ukraine, Eastern Poland, and Romania. She photographed German women cooking, assisting the settlers, and caring for the children. Her work also depicted the apparent delight of the settlers as they journeyed toward a new life as members of Hitler's *Volksgemeinschaft*.[61] In reality, these settlers often faced arduous journeys followed by difficult circumstances on arrival. It was not uncommon for the very young and the elderly to die en route. Once they arrived on German territory, they often spent months in camps prior to being settled in longer-term housing.[62] Purper's photos glossed over the suffering endured by the *Volksdeutsche* communities Germany claimed to be helping (figure 5.3). Her work had a wide resonance. She published frequently in the *Ostdeutscher Beobachter* as well as publications in Germany proper,

5.3 Reception of *Volksdeutsche* resettlers from Dobrudscha, Romania, in the camp of Puntigam, Austria, by Liselotte Purper, 1940

Photo credit: bpk Bildagentur / Liselotte Purper / Art Resource, NY

including the *Deutsche Allgemeine Zeitung, Mutter und Kind, NS Frauen-Warte,* and the *Luftwaffenkurier.*

Erika Schmachtenberger also travelled extensively in occupied Europe and later described her wartime travels as "adventures."[63] In late 1940 or early 1941, she arrived in the Wartheland to shoot a travel feature on the city of Lodz – renamed Litzmannstadt by the Nazis – which she published in the *Münchner Illustrierte Presse* in January 1941 (figures 5.4 and 5.5). Her work functioned to legitimate the German

5.4 and 5.5  (this page and opposite) *Münchner Illustrierte Presse* photo reportage, "Germany's Sixth Largest City: Litzmannstadt," by Erika Groth-Schmachtenberger, January 1941

Photo credit: Institute für Zeitungsforschung Dortmund / Erika Groth-Schmachtenberger

Eine Brücke nur für Juden

Aus Lodz wurde Litzmannstadt. Dieser Wandel, welcher der Stadt endgültig das deutsche Gesicht gibt, bedingte die Zusammenfassung der hier sich einst als unbeschränkte Herren gebärdenden Juden in einem eigenen Stadtteil. Die der allgemeinen Benutzung zugängliche Ausfallstraße, die hier hindurchführt, ist von Holzbrücken überquert, über die sich der jüdische Passantenverkehr vollzieht

geheimnisvollen Energie erfüllt, die ihr heute, da sie die ordnende, planende Hand erhielt, eine neue Blüte verheißt. Die deutsche Verwaltung ist mit äußerster Tatkraft nicht nur an die Reinigung von landfremden, parasitären Elementen und an die Beseitigung polnischer Verwahrlosung herangegangen. Darüber hinaus sind heute schon Baukolonnen überall eifrig dabei, die Sünden der Vergangenheit zu überwinden. Ein großzügiger Stadtbebauungsplan sieht die Sonderung in Industrie-, Geschäfts-, Verwaltungs- und Wohnviertel vor.

Ein Blick in das streng abgeschlossene jüdische Viertel. Die Holzhäuser sind charakteristisch für große Partien des Stadtbildes

Rechts:
Litzmannstadts Zukunft liegt bei der volksdeutschen Jugend, die freudig in den Reihen des BDM. und der HJ. marschiert, in besten Händen

occupation of Poland. Indeed, she positioned what she termed "Germany's sixth largest city," as a modern, vibrant centre for business and entertainment thanks to German planning and industriousness.[64] Her photographs illustrated the development taking place in the city under Nazi rule, including abundant housing and factories as well as a casino, which highlighted the lively nightlife the city offered.

Juxtaposed with photographs emphasizing progress and modernity were two photos of the Litzmannstadt ghetto. "A Bridge for the Jews Only" showed the residents of the ghetto crossing over the bridge that connected its two parts. Schmachtenberger's text implied that the modern development of Litzmannstadt necessitated the concentration of the Jews in a separate part of the city.[65] The other picture, taken through the ghetto fence, showed faceless, dark figures near a dilapidated wooden structure and provided the reader with a view into the "Jewish quarter." These photos contrasted the vision of a modern, recently re-Germanized city with depictions of a squalid Jewish and Polish history. Schmachtenberger's accompanying text read: "With astounding energy, the German administration had not only cleansed the city of foreign, parasitic elements, but also reversed the damages of Polish neglect."[66] Her photo reportage cast Litzmannstadt as a welcoming and exciting place for Germans to visit or live, and a city in which the Jewish population no longer factored. Schmachtenberger's travels in Poland meant that she not only witnessed the persecution of Polish Jews, but that she was also complicit in the production of propaganda that positioned them as dangerous "sub-humans."

While Schmachtenberger produced negative images of Germany's "racial enemies," her work also promoted its allies and obscured the violence they perpetrated. In April 1942, she visited Croatia to shoot a series celebrating a national holiday in the newly established country. The Independent State of Croatia (which included Bosnia-Herzegovina) was founded shortly after the German invasion of April 1941. In reality a puppet state of the Nazi government, Croatia was ruled by the fascist *Ustaša* regime under the leadership of Ante Pavelić, who took the title *Poglavnik* (supreme leader). Shortly after coming to power, the *Ustaša* immediately embarked on a campaign of terror targeted primarily toward Serbs and Jews. By the time Schmachtenberger visited the region, the regime had murdered or expelled hundreds of thousands of Serbs and sent about two-thirds of Croatian Jews to concentration camps, where most were killed on arrival. Deportations to the killing centres began in August 1942.[67] Behind colourful photographs of Croatians celebrating and parading in traditional costumes, Schmachtenberger obscured the mass violence perpetrated under Pavelić's direction. Her

5.6  *Berliner Illustrierte Zeitung* photo reportage, "One Year of a Free Croatia,"
by Erika Groth-Schmachtenberger, 1942

Photo credit: Institute für Zeitungsforschung Dortmund / Erika Groth-Schmachtenberger

photo reportage celebrating Pavelić and his movement, entitled "One Year of a Free Croatia" (figure 5.6), appeared in the *Berliner Illustrierte Zeitung*, one of the most popular illustrated magazines in Germany. The report included a photograph of Pavelić raising his arm in the Nazi salute. Schmachtenberger's text described how "Poglavnik greets his avant-garde" and celebrated how Croatians travelled far and wide to catch a glimpse of their leader.[68]

The work of Feldweg, Purper, Schmachtenberger, and other female photojournalists assisted in creating the illusion of a war without violence and without victims. The medium of photojournalism lent a credibility to this cozy depiction of Nazi aggression; the women's cheerful and emotive photographs appeared in a variety of popular and respected publications inside Germany and the occupied regions.[69]

## Germanizing the Future Generation, Justifying the Occupation

While some women reported on and photographed the resettling of the *Volksdeutsche* and the processes of Germanization taking place in the annexed region of Poland, others focused on topics that concerned the General Government. They too published in high-profile media outlets, including the region's most important occupation paper, the *Krakauer Zeitung* (*KZ*). The Germans quickly established the paper in the fall of 1939. It proved a huge success, with a daily circulation of over 100,000.[70] Women journalists writing for the *KZ* did so for a dual audience, since the paper was popular in both Germany and occupied Poland. It was intended, however, only for ethnic and Reich Germans, employees of German companies, civil servants, and members of the Wehrmacht and SS. While German-occupation papers in Northern and Western Europe attempted to attract local readers and establish a feeling of good will and positivity on behalf of the locals toward the German occupiers, the *KZ* did little to draw a Polish audience until its final months. The dominant Nazi view of Poles as inferior meant that the Germans put little effort into placating the local population. As Lars Jockheck has shown, in line with Germany's propaganda strategy for all of occupied Poland, the primary purpose of the *KZ* was to legitimate Germany's claim to Polish territory and showcase German power. According to the Governor General Hans Frank, propaganda had to convey the feeling of belonging to the "master race" and give Germans a feeling of superiority and community.[71] Emil Gassner, the Nazi official in charge of the press in the region, praised the *KZ* as *the* publication that provided Germans in the region with the "political ammunition" for their work.[72]

Women writing for the *Krakauer Zeitung* focused largely on culture and material directed specifically toward women. The Nazi children's evacuation scheme, the *Kinderlandverschickung* (KLV), in particular received much attention. The KLV was ostensibly designed to ensure the safety of ethnic and Reich German children by relocating them from cities that were subjected to bombing to special camps in the countryside. Articles by women journalists were designed to encourage parents to send their children to the KLV camps and to ease their doubts about the possibility of a long separation. Hedwig Franz began her journalistic training with the magazine *Das Deutsche Rote Kreuz* in 1940. She soon began to write for the League of German Girls magazine *Das deutsche Mädel* and the *Krakauer Zeitung* on topics related to the KLV. As a woman, Franz had the authority to talk about issues related to families and care as Nazi rhetoric and press policy dictated. Franz began her July 1942 article "Germany – Fatherland" in a playful manner: "'I want to go to Germany too,' sobs the 12-year-old boy in Warsaw, who has been told for the tenth time that he is too young to take part in this year's *Kinderlandverschickung* program."[73] Franz wrote of the children's excitement about the prospect of their trip to Germany and emphasized the alleged neglect and persecution the children had suffered living as a German minority in Poland throughout the interwar period: "One can see the long years of deprivation on most of their faces … A rest in the Reich will do them good."[74]

In a follow-up piece, Franz described the material goods the children would receive: mattresses, blankets, uniforms, sweaters, warm jackets, underwear, and new leather shoes. These items provided an incentive for often poor ethnic German families to enrol their children in the KLV program.[75] In an empathetic tone, Franz addressed parental concerns about the conditions in the camps: Would the children have enough food and warm clothing? Would they be homesick? Where was the camp located? Her article provided the answer to such questions, describing the abundant food, activities, and sense of community the children would enjoy at the camp situated in a health resort in the Zittau mountains.[76]

Articles by women journalists promoted the program's stated purpose: to ensure the well-being of children. By presenting the KLV camps as fairy tale–like settings where children enjoyed fresh air, nutritious food, and a thorough education, including instruction in German culture, the writing of women such as Franz masked the program's underlying goal: to indoctrinate children in Nazi ideology without parental interference.[77] In an effort to separate children from their families, KLV authorities often sent ethnic German children from Poland to camps in Germany, while children from the Reich proper regularly ended up in camps in the Wartheland or General Government. The regime's goal for ethnic German children was to bring them up to the "standards" of the Reich Germans, and the KLV program was an important component of this effort.

The reality of everyday life within the camps was markedly different from the cozy depictions that Franz and other women journalists provided. Many of the camps for boys functioned as quasi-military training centres, which were based on a strict regime and, for older boys, included pre-military training in activities such as marching and shooting.[78] Jost Hermand, a former KLV child from Germany proper, recalled

that most of the exercises were designed to teach children that comradeship is formed in battle:

> In addition to instructing us in the use of maps and compasses, delivering
> messages, estimating distances, target identification, and terrain evalua-
> tion, games like these were above all supposed to turn us into ruthless
> warriors. Therefore, we were repeatedly urged by our platoon leaders
> not to show any pity for our opponents and to bring down anyone who
> opposed us with a hook to the jaw.[79]

In 1943–4 at the Gross-Oettingen camp in Poland, KLV children
received neither formal schooling nor cultural education but, rather,
were trained to be "physically steeled young men."[80] The "training"
designed to effect this transformation called for aggressive behaviour,
which led to the brutalization of children. Toward the end of the war,
the deteriorating diet and appalling hygienic conditions led to widespread illness in the camp. The camp instructors were often tyrannical
toward the children. Jost attested that they taught them to despise Poles
and encouraged the perpetration of violence against the local population. The children also learned to sing obscene songs about European
Jewry.

The KLV camps women journalists wrote about so romantically were
in fact a part of the violent Germanization process taking place during
the war and of the regime's efforts at indoctrinating all German youth
in its ideology. Articles masquerading as soft news about the well-being
of children were intended to replace parental authority with that of the
state, and they contributed to the racialized brutality of the war in the
East.

In the context of the occupation of Poland, reportage on culture and
the everyday lives of women was intended to strengthen the population's commitment to maintaining German control over these regions
and its willingness to hold out as the tides of war turned against Germany. Gerda Pelz contributed to both genres in her work as a full-time
journalist in the General Government. Pelz was born in Westfalia in
1914. A trained musician, she worked as a music teacher and a reporter
for the arts section of a daily paper in Hagen prior to relocating to
Krakow.[81]

In November 1940, she obtained her first position in Poland, with the
Institute for German Eastern Studies (Institute für Deutsche Ostarbeit –
IDO), which had been founded by Hans Frank and was housed in Krakow's Jagiellonian University. Designated as the centre of German intellectual life in the Eastern occupied territories, the IDO was intended

to build an "intellectual bulwark for Germandom," fashion "intellectual weapons" for Hitler's campaign against Germany's enemies, and "intellectually secure the military victory and political leadership of the German people in this region."[82] In other words, the institute was to validate the occupation through purportedly scientific study and put a historical and scholarly seal of approval on the regime's repressive actions against Poles and Jews.[83]

Pelz worked in the IDO's editorial department and was responsible for coordinating reporting in and publication of the institute's journals, *Die Burg* and *Deutsche Forschung im Osten*. Published quarterly, *Die Burg* was the primary propaganda vehicle through which the institute disseminated its research to the German-speaking population in the General Government. The articles covered a range of topics that emphasized how German culture, past and present, had produced order in the otherwise chaotic and backward region. The journal was rife with Nazified language and linguistic violence targeting the region's Polish and Jewish populations. Despite the fact that she was a qualified journalist, Pelz was tasked only with coordinating the publication and, as far as the sources indicate, did not produce any of the material herself. Still, her time at the IDO provided a stepping stone to a fruitful career in occupied Poland.

In February 1942, Pelz landed a full-time position on the *Krakauer Zeitung*, writing for the cultural and local news sections. The editor, Rudolf Sparing, recognized that the *KZ* had to offer more than simply news related to politics and war if it was to be both a commercial and propaganda success. Accordingly, Sparing devoted about 30 per cent of the content to culture and light entertainment and ensured that, compared to other occupation newspapers, the *KZ*'s offerings in these realms were of a relatively high quality.[84] To appeal to its large male readership, including the SS and Order Police units, the paper also included pictures, anecdotes, and jokes with a pornographic slant.[85] Overall, the paper was an important mouthpiece for communications designed to reinforce the subjugation of Poland: according to Emil Gassner, the cultural pages were "tirelessly active in bringing all fellow countrymen closer to the desired goals of Germanization and victory in the East."[86]

Pelz specialized in music, and her writing functioned both as entertainment and as an instrument intended to bestow a sense of legitimacy on the occupation and a sense of pride on the German community. By emphasizing Germany's long-standing cultural influence on the region, Pelz implied that it had a rightful claim to the land. In September 1941, even before she had secured a permanent position on the paper, she published an article about the German opera *Der Freischütz*, which had opened at Krakow's state theatre. The opera, based on a

German folk legend, was widely considered the first German nationalist opera. The performance, Pelz wrote, was a fitting symbol of the spirit of German opera, "which from now on will receive a permanent home in the Krakow State Theatre."[87] Such writing cast the German presence in the region as just and permanent. According to Pelz, watching *Der Freischütz* in the General Government rather than in Germany itself provided one with a more meaningful experience, since it invoked Germany's folklore and the notion that the nation had rightfully laid claim to this territory.[88]

As the war turned against Germany in 1943 and 1944, the tone of Pelz's writing changed. Her articles increasingly functioned to discourage defeatism and bolster the morale of both the Wehrmacht and German civilians living in the region. Rather than highlighting the historical and present-day importance of German culture, articles like "The Miraculous Healing Power of Music: Women Musicians Play for the Wounded," emphasized the necessity of music in times of crisis.[89] On 6 October 1944, with the Red Army already on pre-war Polish territory, Pelz published a piece that suggested one could experience more gratitude and an enhanced sense of *Gemütlichkeit* as a result of the fighting: "The glow of the lamp in one's own home, books, and music have seldom exerted such a compelling charm as [they do] now that life has been diverted to other paths for a while."[90] Such everyday pleasures, Pelz suggested, became commonplace and underappreciated in peacetime. In another piece, Pelz insisted that music could not only help one bear the burden of the war, but that the war made one's appreciation of German (or Austrian) culture all the greater: "Did you ever hear Schubert so soft and full of sweetness?" she asked.[91] One could lose sight of the beauty in life when huddled in bunkers with the sirens howling, Pelz acknowledged, but it was important to make time to enjoy art and appreciate beauty in the midst of destruction. She concluded her article by encouraging Germans to "arm themselves against the worry about material belongings" with the assurance that "we remain rich as long as the higher awareness of life that has been sparked in us by music remains."[92]

As the Red Army pushed the Wehrmacht westward, Pelz wrote of German heroism and noted that German music historically exposed the "victory of order over chaos."[93] In her last article for the *KZ*, published on 2 January 1945, she described the Krakow Philharmonic's final performance of the Eroica Symphony, which marked the end of a "heroic" year. She concluded that Germans could draw reassuring lessons from the representation of "militant and heroic motives in art," which "demonstrate that under circumstances similar to today, the healthy power has always been able to persevere."[94] According to Pelz, artistic themes foreshadowed how Germany, as the righteous power, would prevail in the long term and thereby softened what would be only a temporary retreat from Poland. Under Pelz's pen, music became a means to affirm violent nationalism and the regime's colonizing actions in the East. More than any other section of the *Krakauer Zeitung*, the cultural news masked the realities of the war, and Pelz's writing provided a sense of comfort and reassurance for her German readers.

Like her colleagues on the home front, Pelz also wrote articles intended for a female audience in order to simultaneously mobilize women for war work and boost their morale. In October 1944, she encouraged women to take up employment in munitions factories in Poland and Germany. Pelz characterized this initiative as heroic and emphasized the important contribution that women had made to the "Fatherland" by working in such factories during the First World War. These women would not have missed the opportunity to serve their country "at any price," Pelz wrote, and could now look at themselves in the mirror with respect and pride.[95] Pelz cast the dire military situation in an optimistic light and warned of the regret women would feel if they did not step up to contribute to Germany's victory.

Pelz's article promoted war service as a means of emancipation that offered women the type of leadership roles normally reserved for men. Young women who had volunteered earlier for the armaments factories, she wrote, had become some of the most capable foremen, in charge of other female and foreign workers. Naturally, Pelz did not mention that many of these "foreign workers" were forced labourers who lived and worked in deplorable conditions. She highlighted instead women's equality to – if not superiority over – men in their production of armaments. Pelz's writing did not stray too far from Nazi ideology related to women's place in the private and professional sphere, however. The reason she gave for women being able to out-perform men in factory piece-work was their experience with handicrafts such as needlepoint: "How much endurance is needed for sewing and stitching and embroidery alone! Series production in the metal industry benefits from these virtues."[96] The article also reassured women that they could "live the good life" by working in a factory. From ample shower facilities to nutritious meals, women working in armaments would be well cared for. From behind her desk, Pelz ended her article by providing women with food for thought: "A good conscience is a gentle cushion of rest," she advised.[97]

Through her journalism, Pelz contributed to several strands of National Socialist ideology and propaganda: German cultural superiority, heroism, perseverance in the face of the country's enemies, and the important role of women in supporting the war and maintaining the Nazi regime, whether in Poland or Germany. Her writing exemplifies how women journalists helped defend the German occupation of Poland and the role soft news played in the midst of wartime violence. Pelz was not the only female journalist to write for the *Krakauer Zeitung*. In its first year, the paper retained approximately twelve full-time employees, at least two of whom were women.[98] In addition, several women journalists contributed freelance articles to the paper.

## Gratification, Complicity, and Repercussions

Women journalists such as Gerda Pelz found success and prominence from their work in the occupied East, even as it deeply entangled them in processes of persecution and violence. As her personal communications and articles indicate, Pelz socialized with some high-ranking Nazi officials, which gave her a sense of status and importance. Melita Maschmann too felt very much at home working in the Wartheland and enjoyed the power that came with her position as a Reich German among Poles. "I would not have wanted to change places with anyone in Germany," she recalled. "My colleagues and I felt it was an honour to be allowed to help in 'conquering' this area for our own nation and for German culture … Almost everyone had a little kingdom of their own."[99] Maschmann revealed that she and her colleagues also felt a sense of superiority with respect to those who remained in Germany proper.

Maschmann, Pelz, and their fellow journalists were early observers of the violence and plunder directed toward indigenous populations in the East, and their writing helped to camouflage such behaviour or cast it as necessary. Niklas Frank, the son of Hans Frank, maintains that Pelz witnessed the indiscriminate shootings of Polish hostages in the streets of Krakow and was well aware of the mass murder of Jews.[100] The Germans established hundreds of ghettos throughout Poland, where Jewish citizens from across Europe were forced to live in miserable conditions before their eventual deportation to the killing centres. Maschmann described how she came across the Kutno Ghetto, which the Germans had established in an old sugar factory in June 1940. The ghetto's housing was so inadequate for the size of its population that many inhabitants were forced to live outdoors. Maschmann felt little sympathy for the marked suffering of the ghetto inhabitants, since she had "learned that they were the most dangerous enemies of Germany."[101] Jews from the Kutno Ghetto were deported to Chelmo in March 1942, when Maschmann was still working in the region. Maschmann, like Erika Groth-Schmachtenberger, also witnessed the wretchedness of life in the Litzmannstadt (Lodz) Ghetto.[102]

Liselotte Purper observed the nature of the war and the results of the German occupation in Polish and Soviet territory. In October 1940, she made her second trip to the Wartheland on a contract for the National Socialist People's Welfare (NS Volkswohlfahrt). In her diary, she described the city of Wielun: "Here everything begins with dirt. Wretchedness. The Jews – star by star – are only allowed to walk on the street. Polish women, wrapped in their large shawls, drag their feet through the place. Much hardship! Lifeless despair in every meter of this town."[103] In October 1940, she took several pictures of the Litzmannstadt/Lodz and Löwenstadt/Stryków Ghettos, including shots of the Jewish population within.[104] The following year she wrote, "I have no illusions over the severity of the fight in the East ... I have seen enough reports and also pictures that are so dreadful, they will never be published."[105] Purper was in Odessa in July 1942 and observed that there was hardly a house that had not suffered from the war. In the General Government city of Krakow on 10 January 1943, she noted: "I do not have the impression at all that I am in Poland or abroad. So many Germans are out and about in the German cityscape. The Poles have their own shops and hotels. Germans, myself included, feel right at home here. One no longer sees any Jews."[106] The Germans began deporting Jewish inhabitants from the Krakow Ghetto to the Belzec killing centre in June 1942. The ghetto's final liquidation took place in March 1943. The SS and police carried out the operation, shooting approximately 2,000 Jews in the ghetto itself and transferring another 2,000 to the Plaszow forced-labour camp. Those remaining were sent to Auschwitz-Birkenau.[107] Purper visited Krakow just prior to the final liquidation, and it is possible that she viewed one of the transports from the ghetto.

Despite witnessing first-hand the violence and suffering in the East, Purper was proud of her status as a Reich German and enthusiastic about the Nazi empire at the height of its power, as her travel diary and private letters indicate. In a letter to her fiancé, Kurt Orgel, she wrote:

There is the Black Sea, the Baltic, Pomerania, Mecklenburg, Carinthia, the High Tatras; there is Goethe's river Ilm and Strasburg's river Ill. And when I lie in bed looking at the pictures I find myself in our whole wonderful Greater German Reich. No sense of being hemmed in, just glorious – I am completely happy! Then I think of the terrible war and am completely unhappy![108]

Purper was an enthusiastic supporter of the colonization processes taking place in the East and was impressed by the young women helping to Germanize the *Volksdeutsche* communities. In her letters to Orgel, Purper displayed her lack of sentiment toward the people in the East. In 1944, Orgel wrote that he had forbidden his troops to shoot the cattle belonging to Latvian farmers during their unit's retreat across the Baltics in spite of the fact that the Red Army would benefit from their benevolence. Purper responded:

> I am filled with rage! I have to tell you: bury your soft German heart under a layer of hardness. No one in the whole world appreciates or respects soft emotions except the Germans themselves. Think only of the cruelties to which your homeland is at the mercy of. Think of the brutality with which we would be raped and murdered; think only of the indescribable misery that air terror alone brings upon our country. No, let the farmers wail when you have to kill the cattle. No, harm the enemy where you can, that's what you are there for, not to make it easier for him to fight you.[109]

Purper was not only a producer of German propaganda but also a consumer of Nazi rhetoric about the brutality of populations in the East and Goebbels's warnings about Soviet reprisals should Germany lose the war. Pelz and Maschmann, too, were devastated by the imminent end of the German occupation and feared the repercussions their country would experience as a result of the violent war that it had waged in the East.

In addition to their work as journalists, and purveyors and consumers of Nazi propaganda, some German women travelling or based abroad were on the radar of Allied intelligence services and suspected of conducting espionage on behalf of Germany. As we saw in chapter 3, they were thought to be engaging in such roles even prior to the war. During the war, the work of women journalists and their visibility in the public realm garnered even more attention from intelligence agencies. The US and British Secret Service monitored Margret Boveri and Petra Vermehren, who were foreign correspondents on the *Frankfurter Zeitung* in Madrid and Lisbon, respectively. Given Germany's alliance with Japan, the British, American, and French intelligence agencies were especially concerned with the actions of Lily Abegg as the *FZ*'s Far East correspondent both prior to and during the war. Allied intelligence believed that Abegg engaged in anti-Allied propaganda and espionage activities in the Far East and inspired the Tokyo Rose broadcasts designed to undermine Allied morale in the South Pacific.

In a September 1943 letter to the American Embassy in London, the director of the US Federal Bureau of Investigation, J. Edgar Hoover, requested information on Abegg, as she was "reportedly involved in German and Japanese espionage."[110] The embassy investigated, and British intelligence agency MI6 responded that Abegg was already well known to British intelligence:

> She first came to notice early in 1940 when we learned that she was in Berlin and was intending to travel to Japan … She was (and may still be) a correspondent for the *Frankfurter Zeitung*. She is violently pro-Nazi and anti-British. In May 1941, Singapore reported that Lily had arrived in Indochina and that she intended to proceed to Bangkok. The French authorities described her as "agent allemande notoire et trés dangereux" [a German agent and very dangerous]. Lily is reported as saying at this time, "The fact that I was sent to Indochina is for me a clear indication of the next theater of hostilities."[111]

British Security Intelligence in the Far East considered Abegg to be "very clever" and charged that she was conducting espionage and propaganda on behalf of Germany and that she broadcast in German on Tokyo radio.[112] Abegg's work in the Far East would have both positive and negative consequences for her personally and professionally in the immediate post-war period.

In the last years of the war, military losses impacted the careers of female journalists working in occupied Eastern and Western Europe. Newspapers closed as Allied armies advanced. Ruth Rosener, who had undertaken her journalistic training in Minsk, found that the war continually thwarted her efforts to graduate to full-fledged journalist. German losses on the military front meant the closure of the papers on which she was training. In a February 1945 memo concerning Rosener, the office of Max Amann, the Reich leader for the press, noted: "The files show that Fräulein R. has had rare bad luck with regard to her employment to date because she was always at a newspaper that fell victim to military events and since then … her files had gone missing and she had to start [her training] from the beginning again."[113] She was still officially a trainee, the memo continued, but should have been designated a full journalist and able to earn a decent salary.

Although women journalists did not function as embedded war reporters or soldiers in occupied Europe, they did have to take precautions to avoid capture by advancing Allied armies as the tide of the war turned. In the fall of 1944, Ewgenia Hausmania fled from Latvia, and Agnes Vesilo fled from Estonia to Frankfurt an der Oder.[114] Hildegard

Faber left Paris just after D-Day in June 1944. She wrote to a colleague a month later that "the invasion chased us over the border."[115] Gerda Pelz escaped from Krakow in January 1945, just prior to the arrival of the Red Army. The war would eventually follow all of these women home to Germany, yet rarely did it put an end to the successful careers they had established.

## Conclusion

The experiences and writing of women journalists working in occupied Europe remind us that travel, adventure, and implication in wartime violence were not simply male experiences. German women sought positions abroad from the beginning of the war until its final months and participated in the occupation of various countries for personal and professional gain. In contrast to German women who worked as secretaries or domestic helpers in the occupied East, female journalists had a broad public platform from which to communicate a peaceful and optimistic version of the occupation, whether for those Germans experiencing it first-hand or for those on the home front. Since they generally wrote on seemingly lighter topics, their work provided the German population, army, and occupation force with an escape from the realities of the war, which helped stabilize the occupation.

By contrast, male journalists frequently functioned as war reporters within the Propaganda Units, covering military developments and highlighting German victories and enemy atrocities. While a small number of women reported directly on topics connected to wartime violence, the majority obscured the brutality of the occupation or contributed to a feminized narrative about the beauty and glory of war. By putting a positive spin on the by-products of German military victories and atrocities, they helped expand the nature of war reporting under a dictatorship, which made them complicit in legitimating the conditions that allowed mass violence to flourish. As we will see in the next chapter, because their work did not appear to connect to the war in the same manner as the writing of male war correspondents, women journalists such as Ilse Urbach, Gerda Pelz, and Liselotte Purper transitioned with relative ease to the post-war press, where they began to write in support of new ideologies and state forms.

# PART III

The Aftermath

## Chapter Six

# New Patrons, New Entanglements: Transitioning to the Post-War Press

In October 1946, Ilse Urbach published an article in the newly founded, British-licensed newspaper *Die Zeit*. The article was about contemporary life in the picturesque mountain town of Garmisch-Partenkirchen, in Bavaria. Urbach's style of writing was not far removed from the seemingly upbeat travel and cultural articles that she had published during the Third Reich. She wrote of the cozy houses and bustling atmosphere of the town, which was preparing for winter. At the same time, the article addressed the ramifications of the war and Germany's defeat. Urbach described how the town was now "besieged" with American military and noted that one "often met Silesians," a reference to German refugees from the country's former territory in the East that had since been annexed to Poland.[1] In her article, Urbach employed the same tactics that she had adopted in her wartime writing, in which she had cast Poles and Jews as a threat to Germany. In such pieces, she had written in a manner that communicated Nazi ideology in a softer and less overt way than much hard-news propaganda. This time, Urbach wrote about the displacement of locals in the face of refugees and the US occupation force. Her words provided an indirect critique of both as a new scourge on Germany. "That distinguished gentleman who now lives in the converted attic of his splendid house encounters difficulties," she wrote, because "the evacuees on the lower floor were inconsiderate." Finally, the article spoke to Allied denazification efforts and the punishment of those she termed "Nazi activists," who were interned in the town's former hunting barracks.[2]

Urbach herself had been an early member of the Nazi Party and had enjoyed a successful career during the Third Reich. Although she was required to go through a denazification process, the British occupation authorities quickly gave her the green light to continue her career. In spite of her contribution to Nazi discourse about the "inferiority" of

Jews and Poles, British authorities considered Urbach's past work in features, travel, and women's news harmless enough to allow her to transition with ease to the post-war press. Her professional success grew in the first decade after the war. In 1946, she began to work in features for the British-licensed national daily newspaper *Die Welt*. By 1954, she had moved to *Der Kurier*, where she soon became the features editor. The French occupation force established *Der Kurier* in November 1945, and it was an immediate success.[3] Urbach's professional path from dictatorship to democracy and the nature of her writing provide insight into women journalists' transition to the post-war press and the ways in which they used their public platform in the interests of the German population and state(s) after 1945.

The tangling of gender, politics, the press, and the ambiguous status of female journalists as both insiders and outsiders in the field during the Third Reich had complex ramifications for women in the post-war period. The transition to the post-war press meant not only new patrons, in the form of the Allied occupation authorities, who maintained control of the German press until September 1949, but also new possibilities, priorities, and problems. While job opportunities initially expanded for women, male journalists returned to the field in greater numbers after the Allies began to abandon their denazification efforts in 1947. Women in all four occupation zones were soon relegated to the periphery of the profession, working largely in the area of soft news, women's issues, and culture, just as they had prior to 1945. The Western Zones labelled these areas apolitical, as it sought to re-establish traditional gender roles, with women's focus to be largely centred on the domestic sphere. For political leaders, restoring the gender order and the nuclear family was a critical part of creating a stable post-war (West) Germany.[4] In the East, due to economic necessity and socialist ideology, the work of women journalists was more overtly political, in terms of both their writing and the expectations placed upon them. Socialist theory considered full-time labour a precondition for women's autonomy and emancipation. Soviet occupation authorities encouraged and expected women's participation in the workforce.[5] Either way, women journalists soon became instrumentalized by, and contributed to, the political agendas in the Eastern and Western sectors of Germany as they had during the Third Reich.

Scholars of the German post-war press have examined denazification and the continuity of journalists' careers after the Third Reich.[6] This chapter highlights the role that assumptions about gender played in these processes. Historians have identified the centrality of gender to each region's national identity and the ways in which women and their perceived roles in society reflected the ideology of the capitalist West and socialist East.[7] Demonstrating how the careers and writings of women journalists reflect ruptures and continuities in gender relations, not only between pre- and post-1945 Germany, but also between East and West Germany, deepens our understanding of how the states continued to instrumentalize gender for political purposes. The careers and lives of women journalists were affected by these processes and the presence of the "other" Germany.

Although the two Germanys attached different meanings to women's writing, female journalists in both the East and West became embroiled in political affairs and exposed to the risks characteristic of the Cold War: surveillance, discipline, and control. At the same time, through their journalism, they were also actors in creating that politicized environment. Their writing functioned to legitimize the policies of either the Eastern or Western Zones – and, later, East or West Germany – and used the other's handling of the repercussions of the war and the burdens it placed on women to disparage its neighbour. Women journalists were therefore both affected by, and became actors in, the processes of identity-building in the West and East as the Federal Republic of Germany (FRG) and the German Democratic Republic (GDR) sought to position themselves as the legitimate successor to the collapsed National Socialist state and gain the loyalty of the population.

The chapter pays particular attention to women who worked throughout the course of the Third Reich and relaunched their careers in the aftermath of the war. It does, however, briefly address women who were new to journalism and those returning to Germany after having emigrated to escape Nazism. Although I concentrate primarily on the period in which the press was under Allied control, with a focus on Berlin as the media centre of the divided Germany, I also touch on women's longer-term careers after the press was once again in the hands of the Germans.

## Opportunities and Continuities, 1945–1949

The structure of the post-war press in the Eastern and Western regions of Germany was characterized by both change and continuity. After the war, Allied forces took immediate control of the German media. All four occupation powers were eager to rebuild the press as a tool to be used to denazify and demilitarize Germany, and "re-educate" the German population in the ways of democracy. The US military occupation authority, for instance, expressed its views about the power of the press in its 1947 *Fair Practice Guide for German Journalists*. The guide was designed to encourage a deeper understanding of the principles underlying "democratic" journalism: "We believe that the success of democratic government depends upon sound public opinion, and that the newspaper should aid in creating and maintaining sound public opinion."[8]

The Soviet occupation authorities tasked the press in the East with a similar level of responsibility. In 1946, the newly founded, Soviet-approved, German Press Association (Verband der Deutschen Presse – VDP) stated that the role of journalists would be to "help ensure that the German population emerges from the rubble to build a state that will once again be respected by the world." Journalists had to become staunch "democrats" and "peacekeepers."[9] If that did not happen, the VDP cautioned, Germany would find itself once again confronting fascism: "Journalists must know the enormous responsibility they bear. They who decisively influence public opinion can either help create a new catastrophe or they can help prevent it."[10]

Officially, the Allies wanted to engage journalists uncompromised by Nazism, although the policy and practice of denazifying and rebuilding the press differed among the four occupation zones and often within the zones themselves. The Soviets and Americans attempted a more vigorous approach to purging the field and selecting journalists they considered politically untarnished. Despite an initial desire for a complete turnover of journalists, the British were ultimately more accommodating than the Americans and tended to turn a blind eye to the return of politically compromised journalists. From the outset, the French took what they considered a pragmatic view and placed more emphasis on a journalist's talent and professional experience than on their past political affiliations.[11] Helene Rahms, who, like Ilse Urbach, had written for *Das Reich* during the war, recalled that the French military force allowed the journalists at *Der Kurier* considerable freedom. New and seasoned journalists were able to write without what Rahms termed a "persnickety" insistence that they conduct any deep "soul-searching" with regard to the recent past.[12]

Despite the differing degrees of commitment to denazifying the press, studies immediately after the war and in the decades since have shown that, within all four occupation zones, the majority of journalists who had worked under the Nazi regime were not especially affected by denazification, at least in the long term.[13] It was difficult, for instance, for Allied press officers to find uncompromised persons to whom they could issue a licence to publish and manage a paper that would eventually become independent of Allied control. Although some licences were given to former journalists who had emigrated from Germany after 1933 or those who had survived the camps, their numbers were too small to satisfy the demand for experienced journalists.[14] As a result, those who had worked within the Nazi press also received licences.

Journalists who had enjoyed careers in Nazi Germany were often subjected to a denazification process, but the nature of their earlier writing was generally not a deciding factor during such proceedings or in the determination of their professional fate. Instead, the Allies tended to focus on membership and rank within the Nazi Party and its subsidiary organizations, involvement in wartime crimes, and whether one had caused harm to others during the Third Reich. Former members of the SS and those who remained outspoken about their adherence to Nazism were typically the only journalists completely banned from the field.[15] Practical matters also came into play. The goal to re-educate Germans via the press meant that the Allies needed experienced and talented journalists. As Helene Rahms attested, for the most part, such journalists were "only to be found in the politically burdened generation." Rahms believed that the need for journalists immediately after the war meant that, with regard to the examination of their past, they "got off more lightly than teachers, judges, professors and so forth."[16] As Axel Schildt has pointed out, the fact that Rahms had reported for such a high-profile – if, ultimately, highly compromised – paper as *Das Reich* in Nazi Germany was likely an advantage for her after the war, as it reflected her journalistic skills.[17]

Women found certain advantages when it came to re-establishing their career with speed and ease after the war. Some benefited from not entirely inaccurate Allied assumptions about gender in Nazi Germany. Women journalists had rarely held positions of prominence during the Third Reich, despite the fact that many practised journalism in a manner that contributed to the goals of the Nazi regime. Their subordinate position in the press, together with Nazi rhetoric about women standing outside of politics, meant that Western Allied press authorities, particularly in the US and British Occupation Zones, perceived the majority of German women as apolitical, at least in comparison to most men.[18] The fact that women journalists in the United States, Britain, and France also reported in seemingly apolitical soft-news areas underscored these beliefs. As a result, the journalistic field in the Western occupation zones initially seemed more accessible to women than it had in the past.[19]

The same accessibility holds true for the Soviet sector (Sowjetische Besatzungszone – SBZ), due to socialist ideology concerning women's integration into the workforce. The post-war press in the East also suffered from a dire shortage of journalists, which led to increased prospects for women immediately after the war. As in other sectors of the workforce, popular dissatisfaction in the zone and the continuing loss of the population to the West contributed to this shortfall. At the first membership meeting of the German Press Association in early 1946, the elected chair, Paul Ufermann, lamented, "There has never been such a lack of journalists in [East] Germany as at this time. People come to us from everywhere and say: 'We need journalists urgently.'"[20] In addition, the VDP did not want a press cohort comprised only of members from the upper-middle class – the milieu that had traditionally dominated the profession.[21] Its desire to hire journalists who did not possess a university degree further opened the field for women, who were traditionally less likely than their male cohorts to have obtained a postsecondary education. The VDP not only accepted but desired increased numbers of women journalists. Ufermann claimed that the press's newfound dependence on women would finally elevate them to a status on par with that of their male counterparts.[22]

Women with communist ties could obtain particularly prominent roles in the press in the Eastern Zone. The VDP, for instance, included two women on its thirteen-member board of directors, Margarete Lode-Pieck and Charlotte Hohmann, both of whom had impeccable anti-Nazi credentials.[23] Lode-Pieck was married to Communist Party official Arthur Pieck and, after the war, wrote for the *Berliner Zeitung*.[24] Hohmann was the first editor of the woman's magazine *Die Frau von Heute* (The woman of today), founded in 1946. She had been a journalist and political activist on behalf of the Communist Party in the 1920s and early 1930s but had retreated from journalism after the Nazi party gained power.[25] Lily Becher was a member of the VDP's extended board of directors and the editor of the *Neue Berliner Illustrierte*, with seventeen men working under her direction. Becher had lived as a German exile in Moscow and returned to Germany in 1945 with her husband, Johannes Becher, a respected writer and politician.

A select group of women uncompromised by Nazism also obtained senior journalistic positions in the Western Zones at the end of the war. In March 1946, the British occupation force launched the *Telegraph* and included a woman as one of its licensees. Annedore Leber had been a staunch opponent of Nazism throughout the Third Reich.[26] She also received her own licence to publish the women's magazine *Mosaik* in 1947 – a rare feat for a female journalist at the time.[27] In 1946, *Der Kurier* included two women on its editorial staff, one as associate editor of the foreign politics section and the other as editor of the sports and fashion pages.[28] Countess Marion von Dönhoff, a refugee from East Prussia, became the most famous female journalist working in the post-war Western press. In early 1946, without any journalistic experience, she joined the editorial staff of the British-licensed liberal paper *Die Zeit*. In 1955, she became associate editor in charge of the political section, and by 1968 was editor-in-chief.[29]

Opportunities in the aftermath of the war did not open only for female journalists who had distanced themselves from Nazism, however. Women accounted for the majority of the population in war-torn Germany, and the Allies hoped to reach this audience through targeted publications; women journalists were important in this endeavour. Already in April 1945, before the official end of hostilities, Soviet occupation authorities issued a licence for the family-oriented magazine the *Neue Berliner Illustrierte*. The women's magazine *Für Dich* (For you) was launched in the Soviet zone in August 1945. In November 1945, the US Military Government's Information Control Division (ICD) approved journalist Ruth Andreas-Friedrich's application to publish a women's magazine entitled *Sie* (She).[30] Both *Für Dich* and *Sie* offered advice on the daily issues affecting German women, including how to obtain food and housing, and celebrated women for the contribution they would make to the rebuilding of a democratic Germany. A range of women's magazines in all zones soon followed, and daily newspapers included women's supplements.[31] Such publications offered women journalists comparatively good opportunities as editors and reporters, although the majority of licences still went to men.[32]

Those new to journalism and those who had worked during the Third Reich recalled stepping quite seamlessly into positions in occupied Germany. The young radio journalist Lore Walb began her career in the aftermath of the war. She later reflected on the opportunities open to women in the American Occupation Zone after 1945: "At that time, women journalists stood under a lucky star. Journalists were rare and the Americans ... implemented a very women-friendly personnel policy. Never again did women have ... such chances as the ones [they] received in the radio and press in the American Occupation Zone shortly after the war."[33] Gerda Pelz had enjoyed her time in German-occupied Poland writing for the cultural pages of the occupation paper the *Krakauer Zeitung*. She returned to Germany in January 1945, and a year later was working in the British zone as the "right hand" of the head of the Press Department for Culture in the town of Siegen.[34] More-prominent positions were soon to come: Pelz eventually wrote for the Stuttgart based publication *Die Leistung: Illustrierte Zeitschrift für die Wirtschaft* and for the women's supplements in the esteemed daily the *Frankfurter Allgemeine Zeitung* (FAZ), founded in 1949 as the successor to the *Frankfurter Zeitung*. The American Occupation Force allowed photojournalist Erika Groth-Schmachtenberger to return to work in July

1945 thanks to her "clean record."[35] Ursula von Kardorff still managed to work for several western-licensed papers, including the French *Der Kurier* and the US-licensed *Tagesspiegel*, in the first year after the war, although American and Soviet press authorities critiqued her Nazi-era articles for what they deemed excessive nationalism and anti-Soviet rhetoric.[36] In 1946, she began to freelance for, and eventually settled into a permanent position in women's news and features at, the U.S.-licensed *Süddeutsche Zeitung* in Munich.

The case of Felicitas Kapteina provides an especially vivid example of how Allied press authorities in the Western Zones did not consider the work of women journalists under the Nazi regime to have been especially political. Kapteina began her journalism internship in the area of local news on the Nazi Party paper the *Westdeutscher Beobachter*. After the war, she feared that her training on a Nazi paper would scuttle any chance for a career in the press: "I thought to myself. 'They resent you so much, they'll never let you be a journalist again.'"[37] Yet by early 1947, Kapteina was able to continue her training at the regional *Neue Ruhr Zeitung* under the tutelage of Erich Brost. Brost, a well-known politician and journalist, had left Germany in 1939 and returned in June 1945 to help rebuild the press in the British sector. He became an important figure in the landscape of the post-war press; the British commissioned him to set up the German News Service, which later became the German Press Agency (Deutsche Presseagentur). "I went to Brost and shared my distress" about not being able to work as a journalist, Kapteina recalled. "He was understanding." Brost asked to see some of Kapteina's wartime writing. "It became clear how harmless I was," Kapteina contended "because I preferred to write reportage and certainly not with political content."[38]

The presentation of her Third Reich work as "harmless" was certainly self-serving on Kapteina's part. Yet the fact remains that Brost, too, viewed her work as uncompromised by Nazi ideology and, as a result, helped her build a successful career. By 1947, the twenty-four-year-old was the head of local news at the *Westdeutsche Allgemeine Zeitung* in Essen. While Kapteina's work in the Nazi press had contributed to the regime's goals of providing distraction in the midst of war via colourful local stories, other women journalists were more entangled with Nazi processes of violence and empire building. The writing of Gerda Pelz, for example, had functioned to legitimate and bolster the occupation of Poland. Yet both Kapteina and Pelz moved on to establish post-war careers that were respectable, if not especially renowned, and not least because of assumptions related to the supposedly apolitical nature of women's journalism.

Women journalists who had contributed to the hard-news realms of foreign policy or domestic politics, as well as to antisemitic and anti-Soviet propaganda, often transitioned without incident to the post-war media in the Western Zones. In this context, they had some advantages over their male counterparts. Male war correspondents had generally written about the war in a more direct and vitriolic manner than women and had often been members of the Wehrmacht's Propaganda Units (Propagandakompanie). Moreover, some now found themselves in Allied captivity. Together with her husband, Gisela Döhrn had established a career as a foreign correspondent in Moscow in the late 1930s. Her work contributed to Nazi antisemitic and anti-Bolshevik discourse. In 1946, her book *That Was Moscow: Four Years as a Reporter in the Soviet Union* was banned in the SBZ. While her ex-husband remained a Soviet prisoner of war until 1955, Döhrn was publishing books on poetry and travel in the Western Zones by 1947. She wrote under the pseudonym Gisela Bonn, which distanced her professionally from her Third Reich articles. She eventually became editor-in-chief of the magazine *Indo-Asia* and achieved national recognition for her contributions to improving Indo-German relations. In 1996, the Indian Council for Cultural Relations established the annual Gisela Bonn Prize in her honour.[39] The award continues to be conferred to this day.

As we saw in earlier chapters, Margret Boveri was a prominent foreign correspondent in Nazi Germany. Her articles harshly critiqued the British and Americans and largely supported Hitler's foreign policy goals. Yet, by April 1946, along with working freelance for various publications, Boveri accepted a permanent contract as the Berlin correspondent for the *Badische Zeitung*, published in the French Occupation Zone. As she began to relaunch her career, Boveri's male colleagues from the *Frankfurter Zeitung* (FZ) and *Das Reich* continued to struggle. The former editor of the *FZ*, Rudolph Kircher, was in Italy, reportedly uncertain about what fate awaited him in Germany.[40] Rudolf Sparing, Boveri's editor at *Das Reich*, was imprisoned in the Soviet Union, where he died in 1955. Still others, including *Das Reich* war correspondent Hans Schwarz van Berk, were banned from the field.

Despite her continued journalistic production, Boveri struggled to regain the professional security and prominence she had obtained in Nazi Germany.[41] Opposed to the Allied denazification program, the division of Germany, and, after 1949, West German chancellor Konrad Adenauer's policy of integration with the West, Boveri found herself politically and professionally isolated. Although she sought to use her journalism as a platform to argue for German reunification and improved relations with the East, publications like the *Badische Zeitung* and the *FAZ* balked at including such viewpoints on their pages. Instead, they chose largely to toe the political line of the Adenauer government, which favoured integration with Western Europe and close ties to the United States. In the 1950s, rather than writing for the political pages of the *FAZ*, Boveri contributed only the occasional literature review or piece for the features section, which was headed by her friend Karl Korn.[42] Still, she was able to make a living from her writing and eventually reconciled with the Federal Republic and its policies.

Like the Western Zones, the SBZ offered opportunities to women journalists irrespective of their connection to Nazism. Soviet policy was based on the necessity for women's labour rather than gendered assumptions about women's inherent aversion to politics. In August 1945, Soviet military authorities hired Annamarie Doherr as a reporter for the *Berliner Rundfunk*, despite the fact that she had written for both women's and more politically oriented publications throughout the Nazi period.[43] Photojournalist Liselotte Purper had built a prominent and profitable career producing harmonious representations of women and communities of ethnic Germans in occupied Poland during the war. After a short stint working as a dental assistant, Purper re-established her career in East Berlin in 1946. She became a member of the Cultural Association for the Democratic Renewal of Germany (Kulturbund zur demokratischen Erneuerung Deutschlands), a group founded for intellectuals and artists with the goal of imparting antifascist, humanistic values to the German population. Press authorities in the East suppressed any references about her propagandistic work for the Third Reich in order to allow her to work unencumbered on behalf of the Soviet-controlled press.[44]

Weimar-era journalist Elfriede Brüning also repositioned her career in East Berlin in 1946. During the Third Reich, Brüning had been able to work as a novelist, despite her earlier membership in the Communist Party of Germany (Kommunistische Partei Deutschlands – KPD) and arrest on suspicion of communist activities. In 1943, the Nazi Ministry of Propaganda declared her work "indispensable" to the continuation of Germany's cultural life and exempted her from compulsory war work. Despite her Third Reich career and lack of editorial experience, Brüning became the features editor for *Sonntag*, the flagship publication of the Kulturbund.[45] In 1946, no fewer than fifteen women were contributing to *Sonntag*, at least four of whom had begun their careers in Nazi Germany.[46] Hannelore Krollpfeiffer started out as an intern at the *Kattowitzer Zeitung* in Silesia in 1944. She returned to her native Berlin in May 1945 and applied to newspapers in all sectors of the city but received offers from only Soviet-licensed papers. With little experience, she began writing on culture and entertainment for East Berlin's *Nacht-Express*. "I was 22. One wouldn't get such an opportunity today," she recalled. "I had absolutely no experience to show for myself."[47] By 1947, Krollpfeiffer was also writing for *Sonntag*.

In the Eastern and Western regions of Germany, several factors helped women transition to the post-war press. In the West, these included gendered assumptions about women and their lack of ties to war reporting and (overt) wartime violence. In the East, opportunities for women resulted from a practical need for journalists and a socialist ideology that encouraged women to enter the workforce as a form of emancipation.

Like their male colleagues some women journalists were held to account, if only briefly, for their contribution to maintaining the Nazi state. Those who had been members of the Nazi Party had a more difficult time re-establishing their careers after 1945, although the application of justice was uneven. Gertrud Villforth had written on fashion and domestic issues for the women's party paper the *NS Frauen-Warte*. She had joined the Nazi Party in 1939. While fellow party member Ilse Urbach received her denazification documents from the British in 1946, Villlforth's process, which began under the Americans, dragged on until 1950, when it was finally concluded by a German court. Villforth was eventually classified as a follower and issued a fine.[48] Ardent Nazi supporter and early party member Renate von Stieda was unable to continue her journalism career after the war. Instead, she worked as a clerk and a housekeeper. By the early 1960s, however, she had once again become a published author.[49] Journalist and Nazi youth activist Melita Maschmann was interned until 1948. She did not re-establish a successful journalism career, although she did occasionally work freelance. In 1963, Maschmann published her memoir, in which she explored her youthful adherence to Nazism.[50] She lived her remaining decades in relative obscurity. The differences and inconsistences of the Allies' denazification programs meant that not all journalists were subjected to the same standards when it came to the judgment of their past.

One did not have to be a party member to face suspicion for one's Third Reich career. As was discussed in earlier chapters, Lily Abegg had been the East Asian correspondent for the *Frankfurter Zeitung*. Although she had not been a member of the Nazi Party, she was imprisoned in Yokohama, Japan, from 20 September 1945 until 24 January 1946 on suspicion of espionage on behalf of Nazi Germany.[51] She remained a person of interest for the British and American intelligence services until her file was closed in September 1956. In 1946, Abegg returned to Switzerland, where she had spent part of her youth, and began to write for the Swiss magazine *Die Weltwoche*, reporting once again on the Middle East and Southeast Asia. Abegg left *Die Weltwoche* in 1950 and fielded several offers from various high-profile newspapers. She freelanced for the *FAZ* until 1954, when she became the paper's foreign correspondent in Asia. It is possible that her trouble with the American and British intelligence services led Abegg to remain in Switzerland, writing for Swiss publications, until the Allies relinquished control over the German media in September 1949.

In spite of these early opportunities for women, journalism in all occupation zones remained male dominated, particularly after the Allies curtailed their denazification programs in 1947 and men largely regained their positions and stature after the founding of the Federal Republic of Germany and the German Democratic Republic in May and October 1949, respectively. At this stage, the attitude toward and opportunities open to women shifted to align with each state's political agenda. West Germany, under Chancellor Konrad Adenauer, the leader of the Christian Democratic Union (Christlich Demokratische Union – CDU), was characterized by conservatism in both the political and social spheres. The government, the churches, and many political and religious associations led a concerted effort to re-establish the traditional family as the heart of West German society and as an important marker of national identity. This return to "tradition" was not only supposed to signal a moral break with Nazism, it was also intended to create stability and a return to "normality" as part of the effort to prevent the spread of communism – a priority of the Western allies and later the Adenauer government.[52] Denise Lynn has shown how fear of communism was closely linked to anxieties about gender. As women claimed roles and rights outside of the home, many conservatives linked the preservation of traditional gender roles to the West's anti-communist identity, charging that communism destroyed the traditional family.[53]

Since their primary role was envisaged to be in the home as a wife and mother, women in the FRG began to suffer renewed discrimination and restrictions in the labour market, including in the press. They were relegated to the margins of the profession and largely restricted to the women's pages.[54] For instance, in an effort to create a democratic press in the FRG and to foster improved relations between the two countries, the Americans developed formal exchange programs for German journalists to learn from colleagues in the United States. These programs were primarily for men: it was not until 1952 that the first German woman journalist was selected to travel to the United States on one such exchange.[55] Thea Fischer lost her role writing theatre reviews on the British-licensed *Ruhr Zeitung* when a male journalist returned from imprisonment.[56] Reminiscent of actions taken during the Weimar Republic and Third Reich, a campaign in the 1950s sought to ban from various professions "double-income earners" (*Doppelverdiener*) – in other words, married women whose husbands worked. Such pressure affected the media. Antje Huber lost her position at the *Neue Ruhr Zeitung* in 1952 because she had married a colleague at the same paper. According to the paper's policy, only one of them could remain.[57]

Some women voluntarily left publications over friction with male colleagues or bosses. In the fall of 1946, Ruth Andreas-Friedrich stepped back from her position as publisher at *Sie* because of conflict with her male partners. Friedrich had wanted to create a woman's magazine devoted to political issues, intending it to help instil democratic values in German society; her male colleagues envisioned a publication that focused on cosmetics, fashion, and domestic topics – notions that were in keeping with traditional views about the "appropriate" role for women – and women journalists – during, and for decades after, the Third Reich.[58] At *Die Welt*, Helene Rahms worked on features and the women's pages. Her editors, she recalled, found her work on the women's supplement "too intellectual." According to Rahms, one colleague claimed that "women's pages can never be too primitive."[59] When Rahms voiced her disagreement, her editor suggested that she resign. Upon her departure, the paper hired a "mellow, blond intern" who followed the editor's instructions. "I realized," Rahms noted, "that the authority of men continued without objection and they retained their old privileges, so that an idiot like the moustache [her editor] could determine the nature and content of the women's pages."[60] One has to account for fragmented memory, bias, and the desire for positive self-representation in Friedrich's and Rahms's depictions of their career struggles. Nonetheless, their experiences reflect those of many female journalists who sought to establish (or re-establish) themselves in the field after the Second World War, not only in Germany, but also in the United States, Britain, and other European countries. Without doubt, marginalization, limitation, and pigeon-holing due to sexism continued.[61]

Helma Huffschmid had begun her journalism career in earnest during the Second World War, when she took over her husband's work the economic pages of the *Frankfurter Zeitung* after his conscription into the army. Her articles appeared under her husband's name. Beginning in 1948, she again began to write about economics and politics for the *Frankfurter Allgemeine Zeitung* under her husband's byline of HD. The editors were onboard with the arrangement and trusted her to cover politics, although she was not given her own byline.[62] Huffschmid's experience reflects how the use of male or gender-neutral pseudonyms continued after the war to help editors bridge any space between societal gender rhetoric and the activities of women journalists. Such pseudonyms continued to hold more legitimacy than a female name in economic and political news in post-war West Germany.

The politics of the Eastern and Western Zones had a demographic effect on the journalistic profession. As a result of ideology, VDP press policies, and the scarcity of labour, female journalists accounted for a greater percentage of the press cohort in the East then they did in the West. By 1951, women constituted 16 per cent of working journalists in the GDR (during the Third Reich, they had never accounted for more than 11 per cent).[63] In the FRG, the percentage of women journalists was much lower: for example, in the Ruhr, women made up only 3 per cent of journalists; in the Rhineland-Pfalz area, the figure was 5 per cent.[64] These two areas are likely representative of the FRG in general, although the archives do not allow for a precise analysis of the number of women working in the West German press in the first decade after the war. What is clear is that women in the East had the scope and pressure to be active in public life in a manner that those in the West did not.

Positions in the press appealed to women in both zones for intellectual reasons, as well as for the material and practical advantages they offered. In the SBZ, artists and writers were placed in the highest ration-card category, for instance.[65] Margret Boveri freelanced for the Soviet-licensed *Neue Zeit*, the first party paper of the CDU in the East. This job was particularly useful to Boveri, since it entitled her to extra rations and allowed her to "fell a tree in the *Grunewald*" during the unusually cold winter of 1945/46.[66] Boveri's position as a correspondent for the *Badische Zeitung* in Berlin also permitted her an interzonal pass, which meant freedom of movement throughout occupied Germany – something most Germans did not have access to in the aftermath of the war. In addition, for single mothers – not an uncommon role in the first post-war decade – journalism allowed for flexible scheduling, which was valued by women in both the East and West. Many cited their love of writing as the primary reason for pursuing the profession. Just as it had in the past, a career in journalism offered status, freedom, travel, and the opportunity to network with interesting people. Whatever the personal or intellectual appeal of the profession, the experiences of women journalists reveal that their different political stances and professional trajectories during the Third Reich did not tend to determine the nature of their post-war careers. They were, however, hampered by other, both new and long-standing, restrictions.

## New Patrons, Old Prejudices

When it came to restarting their careers, women journalists were dependent on the policies of Allied press officers and the relationships they had with individuals the Allies placed in key publishing and editorial positions, most of whom were men. To negotiate the barriers they continued to face in the patriarchal field, women tapped into the networks they had established during the Third Reich, once again seeking out and relying on a male patron. Women's inclusion in the Nazi press, even if on the margins, and the camaraderie they experienced within the field proved useful after 1945. Lily Abegg had her former political editor on the *Frankfurter Zeitung*, Benno Reifenberg, to thank for her post-war position on the *Frankfurter Allgemeine Zeitung*. Abegg anticipated that working for the *FAZ* would give her the same sense of pleasure and collegiality that she had enjoyed during the Third Reich. She was thrilled that she would once again be published "alongside the old gang."[67]

Helene Rahms spent the last days of the war and the first year after it living with her in-laws in the town of Oldenburg in the British Occupation Zone. When she was reading through *Der Kurier*, a familiar name caught her eye: Christa Rotzoll, an old colleague from *Das Reich*, was now writing for the features section of the paper. According to Rahms, she felt a sense of envy about the interesting people and intellectual discussions Rotzoll would be enjoying in her role as journalist. "She had made it," stated Rahms. "She belonged to that elite clique again."[68] Through Rotzoll, Rahms was able to get in touch with Werner Oehlmann, a former writer for *Das Reich*. Oehlmann, now editor of the features section of the *Hannoversche Zeitung*, hired Rahms on a freelance basis. Rahms spoke of the pride that she felt at having relaunched her career: "I am once again what I was, a journalist."[69] Rahms sought to regain the stature and sense of "being somebody" that she had held in Nazi Germany. When she later joined *Die Welt* in Hamburg, in 1947, she recalled that colleagues from Berlin found each other and pushed aside any sense of complicity or scruples over their work on behalf of the Nazi regime to celebrate the resurgence of their professional lives. "The clique lives" the former journalist on the *FZ* and co-founder of *Der Kurier*, Carl Linfert, supposedly murmured to Rahms.[70]

There may have been an atmosphere of collegiality among former colleagues who had worked throughout the Third Reich, but hostilities did arise between journalists and the occupation authorities. Tensions largely centred around Allied denazification and re-education policies. Despite the fact that the press was not significantly impacted in the long term by denazification, male and female journalists resented these processes. Some expressed their antipathy in antisemitic or derogatory language reminiscent of the Third Reich, which labelled the Americans as uncultured and the Soviets as beasts. In her memoir, Rahms employed antisemitic rhetoric to describe her interactions with a purportedly aggressive German-speaking American information control officer after US occupation authorities arrested her at the end of the war. Rahms claimed that she was unclear of the reason for her arrest, and her portrayal of events, although murky, does imply that it was not due to her Third Reich journalism. In the end, she felt that the CIA wanted to recruit her.

Rahms's description of her discussion with the officer who questioned her is striking: "The young man who had interrogated me, with the bent nose, the broad, slightly downward curved lower lip, the sniveling voice, was he Jewish? Probably. How could he speak German so fluently."[71] For Rahms, the meeting led to "a confusing experience: anti-Jewish feelings. Such feelings," she claimed, "had remained alien to me before and during the worst years. But now?"[72] The use of such language suggests deep and long-standing prejudices and implies that, while Rahms carefully avoided antisemitic language when talking about her Third Reich experiences, she sought to insinuate that Jews reveled in positions of power over Germans after the war.[73] In reality, after 1949, émigrés who had opposed the Nazi regime or who now returned to (re)establish their careers were not always welcome, personally or professionally. Some returnees found themselves pushed to the margins, while those who had remained in the Nazified press rebuilt prominent careers.[74]

Rahms described re-education as "an unbearable word" and noted that "the Americans want to scold us, accuse us, one for all and all for one. In the eyes of the world, we were deserving of punishment, black sheep surrounded by pure, white ones."[75] She went on to deride what she viewed as a lack of culture among the Americans – which she described as a "Coca Cola culture" – as well as an "infantile moralism" and "blind faith in money."[76] Tropes about American materialism, superficial culture, and lack of education, which had often been employed in Nazi propaganda, were echoed by intellectuals such as Rahms in the post-war years.

Ursula von Kardorff also resided in the American Occupation Zone and had little respect for the occupiers, whom she described in her diary as "a little simple-minded."[77] She too criticized US denazification and re-education efforts, writing in June 1945:

> The Allies no longer threaten to bomb us, but now they talk to us like a governess. One has the feeling that one is sitting in a classroom and being

continually rapped over the knuckles ... They talk about educating us in the ways of democracy, and, at the same time, try to peer into everybody's private affairs.[78]

Kardorff complained to her former colleague Jürgen Schüddekopf that she had to undergo a denazification process due to "an idiotic article about the Soviet woman" that she had written during the Third Reich.[79] Although she disliked the Western Allies, Kardorff saved her harshest criticism for the Soviets, referring to them in such disparaging terms as "the red pest" and "red flood."[80] Kardorff loathed the Russians, both during and after the Third Reich, and felt that communism was the same, if not worse, than Nazism. The Red Army's seizure of the Kardorff family's two estates in the East only added to her hatred. So too did the fate of her family: when the Soviets arrived at the Kardorff estate of Böhlendorf in May 1945, three of her relatives committed suicide.[81]

Residing in post-war West Berlin, Margret Boveri critiqued the Russians for what she viewed as their overzealous approach to denazification, which targeted party members irrespective of whether, in her opinion, they had been committed Nazis.[82] In her public and private writing, however, Boveri was most scornful of the Americans. Like Kardorff, Boveri regarded the Americans as ignorant. Shortly after their arrival in Berlin, she wrote, "I can already see that my experience with the American army, if I ever get into a conversation with them, will be similar to that of New York, the majority of Americans know less English than I do."[83] Her low opinion of Americans was also reflected in her resentment that she and fellow colleagues who had written during the Third Reich were included in denazification processes: "From my stay in America and the continued reading of the Anglo-American press, I knew that it would be a long time before the Allies would begin to realize that even among non-emigrated, non-democratic Germans, there were people who combined intelligence with integrity and good will."[84]

In 1946, Boveri published her *American Primer for Grown-Up Germans*, which was supposedly based on her understanding of the United States gained during her time in that country as a foreign correspondent. She claimed that the book was intended to foster understanding between the two countries. In reality, it advanced the same anti-American stereotypes she had propagated throughout the 1930s and 1940s, ignored Germany's wartime crimes, implied her country's victimhood, and compared aspects of US policy with Nazi practice.[85] As Boveri's biographer, Heike Görtemaker, asserts, the book was intended to counter the notion of collective guilt and the re-education policies propagated by the US occupation authorities, which Boveri considered an affront.[86] *American Primer* became a bestseller in the French and British sectors of occupied Germany, although the Americans prevented her from publishing it in their zone. The book angered American authorities to the point where they refused to grant her a visa to visit the United States.[87] Regardless of their disdain for the Allies, journalists such as Rahms, Kardorff, and Boveri were able to re-establish rewarding careers. But, they were also vulnerable to the risks posed by the changing political landscape, particularly in Berlin.

## Berlin: Between Possibility and Vulnerability

Berlin, the traditional media centre of Germany, offered more opportunities for journalists than could be found elsewhere. But the presence of four administrative powers in the former capital led to new tensions and unexpected threats. By the end of 1945, the four occupation zones together published twelve daily newspapers in the city, with a circulation of two million; by the beginning of 1948, this number had grown to nineteen, with a total circulation of 4.7 million.[88] In June 1948, Berlin, with just over three million inhabitants, made up 5 per cent of the total German population but accounted for 24 per cent of the total circulation of German newspapers.[89] Moreover, sixty newspapers from the four occupation zones had permanent correspondents in the city.

Berlin was at the centre of German and European events, particularly as the Cold War took hold. Throngs of foreign journalists were based in Berlin, given that it was the headquarters of the Allied Control Council (the governing body of the four occupation powers) and of the Soviet, American, British, and French occupation authorities. The city also received important international visitors. The activity and interest in Berlin, the permeability of the city's zonal borders, and the fact that journalistic relations between East and West Berlin were initially marked by a degree of communication and crossover contributed to enhanced professional opportunities.[90] As Margret Boveri recalled, throughout the autumn of 1945 and into 1946, former colleagues flocked to Berlin to take advantage of the opportunities it offered. "For journalists," she wrote, "the division of the city among four occupying powers had its advantages. Those who had a black mark against them with one military government were better off with another."[91] Journalists also journeyed back and forth between the East and West zones. Liselotte Thomas and Cläre Jung, for instance, were based in West Berlin but wrote for the Eastern publications *Sonntag* and *Für Dich*, respectively.

Still, there were tensions in the early post-war years as competition between the East and West zones in Berlin (and Germany as a whole) took hold in the economic, political, and ideological arenas. Having been the first of the Allies to reach Germany's capital, the Soviets had launched half a dozen newspapers by the time British and American troops arrived in July 1945; at that stage, Berlin's entire press was under the control of Soviet military authorities.[92] Western officials worried that the material published in Soviet papers was one-sided and oriented only toward the Soviet Union and its aims to establish a socialist post-war Germany. British press officer Peter de Mendelssohn wrote in a July 1945 memo that, in Berlin, western-licensed papers would surely experience fierce competition.[93] Just as Western press officers worried about Soviet influence, Soviet authorities were concerned about the growth of West Berlin newspapers. Yet, as de Mendelssohn recalled, "although a 'newspaper front,' was emerging ever more clearly between East and West Berlin, it was still possible to speak of the 'Berliner Press' as a whole" for the first three years after the war.[94]

East German press authorities in particular sought and encouraged connections with Western journalists in the first post-war years. The VDP was principally an East German organization, but it also included West Berlin–based journalists in its membership: "Although the association primarily represents the professional interests of journalists in the Eastern Zone, the VDP also maintains an interzonal working group with journalist associations in the western and southern regions of Germany," the association's protocol claimed.[95] Even after the German Journalists' Association (Deutscher Journalisten-Verband) was founded in West Berlin in 1949, some journalists in the Western sectors retained their VDP membership.[96]

The post-war press in all zones comprised people with commonalities and similar experiences, but also those who had fundamentally different responses to the Nazi regime and the war. Some had remained in Germany throughout the Third Reich and lived through the destruction of the war, while others had experienced the realities of persecution and the difficulties of emigration and had returned to Germany after the Nazi regime's downfall. Despite these differences, Christina von Hodenberg has described a sense of camaraderie among journalists.[97] In a report on the first meeting of the VDP on 7 April 1946, Paul Ufermann addressed the need for a network of former colleagues in the chaos of post-war Berlin, and the challenge of establishing such an organization.[98] He went on to acknowledge how the VDP's gathering gave journalists the chance to come together "for the first time since the collapse" to discuss "their experiences, their present situation, their hopes for the future and, often, also their current needs."[99]

The Allies viewed the press as a critical tool in its goal to eradicate National Socialist sentiments from the German population. Here, it seemed as if the press in both the Eastern and Western Zones was working toward a similar purpose and using similar tools: both the Western Allies and the Soviet Union had significant confidence in the educational role of the press to help build an antifascist, antimilitaristic, and democratic (or socialist) Germany. Press authorities in the East also viewed connections with the Western press as a way to influence politics and the representation of the Soviet Zone in the West. Moreover, prior to 1949, the division of Germany was not yet deemed final, and Stalin had ambitions to gain a unified state, and therefore, press.

Yet, the spirit and rhetoric of working together constantly shifted, and it all but disappeared by 1949 as macropolitical events heightened the Cold War climate. The first such event, in April 1946, was the forced merger, in the Soviet Zone, of the Communist Party of Germany and Social Democratic Party of Germany (Sozialdemokratische Partei Deutschlands – SPD) into the Socialist Unity Party (Sozialistische Einheitspartei Deutschlands – SED). In March 1947, the US government promulgated the Truman Doctrine, aimed at containing communism. Relations between West and East further deteriorated with the Communist takeover in Czechoslovakia in February 1948. In response to monetary reform in the Western Zones in June 1948, the Soviet imposed a blockade of West Berlin, which, in turn, led to the American and British Berlin Airlift (from June 1948 to May 1949). In April 1949, the Western Allies and other nations established the North Atlantic Treaty Organization (NATO). Finally in 1949, the gulf between East and West was formalized, with the establishment of the FRG and the GDR.

Collectively, these events led to increasing professional threats for journalists traversing the boundaries between East and West both physically and intellectually. After the war, Eva Siewert who lived in the Western sector of Berlin, freelanced for Western publications, including *Der Spiegel* and the *Telegraph*, but also for the East's *Die Weltbühne*, writing primarily about art, music, the ramifications of the war, and lingering antisemitism in Germany. She feared that writing under her own name for the Eastern paper would hinder her career. And, indeed, her work for *Die Weltbühne* brought her unwanted attention in the West. In a July 1947 letter to the paper's editor, Hans Leonard, Siewert complained that a "dark shadow" had fallen over her name in British-American military circles due to the fact that she wrote openly for the paper: "I am ... aware that a number of journalists with similar intellectual or world outlooks to me … write for you under pseudonyms while I was courageous enough to use my own name, which has already sufficiently damaged my work on the other side of this, unfortunately prevailing, border."[100] Susanne Kerckhoff, who had worked as an author during the Third Reich, moved from the Western to the Eastern sector of Berlin after the American occupation authorities deemed the magazine *Uhlenspiegel*, for which she wrote, too left wing. In 1948, she became a reporter for the features section of the *Berliner Zeitung*, which was based in the SBZ.

While Western occupation powers could make life difficult for journalists, the real threat came from Soviet and, later, East German authorities. The vicissitudes of Soviet policy and actions regarding the questions of unification and connections with the Western Zones made it difficult for journalists to recognize and navigate the hazardous political landscape. In 1946, for instance, press authorities in the SBZ sought closer relations with the press in the Western sectors. At the same time, police in the East were warning their citizens that subscribing to West Berlin–based newspapers could subject them to punishment.[101] Stark differences in the nature of the press in the Western and Eastern Zones also made life precarious for journalists writing for Eastern-based papers. While the Western occupation powers fostered the notion of "objective" journalism, stressed the importance of a free press, and published a range of viewpoints about contemporary issues, the Soviets and, later, their East German counterparts established and maintained a controlled press that acted as a mouthpiece for Moscow and the SED. As Volker Berghahn has demonstrated, although journalists in the Western Zones could find their voices limited at certain newspapers if their views went against the publication's political leaning, there was no overarching political line such as they had experienced in Nazi Germany – or that their colleagues experienced in the SBZ.[102] If a journalist felt restricted at one paper, they could simply work for another that was more open to their views.

A system of media control existed in the East from the re-establishment of the press onward. The Soviet Military Administration in Germany (Sowjetische Militäradministration in Deutschland) initially subjected newspapers to pre-publishing censorship. In November 1946, this system was changed to post-publication censoring, which was not abolished until September 1949.[103] The controlled nature of the press remained in place after this date, however. In the GDR, media work was first and foremost political, and its guidelines were established by the party leadership. Verbal and written directives were an important element of press control, and arbitrary repression and punishment of journalists or editors accused of acting against the interests of the state (or the Soviet Union) were not uncommon.[104] After the founding, in February 1950, of the GDR Ministry for State Security (Ministerium für Staatssicherheit – the Stasi), journalists had the additional worry that colleagues could be informers.[105]

By the late 1940s, an increasing number of Eastern-based journalists began relocating to West Berlin, regardless of the status of their careers. In 1949, Annamarie Doherr left her position as a reporter for the East German radio station Berliner Rundfunk, where she had progressed to having her own show, to work as the West Berlin correspondent for the daily newspaper the *Frankfurter Rundschau*. Liselotte Purper left the GDR in 1950 and worked as a photographer in West Berlin, where she became a member of the western Deutscher Journalisten-Verband.[106] Hannelore Krollpfeiffer, whose work focused largely on culture and entertainment, fled from East to West Berlin in 1950 after the Stasi attempted to recruit her as an informant. As she began to establish a career at the *Tagesspiegel*, Krollpfeiffer faced accusations in the Western press that she was an East German spy. Having evaded the Soviet threat, Krollpfeiffer unknowingly traded one risk for another.[107] Seeking to escape the Cold War atmosphere of Berlin, Krollpfeiffer soon relocated to Hamburg, where she eventually became editor of the women's magazine *Brigitte*. Christa Rotzoll, who lived and worked in West Berlin between 1946 and 1958, wrote for Western publications about film and theatre productions in the East. As she later recalled, "Not once in all of those years did I lose the unpleasant feeling that at any time I could be stopped and accused of stirring tensions or spying."[108]

Rotzoll's fear about the East was not unfounded. Although she was never arrested, others were not so fortunate. Ursula Rumin had begun her journalism career in West Berlin in the wake of the war, writing primarily about film, culture, local news, and "women's affairs." Her work appeared in both West and East German publications. In 1950, she found lucrative work as a freelance journalist and screenwriter for the East German Film Company (Deutsche Film Aktiengesellschaft – DEFA). Although Rumin had become increasingly uneasy about travelling back and forth between West and East Berlin, her reporting for DEFA constituted a large proportion of her income.[109] Rumin's intuition proved correct. On 25 September 1952, she crossed over to East Berlin on her way to a meeting at DEFA to discuss a new film project. A Soviet agent seized her at the Friedrichstraße train station and took her to the Soviet prison in Berlin-Karlshorst. She was charged with spying for the Americans and sentenced her to fifteen years of forced labour at the Siberian Gulag Vorkuta.[110] After Stalin's death in March 1953, the Soviets amnestied Rumin, who returned to West Germany in early 1954.

While women and men from any walk of life could find themselves inadvertently coming to the attention of Soviet and/or East German authorities, journalism proved an especially risky activity. The importance that the allies in West Germany, the Soviets, and the East Germans placed on the press gave women journalists greater visibility and status in the public realm than other professions afforded. As a result, their professional role connected them to the Cold War in a manner not experienced by most women. According to Rumin, a number of "Western" German women with whom she was imprisoned in Vorkuta belonged to the intelligentsia, mostly journalists, teachers, or artists. Rumin counted fifteen journalists in her circle in the Siberian camp.[111]

Brigitte Gerland was one such journalist. Abducted by the Soviet Ministry of State Security while travelling in the SBZ in October 1946, she was tried by a Soviet "Special Committee" in Dresden, found guilty of spying for England, and sentenced to ten years at Vorkuta. Born in 1918, Gerland had worked as a reporter in Berlin before she fled Nazi Germany for France in 1938. She returned to Berlin after the collapse of the Third Reich in the spring of 1945, joined the KPD and re-established her journalism career in East Berlin. She was initially a reporter for the news agency of the Soviet military. She soon felt hampered by the limited intellectual freedom her work afforded. Gerland left the party and moved to West Berlin, where she worked as a freelance journalist for several West Berlin papers. Her reporting focused on the Eastern Zone, drawing on her professional experience there, and her relationships with, as she put it, "influential circles."[112] Still a committed socialist, Gerland became a member of the SPD. At the time of her arrest, she was writing primarily for its paper *Der Sozialdemokrat*, which was licensed in the British sector. During her trial, Gerland was classified as a dangerous intelligence agent.[113]

Gerland's crossover from East to West and her writing for the SPD's flagship paper about life in the East in the wake of the forced merger between the KPD and SPD bore wider consequences in the emerging Cold War. Among other factors, it undoubtedly fuelled ongoing Soviet and, later, East German suspicions about continuing support for the SPD in the East. The Soviets increasingly viewed the Social Democrats as the primary obstacle to Soviet influence in the Eastern Zone, particularly after the party set up an eastern bureau (Ostbüro) in West Berlin in April 1946 to gather information about and sustain contacts with Social Democrats in the East. The Soviet Union viewed the bureau as a US endeavour to deprive it of its rightful place in shaping post-war Germany.[114] Gerland's case represents a precursor to the SED's repression of former Social Democrats beginning in 1947.[115] Her fate exemplifies the risks faced by politically minded journalists caught in the middle of the escalating Cold War.

But it was not just political journalists who faced grave occupational hazards in early Cold War Germany. Even those journalists not aligned with political parties had difficulties. Cub reporter Charlotte Fischer-Lamberg disappeared in June 1946 while on assignment in Brandenburg in the Soviet zone. Employed by the US-licensed *Weser-Kurier*, Fischer-Lamberg had planned to cover a convention of the socialist youth organization Free German Youth (Freie Deutsche Jugend – FDJ). After almost a year of inquiries, the US military's Information Control Division discovered that Fischer-Lamberg had been arrested and sentenced to prison for travelling in the Soviet zone without the correct authorization. Although she had been carrying both an invitation from the FDJ and travel authorization from the American military authorities, these provided insufficient protection. The director of the ICD wrote to the director of propaganda for the Soviet military administration, Colonel Sergei Tiulpanov, requesting Fischer-Lamberg's release. "I realize," he wrote, "that undoubtedly further Soviet approval probably should have been obtained but it is clear that Fräulein Fischer-Lamberg made the trip in good faith. I am sure you will agree with me that this is a case which deserves every consideration if a miscarriage of justice is to be avoided."[116] Fischer-Lamberg spent six years in prison in the East, eventually returning to the *Weser-Kurier* and continuing her career.[117] Her colleague Liselotte Weinsheimer believed that she had been arrested "only because she [was] a West German journalist."[118]

The physical and ideological border could also be dangerous for East German journalists. The successful career of committed socialist Gerda Zorn ended abruptly in 1951. In 1950, Zorn had begun work in the SED's press office. In the fall of 1951, she was selected to look after Western journalists visiting the GDR. The visit was part of the SED's campaign Germans at One Table (*Deutsche an einen Tisch*), a significant political undertaking – and one of the last of its kind – that aimed to lay the foundation for negotiating the unification of Germany. Zorn's task was to encourage Western journalists to write positive articles about the new social order that the GDR had built, a huge responsibility given the importance of the *Deutsche an einen Tisch* campaign. She escorted Western journalists through factories, organized discussions with women workers, and visited cultural events, the very subjects that Zorn and other women journalists were expected to cover and that were politically critical in the GDR.[119]

One evening, two of these journalists planned to travel to West Berlin for a night out and challenged Zorn to join them. Wishing to prove that the GDR was not a repressive state and considering that she had never been forbidden to travel to the West, Zorn spent the evening in West Berlin watching an American film. Her intention, she recalled, had been to compare Western to Eastern culture, with the goal of helping the GDR's cultural efforts gain traction in both regions of Germany. The deputy head of her department, a Russian woman, promptly told Zorn that she would face severe repercussions: "As a party member … [you] should have known better than to go to West Berlin."[120] According to the SED press office, Zorn had placed herself at risk of becoming unwittingly entangled in an American espionage network. "The Russians could have sent you to Siberia for 10 years," another colleague warned.[121] Although not expelled from the party, Zorn lost her coveted position and was sent to work in a factory, ostensibly to reconnect with workers. She eventually reignited her journalism career in the GDR but left for West Germany in 1956.

Zorn's experience must be viewed against the backdrop of the relationship between the GDR and FRG, as both states sought legitimacy, domestically and internationally. As West Germany became more prosperous and East Germany more insecure, the SED developed increasingly repressive policies aimed at intimidating alleged nonconformist forces within society. The SED used events and transformations in the FRG as a catalyst for its actions and reactions and led a campaign that was especially active in the cultural arena – Zorn's area of expertise – against the threatening influence of cosmopolitanism and Americanism.[122] The open border to West Berlin functioned as a doorway to Western culture and prosperity. Despite their vacillating rhetoric on the subject, party leaders became suspicious of any actions aimed at promoting closer links with the West. Zorn had crossed not only the GDR's physical border but also the SED's shifting boundary of what it considered ideologically acceptable behaviour.

## Writing the Occupation and the Ramifications of the War

Journalists were not always cognizant of the physical or professional dangers they faced in the shifting atmosphere of the Cold War, but many were aware of the ways in which their writing could be utilized to suit the needs of the German population and to contribute to a narrative about the impact of the war and the challenges of its aftermath. Some were also mindful of how their work could be exploited by the Allies in the Cold War battle for German loyalty. Although the Allies initially intended the press as a vehicle for the re-education and democratization of Germany – which the Soviets and Western powers interpreted differently – it increasingly became a medium through which East and West sought to legitimate and popularize their own politics and ideology in the post-war battle for hearts and minds. For the Western allies, especially the United States, the goal was a democratic, free-market, and, above all, anti-communist West Germany. For the Soviets, it was the establishment of a socialist state tied to Moscow. Both powers sought to weaken the other's influence on the German population via the media.

The Allied Control Council issued Directive No. 40 on 12 October 1946, which allowed the media to discuss German social and political problems.[123] Targeting the "other" Germany as a cause of current difficulties became a part of the media strategy of the licensed press in both the Eastern and Western Zones. Female journalists in the respective sectors contributed to this discourse by critiquing the other's handling of the repercussions of the war – above all, its impact on the female population – in a manner that sought to establish their own zone as the rightful Germany. In doing so, they became part of the process that increasingly set East and West against each other.

Margret Boveri was particularly concerned about this phenomenon. In her post-war recollections, she described conversations with a colleague by the name of Herr v. d. Dekken, who had asked her to write for a newspaper that the publisher Heinz Ullstein was planning to launch with the Americans. Boveri did not want to contribute to the Cold War atmosphere or fuel what she feared would be the permanent division of Germany and, ultimately, Europe. She agreed to write for the American-sponsored paper, only if she could work at the same time for a newspaper published in the Russian zone.[124] Just as she had during the Third Reich, Boveri continued to write about politics and foreign affairs after 1945. In the early post-war years, she critiqued the foreign policy of the Western Allies in such articles as "No-Man's Land Europe: Ideology-Power Struggles, Dollar Politics." She wrote that England and the United States were refusing to cooperate with the Soviet Union out of a desire for hegemony. Both countries, she argued, sacrificed peace for power politics, aided by an "ideologically oriented economic policy."[125] Boveri also felt that the 1948 American Marshall Plan was intended to isolate the Soviet Union economically and feared that it would further cement the division of Germany.

Other women who had been released from incarceration, such as Eva Siewert, or those who had launched their journalism careers after 1945, such as Marion von Dönhoff, also succeeded in reporting on the traditionally male-dominated fields of politics and economics. Through their writing, they were able to assert their views on Germany's current political situation and its future path, including the question of German reunification and the relationship between the two zones – and, later, states.[126] Like their male colleagues, female journalists were sometimes at odds over such issues. Boveri, for instance, pressed for closer relations with the

Soviets and charged that von Dönhoff's writing helped to fuel the Cold War.[127] Von Dönhoff desired a democratic Germany and the "reconstruction of the honour and dignity" of the German population based on the ideals of those who had plotted to assassinate Hitler in July 1944.[128] She viewed the values and actions of this largely aristocratic group as providing a moral benchmark for a new Germany, despite the fact that much of the aristocracy had supported Nazism, at least prior to Hitler's invasion of the Soviet Union.[129] Having lost her home in East Prussia to the Soviets, she too called for German reunification but desired a return to the country's 1937 borders. As a staunch anti-communist, however, von Dönhoff was also an advocate for "Atlanticism," and backed the rearmament of West Germany and its integration into NATO.[130]

Women such as von Dönhoff and Boveri who published their political views remained the exception to the rule. The majority of female journalists continued to be restricted to the local, cultural, features, and women's pages, whether by choice or professional norms. In the early post-war years, journalists in both regions focused on the difficulties of everyday life and how best to cope. Not surprisingly, in the chaos of post-war Germany, where the basic requirements of housing, clothing, food, and medical supplies were hard to come by, and where women bore the primary responsibility for caring for their families, women journalists addressed topics that mattered most to their female readers: paid employment, household management, food security, health and well-being, and pressing social issues like single motherhood. Between 1945 and 1949, the articles in women's magazines were primarily on these issues.[131] Women's magazines also included some political news, but this usually took a back seat to these practical considerations.

*Der Regenbogen: Zeitschrift für die Frau* (The rainbow: magazine for the woman) was founded in the US Zone in 1946. In the first issue, the editor, Maria Pfeffer, introduced the publication to her readers:

> Before we went to work, we talked with many women from a wide variety of circles and asked them, "What do you expect from a new women's magazine?" The answer was pretty uniform. They all wanted a lot of practical things: recipes, useful hints, a fashion page ... in short, advice and help with the worries of everyday life.[132]

In the fall of 1946, the East German magazine *Für Dich* published an article that asked women, "In your opinion, what measures need to be taken in order to control hardships this winter?[133] During its first year, *Für Dich* typically published such pieces as "Warm Clothes for the Woman, Man and Child."[134]

Marta Hillers, who had written about women's social and domestic concerns during the Third Reich, continued her career after 1945, publishing articles in both Eastern and Western newspapers and magazines intended to help women navigate their new reality. Titles included "New Professions in Berlin: The Female Landlord" and various articles about *Trümmerfrauen* (rubble women).[135] She also provided practical advice in articles such as "We are Learning Russian."[136] Other journalists, including Ursula von Kardorff and Pauline Nardi, wrote about non-material concerns in articles such as "Does Happiness Still Exist?" and "Humour after War."[137] By demonstrating that many women were struggling with the same practical and existential concerns, such pieces fostered a sense of community among the female population. At the same time, material that focused on happiness and humour suggested an eventual return to normality or allowed readers a break from worry over material deprivations.

Women's magazines devoted much attention to women's roles in rebuilding Germany physically, socially, and, most important, morally, whether based on a democratic or socialist outlook. In July 1945, US journalist Frances McFadden was working on the draft of a magazine titled *Wir Frauen*, to be published in the American Zone of Occupation. For the first issue, McFadden wanted to publish the results of a survey of German women answering questions related to the theme of peace, including "What can its women do to help Germany win back the respect of other nations?"[138] She also requested a photo of a German woman clearing up rubble with broom in hand to accompany an article fittingly entitled "Woman with a Broom." "The woman with a broom is both a symbol and promise," McFadden wrote. "Everywhere, before the monster bulldozers arrived to clear paths for the armies through the debris left by the bombers, women instinctively seized their brooms in this futile age-old gesture of cleaning up the mess."[139] McFadden believed that Germany's women could not only "clean up the mess" of their destroyed cities, but also help re-establish a society that would earn international respect. Newspapers and magazines from the Eastern Zone likewise focused on women's important contribution to the resurgence of Germany. In the summer of 1946, *Für Dich* published an article titled "A New Berlin! We Can Do It, We Will Do It."[140] The article celebrated women's contribution to various aspects of the rebuilding, from cleaning up the rubble to ensuring the welfare of their fellow Germans. It was accompanied by several pictures of *Trümmerfrauen*, a common visual in post-war newspapers and magazines.

While, as was discussed in the preceding chapter, female photojournalists both veiled and beautified processes of violence perpetrated by the Germans during the war, their post-war work directly addressed

6.1  Woman with baby tending graves on a plot of rubble, by Ursula Litzmann, 1945

Photo credit: akg images / Ursula Litzmann

the consequences of the war in Germany, the suffering of its population, and the devastation of its towns and cities. Photographs that highlighted the ramifications of wartime violence in Germany stood in contrast to the life-affirming photos of peaceful landscapes and charming villages that had constituted much of women's photojournalism in the Third Reich. Erika Groth-Schmachtenberger's first reportage at the end of the war, for instance, captured the destruction of Würzburg, which had sustained an intense bombing raid in March 1945.[141] Liselotte Purper, Hildegard Zenker, and Ursula Litzmann had all travelled to the occupied East during the war. There, they had, respectively, produced images of German women peacefully tending to the "resettled" *Volksdeutsche* communities, nurses caring for injured soldiers, and parading Hitler Youth groups. In publications in the Eastern and Western Zones after 1945, they published a stream of reportage on women coping with everyday life and death among the ruins; the influx of refugees; the destruction of Berlin, Hamburg, and Cologne; and the ubiquitous *Trümmerfrauen* who worked to rebuild the cities (figures 6.1 and 6.2).

6.2  A woman takes a break in the sun on the damaged steps of the National Theatre in Munich, by Erika Groth-Schmachtenberger, 1946

Photo credit: bpk Bildagentur/Erika Groth-Schmachtenberger / Art Resource, NY

For non-German audiences, such photographs functioned to elicit sympathy and respect for German women. For German audiences, these images of loss and destruction were not only a reminder of the ramifications of war and collapse, but they also helped to create an iconography of hope and offered a visual celebration of women's contribution to rebuilding and renewal.[142]

Women journalists' writing about everyday life had political importance after the war, just as it had during the Third Reich. Those writing in the Eastern and Western Zones addressed common themes related to the aftermath of the war, including hunger, refugees, and the processes of justice. In doing so, they focused on the alleged suffering in the "other" Germany in a manner that functioned to establish their own zone or region as the legitimate German state. In the summer of 1946, Elfriede Brüning was writing for the SBZ publication *Sonntag*. The division of Germany immediately encroached on her work, as the paper rejected her first article on German refugees: Brüning had written of her trip to Berlin on the back of a truck with East German expellees, describing "the starving people who besieged our car, begging for a carrot."[143] Her editor advised that, if this article represented her approach to social issues in the SBZ, she would be better off submitting it to the *Tagesspiegel* in the West. Naturally, he warned, she would no longer be welcome at *Sonntag* if she did so. Brüning keenly observed that the *Tagesspiegel* would have welcomed reports about misery in the East, but that *Sonntag* required optimism about everyday life in its region.[144]

Brüning's future writing about refugees reflected this required optimism and demonstrated how women journalists produced narratives that legitimized the Eastern Zone's policies and responses to contemporary issues. In March 1948, she published an article entitled "In Good Hands, Well Cared For" in *Die neue Heimat* (The new home), a magazine produced by the Central Administration for Resettlers in the Soviet Zone. The purpose of *Die neue Heimat* was to help settle Germans displaced or returning from Eastern territories. In the chaos of the post-war years, Soviet authorities, often arbitrarily, deported Germans to the Soviet Union for use as forced labour to rebuild what Nazi violence had destroyed. Brüning described the experiences of a group of East Prussian women who were repatriated after imprisonment in a Siberian gulag. She wrote of the women's arrival at the resettlement camp in Saxony and described how they had maintained their beauty and femininity under the duress of "intense" work. Although the women found the separation from family painful and the work strenuous, they did not regret the experience. They raved about the beauty of the northeast, Brüning wrote: "the midnight sun," "blueberries as large as grapes," "the colorful sky," "the northern lights," "the multiple rainbows."[145] Brüning's words expressed the press's obligatory positivity about events in the East and the actions of the Soviet Union, while keeping silent on the harsh reality of Russian repression.

Western publications addressed the Soviet's use of forced labour, using it to promote the superiority of their own zone. Women journalists had a role to play in such discourse.[146] In the winter of 1946, Ursula von Kardorff planned an article in the *Süddeutsche Zeitung* about German women returning from captivity in the East. The article focused on their fate in Russia and the psychological and physical toll of their experience.[147] Kardorff was a staunch anti-communist, and many of her post-war articles dealt with the victimization of Germans at the hands of the Soviets. The East German *Die Weltbühne* published a scathing response to Kardorff's article. Entitled "Unholy Ursula," the article referred to Kardorff's wartime writing, in particular her article promoting the role of women as *Flakhelferinnen* (see chapter 4). *Die Weltbühne* argued that Kardorff had encouraged women to take on the type of war work that had led to their eventual incarceration in the Soviet Union. Now, the article proclaimed, Kardorff cried "crocodile tears" for the women's fate that she had helped set in motion. According to the paper, anti-flak gunnery assistants were soldiers and, regardless of their gender, had to pay the price for their "military" actions in support of the Nazi war effort. The article also accused Kardorff of downplaying any "favorable statements" her interviewees may have expressed toward the the Soviet Union while highlighting "a torrent of unfavorable statements."[148] It also charged that Kardorff implicitly questioned why German women, far removed from Nazi politics, would be incarcerated at all.[149]

Kardorff's article and *Die Weltbühne*'s response embody Western and Eastern post-war rhetoric about gender and who bore responsibility for Nazi violence and its repercussions. In West Germany, women were viewed for decades after the war either as apolitical, and therefore not responsible for National Socialist crimes, or as primarily victims of Hitler's misogynistic regime. *Die Weltbühne* adopted the Soviet line that women were equal to men and therefore had to pay for alleged crimes in the same manner as men. The original article and the response reflected each region's attitude toward post-war justice as well their differing views of gender within the Third Reich and in the period of reconstruction.

The West linked communism to Nazism, given their totalitarian nature, while socialist rhetoric argued that Nazism derived from capitalism and that the return to the political and economic system of the Weimar Republic threatened the reappearance of fascism in West Germany. The East women's magazine *Für Dich* adopted this line with its articles on suffering in the "other" Germany. In the fall of 1946, for instance, the magazine addressed widespread hunger in the Western Zones and attributed it to capitalism and the inclusion of former Nazis in the administration of this sector. In "Hunger in the West," *Für Dich* claimed that the Western region "has tolerated the fact that the food industry of an entire country is still in the hands of the former Nazi imperial food empire."[150] According to *Für Dich*, the Soviet zone was helping fulfil the nutritional needs of the population in the Western region of Germany.[151] While Kardorff's writing depicted women as apolitical both during and after the Third Reich, *Für Dich* questioned why women in the Western Zones did not become politically active. "Why did the half-starved women not join forces long ago and demand the resignation of the Minister of Food Schlange-Schöningen, who is still deaf to the hunger of the population but has an open hand for to his aristocratic friends?" the article asked.[152]

In the midst of heightened Cold War tensions and the 1948 Berlin blockade, Kardorff wrote a piece that echoed Western views about the totalitarian nature of both the Nazi and communist regimes. In her writing, she depicted the Soviet zone as a mirror image of Nazi Germany and wrote of the victimization of all Berliners in the wake of the war and particularly during the Soviet blockade. She described a series of documents she had recently been shown about Germans deported to the Soviet Union as a "registry of horror." "This is the reality in Berlin," she wrote, "and this is the reality in the Eastern zone."[153] Her terminology called to mind German crimes in occupied Europe – "burned out apartments," "frozen in the east," "shot," "murdered," "gassed," "death in old and new Buchenwald," "transported," "impoverished" – but she applied them to the suffering of the German population.[154] Her text fit into the Cold War atmosphere in the West as she retooled language related to the Nazi regime and applied it the Soviet Union's treatment of Germans.

## Conclusion

Immediately after the war, it seemed that gender roles in both the Eastern and Western Zones were expanding and shifting, as were opportunities for women in journalism. Their transition to the post-war press, however, was uneven and not specifically tied to the nature of their Third Reich journalism or their entanglement with the Nazi regime. Adherence to the new political line seemed a more important factor in the reconstruction of a journalist's post-war career. Yet as Cold War dogma began to dominate the political sphere, women's roles in West Germany quickly reverted to more traditionally defined functions. In contrast, the East was (at least officially) committed ideologically to women's economic and political emancipation. Thus, ideas about women were central to both democratic and socialist discourse and formed an important part of the national identities of the FRG and

GDR. The careers and writing of women journalists in the Eastern Zone more clearly represented a break with traditional perspectives and rhetoric on gender. Nevertheless, in both halves of Germany, women were largely relegated to the areas of soft news, as they had been in the past.

In the FRG, these areas were constructed as apolitical – much as they had been characterized in the Third Reich – while, in the GDR, they were more overtly tied to politics. In this way, women journalists and their work came to symbolize the gender policies and perspectives of two rival states. At the same time, the confidence that all the Allies placed in the press as a vehicle for re-education, and the visibility the profession afforded, meant that female journalists, despite the seemingly harmless areas in which they worked, were more involved than most women in the Cold War. Through their writing, however, they were also actors in creating this context. Women's publications set East against West, as each used their counterpart's approach to the repercussions of the war to delegitimize the "other" Germany. While women journalists contributed to the processes of identity-building in the FRG and the GDR, it was the autobiographical writing of a small group of female jounalists that secured these women an important place in discourses about the Nazi past, particularly in the FRG and, later, in a reunified Germany.

## Chapter Seven

# Rewriting the Third Reich: Female Journalists, Autobiography, and the Legacies of National Socialism

The many millions of Germans who, in a situation of desperate poverty, sometimes misguided, sometimes blameless, came under the rule of a dictator whom they had never voted for by a majority, who first were led into oppression, then against their will entered into war and defeat, who often lost everything and now, at the end of the war, stood starving, helpless and disoriented, have, in my opinion, earned more understanding, more compassion than is often shown to them today.

Elisabeth Noelle-Neumann, *Die Erinnerungen*

Former journalist turned public opinion researcher Elisabeth Noelle-Neumann wrote these words in her 2006 memoir *Die Erinnerungen* (Memories).[1] Her memoir attempted to ensure a positive posthumous legacy for herself after she was accused in the US media of having been a Nazi supporter and antisemite, due to the nature of her Third Reich journalism.[2] Noelle-Neumann never acknowledged her entanglement with Nazi propaganda. Instead, in a 1997 interview she claimed that "I did my duty and would do my duty again in a second life. I'd even say I was proud of what I did back then because I opposed the Nazis by working from within."[3] Full of anecdotes about the inner opposition she supposedly expressed through her journalism, Noelle-Neumann's book attempted to rehabilitate not only its author, but also the press, and an entire generation of Germans who had lived under the Nazi regime.

Although *Die Erinnerungen* appeared decades after the war, when discussions of Germany's Nazi past had become commonplace, and tales of heroism and victimization were debated and disputed, the book reflects a larger and enduring historical trend. Immediately after the war, and throughout the following decades, women journalists published diaries, memoires, and articles about their experiences in Nazi Germany and during its collapse. Through four case studies, based on the texts of Ruth Andreas-Friedrich, Ursula von Kardorff, Margret Boveri, and Helene Rahms, this chapter examines the long-term impact of such autobiographical writing on discussions about the nature of the Third Reich and its memory, in West Germany and, later, a reunified Germany. Written by actors and witnesses to life in the Third Reich, the personal narratives of these female journalists provided a particularly powerful voice in the fashioning and durability of Germany's post-war image – an image founded on the dual notions of decency and victimhood. There is a rich vein of literature on the trope of victimization and heroism that emerged through various West German media after 1945 and on its impact on the country's national identity and bumpy path to "coming to terms with its past."[4] By analysing how gender influenced the portrayal and perception of moral agency after 1945, this chapter recovers the role that female journalists played in these processes.

Settled in what became the Federal Republic of Germany (FRG), these women produced some of the most famous autobiographical narratives by female journalists who had worked throughout the Third Reich.[5] As the West German publishing field became increasingly open, the East German public realm came under stringent state control. Unlike their counterparts in East Germany, then, women journalists in the FRG had the opportunity to publish works in which they attempted to exonerate themselves from responsibility for Nazi propaganda. Their writing included criticisms of the Allies, in particular the Soviets, which proved important to tales about the Nazi past and its ramifications. East German journalists who published autobiographical texts about their Third Reich experiences tended to do so after reunification. These works did not prove as popular in the academic or public realm as those of Friedrich, Kardorff, Boveri, and Rahms, which found a ready audience in the decades of, and after, the Cold War.[6]

Just as these women's contributions to the Nazi press differed, so too did their post-war acknowledgment of their own complicity. The texts also reflect distinct autobiographical styles and were published in different decades, each representing specific moments in Germany's navigation of its violent past and the national discourse this process engendered. Yet, irrespective of temporal and stylistic particularities, each woman offered a detailed depiction of Germany as a nation of victims and opponents of Nazism, alongside, to varying degrees, an acknowledgment of the country's crimes. The mixture of forgetting, distorting, and remembering in these narratives made their version of the past palatable to the German population and largely acceptable to an international audience. Tony Judt has argued that some measure of neglect of Nazism and violent upheaval in Europe was needed in the post-war years to ensure the civic health, reconstruction, and survival of democracy in Western Europe. A combination of forgetting or distorted memory in the political and economic spheres, with pockets for remembering in the cultural sphere, allowed for the rebuilding and stability of Europe.[7] A small group of women journalists contributed to this dual process of remembering and misremembering in West Germany by writing about Jewish persecution by the Nazi state, their gendered experiences in the Nazi press, and the purported spirit of resistance to, or at least non-compliance with, Nazi policies that existed in the German press throughout the course of the Third Reich.

A focus on the experiences and writing of individual journalists can reveal signs of frustration or dislike of Nazism. Volker Berghahn, for instance, has examined the personal and professional trajectories of Paul Sethe, Marion von Dönhoff, and Hans Zehrer to argue that each negotiated a thin line between adaptability and non-compliance in Nazi Germany. Berghahn determined that these same individuals then worked to confront Nazi crimes after 1945 and played a role in providing political and moral guidance to the FRG.[8] If one steps back to look at the bigger picture, however, the perspective changes. As the preceding chapters demonstrate, it was not only difficult, but virtually impossible, for journalists to retreat to a form of "inner emigration" – the act of psychologically distancing oneself from Nazism while remaining in the country – and remain disentangled from Nazi policies, incentives, and propaganda goals, whatever individuals' personal preferences and beliefs, and irrespective of the areas in which they wrote. As we have seen, Ruth Andreas-Friedrich is one example of a journalist who detested the regime but still served it by way of her journalism.

Friedrich, Kardorff, Boveri, and Rahms presented, and represented, an appealing narrative that combined suffering and rejuvenation. Because they offered "both sides of the story," their work had the appearance – albeit to varying degrees – of fairness and balance and fit into changing discussions of Germany's past throughout the post-war decades. Their personal narratives functioned as a mechanism to allow the population to sidestep a sense of national or personal shame over the war and the Holocaust, and also as a small release for that shame. As women, they were not publicly lauded as heroes for their opposition to the Nazi regime, in the manner of some male journalists such as Theodor Heuss and Sebastian Haffner; nor were they associated with the crimes of the Nazis and punished as villains, as were Julius Streicher and Otto Dietrich. On the stage of Germany's post-war transition, these four women did not operate entirely behind the scenes, but neither did they occupy leading roles. From the wings, they played a subtle part in the creation and maintenance of a positive post-war image for the FRG and, later, for a reunified Germany.

The narratives of these four women had a powerful and sustained impact on the presentation of Germany's Nazi past for three reasons: their status as women, their status as journalists, and their chosen genre of autobiography. The ways in which these women presented aspects of journalism and everyday life in the Third Reich were not, for the most part, unique: male journalists, too, described why and how they were not entangled with Nazism. But, unlike their male counterparts, women could claim the status of being "outside of politics" and/or victims during the Third Reich, based either on their journalistic activities or their gender, and they referred to Nazi gender ideology to strengthen this claim. The idea that all women were repressed by Nazi gender politics was a widely held belief that lasted decades after the war. By leveraging this idea, women journalists could make a representative and more powerful statement than most men, who could speak only to their individual circumstances.

A journalist's importance in the public sphere means that individuals in the field command a certain authority and cultural capital: they have the professional status, skills, and contacts to affect public opinion and reach domestic and overseas audiences. As a result, journalists' arguments that their country was a victim of National Socialism carry considerably more weight than similar claims from "ordinary" Germans. Unlike most German women, these four journalists enjoyed a public role, had domestic and foreign contacts in the press, and could expect that their work would be published and reviewed. Based on their professions, they also enjoyed the status of "observer." Thus, they could speak on behalf of the population about everyday experiences within the Third Reich; they presented a past that was not just their own, and they did so as seemingly objective witnesses. As journalists, they also symbolized democracy in the form of freedom of the press – a right firmly embedded in the Basic Law (the constitution) and one that West German citizens came to value after the press controls under the Third Reich. These women's message that the Nazi press, or at least elements within it, had been a breeding ground for opposition strengthened the idea that the post-war press would represent and act as a guarantor of free speech within a democratic system.

The women's use of the autobiographical genre was an important aspect of the positive reception their narratives received. Autobiography, regardless of the degree to which it distorts truth, offers readers a compelling narrative that merges history with literature and provides a sense of "having been there." In other words, the genre makes history accessible and appealing. Moreover, all four women focused on their experiences in Berlin, the former Nazi capital, which continued to hold importance and fascination throughout the Cold War, and with the fall of the Berlin Wall in 1989 and the reunification of Germany in 1990.

The journalists considered here utilized their profession and their professional skills for their own purposes and on behalf of West Germany. Ruth Andreas-Friedrich was primarily concerned with eliciting understanding from the international community for Germany itself. Ursula von Kardorff, Margret Boveri, and Helene Rahms wanted postwar audiences to understand the challenges they had faced in their experiences as female journalists within the Third Reich and sought to exonerate themselves from an affiliation with Nazi propaganda. Presenting the journalistic profession as a stronghold of opposition to the regime strengthened this narrative.

## Ruth Andreas-Friedrich (1901–1977)

In the foreword to her diary, published first in the United States in early 1947 as *Berlin Underground* and shortly afterwards in Berlin, Ruth Andreas-Friedrich wrote the following:

> Germany today is the bad child of the world. The tendency is to identify the whole people with the outrages of its leaders. Yet thousands upon thousands had nothing whatever to do with those outrages. On the contrary, year in and year out they risked life and liberty – with no help from foreign nations – to serve humanity wherever they could ... May it go out into the world to testify that there were human beings living even under Hitler in Germany – human beings who do not deserve to be despised along with their whole nation, because of an irresponsible government. If that be accomplished, these notes will have fulfilled their purpose by helping in some small measure to raise the German people a hairsbreadth from [their] present low degree in the eyes of the world.[9]

As these words indicate, Friedrich wrote and sought to publish her diary in the hope that it would help alter the world's view of Germans after the collapse of the Third Reich. Already in November 1945, the United States Information Control Division (ICD) had cleared Friedrich as "nicht betroffen" (unaffected) by Nazism and issued her a licence to publish a women's magazine titled *Sie*. Consistent with the Nazis' narrative about the "soft" nature of female journalism, the

ICD's report stated that, during her career in Nazi Germany, Friedrich had written only on themes that were "of an unpolitical nature." It did note, however, that two of her books "commended Nazi institutions," including the League of German Girls (Bund Deutscher Mädel).[10] Friedrich received this apolitical declaration with regard to her work, in spite of her editorship of *Kamerad Frau* – a magazine that included overt antisemitic articles. ICD officials did not refer to Friedrich's involvement with *Kamerad Frau* after the war because it considered her to be precisely the type of figure they wanted as a conduit to the German population.

American assumptions about women and the nature of women's journalism during the Third Reich, as well as Friedrich's wartime involvement in the resistance group Uncle Emil, can help explain this silence. Prior to and during the war, Friedrich and a close circle of family and friends assisted Jewish and other Germans in danger by providing hiding places, documents, and food. Friedrich was eventually honoured by Yad Vashem as a Righteous among the Nations for her bravery.[11] Wartime and post-war correspondence between Friedrich and those she had helped demonstrates not only the risks that she had taken to provide such aid, but also the ongoing gratitude of those she had helped save.[12] Despite serving the regime in a journalistic capacity, Friedrich loathed Nazism and privately fought to resist it – a record that gave her autobiographical writing added authority and veracity for non-German audiences.

Despite the fact that she was an active journalist, it was through the publication of *Berlin Underground, 1938–1945* that Friedrich became an important and well-known voice in post-war discourses about Germany's Nazi past. Her intention was to draw a distinction between the Nazi regime and the country as a whole and to highlight what she viewed as the "good" Germany that fell victim to Nazism. It is therefore not surprising that she included little about her journalistic work in the book, nor did she mention her position at *Kamerad Frau*. Friedrich used her transatlantic connections to get her message about Germany out to a larger audience. Indeed, she deliberately sought to publish abroad before releasing the book in Germany.[13] In late 1945, she sent her manuscript, based on her wartime diary, through an American press officer to a friend in the United States, who, in turn, forwarded it to the Jewish-German émigré author Carl Zuckmayer, who recommended the manuscript to New York publisher Henry Holt.[14] When *Berlin Underground* appeared in the United States in early 1947, it was the first post-war book that Holt had published by a German who had not emigrated from Nazi Germany.

According to Friedrich, in the summer of 1938 she decided she would become a witness to this "good" Germany. While on a trip to Sweden, Friedrich had tried to speak with Rosalind von Ossietzky, the daughter of the deceased German pacifist and publisher Carl von Ossietzky.[15] But, after learning that Friedrich did not intend to leave Germany, Rosalind refused to speak with her. It was at that moment, Friedrich asserted, that she decided to keep a diary. She believed that, at some point, Germans would face the difficult task of having to "prove to those outside that not every German who stayed in Germany was a Nazi."[16] In other words, Friedrich viewed her diary as a testimony that would later help facilitate understanding between Germans and the international community.

In the aftermath of the war, Friedrich wrote of her intention to rehabilitate the reputation of those who, like her, had remained in Germany throughout the Third Reich. On 23 August 1945, she noted that she was pleased to meet Americans as often as she could, since it allowed for opportunities to show the victors that Germans were no different from other people.[17] For Friedrich, it was crucial that Germany be viewed as more than "a country comprised of just Nazis and antisemites."[18] She sought to achieve this goal by documenting the escalating persecution of Jews and the actions that she and others took to assist Jewish friends and acquaintances. In an entry dated 19 September 1941, Friedrich bemoaned how Jews were forced to wear the yellow Star of David. She also documented the regime's appropriation of Jewish apartments and the ensuing deportations. "To Jewish concentration camps in Poland, some predict. To certain death say others," she wrote.[19] In both precise and emotive ways, *Berlin Underground* provided not only an early post-war testimony about Jewish oppression, but also acknowledged that some Germans did know what was transpiring.

Friedrich's text also distanced the journalistic profession and the country as a whole from the stigma of Nazism by attributing responsibility for the escalating crimes against Jewish Germans to only a handful of Nazis. Several passages depict fellow journalists, and indeed most Germans, as either mortified by the regime or as heroically assisting Jews. By Friedrich's account, the morning after *Kristallnacht*, on 9 November 1938, her journalist colleagues discussed the pogrom and the deep shame they felt, with her editor purportedly lamenting, "My dear girl, I shan't live through this. We ought to be so ashamed we could sink into the floor. Synagogues – houses of God – temples of the Lord simply soaked down with gasoline."[20] Friedrich wrote that her publisher had joined the Nazi Party only to have access to party bigwigs because they might prove useful at some stage.[21] In post-war Germany,

Friedrich's insinuation that even some Nazis were not "real" Nazis was useful to journalists and the population at large. Coming from a figure like Friedrich, who had an established record as a Nazi opponent and who had garnered respect from US occupation authorities, such a suggestion could help legitimate the claims of others that they joined the party for noble or selfless reasons.

In Friedrich's narrative, much of the non-Jewish German population strove to help Jews during the war. In June 1942, nine months after the deportations to the East had begun, she noted that many Germans were helping to feed Jews: "A great many people with guilty looks are lugging shopping nets full of vegetables through the streets of Berlin."[22] As the end of the war loomed, she claimed that "we who are in our eleventh year under Hitler's dominion have little cause to boast. But, if ever anyone risked his life for his Jewish brothers, it has been the German Aryans – hundreds, thousands, tens of thousands, risking their necks every day and every hour."[23] Friedrich and her small circle certainly took risks to help Jewish Germans. Yet her book constructed for US and German readers a myth of widespread German resistance to Jewish persecution. As later accounts would show, this depiction distorted reality: much of the population was, at best, apathetic to Jewish suffering.[24]

Friedrich also contributed to the popular idea that Hitler had led unwilling and victimized Germans to the abyss, a view that reimagined the level of support the Nazis had enjoyed from much of the population. In Friedrich's view, Germans had twice been victims: first of a chaotic interwar period, and then of the Nazi regime. She wrote that Germans had tolerated Nazism only because they had "feared for their livelihood, for the life and welfare of their wives and children. Because they were afraid of hunger and unemployment, of denunciations, the Gestapo, the scaffold."[25] Friedrich also advanced the notion of "inner emigration." Such a concept could reasonably be applied to Friedrich, but her words on this subject also helped legitimize it for droves of Germans who claimed the same in the post-war years. The question was perhaps especially critical for journalists, because former colleagues who had fled the country when Hitler came to power returned and took up positions in the post-war press. The returning émigrés provided a moral counterbalance to those who had stayed and had enjoyed successful careers in Nazi Germany.

While, given her actions, Friedrich's claim that she had remained in Germany out of a sense of duty rings true, her diary implied that those who suffered the most under the regime were those who stayed – not the émigrés who had fled, often in fear for their lives. Angered by radio broadcasts from Thomas Mann urging Germans to "get out on the barricades," Friedrich wrote in February 1944: "No one who does not himself live in the country and suffer from the country has any idea what it means to be bound with the chains of dictatorship. Those who did not leave here until after 1933 know least of all and forgot the soonest. That is why we bear most of our émigrés such a grudge," she continued, "because they demand of us what they themselves could not accomplish."[26]

Friedrich presented a view of Germans as resisters and victims, but, importantly, she also spoke about German responsibility for Nazism. In an entry from February 1943, she discussed the recent massive roundup of the remaining Jews in Berlin, describing an English bombing raid as retribution for "the monstrous deed." She criticized the German population's focus on its own suffering and its inability to connect its support of the regime to its present circumstance: "From cause to effect is a long road. Very few people know enough to follow it," she noted.[27] As reviews of her book suggested, Friedrich's description of such events presented a seemingly objective balance that, in the eyes of US occupation authorities and audiences, lent her work credibility that went beyond her status as a woman and member of a resistance group.

In the mid to late 1940s, the German press was not (yet) silent about German atrocities committed during the war. German newspapers covered the Nuremberg trials more intensively than later war crimes proceedings. Whether they would have done so if the Allies had not been in control of the press is another question.[28] In their reporting of the trials, however, German journalists tended to place responsibility for German crimes on a small gang of Nazi criminals, which gave ordinary Germans an opportunity to absolve themselves of guilt and responsibility. In addition, the trials did not focus on the genocide of the Jews as a specific and separate part of Nazi atrocities. Friedrich's narrative not only fit into but also expanded this type of media discourse.

Friedrich's book struck a balance between the presentation of German crimes and the suffering of ordinary Germans in a manner that was both acceptable and appealing to Germans, US press authorities in Germany, and American audiences at home. The ICD generally sought to curb the publication of material that focused too heavily on German suffering. The American *Fair Practice Guide for German Journalists* acknowledged the difficult circumstances the population faced but warned that "editorial writers in particular should remember the theme of 'poor suffering Germany' was so overworked by Nationalist and Nazi propaganda before and during the Third Reich." "A better solution," it advised, "is good, honest journalism, free of sarcasm, nagging, cajolery, yelled threats and whining. Understatement is more effective than overstatement."[29] Still, the ICD did take steps to ensure that what was published was well received by Germans.[30] Friedrich's narrative satisfied both criteria.

Little is known about the editing process of Friedrich's diary before publication, including the degree of input editors at Henry Holt may have had on the final text.[31] The nature of her text does suggest post-war editing. She does not record any fear about keeping a diary or describe the logistics of hiding it. There is no repetition in the text, and Friedrich presents herself as remarkably astute with regard to the steps the regime took to isolate and persecute Jewish Germans and, later, the course of the war.[32] At the same time, editing was likely not extensive, given that the diaries were translated and published just over a year from their submission. In addition, letters written about Friedrich to Yad Vashem from those she had helped during the war corroborate diary entries in which she described the actions of Uncle Emil to aid the persecuted.[33]

Irrespective of whether it was composed largely during or immediately after the collapse of the Third Reich, what is clear is that *Berlin Underground* enjoyed a positive reception and that Friedrich's narrative about everyday life in National Socialist Berlin endured. The book was republished multiple times in English and German, most recently in 2000.[34] In addition, extracts were used in articles about the German war experience, including a popular series that appeared in *Die Welt* in 1962, *Chronik unserer schwersten Tage* (Chronicle of our most difficult days). In his introduction to Friedrich's book, US journalist and war correspondent Joel Sayre, who covered the final days of the war in Germany for the *New Yorker*, praised her work and noted how Germans like Friedrich could help build a bridge of reconciliation between the two wartime foes: "We, the people of the United States, have undertaken to educate the Germans under our control in the best ways of our democracy. If we are ever to get anywhere with such a staggering project, it is with Germans like Ruth and her friends that we must work."[35] Reviews, in publications ranging from the *New York Times* to small academic journals, presented American audiences with similarly positive assessments of her work. They lauded Friedrich's presentation of a good Germany and the supposed authenticity of her words. Her writing skills, and her status as a resister and woman journalist who wrote on supposedly apolitical issues, ensured that – as historian Hans Rothfels, a German émigré, noted in his 1948 book *The German Opposition to Hitler* – her work had "all the ring of truth."[36]

Friedrich's views may have been particularly well received in the United States because of the context in which her work appeared. As the Cold War developed, the Soviet Union quickly replaced Germany as the West's enemy – a shift that provided fertile ground for a narrative depicting German victimization and heroism. In a rapid readjustment of their perspective on Nazi Germany, US occupation forces and the American public quickly "feminized" the defeated country and cast themselves in the role of the "masculine" provider and protector. This sentiment would aid in making US audiences more receptive to the autobiographical works of German women journalists in the following decades.[37] The fact that American views on Nazi Germany prior to and even throughout the war were mixed and often generous helped precipitate this quick realignment and likely the enthusiastic reception of Friedrich's book.[38] Around the same time that *Berlin Underground* first appeared in the United States and Germany, US president Harry Truman announced the eponymous doctrine designed to fight Soviet expansionism. In 1948, the United States also began a massive aid program under the Marshall Plan to assist European economic recovery and reduce the appeal of communism. The Berlin blockade and airlift, an important event in establishing Germany as a victim in the eyes of the West, began in June 1948, and Friedrich's book was published in England that same year.[39]

During the blockade, US occupation authorities actively sought to present Berlin as a victim of the Soviets and, coincidently, used *Sie* – the woman's magazine that Friedrich had co-founded but had since left – as a vehicle to transmit their message. The July 1948 issue included a pictorial supplement titled "Berlin, a Fight for Freedom" that had been prepared by the US Information Control Division. The ICD recommended that an English version be distributed in the United States in order to gain American sympathy and support for West Berliners.[40] Articles profiled refugees who had fled from the communist East and detailed the fear in which those in the Eastern Zone continued to live. Captions and pictures in the supplement especially emphasized women's suffering and fortitude.[41] The depiction of women as particular victims of "totalitarian" repression during and after the Third Reich gained audiences in both Germany and the United States. Ursula von Kardorff devoted much of her writing to this claim.

## Ursula von Kardorff (1911–1988)

In the immediate post-war years, Ursula von Kardorff also sought to improve Germany's image abroad. At the same time, she wanted to distance her journalistic activities during the Third Reich from any connection with Nazi propaganda. She did so through press articles and an autobiographical narrative that emphasized Germany's – especially women's – heroism and suffering at the hands of the Nazis and later the Allies. As she communicated to friends and colleagues during the war, Kardorff was not always given a choice about, and was not always pleased with, the topics on which was assigned to write.[42] Given the nature of the press in the Third Reich, it is not surprising that Kardorff was sometimes tasked with writing on subjects that she found unsavoury. Still, she did have some flexibility, given that instructions issued to the press centred more on what journalists were forbidden to write, rather than on what they must write.[43] Later in the war, many of her articles focused on the bravery and resilience of German women amidst the bombings. In the immediate post-war years, when she enjoyed more freedom of choice, Kardorff addressed topics ranging from the hardships of expellees, widows, and prisoners of war to trends in fashion and decorating.[44] As discussed in chapter 4, during the Third Reich her articles depicted Nazism as a vehicle for female empowerment. After the war she emphasized women's victimization at the hands of the regime and the war it had waged.

Despite the importance of the topics on which she wrote during the Nazi period and after, Kardorff depicted herself as apolitical.[45] In personal and professional correspondence, she discussed her distaste for what she described as "political women."[46] Kardorff freelanced for the *Süddeutsche*'s culture editor, Franz Joseph Schöningh, with whom she shared the view that the German population had suffered greatly under Hitler and continued to do so under the Allies.[47] The nature of Kardorff's journalism in the mid-1940s and 1950s and her claim to be apolitical corresponded to Schöningh's perspective on the past and his view of women journalists. In 1946, he assigned Kardorff to cover the Nuremberg trials because he wanted a female correspondent who would offer a different perspective than a male journalist. No background in politics was required, he emphasized.[48] Kardorff's writing on the trials reveals the contradictory nature of her thinking. She appeared distressed by the horrors committed by, and in the name of, Germans, and confronted those atrocities in her articles. Yet much of her work placed responsibility for such crimes in the hands of only a few. In one piece, she noted that nothing the defendants could say would "bridge the abyss of guilt and despair into which the German people have been thrown."[49] On the surface, Kardorff's work acknowledged German responsibility, but the underlying message was that only a small circle had been responsible for leading Germany to that abyss.

In the early post-war years, Kardorff received foreign newspapers from acquaintances abroad and was well aware of international opinion about her country. Like Friedrich, she too turned to her transatlantic contacts in her effort to influence the world's view of Germany. During or shortly after the Berlin Blockade, Kardorff forwarded a series of articles that she had written about the living conditions of West Berliners to Hans Wolfgang Schwerin, a Jewish-German émigré living in New York: "I would be pleased if you happen to know of a German [language] newspaper over there that would be interested." She stressed that no payment would be necessary as long as the publication of the articles "did anything to encourage understanding for Berliners."[50]

Although a prominent journalist, Kardorff became best known for her book *Berliner Aufzeichnungen aus den Jahren 1942 bis 1945*, referred to and promoted as a diary. It was based on her wartime notes, personal correspondence, and post-war feedback from friends and colleagues in Germany and abroad.[51] Like Friedrich, Kardorff wanted *Berliner Aufzeichnungen* to solicit more understanding for Germany and help her country improve its reputation. She also felt that it was important to offer a narrative of Germany's wartime experience from a woman's perspective.[52] Kardorff hoped to publish her manuscript abroad first and initiated communication with contacts in Switzerland, Great Britain, and the United States to that end. She sent a rough draft of her manuscript to a contact in England, noting that, "most of all, I would like it to be published abroad in order to awaken more understanding for our disastrous fate."[53] In 1947, Kardorff wrote to a friend that the purpose of her book was to "make something of the German situation clear to the idiotic *Ausland*, which does not grasp anything about it."[54]

The book was not published abroad or in Germany until the early 1960s. Several factors contributed to this delay. First, Kardorff was reluctant to publish in Germany right after the war because she feared a backlash to her positive depiction of the 20 July plotters: in the immediate post-war years, a considerable segment of the German population continued to view the attempted assassination as treason. She also worried that the book's focus on the German aristocracy – the circles in which Kardorff moved – "would not please the masses."[55] When Kardorff sent the manuscript to a German publishing house for feedback in 1948, the publisher encouraged her to continue to work on it. In its present state, he could not envision much interest beyond her "narrow circle" of friends and associates.[56] Kardorff's aristocratic lineage and the nature of her manuscript initially also hampered her chances of publishing abroad. One US reviewer expressed concern about Kardorff's limited experience of the war, given that she was a privileged aristocrat and had not known the experiences of those in working-class districts.[57]

Kardorff also presented a far more problematic figure than Friedrich because of her nationalism and the nature of her journalism during the Third Reich. She was shut out of the Nuremberg trial proceedings for a short time by a US press officer because he deemed her article on Albert Speer too nationalistic.[58] But, since it had been American press authorities who had cleared Kardorff to cover the trials in the first place, she was soon allowed to return.[59] In 1948, the American-sponsored paper *Die Neue Zeitung* reneged on an offer of employment to Kardorff, in response to a critique by the Soviet Zone's *Weltbühne* about the nationalistic nature of some of her wartime articles.[60] The US control officer in charge wrote to Kardorff:

> I have read the articles carefully and regret to have to inform you that in view of this we can no longer claim your services. I admit that this is embarrassing for me, and probably for you as well, but I hope that you will understand that we, an organization of the Military Government, must be particularly careful in the selection of our German employees with regard to their political and ideological past. I believe you could have been given some concessions had your articles been written in the early stages of the war, but to my surprise they appeared in 1944, even as late as November 15.[61]

In addition to these concerns, Kardorff was anxious about the quality of her manuscript, and she continued to massage it until its publication. Throughout the 1940s and 1950s, she sent it to several friends and colleagues in Germany and abroad for feedback. In numerous letters she described to them her lack of confidence and her ongoing struggle with the book.[62]

*Berliner Aufzeichnungen* was first published in Germany in 1962 and in the United States in 1966 under the title *Diary of a Nightmare: Berlin, 1942–1945*. It received rave reviews in both countries. The book was republished in German in 1976 and again in 1992, shortly after German reunification. *Berliner Aufzeichnungen* combined the genres of literary work, diary, and memoir, with Kardorff's wartime notes providing its foundation. Prior to the publication of the 1992 edition, journalist and historian Peter Hartl compared the finished product with Kardorff's original diary, notes, and wartime correspondence. While Hartl confirmed that the finished product was "not a faithful transcription," he deemed it "a reliable and authentic testimony of the atmosphere and attitude to life in the Nazi era."[63] Some original entries did contain a disdain for Nazism and coded concern for Jewish Germans. In an entry from 30 October 1942, for instance, Kardorff recorded that she had encountered "a poor, old Jewish woman on the street with a young girl. Both with the star."[64] In September 1943, she critiqued the futility of the war: "Almost every fifth day we give up another city in the East that had been conquered with so much blood. Did Jürgen [her brother] have to die for that? … Perhaps this is the beginning of the end of this all too crass nationalism."[65]

As Hartl and others (myself included) discovered, however, the book contains passages for which there are no equivalents in the handwritten records. It was only after the war that Kardorff added important scenarios and viewpoints that reviewers praised. In the first edition, she included "flashbacks" that expressed her hatred for the Nazis, as well as references to Jewish persecution and the aid that she and others provided.[66] This is a complicated issue to navigate. Overt anti-Nazi statements, admissions of assisting Jews, or discussions of resistance activities were terribly risky to document in a diary. Peter Hartl argues that, in writing *Berliner Aufzeichnungen*, Kardorff "deciphered carefully formulated allusions, put unspoken ulterior motives into words, opened up connections without which the diary text would have revealed only half the truth to an uninitiated reader."[67] There are some credible examples of such incidences. In the finished book, Kardorff recounted an argument between war correspondent and SS member Hans Schwarz van Berk and the lawyer Konrad Zweigert. She describes how Zweigert angrily critiqued the Nazi regime and the war it waged. The original entry reads "Krach [Clash] Zweigert Schwarz."[68] Since most diarists would not have compromised others by including full names and recounting anti-Nazi statements, Kardorff's original note can be read as a coded reference to the dispute.

Yet Hartl's claim is not entirely convincing. Kardorff made other alterations during the post-war years that were entirely self-serving. She changed all references from the "Führer" to "Hitler," which helped to make the manuscript more acceptable to an audience outside Germany and further disassociated her from Nazism. She removed nationalistic statements and made no mention of her work for the Nazi paper *Der Angriff* or her brother Klaus's membership in the Storm Troopers (SA). No corresponding notes exist to corroborate her descriptions of her own, her family's, or her friends' assistance to German Jews. Moreover, as Axel Schildt has shown, some of Kardorff's correspondence into the 1960s contained hints of antisemitism.[69] This does not negate the possibility that she and her family helped Jewish acquaintances, but we may never know whether such aid took place and, if so, to what extent. The nature of Kardorff's correspondence about her draft manuscript suggests that she was very aware of what would – and would not – appeal to an international audience. She understood that one's anti-Nazi credentials could be used as a post-war negotiating tool to gain legitimacy or favours. According to Kardorff, no matter how distasteful, "one now has to make a kind of trade in these things … and thereby gain advantages."[70]

Kardorff sought to use *Berliner Aufzeichnungen* not only to improve Germany's post-war reputation, but also to secure her own. This helps explain why she highlighted her professional focus on culture, everyday life, and "women's topics" during the Third Reich. Doing so was meant to demonstrate that she had avoided political discussion and had therefore not been complicit with the dissemination of Nazi propaganda. In an entry dated February 1945, but which was added at some point after the war, Kardorff wrote: "So this is the end of six years' work. I hope that during those years I never sold out to the Promi [Propaganda Ministry] and that I never wrote anything really opposed to my convictions. Anyhow, I had the good fortune to be working in features, which saved me from having to do a lot of unpleasant things."[71] In addition to presenting herself as a journalist uncompromised by Nazism, she portrayed the newspaper for which she worked in the same manner. She described the *Deutsche Allgemeine Zeitung* as a newspaper read by Germans but not Nazis.[72] Kardorff dated this passage 12 May 1943 but, in fact, she added it after the war, and no similar entry is recorded in her original notes.

Her treatment of former SS member Hans Schwarz van Berk demonstrates her attempt to rehabilitate the reputation of a colleague closely tied to the regime – and, by extension, to redeem the German press more generally. In 1962, she received a letter from Joachim Friedrich Goldman, asking about the wartime record of Schwarz van Berk, who had been a close colleague of Joseph Goebbels as well as the editor of *Der Angriff* at the time Kardorff joined the paper as a volunteer. The Nazis' "most prominent journalist," Goldman wrote, was now working as an advertising consultant for a group of manufacturers. A Jewish member of the group was seeking evidence against Schwarz van Berk's appointment. After learning that Kardorff had featured Schwarz van Berk in the recently published *Berliner Aufzeichnungen*, Goldman hoped that she would testify about his "inglorious past."[73]

"I don't think I have ever answered a letter so quickly," Kardorff responded. "He [Schwarz van Berk] was in the Waffen SS and also a journalist for [the newspaper] *Das Reich*. He was a Nazi, but one of the most upstanding that I knew."[74] Kardorff attested to Schwarz van Berk's supposed decency, noting that she and others had been open with him about their anti-Nazi views. She emphasized that he had not tried to return to journalism and was no longer engaged in politics – "not because of a bad conscience," Kardorff stressed, "but rather because, I believe, he had already seen and realized how gruesome everything was."[75] Although there are indications in her wartime correspondence that she and her close circle were able to talk somewhat frankly in front of Schwarz van Berk, Kardorff did not address details about his wartime activities in her letter. Despite having witnessed German atrocities on the Eastern front, for instance, Schwarz van Berk had written virulent articles describing Soviet citizens in dehumanizing terms. Kardorff also failed to mention that he had remained a committed Nazi to the bitter end, and that he had encouraged Germans to continue fighting to avoid occupation by a supposedly inferior race.[76] Kardorff's defence of her former colleague as a "good" Nazi mirrored Friedrich's description of a professional circle in which most journalists, even those who belonged to the party, were, if not disdainful of Nazism themselves, certainly tolerant of those who were.

If Kardorff sought to distance herself and other journalists from the Nazi regime through her writing, she also hoped to elicit sympathy for the German people. To that end, she described what she viewed as wartime and post-war injustices against the Germans, first by the Nazi regime and then by the Allies. She wrote about the reach of the Gestapo, the bombings, the nature of the Allied occupation, and what she considered to be Allied hypocrisy:

> Dr. Meier said that when the war was over, we would be horribly punished and that the Allies would resort to measures that would affect every one of us. Of course, we do bear a dreadful weight of guilt, but so do the others – for instance, the British and Americans, who made it so difficult for the Jews who were trying to escape from Germany to enter their countries. They have no right to sit in judgement on us.[77]

Kardorff's presentation of women's experiences in the war and its aftermath provide a telling example of how her book helped create, legitimize, and maintain the idea that women had been innocent victims of Nazism, while providing a small space for acknowledging Germany's crimes. In Kardorff's presentation, the war and its consequences belonged to men; Germany's resurgence would belong to its women. "Perhaps we women now face our hardest job … to give understanding, comfort, support, and courage to so many utterly defeated men," she wrote in the summer of 1945, thereby associating Germany's defeat with men and the courage to move forward with women.[78] Kardorff wrote of the hardship women faced due to the war and the violence they experienced at the hands of Soviet soldiers. Historians have documented that the Red Army perpetrated extreme brutality toward the German population, most notably through the mass rape of women. Soviet violence in Germany was motivated by a series of factors, including a desire for revenge against German atrocities perpetrated in the Soviet Union.[79] Women's experiences came to symbolize the rape of Germany by the Soviet Union and German victimhood in general.[80] Kardorff's numerous references to the Soviets helped create and support this appropriation. Her 23 September 1945 diary entry reads:

> All the women here aged more than thirty look old, sad, and broken. "Come here, woman." The cry that rang through the city when the victors decided to rape, loot, and shoot anyone they chose still rings in everybody's ears. Hitler and his war have broken down the dam, which protected us. The red flood, which threatens to swamp half of Germany, is his doing.[81]

Kardorff's text placed the blame for Germany's current situation on a small group of Nazis. At the same time, her words "red flood" depicted the Soviets as uncivilized and inferior to Germans, a common trope in Nazi propaganda.

Juxtaposed with Kardorff's depiction of the German plight was her portrait of German heroism and sacrifice during the war. In the postwar years, publicizing the 20 July 1944 assassination attempt on Hitler became Kardorff's personal mission, and *Berliner Aufzeichnungen* her tool. Much of her writing focused on the valour of the conspirators, the price they paid for their actions, and the impact such bravery should have in Germany and abroad.[82] Already in August 1945, she described an English radio program about the assassination attempt: "Beautifully made, not even the most crazed propagandist could have done it better." "I believe it to be a quasi-duty of mine," she continued "to provide a sweeping advertisement for these types of things."[83] Kardorff had a personal stake in publicizing the heroism of this group. As a member of the Prussian aristocracy, she was socially acquainted with the small circle of army officers that planned the assassination attempt. She played a minor role in the aftermath by delivering a message to a conspirator's wife and was questioned by the Gestapo.[84]

Yet Kardorff also addressed German crimes. She drew particular attention to the persecution and murder of European Jews, and her original diary and wartime correspondence indicates that, as a German, she felt some guilt at the time. On 3 April 1933, two days after the regime launched its boycott of Jewish business, Kardorff wrote to a friend: "Yesterday was so gruesome that we just sat and cried. It's a disgrace that one has to watch this without being able to help."[85] She also continued to visit Martha Liebermann, the Jewish widow of artist Max Liebermann, until the spring of 1943, when the eighty-five-year-old committed suicide prior to her deportation.[86] But in her frequent comparisons of wartime Jewish experiences and post-war non-Jewish ones, Kardorff suggested that Germans had suffered from the war just as much as Jews. In one case, Kardorff described a conversation with US military personnel in July 1945, writing that Americans seemed naive: "When you are with them you suddenly feel burdened with the weight of centuries, old as the hills and complicated – a feeling which, apart from ourselves, perhaps only the Jews experience. What a similarity there is between the Germans and the Jews."[87]

Kardorff's thoughts on injustice were clearly related to her status as a member of the Prussian nobility (*Junkers*). She frequently complained that the occupying powers hated the *Junkers*, and she compared their post-war situation with that of German Jews during the Third Reich. When completing an American questionnaire in July 1945, Kardorff was scornful of the questions: "Among other things they wanted to know … whether our forebears had ever had any titles of nobility … In the old days, a Jewish grandmother was the thing not to have had, but now the same applies to an aristocratic one."[88] Kardorff had written about the questionnaire in her original diary notes but added the sentence about "a Jewish grandmother" specifically for the book – an addition that indicates her desire to underscore the notion of German victimhood by comparing the suffering of Germans with those of European Jews.

A number of years elapsed between when Kardorff began to prepare her manuscript for publication and its eventual appearance. The reception of her work demonstrates how a woman journalist's words reflected and informed several discursive trends about the Nazi past that developed in the immediate post-war years and in the 1960s. After initial discussion during the Nuremberg trials, the German political, academic, and public spheres were relatively – although not completely – silent during the late 1940s and 1950s about German crimes committed under National Socialism. The Federal Republic did take some early steps to redress Third Reich atrocities, such as the 1952 Luxembourg agreement, which provided restitution to Israel. Yet, media discussion about the war and its aftermath focused largely on the German experience.[89]

This was a time when, in the words of Raul Hilberg, "the destruction of the European Jews has not yet been absorbed as a historical event."[90]

It was not until the late 1950s and early 1960s that West Germany began slowly to confront its violent past. The Central Office of the State Justice Adminstrations for the Investigation of National Socialist Crimes (Zentrale Stelle der Landesjustizverwaltungen zur Aufklärung nationalsozialistischer Verbrechen) was established in Ludwigsburg in 1958. The West German Einsatzgruppen trial took place in Ulm that same year.[91] The 1961 Eichmann trial attracted global media interest and sparked more discussion about the Holocaust in the United States and Germany. The Auschwitz trials that took place in Frankfurt between 1963 and 1965 also marked a significant change in the German perspective on the war. Whereas the German population viewed the Nuremberg trials largely as a victor's justice, there was no such concern over the Frankfurt process, because the defendants were judged by the German justice system.[92] While these events increased awareness of the crimes against European Jews, the building of the Berlin Wall in August 1961 heightened the Cold War and reinforced the view of West Germans that they were victims of the Soviets – a view shared by many Americans. The publication of Kardorff's book and its reception need to be situated in this context of renewed discussion about German victimization as well as an emerging focus on the Holocaust. *Berliner Aufzeichnungen* spoke to both German victimization and German crimes against European Jews. At the same time, Kardorff's criticisms of the Soviet Union and her fears of communist aggression chimed with contemporary US and West German opinion.

Widely reviewed at the time, Kardorff's book found a receptive audience in Germany and the United States. Her account of the Nazi period and of the war years was lauded for its supposed honesty and candour. Reviewers emphasized the fact that Kardorff was a female journalist, implying that this identity made her take on Germany's wartime experience particularly believable. *Berliner Aufzeichnungen* was on the bestseller list in Germany for several weeks in 1962 and, like Friedrich's text, ran in the popular series *Chronik unserer schwersten Tage*.[93] The *Neue Zürcher Zeitung* praised Kardorff as an "unsuspicious witness," because of her profession.[94] She also received positive reviews in the *Frankfurter Allgemeine Zeitung* and *Der Spiegel*.

Private letters to Kardorff were mostly enthusiastic. One man who understood the public relations value of the book wrote that someone had finally shown that one could not paint the behaviour of Germans during those difficult years in only black and white; he hoped, moreover, that the book would be widely published, particularly overseas.[95] After having read the final manuscript, a friend of Kardorff's commented that, "all of these years, we were more ashamed than we had reason [to be]; the shame and disgrace has covered up everything else."[96] The reception in the United States was equally favourable, with respect to both Kardorff's self-presentation and the image she created of Germany. One review spoke to her status as a journalist and a woman, praising Kardorff for having helped the average American gain insights into the German war experience.[97] Another described Kardorff as "a journalist who [had] kept her sympathies in check [during the Third Reich] by not taking on any political assignments."[98] The *New Yorker* wrote that, as a journalist, Kardorff was "a well-placed observer" of events.[99] The American author Bernardine Kielty Scherman remarked: "This is the first expression of anti-Nazism from a German in which this reader has felt trust … We on the outside have had an accumulation of Jewish atrocity stories, but here we see the growing realization of those horrors among decent Germans."[100] In light of such positive reviews, the American Library Association suggested that even small US libraries buy Kardorff's book.[101]

## Margret Boveri (1900–1975)

In the late 1960s, a wave of student protests swept through West Germany. Among other things, they demanded social change, an end to the hierarchical nature of German universities, and an exploration of their parents' and grandparents' actions during the Third Reich.[102] The political climate shifted left, and the Social Democrats took power. Willy Brandt's *Ostpolitik* was an important step in Germany's reconciliation with the East and acknowledgment of the genocidal war on the Eastern front. Change was also taking place in the academic realm, as scholars, in ever-increasing numbers, were exploring the roots of Nazism and the genocide of European Jews.[103] In addition, in the mid to late 1970s, historians began to analyse the role of women in the Third Reich, showcasing the diversity of experiences and disputing the notion that women were primarily victims of the regime.[104]

It was during this period of investigation and confrontation with the past that Margret Boveri published three books about her experiences under the Nazi regime. *Wir lügen alle: Eine Hauptstadtzeitung unter Hitler* (Everyone lies: a capital newspaper under Hitler), published in 1965, depicted the history of the *Berliner Tageblatt* and its 1939 demise.[105] *Tage des Überlebens: Berlin 1945* (Survival in Berlin), published in 1968, 1996, and again in 2004, centred on the last days of the war in Germany's capital and was based on Boveri's diary notes. Because it detailed the Red Army's often violent behaviour in Berlin, Boveri was concerned that her book would become a weapon in the Cold War. In a 1966 letter to a friend, she described her fear that her work could be used by Western "cold warriors against the Soviets."[106] Her worry highlights an important fact: a German journalist's voice, even in works focused on personal experience and observation, could affect public opinion within Germany and abroad. Both *Wir lügen alle* and *Tage des Überlebens* were widely reviewed and, for the most part, positively received in West Germany.

A third book, Boveri's memoir *Verzweigungen* (Crossroads), appeared in 1977 and was republished in 1996. It is the primary focus of this section. Unlike Friedrich's and Kardorff's volumes, *Verzweigungen* was not written in an attempt to secure understanding for Germany from the international community. Boveri wrote the book near the end of her life and more than three decades after the war. In it she endeavoured to explain and justify her activities during the Third Reich to German audiences and, in particular, to her co-author and interviewer, Uwe Johnson, a respected novelist and editor from East Germany. Thanks to Johnson's insistence, *Verzweigungen* offered a more introspective look at Germany's Nazi past and Boveri's career than her earlier writing had.[107] In many parts, the book reads as a dialogue between Johnson and Boveri, with Johnson pushing Boveri to address difficult questions concerning her role in Nazi Germany. Johnson confronted Boveri, for instance, with what he viewed as excuses or alibis in her presentation of her past. The narratives of Friedrich and Kardorff were not held to account in the same manner prior to publication. But neither Friedrich nor Kardorff had achieved the same level of prominence, nor displayed the same pro-Nazi tendencies, as Boveri throughout the Third Reich. Moreover, they had not lauded Nazi foreign policy in their journalism, as Boveri had done.

Johnson challenged Boveri on her decision to remain in Germany, her claims about inner emigration, her alleged opposition toward the regime, and her notion that, as Friedrich and Kardorff had also asserted, one could be more help to Germany if one remained.[108] Boveri appeared to reflect on the question of emigration and conceded that it was *possible* that she had deceived herself into thinking that she would be a more effective opponent of Nazism if she remained when she simply did not want to leave Germany. Still, she continued to claim that one did not leave one's country when things were going badly – a stance she expressed in much of her post-war writing. The trope of personal and national victimization and resistance also remained firmly rooted in her narrative, despite evidence to the contrary. Even in the face of her professional success and the enthusiasm she displayed for her work, Boveri claimed that any sense of enjoyment had disappeared from her life after 1933.[109]

Because she had worked as a foreign correspondent during the Third Reich, Boveri could not claim that her journalism was centred on the seemingly apolitical world of women's stories, as Kardorff had done. She did, nevertheless, use her gender to distance herself from Nazism. Boveri focused much attention on sexist Nazi rhetoric, and the subsequent discrimination and roadblocks she faced as a female journalist, to cast herself as an outsider in the eyes of the regime.[110] She also emphasized her own vulnerability as a journalist. Boveri had been arrested and briefly detained by the Gestapo in 1935, an experience that left her shaken. She had not come to the attention of Germany's secret police due to her journalism, however, but rather as a result of the vast newspaper archive that she kept. More specifically, she was targeted because one of the employees she had hired to maintain the archive belonged to the banned Socialist Worker's Party and it was his arrest that the Gestapo sought.[111] Boveri was released after one day in custody, and her archive was returned to her.

Boveri utilized what she described as her friendly relationships with Jews to demonstrate her supposed anti-Nazi stance and personal victimization during the Third Reich, and then transferred this presentation to the population as whole. She emphasized how she, too, tried to aid victims of Nazism: "My main assistance," she wrote, "consisted of helping various Jews earn money through secretarial and archival work."[112] Boveri did employ Erika Schmidt-Landry, a Jewish woman, to work on her archive from the fall of 1934 to the spring of 1935.[113] Later, in 1940 and 1941, Boveri worked as a foreign correspondent for the *Frankfurter Zeitung* in the United States. After that country entered the war in December 1941, she was interned, along with other Germans, until her return to Europe could be arranged. According to Boveri, American authorities considered her a "foreign agent" due to her status as a journalist. "No one thought about the fact that I could not be a genuine Nazi because I was friendly with Jewish colleagues who had emigrated," she declared.[114]

To further distance herself from Nazism, Boveri emphasized that the papers for which she wrote provided quality news, to the degree possible under Nazi press controls, and largely employed journalists and editors opposed to the regime. Such claims created a narrative that distanced the profession from its general accommodation with the regime. Like Friedrich and Kardorff, she utilized the persecution of Germany's Jews to achieve this objective. Boveri labelled two of the papers for which she wrote, the *Berliner Tageblatt* (*BT*) and the *Frankfurter Zeitung* (*FZ*), as "pro-Jewish." The *BT*, according to Boveri, was "the newspaper of the Jews" and therefore was despised by the Nazis. "Their business flyers, obituaries and new addresses for those who had emigrated appeared in our paper," she told Johnson. "We sat in the middle [between the regime and Germany's Jews] so to speak."[115] There was some truth to Boveri's claim. Compared to the rest of the coordinated press, the *FZ* and the *BT* did provide a degree of quality reporting. The publishing chief at the *Berliner Tageblatt*, Karl Vetter, had initially attempted to retain some of the paper's most respected reporters, including Jewish colleagues and those on the political left. But Vetter also conformed to Nazi press directives so that the paper would not be shut down. Throughout 1933, the *BT* had continued to include a degree of quality reporting by well-known voices. By the time Boveri joined the paper in 1934, however, its liberal leanings were largely no longer apparent.[116] Moreover, it published articles that Jewish readers and opponents of the Nazi regime would have found repugnant.

In the winter of 1936, Boveri herself wrote about a *Rassenschande* (race defilement) trial in Hamburg in which two Jewish men were accused due to their relationships with "Aryan" women.[117] Such articles contributed to, and normalized, racial categorization, and readers eagerly consumed titillating material that helped reinforce Jewish otherness and social isolation.[118] For Jewish men, charges of race defilement could lead to incarceration in a concentration camp and eventual death.[119] When asked by Johnson what she would have done if someone outside of Germany had confronted her with the article, Boveri responded, "I would have possibly found it [i.e., the confrontation] tactless, but I also would have found it justified. I probably would have blushed."[120] Boveri acknowledged her contribution to racial propaganda in a most tepid manner while maintaining that Germans recognized the pro-Jewish nature of the paper. Although she admitted that Jewish readers would have been upset by the race defilement article and many others like it, Boveri asserted that they understood why the *BT* published such material and that they recognized the paper's overall worth.[121] By Boveri's account, the paper produced antisemitic pieces as a cover for its opposition to the regime; she neglected to mention to Johnson that, when searching for a journalistic position herself, she placed an ad in which she mentioned her status as an "Aryan," thereby adopting the regime's language and capitalizing on its policy of exclusion.[122]

Dubious about her assertation that she believed her role as a foreign correspondent would benefit the German population under Nazi rule, Johnson questioned how Boveri could reconcile her professional success with her claim to have been an opponent of the regime. Boveri responded that her position allowed her more access to international news than most Germans, and that she sought to stay informed on behalf of her compatriots. She did not discuss that foreign newspapers provided more detailed information about atrocities perpetrated by Germany than domestic publications could provide. Instead, she offered the feeble argument that she used her writing to demonstrate to Germans how politics in other countries were conducted. Her articles, she claimed, offered "a kind of counter-image to the possibilities for public discourse that the Nazis tried to make us accept."[123] Yet, clearly, Boveri's Third Reich reporting in no way provided such a "counter-image."

Like Friedrich and Kardorff, Boveri also contributed to the rehabilitation of Nazi journalists. Boveri had contributed to *Das Reich* in the later years of the war. In 1955, she wrote an article for the *Frankfurter Allgemeine Zeitung* (*FAZ*) about the death of *Das Reich*'s former editor Rudolf Sparing, who had been in Soviet captivity since the end of the war. She declared that, although she had had reservations about joining *Das Reich*, she overcame her inhibitions after a few weeks because she worked with esteemed journalists who said what they thought and "thought much differently than Hitler and his followers."[124] Boveri credited Sparing's broad shoulders for the open and intellectual atmosphere at *Das Reich*: "He was, as far as I could see, a Nazi, and also a fanatic in his German patriotism. But the injustices that happened during the war years were surely repugnant to him in his soul, even if in his critiques he did not speak of injustice but rather of the 'wrong policy' or 'wrong measures.'"[125] In response to a reader's letter about her article, Boveri maintained that she had known no commited Nazis in Germany and that even those members of the press who were "allegedly Nazis were in reality not Nazis."[126] Hans Schwarz van Berk, whom Kardorff would defend only a few years later, applauded Boveri's article on Sparing.[127]

The similarity of the narratives of Friedrich, Kardorff, and Boveri about their relationships with their coworkers during the Third Reich suggests that there was a degree of comfort and open discussion within certain elements of the press. Helene Rahms, who will be discussed shortly, also spoke of informal evenings with colleagues, including Kardorff, where they were able to express whatever reservations they may have had about the Nazi regime. As all four women continued their careers in the post-war years, however, they also shared a need to defend the role of the press, or at least the papers and colleagues with whom they had been associated. By describing the editor of *Das Reich* as upstanding, despite his politics, Boveri strengthened her own claim that, by working for the paper, she had served not the regime, but rather the German population by providing "real news." Boveri's depiction of the press under National Socialism benefited journalists and Germans alike. The rebuilding of a free press in the post-war years was an important achievement and a symbol of democracy. The idea that it was made up of those who had resisted the Nazi regime by attempting to provide real news could function as a source of pride for the German nation.

Pressed by Johnson, Boveri grudgingly conceded that she had established and enjoyed a prominent career during the Third Reich.[128] While she may have entertained some initial doubts about writing for the Nazi regime, Boveri was a self-proclaimed nationalist and her pride in Germany, coupled with her professional ambition, held firm even in the midst of the persecution of her fellow Germans and, later, other European citizens. One therefore cannot give credence to her post-war denials about her pro-Nazi attitude. Yet the very appearance of her grappling with her own agency and the responsibility she bore for service to the regime could benefit the country as a whole, as Michela Hoenicke Moore has argued in her analysis of Boveri's 1946 book, *American Primer for Grown-Up Germans*.[129] The content of Boveri's memoir did address opportunism within the Third Reich and chimed with contemporary academic and public discussion about the popular support the regime enjoyed, even if Boveri mostly denied her own adherence. At the same time, Boveri provided a narrative that included a trope of personal and national resistance and suffering and allowed for a relatively positive view of the German nation under Nazism.

Margret Boveri remained one of the most well-known journalists and public intellectuals in Germany. After the war, she continued as a prolific writer and political critic, in particular of the Cold War and the demonization of the GDR.[130] The publication of Boveri's memoir was announced in newspapers across Germany. Prior to this, she had been awarded the *Preis Deutscher Kritiker* (German Critic's Prize) in 1968 and, in 1970, the *Bundesverdienstkreuz* (Federal Cross of Merit), the highest civilian honour, for promoting understanding between East and West Germany.[131] Her awards and prominence added credibility to her dubious narrative about the Third Reich. Yet, exposés of her career and reviews of her work continue to be published today. For instance, an article on "great" journalists of the twentieth century appeared in the well-regarded *Süddeutsche Zeitung* in 2010. The author spoke to the accommodations that Boveri had made in the Third Reich in pursuit of her career, noting "Margret Boveri came to terms with those in power. She was not a National Socialist, but she knew how to make compromises."[132] The journalist also discussed how Boveri had contributed to Nazi propaganda, while at the same time pointing out that she was a female pioneer in the field of foreign correspondence. The article ended with this appraisal: "Despite all the political aberrations, Margret Boveri remains one of the great journalists of the past century. She was a woman who asserted herself in a formerly male profession and made a name for herself with her judgments."[133] Such a designation would likely have pleased Boveri – it certainly corresponded to her own self-presentation.

## Helene Rahms (1918–1999)

In 1997, just one year after the republication of Boveri's autobiography, Helene Rahms published her memoir, *Zwischen den Zeilen: Mein Leben als Journalistin im Dritten Reich* (Between the lines: my life as a journalist in the Third Reich). Most of her text traversed the same well-trodden territory that Friedrich, Kardorff, and Boveri had covered decades earlier: a lack of agency due to gender, the decency of the press, the population's distaste for the regime, and silent or overt acts of opposition. Rahms believed that her generation was still being held collectively accountable for the "mistakes, errors, and crimes of the Nazi era."[134] In response, her narrative emphasized her own, her colleagues', and the German population's vulnerability and bravery amidst the danger in which they had lived. The nature of Rahms's writing and the structure of her memoir are curious. She rarely included dates, and instead collapsed chronology, while giving critical moments, such as *Kristallnacht* or the invasion of the Soviet Union, a haziness that served to soften such events.

By the time she published her book, a reunified Germany was a respected member of the international community and a model of a strong democracy. Among the upheavals that accompanied reunification, however, was a resurgence, in the 1990s, of right-wing extremism and violence toward minorities, particularly in the former GDR. Headlines about such violence in Germany sent shockwaves through the country and the international community. Discussions about Germany's past took on a special resonance, as fears of neo-Nazism grew, despite the fact that the nature of Germany's violent past had largely been accepted and the victimization trope disputed. In this context, at least one review of her work pointed out the predictability of Rahms's story of opposition and German suffering.[135] But others lauded her memoir. That the prestigious *Frankfurter Allgemeine Zeitung*, where Rahms worked for many years, promoted her book, indicates a continuing desire for, and acceptance of, the portrait of Nazi Germany offered by women journalists like Rahms.[136]

The 1980s marked steps forward and backward in Germany's attempts to investigate and situate its past. Coinciding with a conservative turn in politics under Chancellor Helmut Kohl, controversies played out in politics, the media, and academic circles that showcased tensions between the enduring discourse of German victimhood and the exploration and acknowledgement of the scale of German wartime crimes and the specificities of the Holocaust. These disputes ensured that Third Reich history remained on the German and international agenda and that it continued to be tied to the FRG's national identity. Two notable events occurred in 1985. In his 8 May 1985 speech to the German parliament, West German president Richard von Weizsäcker demonstrated forward movement by speaking to the genocide of European Jews and underscoring the importance of its memory and memorialization. Weizsäcker noted that 8 May was a day of remembrance, but that remembrance meant recalling events honestly, without distortion. "This," he stated, "places high demands on our truthfulness ... Everyone who directly experienced that era should today quietly ask himself about his involvement then."[137]

Later that year, to mark the fortieth anniversary of V-E Day, US president Ronald Reagan and Chancellor Kohl visited the Bitburg cemetery, which contained the graves of SS men. The event was meant to function as an indication of the strength of the German-American relationship and the two countries' successful post-war reconciliation. But the visit blurred the distinction between German victimhood and the victims of the Germans. Reagan's comments that the young men buried in Bitburg were victims of one man, Hitler, just as surely as those who died in concentration camps were victims, underscored and further legitimized the conflation of Jewish and German victimhood during the war.[138] Reagan's words also demonstrated that this narrative remained one strand of American opinion with regard to Germany's Second World War experience.

The *Historikerstreit* (historians' dispute) that began in the summer of 1986 added to the discussion and controversy. It focused on the place of Nazism in German history, the singularity of the Holocaust, and the question of German national identity. Historian Andreas Hillgruber published *Zweierlei Untergang*, in which he argued that the Holocaust and the loss of East Germany to the Soviet Union were the two tragedies of the Second World War. But Hillgruber's text focused more attention on Germany's loss in the East.[139] In June, the controversy became public. Conservative historian Ernst Nolte published an article in the *Frankfurter Allgemeine Zeitung* in which he argued that the Holocaust was a "reaction, born from fear of the annihilation processes of the Russian Revolution."[140] By Nolte's account, German crimes were just one example of atrocities in a long list of twentieth-century violence. He believed that Germany's past (and national identity) should be destigmatized. Jürgen Habermas labelled Nolte's argument an attempt to cancel out the damages of the Holocaust. The *Historikerstreit* brought even more attention to discussions about Germany's past and its connection to the country's contemporary image.

In the 1980s and 1990s, an increased focus on social history, the history of everyday life, and women's history brought significant strides in academic exploration of Nazism, the unfolding of the events of the Holocaust and the involvement of various segments of German society. Scholars demonstrated the broad support Nazism had enjoyed and pointed to how various groups had helped maintain the regime. Difficulties in accepting the past still remained, however. Despite much academic work about the war on the Eastern front, there was a public outcry when an exhibit on the crimes of the Wehrmacht toured Germany – the myth of the "clean Wehrmacht" was still thriving in the 1990s.[141] Rahms's 1997 memoir is another example of the endurance of Germany's victimization narrative and its entanglement with German national identity. Flying in the face of extensive research and public discourse on Nazi Germany, Rahms's memoir functioned to help those who desired to ignore the historical record.

Rahms claimed that her book was directed toward Germany's youth, to demonstrate how ambition and curiosity, qualities she attributed to journalists, led to entanglement with the regime's interests. Some sections of her work do suggest that she was attempting to discuss the ways in which she engaged with and benefited from Nazism. She described how two former colleagues had left the profession due to their distaste for the Nazi-controlled press: one ended up on a chicken farm and the other became a nurse. Rahms made it clear that, given her professional dreams, leaving journalism was not something she ever considered: "I didn't want to feed chickens [or] care for the sick. I was ambitious, I wanted to write."[142] Perhaps not surprisingly, given the determination with which she pursued this ambition, her memoir functioned as a vehicle to rehabilitate her Third Reich career.

Rahms recounted the difficulty she had had entering the profession due to her gender. Like Kardorff, she implied that her work in features was of little importance, and that she was not responsible for the production of Nazified news. Her editor, she assured readers, classified her journalism as "pretty filler."[143] Moreover, she wrote about herself in the third person, describing herself as "the volunteer" or the "young reporter," which further distanced her from the notion that she bore agency for serving the regime.[144]

Along with her gender and the apolitical nature of her work, Rahms emphasized how her youth and naivety affected her (lack of) understanding of Nazism and its ramifications. She wrote about a trip to Prague with her editor that took place after Germany's March 1939 occupation of Czechoslovakia. Rahms presented herself as a student of her editor's superior experience and knowledge with regard to political events. In her depiction, she listened intently while he described how the Czechs persecuted ethnic Germans, and how Germans were "tidier and harder working." The Czechs, he allegedly advised, "are smart but lazy. Simply Slavs."[145] Rahms positioned herself as young and believing.

*Zwischen den Zeilen* painted a rosy picture of the upstanding journalistic profession despite Nazi control. As with other memoirists, Rahms used the persecution of German Jews to demonstrate her colleagues' true feelings about National Socialism. Although outwardly accommodating to the regime, the *Saale-Zeitung*, according to Rahms, did not blacken the name of anyone, did not betray anyone, and did not include diatribes against the Jews.[146] "The word 'decency' was often used in our editorial office," Rahms claimed.[147] Her memoir contains an interesting tension between her depiction of Nazi control over the press and the narrow scope that journalists and editors had for independent decisions, which allowed some papers to supposedly avoid printing antisemitic pieces. Like Friedrich and Boveri, Rahms used *Kristallnacht* to demonstrate the extent of her colleagues' supposed loathing for the regime and the care the paper had taken not to publish articles that were disrespectful to Germany's Jewish community. She claimed that the morning after the pogrom, the paper's editor, Bernd Olaf, announced: "It is now clear to us that this state in which we live is not a *Rechtsstaat* [a state founded on the rule of law]." He told staff that they should act according to their consciences. "Our paper reported the fire [at the synagogue] briefly in an objective tone," Rahms wrote. "It respectfully called the synagogue 'the Jewish house of worship'."[148]

Rahms repeatedly used the term "clique" to position journalists as an elite group who "existed as islands in the '*Volksgemeinschaft*'… half-cowered artists and intellectuals who had shut themselves in for what they thought was a period of transition." "We never spoke about politics," Rahms alleged. "The name Hitler did not come up, rather [one spoke] about one's own work, literature, music."[149] Rahms presented those she classified as intellectuals as separate from the regime and the war it waged. By her account, journalists and the military despised each other. "Bespectacled, with wrinkled pants and worn-out shoes, [journalists] felt themselves to be the opposite of those wearing uniforms, who still wore their highly polished boots in the midst of the bombed-out cities," she wrote.[150] Certainly, like any segment of German society, there had been journalists working in the Third Reich who were not enthralled with Nazism and even those who opposed the regime. But Rahms also positioned colleagues who were party members as dissociated from Nazism.

Discussing Ilse Urbach, a colleague on *Das Reich*, Rahms noted that, even though Urbach had an early party number, she had rarely worn her badge, had never said a word about the regime, and had despised many of her fellow party members. Toward the end of the war, a *Gauleiter* (district leader) by the name of Franke visited the newspaper office. By Rahms's account, Urbach whispered to another colleague that she could "never drink a beer with such a pig." Later at the pub, Urbach told an "amusing" childhood story in which she referred to a Jewish child who had been harassed. Rahms maintained that the telling of the story was unusual and described Urbach's laughter as "nervous." Why, Rahms wondered, would Urbach tell such a story to a group who never spoke about the Jews and to whom antisemitic remarks were taboo? Her conclusion: Urbach was the Jewish child.[151] Urbach was not in fact Jewish and had written antisemitic articles during the war. Still, the persecution of German Jews proved useful for Rahms's depiction of fellow journalists as opponents of Nazism. After the war, Rahms and Urbach worked together on *Die Welt* in Hamburg.

Rahms portrayed other women who had enjoyed successful careers in Nazi Germany as courageous and outspoken. She described how a young Christa Rotzoll entered into a heated debate with a Nazi colleague who had argued that the regime and the paper *Das Reich* should not tolerate critiques of Nazism by "intellectuals." Allegedly, an enraged Rotzoll had responded, "What do you want to do with them? Have them arrested and stuffed into concentration camps?"[152] Rahms likewise described herself as daringly outspoken. She wrote that Goebbels had invited her to a private meeting that took place sometime in 1943. During their alleged exchange, Rahms boldly and naively challenged his belief in a "special peace" with England. By describing this incident, Rahms simultaneously implied her importance as a journalist – a private invitation by Goebbels suggested a certain prominence – and her lack of entanglement with the regime and its ideology. She wrote, "My admittedly vain provocation had no consequences. I was insignificant to him [and] not to be taken seriously."[153]

In her memoir, Rahms cast members of the Wehrmacht as victims of the Soviets. She maintained that what German soldiers endured as prisoners of war in the Soviet Union was unthinkable to the rest of the population: "They returned with faces bloated and disfigured from hunger, explained in fragments what we, who remained at home, could not imagine."[154] Extensive public and academic discussion about the German occupation of Soviet territory had taken place by the time Rahms published her memoir, but, like Friedrich, Kardorff, and Boveri, she included no discussion of German violence on the Eastern front or the crimes perpetrated against Soviet prisoners of war and other citizens. For Rahms, the presentation of downtrodden and mistreated German POWs was personal, since her husband, a high-ranking officer in the Wehrmacht, had spent time in Soviet captivity. Rahms stated that she wrote her memoir for later generations of Germans that included her children and grandchildren; her own private and public legacy was thus at stake.

Rahms provided some balance to her narrative and acknowledged that she and her cohort were able to put their consciences aside and went on "writing, editing, eating and drinking, dancing and loving" during the war.[155] She also referred to the press as an arm of Nazi propaganda, albeit in an indirect way. She noted that the press club was jokingly called "The Duck," which, in newspaper jargon, alluded to fake news. The name, Rahms wrote "fitted all too well into the time when the journalistic craft was mainly used to gloss over and disguise reality."[156] Rahms also addressed the population's general lack of interest in the violence taking place in their midst: "Everyone knew that those who had been towed away and locked up in camps were in bad shape," she wrote. "But no one dared to imagine what happened to them in detail. The rare, accidental authentic information that I remember did not have a calming effect, but neither did it have the effect of a constant nightmare."[157]

Similar to the other women discussed in this chapter, Helene Rahms built a brilliant, successful post-war career. She spent twenty-five years in features at the prestigious *Frankfurter Allgemeine Zeitung* and many years as the head of its women's section. For her writing on architecture, she won silver in the *Deutscher Preis für Denkmalschutz* (Prize for the Protection of German Cultural Heritage) in 1979 – the highest honor in this arena. Her prominence suggests that, although its degree of distortion was quite high, her memoir was more likely to be read, and likely to be considered more authentic, than works of "ordinary" Germans.

## Conclusion

By default or design, a small group of women journalists marketed a distorted version of Germany's Third Reich experience to German and transnational audiences after 1945. The autobiographical writing of these women aided in refashioning the memory of Nazism in the decades following the end of the Second World War in a manner that helped the FRG, and later a reunified Germany, process the past. By offering, to differing degrees, ostensibly balanced narratives that acknowledged individual and national responsibility – however modest – for Nazism and its repercussions, together with a more overt message about the population's resistance, oppression, and resilience, these women helped provide Germans and even international audiences with a palatable version of the Third Reich.

Their status as women and as professional journalists was an important part of their influence. As women, they had not occupied leadership positions in the Nazi press. Although prominent, they could also represent themselves as "ordinary" journalists and ordinary Germans. In the post-war years, Nazi discourse proved beneficial for women. The party's repeated declaration of politics as a male domain allowed women to claim that the crimes of Nazism and the German nation were products of a state controlled exclusively by men.[158] These women's gender also underscored the perceived authenticity of their version of Germany's past. Friedrich's writing and her status as a woman who worked in an "apolitical" realm during the Nazi period helped set the stage for the narratives of the women that followed, and for their acceptance by both German and international audiences. Kardorff and Rahms highlighted how their work was not political; Boveri emphasized the gender discrimination she faced as a woman in a man's realm.

In the post-war years, these four women journalists were better positioned than their male colleagues to portray their own and the country's oppression at the hands of the Nazis and Allies. Male journalists also wrote post-war memoirs that addressed their Third Reich careers. These works, however, did not typically enjoy the same traction or popularity as those of the female journalists discussed in this chapter. In *Journalismus im Dritten Reich*, Norbert Frei and Johannes Schmitz drew on eleven memoirs, four (36 per cent) of them from women journalists, including Friedrich, Boveri, and Kardorff. The men's memoirs referenced in this study were published only in German from the late 1960s to the early 1980s, with most appearing in the 1970s. They have not been translated or reissued. In contrast, the personal narratives of Friedrich, Kardorff, Boveri, and Rahms together have been published at an average rate of two per decade in German and/or English since the end of the Second World War.[159] To varying degrees, the media, academia, and the public in Germany and abroad considered these women authentic chroniclers of Germany's wartime experience. Their work was reviewed in prestigious newspapers in Germany, and often abroad, and is included in important academic works on Nazism.[160]

To achieve their goals, the women veiled, misrepresented, and/or ignored the nature of their writing during the Third Reich. They downplayed the advantages and opportunities they had garnered as members of Hitler's *Volksgemeinschaft*, instead focusing on the obstacles they had faced as women; masked the self-coordination or *Gleichschaltung* that took place in the press during the Nazi period; and utilized the Jewish experience of persecution to highlight German resistance, suffering, and heroism. Their personal narratives were published in the decades ranging from the 1940s to the 2000s and in different political, social, and cultural climates. Although these women traversed distinct paths from dictatorship to democracy, the continuity of their presentations of Germany's Nazi experience, along with the ongoing popularity of their publications, helped ensure not only that the victimization narrative endured in Germany's memory culture, but also that the country continued the process of acknowledging its crimes. Coming to terms with the past was not always a virtuous process.

# Influence and Complicity

In 1884, British journalist and feminist Florence Fenwick-Miller aptly noted that

> For every hundred persons who listen to the priest, the journalist … speaks to a thousand; and while the words of the one are often heard merely as a formality, those of the other … may effectively influence the thoughts and consciences and actions of thousands in the near future. Shallow, indeed, would be the mind which undervalued the power of the journalist, or underrated the seriousness of his vocation.[1]

Fenwick-Miller's view of the importance of journalism applies to the profession as practised in democratic systems but, arguably, even more so under authoritarian regimes that effectively controlled and harnessed the power of the mass media to pursue their social and political goals. As a journalist herself, Fenwick-Miller also spoke to the work and influence of female journalists. From the late nineteenth century onward, opportunities within the press began to open for women throughout Europe and North America. They were, however, generally clustered in the lower-prestige fields associated with their gender: soft news that focused on the private sphere and everyday life. As this book has shown, press authorities in Nazi Germany wanted and needed female journalists in these areas, to act as a conduit to Germany's women and write about the various facets of a women's life and duty to the Nazi state.

Yet women journalists occupied a range of roles in the Nazi press, and their contributions to it varied. The analysis of the different personal and professional trajectories of women in the preceding chapters has revealed a range of motivations, ambitions, opportunities, and experiences. While most worked in the realm of soft news – due to the expectations of Nazi press authorities as well as long-standing ideas about the competencies and responsibilities of men and women – the Third Reich allowed space for women to be involved in almost all areas of journalism. Just as their peers did in less nationalistic and militaristic systems, a small number of German women established prominent careers in the hard-news arena. At the same time, women journalists in Nazi Germany experienced the professional roadblocks, pigeonholing, and hostility from press authorities and male colleagues that marked the experience of most women in the field. They adopted strategies to overcome such limitations: while some used their femininity to access opportunities or to give them a voice of authority when writing about issues traditionally deemed women's news, others attempted to adapt to the "masculine" rules of the game.

What differentiated women working under the Nazi dictatorship from their counterparts in democratic systems was, therefore, *not* dissenting views about what female journalists could and should do, or more rigid professional restrictions. As Liesbet van Zoonen has shown, regardless of the focus – Norway, Germany, Senegal, or the United States – the story is the same: daily journalism was, and largely remains, dominated by men.[2] What did set female journalists in the Third Reich apart was the intended purpose of their work: they were tasked with normalizing the abnormal. Those who worked in soft news helped to ease the cognitive dissonance between the illusion of normality and contentedness in everyday life that the regime sought to project, and the political and ideological aims of a repressive and violent system. The few women who worked in hard news affirmed the regime's aggressive policies related to race and space. Certainly the controlled nature of the press, coupled with women's precarious status within it, left little margin for journalistic independence or open dissent, perhaps even less so for women than for men, who enjoyed more stable positions. But women found the profession appealing and entered it voluntarily. Despite endemic discrimination, journalism provided women a level of prestige, flexibility, and opportunities to travel and mix with prominent individuals. The status of journalist also afforded women some opportunities to step out of traditional gender roles, even if their writing upheld such norms. The work of women journalists helped manage the relationship between the Nazi state and the German public and afforded them an – often opaque – form of soft-power influence at a time when notions about men's responsibility in the public sphere and women's role in the private sphere were firmly entrenched in Nazi rhetoric and traditional beliefs about gender.

In this way, women journalists in Nazi Germany provide an important case study on the interrelation of gender, discrimination, agency, ambition, and political and moral complicity in a patriarchal and authoritarian dictatorship. Although some women stepped back from the field after Hitler's ascension to power, most, like their male counterparts, found ways to accommodate themselves to the demands of the profession regardless of their feelings toward the regime and its ideology. Women entered the field through the pathways open to them and equipped with a clear understanding of what the Nazi state expected of journalists. This is not to say that all journalists wished to, or anticipated that they would have to, write in support of a regime that would persecute its own citizens, wage an expansionist war, and perpetrate genocide. Rather, the party made clear the purpose of the press in service to the state prior to its gaining power, and consistently thereafter. In 1937, Reich press chief Otto Dietrich captured Nazi press policy in a nutshell:

> With us, the newspaper is not a playground for irresponsibility and the unbridled criticism of a few, who, as the vanguard of anonymous interests, abuse the right of criticism to undermine the authority of the state. With us, who possess better methods to keep the state close to the people, the newspaper is the journalistic conscience of the nation, destined to promote the action of the state instead of paralysing it![3]

For the sake of their careers, women journalists generally tolerated the restrictions placed on the press. As their positive recollections indicate, the perks of the profession helped to counter the lack of professional freedom. Women thus took a professional route to become "implicated subjects" in a dictatorship that led to the persecution of those not included in the vaunted *Volksgemeinschaft*.

Just as women's experiences and the nature of their journalism differed within the Nazi press, so too did the extent of their engagement or complicity with regard to affirming Nazi aggression. Carola Ihlenberg's articles on selecting German-made gifts or Ruth Andreas-Friedrich's advice on how to work through wartime grief played an important role in the regime's desire to preserve a sense of normality and bolster women's morale during the war, respectively. But such material did not entangle its authors in promoting processes of violence in the same manner as Margret Boveri's reporting on Nazi foreign policy successes or Lily Abegg's coverage of Germany's invasion of France. Some women journalists may have preferred to work in soft news precisely because they believed that they would not have to promote the regime's repressive policies or warn of the danger of Germany's alleged racial and ideological enemies – at least to the same degree as those working in more overt political areas. At the same time, those few women working in hard news may have been more adaptable to fulfilling the demands of the regime in order to prove that they were just as capable as men in an arena where discrimination made their presence, let alone their success, unlikely.

These are speculations, however, and difficult to substantiate. Given that many women worked freelance, they often crossed over between writing on seemingly benign topics, or for non-party publications, and those that aligned more closely with Nazism. Marta Hillers provides one example. While her writing for the women's magazine *Die neue Gartenlaube* did not ostensibly connect with Nazi ideology, she also wrote for *Hilf mit* and *Das Deutsche Mädel* – two party publications aimed at indoctrinating young children in Nazism. As a freelancer, journalists such as Hillers often accepted assignments where and when they could. For those who forged especially prominent careers, like Margret Boveri or Elisabeth Noelle-Neumann, it is possible that the more opportunities they acquired in the male-dominated field, the more they grew to respect the Third Reich and its policies.

Regardless of their motivations or intentions at the time, the experiences of women journalists in Nazi Germany make clear that participation in a public institution like the press within an authoritarian system leads to relationships of complicity and reward, regardless of one's adherence to the system. The more extensive the contribution to directly affirming the state's ideology, the higher the rewards, in whatever form they may take – prestige, travel, remuneration. This study of women journalists in the Nazi and post-war press also has shown how gender can affect the perception of complicity and effectively minimize women's professional contribution to a repressive system after its collapse. After 1945, German women journalists successfully downplayed the agency and privilege they had enjoyed in Nazi Germany. Their gender, tropes of feminine weakness, and Nazi rhetoric about women's place in German society often (although not always) proved a useful exculpatory strategy. This mixture of opportunism and collusion, marginalization and evasion, experienced and carried out by women journalists to the benefit of an authoritarian system did not disappear with the Nazi state. The masculine image of what constituted "hard" or "real" journalism, contrasted with soft-news realms focused on everyday experiences in the so-called private sphere, can work to the benefit of nefarious systems that cloak violent ideology behind soft news, as we continue to see today.

# Notes

**Introduction**

1 Ursula von Kardorff, *Berliner Aufzeichnungen aus den Jahren 1942 bis 1945* (Munich: Beck, 1992), 290.

2 Ursula von Kardorff, *Diary of a Nightmare: Berlin, 1942–1945* (New York: John Day, 1966); *Berliner Aufzeichnungen aus den Jahren 1942 bis 1945* (Munich: Beck, 1992).

3 Michael Rothberg, *The Implicated Subject: Beyond Victims and Perpetrators* (Stanford, CA: Stanford University Press, 2019), 1.

4 Jana F. Bruns, *Nazi Cinema's New Women* (Cambridge: Cambridge University Press, 2009), 3.

5 Susan Tegel, *Nazis and the Cinema* (London: Continuum, 2007), 76–7.

6 Kate Lacey, *Feminine Frequencies: Gender, German Radio, and the Public Sphere, 1923–1945* (Ann Arbor: University of Michigan Press, 1996), 102.

7 Ibid., 117–18.

8 Frauensendungen der Woche 20–26 June 1937, Reichssender Breslau, Bundesarchiv Berlin-Lichterfelde (BArch-B), NS44/45.

9 Lacey, *Feminine Frequencies*, 102.

10 See Oron J. Hale, *The Captive Press in the Third Reich* (Princeton, NJ: University Press, 1964) and Judith Prokasky, ed. *Zwischen den Zeilen? Zeitungspresse als NS-Machtinstrument* (Berlin: Stiftung Topografie des Terrors, 2013).

11 See Heike B. Görtemaker, *Ein deutsches Leben: Die Geschichte der Margret Boveri* (Munich: Beck, 2005) and Else Frobenius, *Erinnerungen einer Journalistin: Zwischen Kaiserreich und Zweitem Weltkrieg*, ed. Lora Wildenthal (Cologne: Böhlau, 2005). There are relatively few studies that focus solely on women journalists. See Carmen Sitter, *"Die eine Hälfte vergisst man(n) leicht!" Zur Situation von Journalistinnen in Deutschland unter besonderer Berücksichtigung des 20. Jahrhunderts* (Pfaffenweiler: Centaurus, 1998).

12  See Norbert Frei and Johannes Schmitz, *Journalismus im Dritten Reich* (Munich: Beck, 1989) and Heidi J.S. Tworek, *News from Germany: The Competition to Control World Communications, 1900–1945* (Cambridge, MA: Harvard University Press, 2019).

13  See Pierre Bourdieu, "The Forms of Capital," in *Handbook for Theory and Research for the Sociology of Education*, ed. J.G. Richardson (Westport, CT: Greenwood Press), 241–58.

14  Joan Scott, *Gender and the Politics of History* (New York: Columbia University Press, 1988), 42. For more on gender theory, see Judith Butler, *Gender Trouble: Feminism and the Subversion of Identity* (New York: Routledge, 2006. For gender in Germany, see Karen Hagemann and Jean H. Quataert, eds., *Gendering Modern German History: Rewriting Historiography* (New York: Berghahn Books, 2007).

15  See Deborah Chambers, Linda Steiner, and Carole Fleming, *Women and Journalism* (London: Routledge, 2004) and Kay Mills, *A Place in the News: From the Women's Pages to the Front Page* (New York: Columbia University Press, 1990).

16  Adolf Dresler, *Die Frau im Journalismus* (Munich: Knorr & Hirth, 1936), 11.

17  Sitter, *Die eine Hälfte*, 224. In his study, professor of journalism studies Adolf Dresler calculates that 687 women were members of the German Press Association in 1935: *Die Frau im Journalismus* (Munich: Knorr & Hirth, 1936), 11. His numbers, however, exclude photographers and illustrators. By the war, the number of women working in the press was approximately 1,500. Sitter, *Die eine Hälfte*, 224.

18  Anja Meyer, Thea Fischer interview, in *Medienfrauen der ersten Stunde:"Wir waren ja die Trümmerfrauen in diesem Beruf,"* ed. Angelika Engler and Lissi Klaus (Zurich: eFeF, 1993), 106.

19  See Robert Gellately, *Backing Hitler: Consent and Coercion in Nazi Germany* (Oxford: Oxford University Press, 2001); Shelley Baranowski, *Strength through Joy: Consumerism and Mass Tourism in the Third Reich* (Cambridge: Cambridge University Press, 2004); and Julia Timpe, *Nazi-Organized Recreation and Entertainment in the Third Reich* (London: Palgrave Macmillan, 2017).

20  See Thomas Kühne, *Belonging and Genocide: Hitler's Community, 1918–1945* (New Haven, CT: Yale University Press, 2010).

21  Pioneering studies include Claudia Koonz, *Mothers in the Fatherland: Women, the Family and Nazi Politics* (London: Jonathan Cape, 1987) and Jill Stephenson, *Women in Nazi Germany* (Toronto: Longman, 2001). Recent scholarship includes Rachel Century, *Female Administrators of the Third Reich* (Palgrave: Macmillan, 2017) and Melissa Kravetz, *Women Doctors in Weimar and Nazi Germany: Maternalism, Eugenics, and Professional Identity* (Toronto: University of Toronto Press, 2019).

22  "Die Arbeitstagung des RDP in Köln," *Deutsche Presse*, 14 December 1935, 662–3. All translations are my own, unless otherwise stated.

23  Reich Press Chief Otto Dietrich, press conference speech, 3 September 1939, as quoted in Jürgen Wilke, *Presseanweisungen im zwanzigsten Jahrhundert: Erster Weltkrieg–Drittes Reich–DDR* (Cologne: Böhlau, 2007), 197. The Westwall was a German defensive line in Western Europe built during the 1930s and the Second World War.

24  Else Boger-Eichler, *Die Schriftleiterin* (Berlin: Akademisches Auskunftsamt der Deutschen Arbeitsfront, 1939), 8; *Der Schriftleiter*, Akademisches Auskunftsamt (AAA), 1 January 1938, BArch-B, R103/125, 18.

25  Boger-Eichler, *Die Schriftleiterin*, 8.

26  Karin Wright, Martin Scott, and Mel Bunce, "Soft Power, Hard News: How Journalists at State-Funded Transnational Media Legitimize Their Work," *International Journal of Press Politics* 25, no. 4 (2020): 608. See also Joseph Nye, *Soft Power: The Means to Success in World Politics* (New York: Public Affairs, 2004), x.

27  See Elizabeth Harvey, Johnanes Hürter, Maiken Umbach, and Andreas Wirsching, eds., *Private Life and Privacy in Nazi Germany* (Cambridge: Cambridge University Press, 2019); Pamela E. Swett, *Selling under the Swastika: Advertising and Commercial Culture in Nazi Germany* (Stanford, CA: Stanford University Press, 2014); Jonathan Wiesen, *Creating the Nazi Marketplace: Commerce and Consumption in the Third Reich* (New York: Cambridge University Press, 2011); Martina Steber and Bernhard Gotto, eds., *Visions of Community in Nazi Germany: Social Engineering and Private Lives* (Oxford: Oxford University Press, 2014); Karl Christian Führer, "Pleasure, Practicality and Propaganda: Popular Magazines in Nazi Germany, 1933–1939," in *Pleasure and Power in Nazi Germany*, ed. Pamela E. Swett, Corey Ross, and Fabrice d'Almeida (New York: Palgrave Macmillan, 2011); and David Welch, *Propaganda and the German Cinema, 1933–1945* (London: I.B. Tauris, 2001).

28  Chambers, Steiner, Fleming, *Women and Journalism*, 8. See also Alice Fahs, *Out on Assignment: Newspaper Women and the Making of Modern Public Space* (Chapel Hill: University of North Carolina Press, 2014.)

29  For more on women and domesticity, see Nancy Reagin, *Sweeping the German Nation: Domesticity and National Identity in Germany, 1870–1945* (Cambridge: Cambridge University Press, 2007).

30  For more on the *Volksgemeinschaft* see Michael Wildt, *Hitler's Volksgemeinschaft and the Dynamics of Racial Exclusion* (New York: Berghahn Books, 2012.)

31  Julia Edwards, *Women of the World: The Great Foreign Correspondents* (Boston: Houghton Mifflin, 1988), 5.

32  See Paul Corner, ed., *Popular Opinion in Totalitarian Regimes: Fascism, Nazism, Communism* (Oxford: Oxford University Press, 2017); Shelley Baranowski, *Nazi Empire: German Colonialism and Imperialism from Bismarck to Hitler* (Cambridge: Cambridge University Press, 2011; and Gerhard L. Weinberg, *Hitler's Foreign Policy, 1933–1939: The Road to World War II* (New York: Enigma Books, 2010).

33  See Olga Shtyrkina, *Mediale Schlachtfelder: Die NS-Propaganda gegen die Sowjetunion (1939–1945)* (Frankfurt: Campus Verlag, 2018); Jeffrey Herf, *The Jewish Enemy: Nazi Propaganda during World War II and the Holocaust* (Cambridge, MA: Harvard University Press, 2006); and Ian Kershaw, "How Effective Was Nazi Propaganda," in *Nazi Propaganda: The Power and the Limitations*, ed. David Welch (New York: Routledge, 2015), 180–205.

34  See Elizabeth Harvey, *Women and the Nazi East: Agents and Witnesses of Germanization* (New Haven, CT: Yale University Press, 2003); Elissa Mailänder, *Gewalt im Dienstalltag: Die SS-Aufseherinnen des Konzentrations- und Vernichtungslagers Majdanek* (Hamburg: Hamburger Edition, 2009); and Wendy Lower, *Hitler's Furies: German Women in the Nazi Killing Fields* (London: Chatto and Windus, 2013).

35  Chambers, Steiner, and Fleming, *Women and Journalism*, 13; For more on foreign correspondents, see John Maxwell Hamilton, *Journalism's Roving Eye: A History of American Foreign Reporting* (Baton Rouge: Louisiana State University Press, 2009), 275, 317.

36  See Karen Hagemann, Donna Harsch, and Friederike Brühöfener, eds., *Gendering Post-1945 German History: Entanglements* (New York: Berghahn, 2019) and Elizabeth Heineman, *What Difference Does a Husband Make? Women and Marital Status in Nazi and Postwar Germany* (Berkeley and Los Angeles: University of California Press, 1999).

37  See Donna Harsch, *Revenge of the Domestic: Women, the Family and Communism in the German Democratic Republic* (Princeton, NJ: Princeton University Press, 2007).

38  See Robert G. Moeller, *War Stories: The Search for a Usable Past in the Federal Republic of Germany* (Berkeley and Los Angeles: University of California Press, 2001).

39  See Konrad Jarausch, *After Hitler: Recivilizing Germans, 1945–1995* (Oxford: Oxford University Press, 2006); Norbert Frei, *Adenauer's Germany and the Nazi Past: The Politics of Amnesty and Integration* (New York: Columbia University Press, 2002); David A. Messenger and Katrin Paehler, eds., *A Nazi Past: Recasting German Identity in Post-war Europe* (Lexington: University Press of Kentucky, 2015); and Elizabeth Heineman, "The Hour of the Woman: Memories of Germany's 'Crisis Years' and West German National Identity," *American Historical Review* 101, no. 2 (1996): 354–96.

40  Ruth Andreas-Friedrich, *Berlin Underground, 1938–1945* (New York: Holt, 1947), foreword.

## 1  On the Peripheries of Power

1  "Frauen als Journalistinnen," *Münchner Neueste Nachrichten*, 26 November 1933, Nr. 48.

2  Ibid.

3  Oron J. Hale, *The Captive Press in the Third Reich* (Princeton, NJ: University Press, 1964); Norbert Frei and Johannes Schmitz, *Journalismus im Dritten Reich* (Munich: Beck, 1989); Sönke Neitzel and Bernd Heidenreich, eds., *Medien im Nationalsozialismus* (Paderborn: Fink, 2010); Judith Prokasky, ed., *Zwischen den Zeilen? Zeitungspresse als NS-Machtinstrument* (Berlin: Stiftung Topografie des Terrors, 2013).

4  See Mary Lynn Stewart, *Gender, Generation, and Journalism in France, 1910–1940* (Montreal and Kingston: McGill-Queen's University Press, 2018); Kay Mills, *A Place in the News: From the Women's Pages to the Front Page* (New York: Columbia University Press, 1990); and Cynthia Carter, Linda Steiner, Stuart Allan, eds., *Journalism, Gender and Power* (New York: Routledge, 2019).

5  Tracy Lucht and Kelsey Batschelet, "'That Was What I Had to Use': Social and Cultural Capital in the Careers of Women Broadcasters," *Journalism and Mass Communications Quarterly* 96, no. 1 (2019): 195.

6  Although its hiring practices were biased – not only against women, but also against minorities – the press in democratic countries was not subject to restructuring and control in the same manner as it was in Nazi Germany.

7  Tim Mason, "Women in Germany," *History Workshop Journal*, no. 17 (1976): 74–113; Jill Stephenson, *Women in Nazi Germany* (Toronto: Longman, 2001); Matthew Stibbe, *Women in the Third Reich* (New York: Oxford University Press, 2003).

8  See Thomas Kühne, *Belonging and Genocide: Hitler's Community, 1918–1945* (New Haven, CT: Yale University Press, 2010).

9  Weiß was a member of the SA, with the rank of *Obergruppenführer*.

10  Peter Fritzsche, *Reading Berlin, 1900* (Cambridge, MA: Harvard University Press, 1998), 53.

11  Hale, *The Captive Press*, 3.

12  Bernhard Fulda, *Press and Politics in the Weimar Republic* (Oxford: Oxford University Press, 2009), 42.

13  Wolfgang Müsse, *Die Reichspresseschule: Journalisten für die Diktatur? Ein Beitrag zur Geschichte des Journalismus im Dritten Reich* (Munich: Sauer, 1995), 76.

14  Lutz Hachmeister, *Theoretische Publizistik: Studien zur Geschichte der Kommunikationswissenschaft in Deutschland* (Berlin: Volker Spiess, 1987), 44, 47. Stefanie Averbeck gives the publication's founding

year as 1926. Stefanie Averbeck and Arnulf Kutsch, "Thesen zur Geschichte der Zeitungs- und Publizistikwissenschaft 1900–1960," in *Die Spirale des Schweigens: Zum Umgang mit der nationalsozialistischen Zeitungswissenschaft*, ed. Wolfgang Duchkowitsch, Fritz Hausjell, and Bernd Semrad (Vienna: Lit Verlag, 2004), 59.

15 Averbeck and Kutsch, "Thesen zur Geschichte."

16 Adolf Hitler, *Mein Kampf*, translated by Ralph Manheim (1925; New York: Reynal and Hitchcock, 1940), 108.

17 Ibid., 51. See also Hachmeister, *Theoretische Publizistik*, 50.

18 "Das Schriftleitergesetz," *Zeitungs-Verlag*, 7 October 1933, Nr. 40, 650–1.

19 The first official anti-Jewish measure was the Law for the Restoration of the Professional Civil Service, promulgated on 7 April 1933.

20 Hilde Walter, "Vorgänge bei der Gleichschaltung und 'Arisierung' des Rudolf-Mosse-Betriebs," *Erinnerungsbericht: Über persönliche Erfahrungen im Dritten Reich bis November 1933*, 8 October 1959, Institut für Zeitgeschichte Munich (IfZ), zs-2031, 7. Walter published in the *Berliner Tageblatt*, *Die Welt am Montag*, and *Die Weltbühne*.

21 Memo, Reichsverband der Deutschen Presse (RDP), Auszug aus dem Schriftleitergesetz, 12 April 1944, Bundesarchiv Berlin-Lichterfelde (BArch-B), R103/25. The law also classified journalists into three categories within the overall professional registrar (*Berufsliste*): List A was for journalists who were authorized to work in any field, B was for those allowed only to work in a specific area (*Fachgebiet*), and C was for journalists in training.

22 Memo, RDP to Regional Press Associations, 2 November 1934, BArch-B, R103/1, Nr. 18.

23 Frei and Schmitz, *Journalismus im Dritten Reich*, 28. See also "Aktionen gegen nichtarische und gegen nichtarisch verheiratete Schriftleiter," undated memo, BArch-B, R103/5.

24 Wilhelm Weiß, "Presseführung und Zeitungsgestaltung: Grundsätzliche Ausführungen über zeitgemäße Fragen der deutschen Presse," *Deutsche Presse*, 20 March 1937, 142.

25 Corey Ross, *Media and the Making of Modern Germany: Mass Communications, Society, and Politics from the Empire to the Third Reich* (Oxford: Oxford University Press, 2008), 270.

26 Adolf Dresler, *Die Frau im Journalismus* (Munich: Knorr & Hirth, 1936), 11. He did not include figures outlining how much the field of journalism grew as a whole and therefore provided no analysis regarding the percentage of women who made up the press corps.

27 Deborah Chambers, Linda Steiner, and Carole Fleming, *Women and Journalism* (London: Routledge, 2004), 55.

28 See "Mitteilungen an die Verbände: Presse und Doppelverdiener," *Deutsche Presse*, 15 September 1933.

29  Rolf Cunz, "Vom Aufgabenkreis der Schriftleiterin," *Zeitungs-Verlag*, 1 January 1934, Nr. 356, 6–7.

30  Annette Lehmann, Helma Huffschmid interview, in *Medienfrauen der ersten Stunde: "Wir waren ja die Trümmerfrauen in diesem Beruf,"* ed. Angelika Engler and Lissi Klaus (Zurich: eFeF, 1993), 40.

31  For example, see Gabriele Tergit (née Elise Hirschmann), Maria Reese, Marcia Kahn, and Martha Maria Gehrke.

32  Irene Below and Ruth Oelze, *Lucy von Jacobi: Journalistin* (Munich: Richard Boorberg, 2009), 15. In 1928, Jacobi was one of the first women to obtain a permanent position at the famous Ullstein-Verlag as features editor on the *Vossische Zeitung*.

33  See Martha Wertheimer, Nationalsozialismus, Holocaust, Widerstand, Exil 1933–1945, online database, http://db.saur.de/DG20/basicFull CitationView.jsf?documentld=DBE-1929.

34  Rolf Sachsse, *Die Erziehung zum Wegsehen: Fotografie im NS-Staat* (Dresden: Philo & Philo Fine Arts, 2003), 113.

35  Else Boger-Eichler, *Die Schriftleiterin* (Berlin: Akademisches Auskunftsamt der Deutschen Arbeitsfront, 1939), 9.

36  Erika Groth-Schmachtenberger, *Meine liebsten Fotos: Erinnerungen einer Bildberichterin aus sechs Jahrzehnten* (Würzberg: Echter, 1984), 15.

37  Ibid.

38  Memo, Wilhelm Weiß, RDP, 29 April 1936, BArch-B, R103/2, Nr. 32.

39  Wolf Meyer-Christian, "Die Erziehung des Schriftleiter-Nachwuchses," *Deutsche Presse*, 29 September 1934.

40  *Schriftleiter*, Akademisches Auskunftsamt (AAA), 1 January 1938, BArch-B, R103/125, 18.

41  Meyer-Christian, "Die Erziehung," *Deutsche Presse*, 29 September 1934.

42  The law specified that one could become a journalist only if one possessed German citizenship; had not lost their citizenship, political rights, or the right to hold public office; had proof of "Aryan" ancestry and/or did not have a "non-Aryan" spouse; was at least twenty-one years old; was considered legally competent; and was trained and accredited in the profession.

43  Memo, RDP, 20 June 1944, BArch-B, R103/25.

44  Wilhelm Weiß, "Die Frau im Schriftleiterberuf," *Deutsche Presse*, 7 March 1936, 118.

45  Aufklärungsblätter über die akademischen Berufe, Schriftleiter (Journalist, Redakteur) akad. Geb. (Leipzig: Sächsisches Akademisches Auskunftsamt für Studien und Berufsfragen, der Landesstelle für Akademische Berufsberatung, 1938), BArch-B, R103/25.

46  Frauengruppe des Landesverbandes Berlin, *Deutsche Presse*, 14 April 1934, Nr. 15, 11.

47 Boger-Eichler, *Die Schriftleiterin*, 14.

48 Weiß, "Die Frau im Schriftleiter Beruf," 118. The quote reads, "even if you are not a male journalist, but a female journalist."

49 Bericht über die Tagung der Gauabteilungsleiterinnen, 2 May 1939, BArch-B, NS44/46.

50 Memo, NSF Press and Propaganda Department, 7 January 1937, BArch-B, NS45, and May 1939, NS44/46.

51 Letter, Erika Kirmsse, Presse-Propaganda, Nachwuchsstelle f. Schriftleiterinnen to Herrn Dr. J. Schäfe, Hauptschriftleiter der *Kölnischen Zeitung*, 14 April 1939, BArch-B, NS44/96.

52 Dresler, *Die Frau im Journalismus*, 12.

53 Helene Rahms, *Zwischen den Zeilen: Mein Leben als Journalistin im Dritten Reich* (Bern: Scherz, 1997), 12.

54 Boger-Eichler, *Die Schriftleiterin*, 14.

55 Stewart, *Gender, Generation, and Journalism*, 76.

56 Elisabeth Noelle-Neumann, *Die Erinnerungen* (Munich: Herbig, 2006), 42.

57 Anja Meyer, Gertrud Uhlhorn interview, in *Medienfrauen*, 120.

58 Ibid.

59 Ursula Roeh, Lebenslauf, undated, BArch-B, Collection Former Berlin Document Centre (BDC), Personenbezogene Unterlagen der Reichskulturkammer (RK), RKI487.

60 See RDP, BArch-B, R103/138. Among others, Käte Lindener, Frieda Brayer, and Erika Lori trained at the paper.

61 Memo, n.d., BArch-B, R103/91.

62 Letter, Kardorff to unnamed friend, 27 March 1937, IfZ, ED348/4.

63 Rahms, *Zwischen den Zeilen*, 11.

64 Ibid., 26.

65 Mills, *A Place in the News*, 24.

66 Ibid.

67 Rahms, *Zwischen den Zeilen*, 34–5.

68 Alice Fahs, *Out on Assignment: Newspaper Women and the Making of Modern Public Space* (Chapel Hill: University of North Carolina Press), 163. See also Martha Gellhorn, *Travels with Myself and Another* (London: Allen Lane, 1978).

69 Noelle-Neumann, *Die Erinnerungen*, 51–2.

70 Ibid., 82.

71 Memo from Wilhelm Weiß, RDP, Schulvorbildung der Schriftleiteranwärter, 28 June 1943, BArch-B, R103/7, Nr. 18.

72 Statistics compiled from RDP, BArch-B, R 103, R 34 and R 55. Of this group, ten (24 per cent) went on to attend university. Eight of these women (19 per cent) were already practising journalism during the Weimar years. Women with a university degree had to complete only a six-month internship.

73 Successful women journalists with doctorates included Margret Boveri, Gertraude Ulmer, Heddy Neumeister, Hanna Holzwart, Hildegard Faber, and Ruth Hildebrand.

74 Dr Else Boger-Eichler, Lebenslauf, 12 April 1935, BArch-B, NS44/174.

75 Jorg Requate, *Journalismus als Beruf: Entstehung und Entwicklung des Journalistenberufs im 19 Jahrhundert. Deutschland im internationalen Vergleich* (Göttingen: Vandenhoeck und Ruprecht, 1995), 17.

76 Although the regime made early attempts to restrict the numbers of female university students, by the mid-1930s it grew increasingly anxious to recruit women, even in areas where they had not traditionally been significantly represented. See Jill Stephenson, "Women and the Professions in Germany, 1900–1945," in *German Professions, 1800–1950*, ed. Geoffrey Cocks and Konrad H. Jarausch (New York: Oxford University Press, 1990), 277.

77 Helmut Sündermann, *Der Weg zum deutschen Journalismus: Hinweise für die Berufswahl junger Nationalsozialisten* (Berlin: Franz Eher, 1938), 17.

78 Carmen Sitter, *"Die eine Hälfte vergisst man(n) leicht!" Zur Situation von Journalistinnen in Deutschland* (Pfaffenweiler: Centaurus, 1998), 218. See also Aufklärungsblätter über die akademischen Berufe, Schriftleiter (Journalist, Redakteur) akad. geb. Nach dem Stand vom 1. January 1938, BArch-B, R103/25.

79 Meyer, Gertraude Uhlhorn interview, in *Medienfrauen*, 121.

80 Sitter, *Die eine Hälfte*, 218.

81 Statistics compiled from RDP, BArch-B, R103/234. Out of 342 trainees, 167 were women.

82 Ibid.

83 Meyer-Christian, "Der erste Kursus der RPS," *Deutsche Presse*, 20 April 1935.

84 Boger-Eichler, *Die Schriftleiterin*, 12.

85 Sitter, *Die eine Hälfte*, 232.

86 Heinrich Holtze, "Reichspresseschule – ein Sieb für den Nachwuchs," *Deutsche Presse*, August 1935.

87 Memo, Wilhelm Weiß, RDP, 29 April 1936, BArch-B, R103/2, Nr. 32.

88 Letter, Kardorff to Hanna, 27 April 1939, IfZ, ED348/4.

89 Gutachten der Reichspresseschule, BArch-B, 17 April 1939, R55/456.

90 Fritz Zeirke, "Was treibt die Reichspresseschule," *Deutsche Presse*, 15 May 1937, 225.

91 For a discussion on culture and "Bildung" in the nineteenth and early twentieth century, see Jennifer Jenkins, *Provincial Modernity: Local Culture and Liberal Politics in Fin-de-Siècle Hamburg* (Ithaca, NY: Cornell University Press, 2003).

92 Meyer-Christian, "Der erste Kursus," *Deutsche Presse*, 20 April 1935.

93 Ibid. In 1938, twenty-five female journalists completed this course. Sitter, *Die eine Hälfte*, 219.

94 Ibid.

95 Chambers, Steiner, and Fleming, *Women and Journalism*, 65.

96 Else Günther, "'Sieben zu Siebzig': Jungschriftleiterinnen in der Gemeinschaft der Reichspresseschule," *Deutsche Presse*, 29 August 1936, Nr. 35, 432.

97 Ibid.

98 See, for instance, Leo Leixner, "Zurück aus Hinterpommern: Eine Studienfahrt der Reichspresseschule," *Deutsche Presse*, 21 August 1937, Nr. 24, 378.

99 Ruth v. Kondratowicz, Personalfragebogen, 22 October 1938, BArch-B, R103/187. Kondratowicz was also employed as the secretary to the head of the school.

100 Heinrich Boltze, "Die Reichspresseschule – ein Sieb für den Nachwuchs," *Deutsche Presse*, 10 August 1935, 382; Karolina Seyboth, Lebenslauf, n.d., BArch-B, R103/197.

101 Protokoll der Landesverbände Leiter, 22 March 1943, BArch-B, R103/127. The surviving documents are fragmentary; most related to exam results are from 1943 and 1944.

102 Rahms, *Zwischen den Zeilen*, 17. See also BArch-B, R103/100.

103 Introduction by Peter Hartl in Ursula von Kardorff, *Berliner Aufzeichnungen aus den Jahren 1942 bis 1945* (Munich: Beck, 1992), 12.

104 Ibid.

105 Rahms, *Zwischen den Zeilen*, 17.

106 Ibid.

107 Protokoll über die Schriftleiteranwärter-Prüfung, RDP, 12 March 1944, BArch-B, R103/94.

108 Memo, RDP, 4 March 1938, BArch-B, R103/4, Nr. 10.

109 See RDP files, R103/91, 119, 120.

110 Compiled numbers based on exam reports from RDP files R103/92, R103/127, R103/122, R103/91. The numbers for the prewar exams are not available.

111 Aufklärungsblätter über die akademischen Berufe, Schriftleiter (Journalist, Redakteur), 1 January 1938, BArch-B, R103/25.

112 Letter, Thimme to Hans Schwarz van Berk, 27 October 1936, Landesarchiv Berlin (LAB), A Rep 250-06-04, Nr. 3.

113 National Socialist Women's League, membership cards, BArch-B, NS44/100, 131.

114 Letter, Schwarz van Berk to Thimme, 19 November 1936, LAB, A Rep 250-06-04, Nr. 3.

115 NS-Frauenschaft, March 1939, BArch-B, NS44/46.

116 Margret Boveri, *Verzweigungen: Eine Autobiographie*, ed. Uwe Johnson (Munich: R. Piper, 1977), 236.

117 Anja Meyer, Waltraud Fest interview, in *Medienfrauen*, 142–3.

118 Jacques Picard, *Edit von Coler: Als Nazi-Agentin in Bukarest* (Bonn: Schiller, 2010), 29.

119 Chambers, Steiner, and Fleming, *Women and Journalism*, 3.

120 Anja Meyer, Thea Fischer interview, in *Medienfrauen*, 103.

121 Neumann, *Die Erinnerungen*, 50.

122 Rahms, *Zwischen den Zeilen*, 16.

123 Ibid., 44.

124 Ibid., 54.

125 Ibid., 14.

126 Ibid., 15.

127 Letter, Herr Lindner to the RDP, 18 December 1939, BArch-B, R103/80.

128 Dresler, *Die Frau im Journalismus*, 11–12.

129 Sitter, *Die eine Hälfte*, 226.

130 Statistics compiled from various files: BArch-B, R103, R55, R34, NS44, NS42; LAB, A Rep 250-06-04, E Rep 200–64; IfZ, ED 324, ED 348. Thirty-five of these women did not indicate one way or another whether they worked freelance or in a full-time position. Assuming that these thirty-five women were freelance journalists, the number increases to 105 (74 per cent). Moreover, the women who listed a position with a newspaper may not have been permanent employees but rather occasional employees.

131 Dr Heddy Neumeister, Lebenslauf, n.d., BArch-B, RK 1483.

132 Dehio wrote for diverse papers, including *Der Angriff*, the women's magazine *Die Frau*, the *Deutsche Allgemeine Zeitung*, and the Deutsches Nachrichtenbüro (DNB; German News Agency).

133 Letter, Dehio to Kränzlein, 5 March 1939, LAB, A Rep 250-06-04, Nr. 5.

134 Letter, Dehio to Kränzlein, 11 June 1937, LAB, A Rep 250-06-04, Nr. 4

135 Letter, Dehio to the editorial department, *Der Angriff*, 30 March 1939, LAB, A Rep 250-06-04, Nr. 5.

136 Letter, Dehio to Kränzlein, 15 January 1938, LAB, A Rep 250-06-04, Nr. 5.

137 Letter, Waldemar Lenz to editorial department, *Der Angriff*, 22 April 1938, LABA Rep 250-06-04, Nr. 4.

138 Letter, *Der Angriff* to Lenz, 26 April 1938, LAB A Rep 250-06-04, Nr. 5.

139 As of November 1938, in a list sent to the German Foreign Ministry, Kränzlein listed Dehio as the paper's only correspondent in Rome. Memo, Kränzlein to the Auswärtiges Amt, 25 November 1938, LAB, A Rep 250-06-04, Nr. 2.

140 Dresler, *Die Frau im Journalismus*, 11.

141 Gertrud Burath, Fragebogen, 1 October 1936, BArch-B, RK I62.

142 Herta Herbst, Lebenslauf, Fragebogen, 23 August 1935, BArch-B, RK I233.
143 André Uzulis, "'Darf nichts bringen': Eine Nachrichtenagentur im Dritten Reich," in *"Diener des Staates" oder "Widerstand zwischen den Zeilen"? Die Rolle der Presse im Dritten Reich*, ed. Christoph Studt (Berlin: Lit, 2007), 110.
144 Statistics compiled from lists of *Decknamen* from BArch-B, R103/92, 4, 5, and 24.
145 Boveri, *Verzweigungen*, 284.
146 For instance, Ilse Thien used the pseudonym "Schuster."
147 Meyer, Gertraude Uhlhorn interview, in *Medienfrauen*, 126
148 Statistics compiled from the lists of *Decknamen* from BArch-B, R103/92, 4, 5, 6, and 24.
149 I have found no cases where a man used a women's pseudonym to publish in a women's magazine.
150 Statistics compiled from various BArch-B, R103 files. It is not possible to break down the figures into those who worked before the war and those who started their career during the war.
151 Senta Ulitz, "Haben Sie Lust zu diesem Beruf?" *Die junge Dame*, 1 June 1941, Nr. 24.
152 Anneliese Schwahl, "Haben Sie Lust zu diesem Beruf?" *Die junge Dame*, 1 June 1941, Nr. 24.
153 Ibid.
154 Marta Hillers, Fragebogen, August 1938, BArch-B, RKB76.
155 Marta Hillers and Trude Sand, "Heimat Landstraße: Zwei Mädel mit Fernfahrern unterwegs," *Berliner Lokal-Anzeiger*, 11–15 December 1934.
156 Groth-Schmachtenberger, *Meine liebsten Fotos*, 15.
157 Ibid., 22.
158 Christine Dippold, "Die Fotografin und ihr Werk. Eine Einführung," in *Im Fokus*, 20.
159 See Shayla Thiel, "Shifting Identities, Creating New Paradigms," *Feminist Media Studies* 4, no. 1 (2004): 23, 28. Thiel looks at online journalism, but her findings can equally be applied to print journalism in the twentieth century.
160 Groth-Schmachtenberger, *Meine liebsten Fotos*, 24.
161 Ibid., 35.
162 Noelle-Neumann, *Die Erinnerungen*, 29, 41.
163 Ibid., 82.
164 Rahms, *Zwischen den Zeilen*, 126.
165 Ibid., 30–3.
166 Ibid., 35.
167 Peter Fritzsche, *Life and Death in the Third Reich* (Cambridge, MA: Harvard University Press, 2008), 37.
168 Letter, Kardorff to unknown, 12 October 1938, IfZ, ED 348/4.
169 Ibid.

## 2 Prettying Up Politics and Normalizing Nazism, 1933–1939

1 Josephine Trampler-Steiner, "Die Frau als Publizistin und Leserin: Deutsche Zeitschriften von und für Frauen" (PhD diss. , University of Munich, 1938), 67. At the University of Munich, Trampler-Steiner worked under the supervision of famed professor of journalism Dr Karl D'Ester.

2 Ibid.

3 "Nachrichtendienst der Presse-Frauenschaft," *Deutsche Presse*, 9 September 1933, Nr. 36, 586.

4 Karin Wright, Martin Scott, Mel Bunce, "Soft Power, Hard News: How Journalists at State-Funded Transnational Media Legitimize Their Work," *International Journal of Press Politics* 25, no. 4 (2020): 608.

5 Joseph Nye, *Soft Power: The Means to Success in World Politics* (New York: Public Affairs, 2004), x.

6 Carmen Sitter, *"Die eine Hälfte vergisst man(n) leicht!" Zur Situation von Journalistinnen in Deutschland unter besonderer Berücksichtigung des 20. Jahrhunderts* (Pfaffenweiler: Centaurus, 1998), 224.

7 See Laurie Marhoefer, *Sex and the Weimar Republic: German Homosexual Emancipation and the Rise of the Nazis* (Toronto: University of Toronto Press, 2015) and Annette Timm, *The Politics of Fertility in Twentieth-Century Berlin* (New York: Cambridge University Press, 2010).

8 See Elizabeth Dixon Whitaker, *Measuring Mamma's Milk: Fascism and the Medicalization of Maternity in Italy* (Ann Arbor: University of Michigan Press, 2009) and Tricia Stark, *The Body Soviet: Propaganda, Hygiene, and the Revolutionary State* (Madison: University of Wisconsin Press, 2008), 160.

9 Karl Christian Führer, "Pleasure, Practicality and Propaganda: Popular Magazines in Nazi Germany, 1933–1939," in *Pleasure and Power in Nazi Germany*, ed. Pamela E. Swett, Corey Ross, and Fabrice d'Almeida (New York: Palgrave Macmillan, 2011), 133.

10 Adolf Dresler, *Die Frau im Journalismus* (Munich: Knorr & Hirth, 1936), 11–12; see also Else Boger-Eichler, *Die Schriftleiterin* (Berlin: Akademisches Auskunftsamt der Deutschen Arbeitsfront, 1939), 8.

11 Deborah Chambers, Linda Steiner, and Carole Fleming, *Women and Journalism* (London: Routledge, 2004), 7; Alice Fahs, *Out on Assignment: Newspaper Women and the Making of Modern Public Space* (Chapel Hill: University of North Carolina Press, 2014), 59.

12 For more on the regime's economic objectives see Adam Tooze, *The Wages of Destruction: The Making and Breaking of the Nazi Economy* (New York: Penguin, 2007).

13 "Das Schriftleitergesetz," *Zeitungs-Verlag*, 7 October 1933, Nr. 40, 650–1.

14 "Die Arbeitstagung des RDP," *Deutsche Presse*, 14 December 1935, 662–3; Helmut Sündermann, *Der Weg zum deutschen Journalismus: Hinweise für die Berufswahl junger Nationalsozialisten* (Berlin: Franz Eher, 1938), 9.

15 Annie Juliane Richert, "Über den Fachausschuss der Schriftleiterinnen," *Deutsche Presse*, 14 December 1935, Nr. 59, 668–9.

16 Ibid.

17 Boger-Eichler, *Die Schriftleiterin*, 8.

18 Wilhelm Weiß, "Die Frau im Schriftleiterberuf," *Deutsche Presse*, 7 March 1936, 118.

19 Ibid.

20 Boger-Eichler, *Die Schriftleiterin*, 8.

21 Dresler, *Die Frau im Journalismus*, 11–12.

22 Weiß, "Die Frau im Schriftleiterberuf," 118.

23 Dresler, *Die Frau im Journalismus*, 11–12.

24 "Schriftleiter muß Kämpfer für den neuen Staat sein," *Völkischer Beobachter*, 21 April 1934, Nr. 111.

25 Boger-Eichler, *Die Schriftleiterin*, 8; Aufklärungsblätter über die akademischen Berufe, Schriftleiter (Journalist, Redakteur), 1 January 1938, Bundesarchiv Berlin-Lichterfelde (BArch-B), R103/25.

26 Boger-Eichler, *Die Schriftleiterin*, 8.

27 Anja Meyer, Gertraude Uhlhorn interview, in *Medienfrauen der ersten Stunde: "Wir waren ja die Trümmerfrauen in diesem Beruf,"* ed. Angelika Engler and Lissi Klaus (Zurich: eFeF, 1993), 138.

28 Annie Juliane Richert, "Die Frauenbeilage in der Tageszeitung," *Deutsche Presse*, 1 September 1935, Nr. 01, 1.

29 Statistics compiled from various files: BArch-B, R103, R55, R34, NS44, NS42; Landesarchiv Berlin (LAB), A Rep 250-06-04, E Rep 200-64; Institut für Zeitgeschichte Munich (IfZ), ED 324, ED 348. Based on 247 women. This statistic may be too low, since other women who indicated that they worked in areas outside of so-called women's issues may also have contributed to women's publications or supplements.

30 Alexa Godbersen, Felicitas Kapteina interview, *Medienfrauen*, 66.

31 Helene Rahms, *Zwischen den Zeilen: Mein Leben als Journalistin im Dritten Reich* (Bern: Scherz, 1997), 11.

32 Ibid.

33 Protokoll über die Schriftleiteranwärter-Prüfung, Reichsverband der Deutschen Presse (RDP), 12 March 1944, BArch-B, R103/94. This report stated: "As usual, most of the candidates lean toward the cultural or entertainment pages … but their exam answers also indicate that they recognize that the role of journalist is first and foremost political and one must be able to grapple with political issues."

34 Führer, "Pleasure, Practicality and Propaganda," 133; Jürgen Wilke, *Presseanweisungen im zwanzigsten Jahrhundert: Erster Weltkrieg–Drittes Reich–DDR* (Cologne: Böhlau, 2007), 253.

35 Judith Prokasky, *Zwischen den Zeilen? Zeitungspresse als NS-Machtinstrument* (Berlin: Stiftung Topografie des Terrors, 2013), 13.

36 Alfred Schmidt, *Publizistik im Dorf* (Dresden: M. Dittert, 1939), 19. According to the 1937 census 380 people – 200 men and 180 women – lived in the area.

37 Führer, "Pleasure, Practicality and Propaganda," 132.

38 Dorothee Goebeler, "Die Frauenzeitschrift von einst und jetzt," *Der Zeitschriften-Verleger*, 21 August 1940, Nr. 34, 236–69.

39 Elisabeth Strietholt, "Noch einmal: Die Frauenbeilage," *Zeitungs-Verlag*, 4 April 1936, Nr. 14, 164–5.

40 Wilke, *Presseanweisungen im zwanzigsten Jahrhundert*, 240.

41 Marta Hillers, Fragebogen, August 1938, BArch-B, RKB76.

42 Marta Hillers, "Friseurin sehr gesucht!" *Die neue Gartenlaube*, January 1938, Nr. 4, 88.

43 See Jennifer Lynn, *Contested Femininities: Representations of Modern Women in the German Illustrated Press, 1920–1960* (forthcoming). See also Norbert Frei and Johannes Schmitz, *Journalismus im Dritten Reich* (Munich: Beck, 1989), 72. Most of the women's magazines in circulation in 1939 were established during the Weimar Republic.

44 Anneliese Reese, "Eines schickt sich nicht für alles," *Berliner Lokal-Anzeiger*, 2 December 1934.

45 "Aus dem weiblichen Berufsleben: Studium der Juristin," *Berliner Lokal-Anzeiger*, 16 December 1934.

46 Carola Ihlenberg "Vater wird plötzlich die Hauptperson! Das Glück des Schenkens und das der Beschenkten," *Berliner Lokaler-Anzeiger*, 2 December 1934, 5.

47 Carola Ihlenberg "Der Monat der Einkäufe," *Berliner Lokaler-Anzeiger*, 2 December 1934, 6.

48 Pamela E. Swett, "Private Life in the People's Economy: Spending and Saving in Nazi Germany," in *Private Life and Privacy in Nazi Germany*, ed. Elizabeth Harvey, Johannes Hürter, Maiken Umbach, and Andreas Wirsching (Cambridge: Cambridge University Press, 2019), 17.

49 Frei and Schmitz, *Journalismus im Dritten Reich*, 76.

50 See Dr Willy Stiewe, *Das Pressefoto als publizistisches Mittel* (Leipzig, 1936).

51 Arthur Gläser, "Die Frau als Fotografin: Zu den Bildern von Ingeborg Hoppe," quoted in Rolf Sachsse, "Im Schatten der Männer: Deutsche Fotografinnen 1940 bis 1950," in *Frauenobjectiv: Fotografinnen 1940 bis 1950* (Cologne: Wienand, 2001), 25.

52  Erika Groth-Schmachtenberger, "Am Lido von Rom," *Illustrierter Rundfunk*, November 1937, Nr. 32, 35.

53  Monika Ständecke, "Idylle und Wirklichkeit: Landleben im Sucher," in *Im Fokus: Die Bildberichterstatterin Erika Groth-Schmachtenberger und ihr Werk*, ed. Christine Dippold and Monika Kania-Schütz (Grossweil: Echter, 2008), 80; see also Elizabeth Harvey, "'Ich war überall': Die NS-Propagandaphotogr/aphin Liselotte Purper," in *Volksgenossinnen: Frauen in der NS-Volksgemeinschaft*, ed. Sybille Steinbacher (Göttingen: Wallstein, 2007), 142.

54  Erika Groth-Schmachtenberger, "Mädel im Landdienst," *Illustrierter Rundfunk*, 1939, Nr. 29, 35.

55  Nancy Reagin, *Sweeping the German Nation: Domesticity and National Identity in Germany, 1870–1945* (Cambridge: Cambridge University Press, 2007), 150.

56  Sitter, *Die eine Hälfte*, 221.

57  Weiß, "Die Frau im Schriftleiterberuf," 118.

58  The paper appeared biweekly from 1932 to 1943, after which it was published monthly until 1945.

59  Memo, Reichsfrauenführerin, Gemeinschaftswerbung für unsere Zeitschriften, 1 November 1937, Nr. 166/37, BArch-B, NS45.

60  Ibid.

61  Erika Kirmsse, *Deutsches Frauenschaffen: Jahrbuch der Reichsfrauenführung* (Berlin: Reichsfrauenführung, 1937), 6; Kirsten Döhring and Renate Feldmann, *Von "N.S. Frauen-Warte" bis "Victory": Konstruktionen von Weiblichkeit in nationalsozialistischen und rechtsextremen Frauenzeitschriften* (Berlin: Logos, 2004), 89.

62  Memo, *N.S. Frauen-Warte*, 30 November 1932, BArch-B, NS44/54.

63  Lydia Gottschweski, "Weibliches Führertum," *N.S. Frauen-Warte*, 1 October 1933, Nr. 7, 179.

64  Döhring and Feldmann, *Von "N.S. Frauen-Warte" bis "Victory,"* 91. Study based on 236 articles. Well-known male journalists, including the editor of the party paper *Der Angriff*, Hans Schwarz van Berk, also published in the paper.

65  Ellen Schwarz-Semmelroth file, BArch-B, Collection Former Berlin Document Center (BDC), Personenbezogene Unterlagen der Reichskulturkammer (RK), RKI549.

66  See *NS Frauen-Warte* issues from July 1933 to August 1939, BArch-B, NS47/12. See also Döhring and Feldmann, *Von "N.S. Frauen-Warte" bis "Victory,"* 92.

67  *NS Frauen-Warte*, August 1936, BArch-B, NSD47.12. For more on Nazi control of food, see Gesine Gerhard, *Nazi Hunger Politics: A History of Food in the Third Reich* (Washington DC: Rowman & Littlefield, 2015).

68  See Reagin, *Sweeping the German Nation*, 6.

69  "Unsere Wohnung wird ein Heim," *NS Frauen-Warte*, June 1938, Nr. 26, 182, BArch-B, NSD47/12.

70  Gertrud Villforth, Meldebogen, 10 March 1950, Staatsarchiv Ludwigsburg (StAL) EL 902–20 BA89419.

71  Gertrud Villforth, "Kleine Modeschau," *NS Frauen-Warte*, April 1936, Nr. 22.

72  Swett, "Private Life in the People's Economy," 17.

73  See Irene Guenther, *Nazi Chic? Fashioning Women in the Third Reich* (Oxford: Berg, 2004).

74  As quoted in Johannes Christoph Moderegger, *Modefotografie in Deutschland* (Norderstedt: Libri, 2000), 84.

75  For more on the regime's pro- and anti-natal policies, see Gisela Bock, *Zwangssterilisation im Nationalsozialismus: Studien zur Rassenpolitik und Frauenpolitik* (Opladen: Westdeutscher, 1986) and Michelle Mouton, *From Nurturing the Nation to Purifying the Volk: Weimar and Nazi Family Policy, 1918–1945* (Cambridge: Cambridge University Press, 2007).

76  Published in *NS Frauen-Warte*, 1934 and 1939, respectively.

77  Renate von Stieda, Lebenslauf, 26 January 1939; RDP Fragebogen, n.d, BArch-B, BDC, RKB211.

78  Renate von Stieda,"Kulturgemeinschaft," *NS Frauen-Warte*, September 1933, Nr. 6.

79  Renate von Stieda, "Von der Kraft des Zeitgeistes in unserem Leben," *NS Frauen-Warte*, March 1936, Nr. 20.

80  Renate von Stieda, "Aufgabe und Leistung der SA. Wehrertüchtigung der jungen Mannschaft: Die ersten NS- Kampfspiele," *NS Frauen-Warte*, October 1937.

81  Renata von Stieda, "Der Reichsparteitag der Arbeit 1937," *NS Frauen-Warte*, October 1937.

82  Wilke, *Presseanweisungen im zwanzigsten Jahrhundert*, 154.

83  Döhring and Feldmann, *Von "N.S. Frauen-Warte" bis "Victory,"* 98–9.

84  Doris Bergen, "The Nazi Concept of 'Volksdeutsche' and the Exacerbation of Anti-Semitism in Eastern Europe, 1939–45," *Journal of Contemporary History* 29, no. 4 (October 1994): 569.

85  For more on Germany's colonial discourse and actions in Poland, see Elizabeth Harvey, *Women and the Nazi East: Agents and Witnesses of Germanization* (New Haven, CT: Yale University Press, 2003) and Kristen Kopp, *Germany's Wild East: Constructing Poland as Colonial Space* (Ann Arbor: University of Michigan Press, 2012).

86  Hanna Koblick, "Schlesien als Grenzland," *NS Frauen-Warte*, July 1935.

87  Bergen, "The Nazi Concept of 'Volksdeutsche,'" 570.

88  Ibid.

89  Koblick, "Schlesien als Grenzland."

90  Ibid.

91  Erika Meyer, "Danzig im Not," *NS Frauen-Warte*, August 1935.

92  Ibid.

93  Renate von Stieda, Lebenslauf, 26 January 1939, BArch-B, BDC, RKB211.

94  Letter, von Stieda to Ernst Jünger, 18 August 1962, Deutsches Literaturarchiv Marbach (DLA), 6 BZ 94.9.

95  Else Frobenius, *Erinnerungen einer Journalistin: Zwischen Kaiserreich und Zweitem Weltkrieg*, ed. Lora Wildenthal (Cologne: Böhlau, 2005), 91.

96  Else Frobenius, Fragebogen, 1938, BArch-B, BDC, RKI120. For more on the colonialist movement and public culture, see Willeke Sandler, *Empire in the Heimat: Colonialism and Public Culture in the Third Reich* (New York: Oxford University Press, 2018).

97  Frobenius, *Erinnerungen*, 193.

98  Ibid., 180. For more on German women and colonialism, see Lora Wildenthal, *German Women for Empire, 1884–1945* (Durham, NC: Duke University Press, 2001).

99  The women's supplements were incorporated into the paper's *Feuilleton* section.

100  Frobenius, *Erinnerungen*, 180.

101  Ibid., 194.

102  Ibid.

103  Ibid.

104  Alice Rilke, "Nationalsozialismus der Tat," *NS Frauen-Warte*, November 1935, Nr. 11.

105  Ibid.

106  Barbara Lüdecke, "Die Lebenshaltung der Berufstätigen Frau," *NS Frauen-Warte*, August 1935, Nr. 3.

107  Antonie Werner, "Etwas über den Krankenpflegerinnen-Beruf und Ausbildungsmöglichkeiten," *NS Frauen-Warte*, January 1936, Nr. 16; Annemarie Bechem, "Froh und gesund: Lehrerin an Bäuerlichen Werkschulen," *NS Frauen-Warte*, January 1936, Nr. 16.

108  M. Schinz, photos by Erna Lendvai-Dirksn, "Frauenberufe," *NS Frauen-Warte*, January 1936, Nr. 16.

109  "Neue Wege der Mädchenbildung: Vom Frauenabitur zum Frauenberuf," *NS Frauen-Warte*, January 1936, Nr. 16.

110  Ibid.

111  Katja Protte, "Beruf: 'Bildberichterstatterin,' in 'Bildberichterstatterin im Dritten Reich': Fotografien aus den Jahren 1937 bis 1944 von Liselotte Purper," *Deutsches Historisches Museum Magazine* 20 (Summer 1997): 4.

112  Ilse Urbach, Lebenslauf, undated, BArch-B, R103/94.

113  Führer, "Pleasure, Practicality and Propaganda," 141.

114 NSDAP Gauleitung Berlin, Politische Beurteilung, Katharina Kleikamp, 28 May 1937, BArch-B, BDC, RKI279.
115 Memo, Amtsgerichtsrat Justitiar, RDP, 1 August 1938, BArch-B, R103/4, Nr. 53.
116 Ruth Andreas-Friedrich, Fragebogen, Reichsschrifttumskammer, 1936, 1938, BArch-B, RKI7; "Probleme um die Ehe: Die ersten Ehemonate," *Berliner Hausfrau*, 15 July 1937, Nr. 42.
117 Ibid. The *Frankfurter Illustrierte Blatt* was Germany's fourteenth most popular magazine. Andreas-Friedrich also published in *Mode und Heim, Fürs Haus, Berliner Hausfrau*, the *DAZ* and the *Neue Illustrierte Zeitung*.
118 Ilse Thien, Lebenslauf, n.d., BArch-B, BDC, RKI57. Thien also wrote for *Deutsche Familien-Illustrierte, Elegante Welt, Für alle*, and *Berliner Hausfrau*.
119 Trampler-Steiner, *Die Frau als Publizistin*, 103.
120 Leondard W. Doob, "Goebbels' Principles of Propaganda," *Public Opinion Quarterly* 14, no. 3 (1950): 442.
121 Andrew Stuart Bergerson, "Integrating in the Accusative: The Daily Papers of Interwar Hildesheim," *Issues in Integrative Studies* 15 (1997): 8.

## 3  Traversing Borders, Pushing Boundaries

1 Petra Vermehren was based in Greece when she wrote for the *Berliner Tageblatt* and, after its cancellation, the *Deutsche Allgemeine Zeitung*. She eventually reported from Lisbon for *Das Reich*.
2 Julia Edwards, *Women of the World: The Great Foreign Correspondents* (Boston: Houghton Mifflin, 1988), 5. See also Sarah Lonsdale, "The 'Awkward' Squad: British Women Foreign Correspondents during the Interwar Years," *Women's History Review*, 23 May 2021, 1–21.
3 For more on foreign correspondents in Germany, see Norman Domeier, *Weltöffentlichkeit und Diktatur: Die amerikanischen Auslandskorrespondenten im "Dritten Reich"* (Göttingen: Wallstein, 2021).
4 See Elizabeth Harvey, *Women and the Nazi East: Agents and Witnesses of Germanization* (New Haven, CT: Yale University Press, 2003) and Melissa Kravetz, *Women Doctors in Weimar and Nazi Germany: Materialism, Eugenics and Professional Identity* (Toronto: University of Toronto Press, 2019).
5 John Maxwell Hamilton, *Journalism's Roving Eye: A History of American Foreign Reporting* (Baton Rouge: Louisiana State University Press, 2009), 47.
6 Ibid., 194.
7 Ibid., 1.
8 Ibid., 9.
9 Margret Boveri, *Verzweigungen: Eine Autobiographie*, ed. Uwe Johnson (Munich: Piper, 1977), 321.

10  Boveri's dissertation was "Personalities and Apparatus of Foreign Policy Management under Sir Edward Gray (1904–1916)."

11  Boveri, *Verzweigungen*, 222, 218.

12  Margret Boveri, Lebenslauf, 21 February 1938, Reichssender Breslau, Bundesarchiv Berlin-Lichterfelde (BArch-B), Collection Former Berlin Document Center (BDC), Personenbezogene Unterlagen der Reichskulturkammer (RK), BDC, RKI50.

13  Norbert Frei and Johannes Schmitz, *Journalismus im Dritten Reich* (Munich: Beck, 1989), 47.

14  Ibid.

15  Boveri, *Verzweigungen*, 230.

16  Ibid., 237, 239. The articles were titled "Das japanisch-englische Bündnis von 1902"; "Empire-Politik"; "Die Flottenfrage und der Status Quo"; "Die Durchdringung des Vorderen Orients"; "Der Kampf der Admiralitäten"; and "Zur Konferenz der Balkanmächte."

17  Ibid., 237.

18  See Heike B. Görtemaker, *Ein deutsches Leben: Die Geschichte der Margret Boveri* (Beck: Munich, 2005).

19  Ibid., 69.

20  Edwards, *Women of the World*, 60–1.

21  Görtemaker, *Ein deutsches Leben*, 76.

22  Ibid., 268.

23  Scheffer to Boveri, 25 June 1935, cited in ibid., 76.

24  See, for instance, Margret Boveri, "Zwischen den Inseln Griechenlands," *Der Welt-Spiegel und Frauen-Spiegel, Berliner Tageblatt*, 21 July 1935, Nr. 29.

25  Boveri, *Verzweigungen*, 276.

26  Jürgen Wilke, *Presseanweisungen im zwanzigsten Jahrhundert: Erster Weltkrieg–Drittes Reich–DDR* (Cologne: Böhlau, 2007), 158.

27  Margret Boveri, "Flug zum Mittelmeer: Erlebnisse auf der Reise nach Malta," *Berliner Tageblatt*, 13 October 1935, Nr. 485, 3.

28  Ibid.

29  Boveri, *Verzweigungen*, 277.

30  Deborah Chambers, Linda Steiner, and Carole Fleming, *Women and Journalism* (London: Routledge, 2004), 203.

31  Boveri, *Verzweigungen*, 282, 284.

32  Görtemaker, *Ein deutsches Leben*, 86.

33  Boveri, *Verzweigungen*, 233.

34  Lonsdale, "The 'Awkward' Squad," 12.

35  Boveri, *Verzweigungen*, 301.

36  Letter, Scheffer to Boveri, 30 October 1936; Görtemaker, *Ein deutsches Leben*, 85.

37  "Drahtmeldung unseres Korrespondenten: Mussolinis große Rede. Stürmische Begeisterung auf dem Domplatz," *Berliner Tageblatt*, 2 November 1936.

38  Italy quit the League of Nations in December 1937.

39  M. Boveri, "Ein Heimkehrer nach Europa: Italiens neue Außenpolitik nach Beendigung der abessinischen Unternehmung," *Berliner Tageblatt*, 8 December 1936, Nr. 580, 2.

40  Margret Boveri, Lebenslauf, 21 February 1938, BArch-B, BDC, RKI50.

41  Boveri, *Verzweigungen*, 319.

42  Ibid., 311.

43  Ibid., 319. Boveri visited Turkey, Syria, Lebanon, Iraq, and Iran.

44  MB, "Erschüttertes Vertrauen," *Frankfurter Zeitung*, 20 August 1939, 3.

45  Görtemaker, *Ein deutsches Leben*, 120.

46  Lily Abegg, *Japans Traum vom Musterland: Der neue Nipponismus* (Munich: Kurt Desch, 1973), 11.

47  LA, "No Denunciation of the Washington Agreement" (Tokyo), 2 April 1934, Deutsches Nachrichtenbüro (DNB).

48  Lily Abegg, *Yamato: Der Sendungsglaube des japanischen Volkes* (Frankfurt: Societats Verlag, 1936).

49  Ricky Law, *Transnational Nazism: Ideology and Culture in German-Japanese Relations, 1919–1936* (Cambridge: Cambridge University Press, 2019), 185, 203.

50  Ibid., 202.

51  Andreas Tobler, "Eine Schweizerin folgt Hitler nach Paris," *Tagesanzeiger*, 29 June 2019, https://www.tagesanzeiger.ch/kultur/diverses/eine-schweizerin-folgt-hitler-nach-paris/story/24854013.

52  Ibid.

53  Letter, Abegg to Richard Kempe, Auswärtiges Amt, 26 February 1939, Politisches Archiv des Auswärtigen Amts (AA/PA), Nachlass Kempe, NL136-1.

54  Boveri, *Verzweigungen*, 349.

55  LA, "Tschiang Kai-schek will Zeit gewinnen: Ein Teil der Zentralarmee noch im Inneren Chinas," Funkmeldung, *Frankfurter Zeitung*, 2 December 1937, Nr. 613–41, 1.

56  LA, Hankau "Ungleicher Kampf: Die Ursachen der japanischen Siege in China," *Frankfurter Zeitung*, 29 December 1937, Nr. 661–2, 1–2.

57  See, for example, Mary Lynne Stewart, *Gender, Generation, and Journalism in France, 1910–1940* (Montreal and Kingston: McGill-Queen's University Press, 2018), 73. Andreé Viollis, a reporter for *Le Petit Parisien* won a prize for her exposé of Japanese militarism in 1933, awarded by *L'Europe nouvelle*, the weekly review of foreign policy.

58  Law, *Transnational Nazism*, 196.

59  See Günther Gillessen, *Auf verlorenem Posten: Die Frankfurter Zeitung im Dritten Reich* (Munich: Siedler, 1992).

60  LA, "Die Männer von Peipiag: Erbitterung in Hankau über die Gegenregierung," *Frankfurter Zeitung*, 23 December 1937, Nr. 652–3, 1.

61  LA, "Das Vordringen der Japaner in Nanking," *Frankfurter Zeitung*, 19 December 1937, Nr. 645–6, 2.

62  See, for instance, Abegg to Kempe, Auswärtiges Amt, 26 February 1939, AA/PA, Nachlass Kempe, NL136-1.

63  Law, *Transnational Nazism*, 198. Law shows that the *Völkischer Beobachter* combined reporting and political advocacy in an effort to build unofficial connections with Japan.

64  Hamilton, *Roving Eye*, 175.

65  Chambers, Steiner, and Fleming, *Women and Journalism*, 3.

66  *Berliner Börsen-Courier*, 30 November 1932, Nr. 560.

67  *Der Tag*, 23 September 1933.

68  Darré served as Reich Minister of Nutrition and Agriculture from 1933 to 1942. He developed a plan for *Rasse und Raum* (race and space), which provided the foundation of the Nazi policy of *Lebensraum*.

69  Richard Evans, *The Third Reich in Power* (New York: Penguin Books, 2006), 347.

70  Von Coler, "Unser Heimatgau in München," *Niederdeutscher Beobachter*, 29 May 1937.

71  Ibid.

72  Von Coler, "Keine Lösung des Bodenproblems," *Nationalsozialistische Landpost*, 23 May 1936.

73  Ibid.

74  "Deutschland wächst," *Flensborg Avis*, 23 June 1935.

75  The sources available do not make it possible to ascertain whether her trip was taken in an unofficial capacity or whether she was on an assignment from one of the German ministries with which she had contact.

76  Edit von Coler, "Sachbearbeiterin im Reichsnährstand, Berlin: Bericht über eine Rumänien-Reise im Mai 1938," 11 June 1938, Institut für Zeitgeschichte Munich (IfZ), ED374/1.

77  Radu Ioanid, *The Holocaust in Romania: The Destruction of Jews and Gypsies under the Antonescu Regime, 1940–1944* (Chicago: Ivan R. Dee, 2000), 37.

78  Report, Edit von Coler, "Bericht über eine Rumänien-Reise im Mai 1938," 11 June 1938, IfZ, ED374/1.

79  "Erzeugungssteigerung – auch in Rumänien: Eine Unterredung unserer Sonderberichterstatterin mit dem rumänischen Landwirtschaftsminister," *Nationalsozialistische Landpost*, 27 May 1938.

80  Report, Edit von Coler, 22 January 1939, IfZ, ED374/1.

81  Edit von Coler, "Rumänien im Zeichen der Aufbauarbeit. Ein Reisebericht," *Berliner Börsen-Zeitung*, 11 June 1938, Nr. 268.

82  Edit von Coler, "Rumänien: Schönes Bauernland," *Deutsche Allgemeine Zeitung*, n.d., BArch-B, R901/60795.

83  Report, Edit von Coler, "Unterredung mit alten Bekannten," 10 November 1938, IfZ, ED374/1.

84  Ethnic Germans represented about 7 per cent of the Romanian population.

85  Reports, Edit von Coler, 2 and 10 November 1938, IfZ, ED374/1.

86  Norbert Götz, "German-Speaking People and Germany Heritage: Nazi Germany and the Problem of Volksgemeinschaft," in *The Heimat Abroad: The Boundaries of Germanness*, ed. Krista O'Donnell, Renate Bridenthal, and Nancy Reagin (Ann Arbor: University of Michigan Press, 2005), 76.

87  Picard, *Edit von Coler*, 73.

88  Ibid., 76.

89  Report from Edit von Coler, 21 April 1939, IfZ, ED374/1.

90  Ioanid, *The Holocaust in Romania*, 49.

91  Ibid., xxi.

92  As quoted in Picard, *Edit von Coler*, 75.

93  Malaxa had business links to Nazi Germany. He advocated for a Romanian-German alliance and eventually used his influence to help with the German war effort

94  Report, Wilhelm Fabricius, Deutsche Gesandtschaft to Auswärtiges Amt, 29 October 1938, BArch-B, R43/4106.

95  Report, Edit von Coler to Reichsnährstand, 10 November 1938, Foreign Office to Reichsnährstand, 10 November 1938, BArch-B, R43/4106.

96  "Hitler Signs Trade Peace with Carol," *Daily Express*, 24 March 1939, 1.

97  Ibid.

98  R.G. Waldeck, *Athene Palace: Hitler's "New Order" Comes to Romania* (Chicago: University of Chicago Press, 1942), 81.

99  Ibid.

100  Ibid., 82.

101  Ibid. 86.

102  Ibid.

103  Picard, *Edit von Coler*, 93.

104  Report, 6 November 1939 Nr. 4913/39 A, BArch-B, R43/4106.

105  Edit von Coler, Report to Reichsminister Dr Lammers, 27 October 1939, BArch-B, R43/4106.

106  Abschrift an Herrn von Ribbentrop, 29 July 1940, BArch-B, R43/4106.

107  Ian Kershaw, "How Effective Was Nazi Propaganda," in *Nazi Propaganda: The Power and the Limitations*, ed. David Welch (London: Routledge, 2015), 184.

108 Gisela Döhrn Fragebogen, Lebenslauf, 20 October 1942, BArch-B, BDC, R9361-V/16661.
109 Döhrn also wrote for the *Leipziger Neueste Nachrichten* and the *Essener Nationalzeitung*.
110 See, for instance, "Die Abreise," *Hamburger Fremdenblatt*, 11 November 1940, 1. Prior to Operation Barbarossa, the Soviets actively traded with Germany, shipping much-needed grain and war materials.
111 "Masseverhaftung von Gelehrten," *Hamburger Fremdenblatt*, 22 May 1937, 2.
112 Chambers, Steiner, and Fleming, *Women and Journalism*, 20.
113 Gisela Döhrn, "Du spielst Pik aus, Brüderchen," *Hamburger Fremdenblatt*, 28 August 1941, Nr. 238, 1.
114 Gisela Döhrn "Genosse Verstorbener zieht um," *Hamburger Fremdenblatt*, 4 September 1941, Nr. 245, 2.
115 Gisela Döhrn, *Das war Moskau: Vier Jahre als Berichterstatterin in der Sowjetunion* (Berlin: Albert Limberg Verland, 1941), 33.
116 Ibid., 75.
117 Ibid., 123.
118 Ibid., 125.
119 Ibid.
120 Friedrich Carl Kobbe, "Über Gisela Döhrn," *Düsseldorfer Nachrichten*, n.d.
121 Russel Lemmons, *Goebbels and Der Angriff* (Lexington: University Press of Kentucky, 1994), 128.
122 Frei and Schmitz, *Journalismus im Dritten Reich*, 98–9.
123 Memo from Kränzlein to Auslandskorrespondenten, *Der Angriff*, Hauptschriftleitung, 13 December 1938, Landesarchiv Berlin (LAB), A Rep 250-06-04, Nr. 4.
124 Der Hauptschriftleiter KRZ/P to Dr Krome, 21 August 1939, LAB, A-Rep 250-06-04, Nr. 1.
125 *Der Angriff*, 18 June 1937, 5; 20 June 1937, 6 and 13. Two examples include "Women in Strength through Joy Sport" and "Enough with the Asparagus Harvest, the First Blueberries Have Arrived."
126 Among those who contributed to the paper prior to the Second World War were Erika Hoffmann, Barbara Willie, Annemarie Lauk, Luise Lehmann, Anna Maletzki, Charlotte Tronier-Funder, Ingeborg Pabel, Adelheid Dehio, Frau Müller-Neudorf, Frau von Scheele-Willich, Ursula von Kardorff, Cecilie Ihlenfeld, and Mia Passini. This list is not exhaustive.
127 Kränzlein to Frau C. von Scheele-Willich, 4 April 1939, LAB, A Rep 250-06-04, Nr. 2.
128 *Der Angriff* to Cecilie Ihlenfeld, 16 May 1936, LAB, A Rep 250-06-04, Nr. 5.
129 Memo, Kränzlein to Dr Theodor Seibert, 1 February 1938, LAB, A Rep 250-06-06, Nr. 1.

130  Mia Passini file, BArch-B, RKB0147.
131  Ursula Huber, "Grete von Urbanitzky – ungeliebte Parteigängerin der Nationalsozialisten," *L'homme*, April 1993, 74–88.
132  Mia Passini file and Fragebogen, BArch-B, BDC, RK B0147. She wrote for newspapers in Switzerland as well as for Germany's *Münchner Neueste Nachrichten*. She also wrote under the pseudonym "Luise Stahl."
133  Letter, Kränzlein to Passini, 28 May 1938, LAB, A Rep 250-06-04, Nr. 5.
134  "Blutbad an der Grenze. 30 von 180 Flüchtlingen entgingen dem Rotmord," *Der Angriff*, 19 May 1939, 1.
135  MP "'Trockengemüse' mit Sprengladung: Paris befahl den Pyrenäen-Zöllnern, die Augen zu schließen," *Der Angriff*, 19 May 1938, 2.
136  See, for instance, Brendan Fay "The Nazi Conspiracy Theory: German Fantasies and Jewish Power in the Third Reich," *Library and Information History* 35, no. 2 (2019): 75–97, and Lorna Waddington, *Hitler's Crusade: Bolshevism and the Myth of the International Jewish Conspiracy* (London: I.B. Tauris, 2007).
137  MP, "Morgenthaus Mission," *Der Angriff*, 25 August 1938, 1–2.
138  Ibid.
139  MP "Großstadtverbot für Emigranten: Sie müssen 50 km außerhalb von Paris wohnen," *Der Angriff*, 23 May 1938, Nr. 22, 2.
140  Passini to Kränzlein, 7 July and 16 August 1938, LAB, A Rep 250-06-04, Nr. 5.
141  Kershaw, "How Effective Was Nazi Propaganda," 184.
142  Kränzlein to Passini, 8 July 1938, LAB, A Rep 250-06-04, Nr. 5.
143  Passini to Kränzlein, 16 August 1938, LAB, A Rep 250-06-04, Nr. 5.
144  Patrick Merziger, "German Humour' in Books: The Attractiveness and Political Significance of Laughter during the Nazi Era," in *Pleasure and Power in Nazi Germany*, ed. Pamela E. Swett, Corey Ross and Fabrice d'Almeida (Houndmills, UK: Palgrave Macmillan, 2011), 109.
145  Memo from Kränzlein, 26 November 1938, LAB, A Rep 250-06-04, Nr. 1.
146  "Die Leiche im Zimmer 13: Die Mordtat aufgeklärt," *Der Angriff am Abend*, 27 January 1939, 7.
147  "Blum schützt Tannenzapf: Die Lawine des Filmjudenskandals," *Der Angriff*, 31 December 1938, Nr. 314, 7.
148  Ibid. In 1911, Natan was convicted of having made erotic films and served a short sentence in prison. The rumours that he continued to make pornographic films after his conviction are unsubstantiated.
149  Kränzlein to Passini, 19 August 1938, LAB, A Rep 250-06-04. Nr. 5.
150  Passini to Kränzlein, 16 August 1938, LAB, A Rep 250-06-04, Nr. 5.
151  See Doris Bergen, "Social Death and International Isolation: Jews in Nazi Germany, 1933–1939," in *Nazi Germany, Canadian Responses: Confronting Antisemitism in the Shadow of War*, ed. Ruth L. Klein (Montreal: McGill-Queen's University Press, 2012), 8.

152 Thomas Pegelow Kaplan, *The Language of Nazi Genocide: Linguistic Violence and the Struggle of Germans of Jewish Ancestry* (Cambridge: Cambridge University Press, 2009), 9. For more on how linguistic violence is still employed, see Judith Butler, *Excitable Speech: A Politics of the Performative* (New York: Routledge, 2021).

153 Anneliese Zander-Mika, "Frau und Presse," in *Handbuch der Zeitungswissenschaft*, ed. Walter Heide (Leipzig: Karl W. Hiersemann, 1940), 1167.

154 Often front-page hard-news editorials did not have bylines, so the true number of women writing in this realm may be larger than the sources indicate.

155 Tracy Lucht and Kelsey Batschelet, "That Was What I Had to Use": Social and Cultural Capital in the Careers of Women Broadcasters," *Journalism and Mass Communications Quarterly* 96, no. 1 (2019): 210–11.

## 4  Opportunity and Influence on the Homefront, 1939–1945

1 Christa Rotzoll, *Frauen und Zeiten* (Munich: Deutscher Taschenbuch Verlag (dtv), 1991), 128.

2 Christa Rotzoll, "Ostarbeiterinnen: Im Lager und in der Fabrik," *Das Reich*, 21 November 1943.

3 Ibid.

4 For more on forced labour, see Ulrich Herbert, *Hitler's Foreign Workers: Enforced Foreign Labor in Germany under the Third Reich* (New York: Cambridge University Press, 1997) and Sophie Hodorowicz, *Wearing the Letter "P": Polish Women as Forced Laborers in Nazi Germany, 1939–1945* (New York: Hippcrene Books, 2016).

5 Corey Ross, *Media and the Making of Modern Germany: Mass Communications, Society, and Politics from the Empire to the Third Reich* (Oxford: Oxford University Press, 2008), 375.

6 See Paul Corner, ed., *Popular Opinion in Totalitarian Regimes: Fascism, Nazism, Communism* (Oxford: Oxford University Press, 2017); Julia Timpe, *Nazi-Organized Recreation and Entertainment in the Third Reich* (London: Palgrave Macmillan, 2017); and David Bankier, *The Germans and the Final Solution: Public Opinion under Nazism* (Oxford: Blackwell, 1996).

7 March 1944, List of Reichsverband der Deutschen Presse (RDP) Members, Bundesarchiv Berlin-Lichterfelde (BArch-B), R 103/234; Reichskulturkammer, January 1942, BArch-B, R 56IV/27.

8 Memo, RDP, 1 January 1945, BArch-B, R103/104. Statistics compiled from RDP files.

9 Ross, *Media and the Making of Modern Germany*, 361, 363.

10 Ibid., 361.

11  By March 1944, 238 journalists were on the Special War List, 51 of whom
    were women.
12  Memo, RDP, 26 June 1940, BArch-B, R103/80, Nr. 21. When the war
    ended, presumably with Germany's victory, journalists entered into
    the Special War List would be required to complete the Nazi journalist-
    training program if they wanted to continue to work in the profession.
13  Statistics compiled from RDP, BArch-B, R103/234.
14  Memo über den Fraueneinsatz im Reichsministerium für Volksaufklärung
    und Propaganda, March 1942, BArch-B, R55/18.
15  Letter, Head of personnel department to Goebbels, Reichsministerium
    für Volksaufklärung und Propaganda (RMVP), 30 April 1942, BAarch-B,
    R55/18. By 15 April, 1942 there were 858 women and 594 men employed
    within the Ministry of Propaganda.
16  Memo, RDP, 21 January 1942, BArch-B, R103/6, Nr. 6.
17  Helene Rahms, *Zwischen den Zeilen: Mein Leben als Journalistin im
    Dritten Reich* (Munich: Scherz, 1997), 99; Elisabeth Noelle-Neumann,
    *Die Erinnerungen* (Munich: Herbig, 2006), 103; Anja Meyer, Thea
    Fischer interview, in *Medienfrauen der ersten Stunde: "Wir waren ja die
    Trümmerfrauen in diesem Beruf,"* ed. Angelika Engler and Lissi Klaus
    (Zurich: eFeF, 1993), 106. All three women maintained that they were able
    to turn down the ministry's offer without consequences.
18  See BArch-B, R55/15.
19  Memo, Fraueneinsatz, Ministerium für Volksaufklärung und Propaganda
    an den Gau-Organisationsleiter der NSDAP, 27 February 1942, BArch-B,
    R55/18.
20  Ibid.
21  Elisabeth Eisenhardt file, Ministerium für Volksaufklärung und
    Propaganda, u.d, BArch-B, R55/30141. In early 1937, at the age of
    twenty-eight, Eisenhardt joined the government's foreign press office
    (*Auslandspressestelle der Reichsleitung*), where she compiled and translated
    reports concerning the French press.
22  Annette Lehmann, Helma Huffschmid interview, in *Medienfrauen*, 42.
23  Meyer, Gertraude Uhlhorn interview, in *Medienfrauen*, 124.
24  Ibid., 128.
25  See BArch-B, R103.
26  Letter, Luise Herklotz to the RDP Baden-Westmark, 25 January 1945,
    BArch-B, R103/119.
27  The paper was the brainchild of Rolf Reinhardt, SA Oberführer and Chief
    of Staff for the Reich Leader of the Press, Max Amann. The first issue
    appeared on 26 May 1940.
28  Jeffrey Herf, *The Jewish Enemy: Nazi Propaganda during World War II and the
    Holocaust* (Cambridge, MA: Harvard University Press, 2006), 21.

29  Noelle-Neumann, *Die Erinnerungen*, 96.
30  Ibid., 65.
31  Ibid., 102–3.
32  Ibid., 106.
33  For example, Karla Höcker, Klara Trost, Elefried Ferber, Karoline Kiege, Edith Tohde, Ingeborg Ritter, and Hilde Weber all contributed to the paper. This list is not exhaustive.
34  Noelle-Neumann, *Die Erinnerungen*, 199.
35  Margret Boveri, *Verzweigungen: Eine Autobiographie*, ed. Uwe Johnson (Munich: Piper, 1978), 319.
36  Boveri became the *Frankfurter Zeitung*'s foreign correspondent in Stockholm in May 1939.
37  Reichskulturkammer, January 1942, BArch-B, R56IV/27. The files indicate only that, as of 1942, no woman had become editor of a major daily. Nevertheless, this likely remained the case throughout the war.
38  Noelle-Neumann, *Die Erinnerungen*, 106.
39  Heike B. Görtemaker, *Ein deutsches Leben: Die Geschichte der Margret Boveri* (Munich: Beck, 2005), 136.
40  For more on the difference gender makes in journalism and the strategies women have adopted to succeed in the field see Linda Steiner, "Failed Theories: Explaining Gender Differences in Journalism," *Review of Communication* 12, no. 3 (2012): 201–23.
41  Letter to the RMVP Personnel Department, 1 June 1943, BArch-B, Collection Former Berlin Document Center (BDC), Personenbezogene Unterlagen der Reichskulturkammer (RK), RK I 242.
42  Maschmann had joined the BDM herself in 1933, when she was fifteen.
43  Melita Maschmann, *Account Rendered: A Dossier on My Former Self* (Lexington, MA: Plunkett Lake Press, 2016), 109.
44  Max Baumann, "Berufsaussichten nach dem Krieg," *Deutsche Presse*, September 1944, Nr. 20, 241. Baumann was a lecturer in journalism and head of the Regional Press Association.
45  Ibid.
46  Letter from the RPD to Officer J.M. Pirwitz, 1 April 1944, BArch-B, R103/25.
47  Letter, Werner Sack to Ministerium für Volksaufklärung und Propaganda, 3 November 1944, BArch-B, R103/87.
48  Memo, RDP, 14 August 1944, BArch-B, R103/93.
49  Memo, RDP to Ministerium für Volksaufklärung und Propaganda, 11 February 1943, BArch-B, R 103/6, Nr. 5.
50  Ursula von Kardorff, *Diary of a Nightmare: Berlin, 1942–1945* (New York: John Day, 1966), 146.
51  Letter, Rita Münchenberg to RDP, 24 July 1944, BArch-B, R103/25.

52  Memo, Elisabeth Grass to RDP, 26 November 1944, BArch, R103/119.

53  File, Charlotte Jossner, 1943, BArch-B, BDC, RKG0036.

54  Memo, RDP, 5 May 1941, BArch-B, R103/5, Rundschreiben Nr. 20.

55  Letter, Renate von Stieda to the Reichsschrifttumskammer, 12 January 1943, BArch-B, BDC, RKB211.

56  Ross, *Media and the Making of Modern Germany*, 361, 373.

57  Memo, RDP, 29 September 1944, BArch-B, R103/131, Nr. 5.

58  Letter, *Bodensee-Rundschau* to RDP Baden-Westmark, 27 February 1945, BArch-B, R103/127.

59  Letter, Magdali Eleonore Buelle to RDP Baden-Westmark, 6 October 1944, BArch-B, R103/126.

60  Ross, *Media and the Making of Modern Germany*, 365.

61  See Senta Ulitz, "Haben Sie Lust zu diesem Beruf?" *Die junge Dame*, 1 June 1941, Nr. 24, and Liselotte Purper, "Mein Weg zur Bildberichterstatterin," *Frauenkultur*, February 1944.

62  For more on the pleasure of travel for German soldiers, see Julia Torrie, *German Soldiers and the Occupation of France, 1940–1944* (Cambridge: Cambridge University Press, 2018).

63  Rahms, *Zwischen den Zeilen*, 92–3.

64  Ibid., 145. For more on the regime's use of material benefits to placate the population, see Shelley Baranowski, *Strength through Joy: Consumerism and Mass Tourism in the Third Reich* (Cambridge: Cambridge University Press, 2004) and Jonathan Wiesen, *Creating the Nazi Marketplace: Commerce and Consumption in the Third Reich* (Cambridge: Cambridge University Press, 2011).

65  Kardorff, *Diary of a Nightmare*, 138.

66  Letter, Ursula Litzmann to Ernst Jünger, 27 January 1943, Deutsches Literaturarchiv Marbach (DLA), 0 58.807/29.

67  Erika Groth-Schmachtenberger, *Meine liebsten Fotos: Erinnerungen einer Bildberichterin aus sechs Jahrzehnten* (Würzburg: Echter, 1984), 50.

68  Ibid., 52.

69  Ibid.

70  Schmachtenberger Lebenslauf, BArch-B, BDC, RK K0004.

71  The title of the film can be translated as "Perhaps We Will See Each Other Again."

72  Groth-Schmachtenberger, *Meine liebsten Fotos*, 58.

73  Alfred Höck, "Bilder aus dem Salzburger Land," in *Im Fokus: Die Bildberichterstatterin Erika Groth-Schmachtenberger und ihr Werk*, ed. Christine Dippold and Monika Kania-Schütz (Grossweil: Echter, 2008), 155.

74  Elizabeth Harvey, "Seeing the World: Photography, Photojournalism and Visual Pleasure in the Third Reich," *in Pleasure and Power in Nazi Germany,*

ed. Pamela Swett, Corey Ross, and Fabrice d'Almeida (New York: Palgrave Macmillan), 191.

75  Liselotte Orgel-Köhne, *Willst du meine Witwe werden? Eine deutsche Liebe im Krieg* (Berlin: Aufbau, 1995), 79.

76  For more on German plunder in Europe, see Götz Aly, *Hitler's Beneficiaries: Plunder, Racial War, and the Nazi Welfare State*, trans. Jefferson Chase (New York: Metropolitan Books / Henry Holt, 2007).

77  Nicholas Stargardt, *The German War: A Nation under Arms, 1939–1945* (New York: Basic Books, 2015), 391.

78  Purper diary entry, 26 July 1942, quoted in "Bildberichterstatterin im Dritten Reich," Fotografien aus den Jahren 1937 bis 1944 von Liselotte Purper, *Deutsches Historisches Museum*, no. 20 (Summer 1997): 19.

79  Ibid.

80  Ion Antonescu governed Romania from 1940 until 1944. After the war, he stood trial in Romania and was convicted of war crimes. He was executed on 1 June 1946.

81  Meyer, Thea Fischer interview, in *Medienfrauen*, 106.

82  Ibid.

83  Noelle-Neumann, *Die Erinnerungen*, 126; Kardorff, *Diary of a Nightmare*, 197.

84  Groth-Schmachtenberger, *Meine liebsten Fotos*, 58.

85  Noelle-Neumann, *Die Erinnerungen*, 101.

86  Ibid., 129.

87  Kardorff, *Diary of a Nightmare*, 73.

88  Noelle-Neumann, *Die Erinnerungen*, 119. Despite attempts, the Nazis could not keep all news from the population. Many Germans turned to the BBC or other foreign radio broadcasts to receive information that the Nazi government suppressed. See Robert Gellately, *Backing Hitler: Consent and Coercion in Nazi Germany* (Oxford: Oxford University Press, 2001), 185–6.

89  Kardorff, *Diary of a Nightmare*, 178.

90  See Rudolf Vrba and Alan Bestic, *Escape from Auschwitz: I Cannot Forgive* (New York: Grove Press, 1986).

91  See Laurel Leff, *Buried by the Times: The Holocaust and America's Most Important Newspaper* (Cambridge: Cambridge University Press, 2005).

92  Rahms, *Zwischen den Zeilen*, 175.

93  Letter, Hans F. Friedrich to Thien, 12 December 1939, BArch-B, BDC, RK I573. The article was titled "Senorita ohne Schal und Schleier."

94  Nachrichtenblatt Nr. 19, RMVP, 30 April 1932, BArch-B, R103/6, Nr. 30.

95  "Konzentration der Zeitschriften: Maßstäbe, Fortbestand, Schließung und Zusammenlegung," *Das Reich,* 14 February 1943. Publications considered "luxury," however, would be closed, likely due to the disparity between the projected images in such publications and the reality of everyday life.

96 Memo, RDP, 30 July 1941, BArch-B, R103/6, Nr. 30. The report anticipated that the importance of such material would grow along with the length and severity of the war.

97 Memo, Kulturpolitik, Hohe Berufung und Vielgestalt, Zehn Jahre Kulturpressearbeit, 1943, Kulturkammer, BArch-B, BDC, R56I/8.

98 Memo, Reichspropagandaleiter der NSDAP, 6 July 1943, BArch-B, NS18/1072. See also Aristotle A. Kallis, *Nazi Propaganda and the Second World War* (New York: Palgrave Macmillan, 2005), 132. From 27 February to 6 March 1943, close to 200 non-Jewish Germans – mostly women – staged a demonstration outside the Jewish community building in Berlin, located at Rosenstraße 2–4 to demand the release of their Jewish husbands and male children of "mixed marriages" who were incarcerated and awaiting deportation to the East. See Nathan Stoltzfus, *Resistance of the Heart: Intermarriage and the Rosenstrasse Protest in Nazi Germany* (New York: Rutgers University Press, 2001).

99 Wilhelm Weiß, "Die Frau im Schriftleiterberuf," *Deutsche Presse*, 7 March 1936, 118.

100 Memo, Reichspropagandaleiter der NSDAP, 20 May 1942, BArch-B, NS18/110.

101 Norbert Frei and Johannes Schmitz, *Journalismus im Dritten Reich* (Munich: Beck, 1989), 110.

102 Ibid.

103 Rahms, *Zwischen den Zeilen*, 97.

104 Ibid., 122.

105 Helene Rahms, "Berlin am See," *Das Reich*, 16 April 1944, Nr. 16.

106 Ibid.

107 Christa Rotzoll, "Bleibt Berlin gesellig?" *Das Reich*, 14 May 1944, Nr. 20.

108 Ibid.

109 Ilse Urbach, "Verlagerte Berliner Luft," *Das Reich*, 30 July 1944, Nr. 31.

110 Peter Fritzsche, *Reading Berlin, 1900* (Cambridge, MA: Harvard University Press, 1998), 59–60. See also Andrew Stuart Bergerson, "Integrating in the Accusative: The Daily Papers of Interwar Hildesheim," *Issues in Integrative Studies* 15 (1997): 57.

111 Correspondence, Deutsches Nachrichtenbüro (DNB), 8 December, 5 July, and 12 December 1943, BArch-B, R34/456.

112 Correspondence, DNB, 9 January 1940, BArch-B, R34/464.

113 Memo, DNB Vienna to Elfriede Meyn, DNB Paris, 1 December 1943, BArch-B, R34/371.

114 Dr Stiewe, "Die Bedeutung der Frauenzeitschriften im Kriege," *Der Zeitschriften-Verleger*, 27 March 1940, Nr. 13, 97–9.

115 Gutachten über die Abschlussprüfung der Schriftleiterin Fräulein Ruth Schultze, 1 October 1944, BArch-B, R103/100.

116 For more on *Kamerad Frau* see Laura Wehr, *Kamerad Frau? Eine Frauenzeitschrift im Nationalsozialismus* (Regensburg: Roderer, 2002).

117 "Müde? Kein Wunder, meinen sie, wenn man neben dem Beruf noch seinen Haushalt halt," *Kamerad Frau*, May 1943; "Mein Liebster ist kriegsversehrt," *Kamerad Frau*, March 1944; "Deine Gesundheit, Deine Schönheit," *Kamerad Frau*, August 1944.

118 Die Schriftleitung, "Liebe Leserinnen, liebe Kameradinnen," *Kamerad Frau*, April 1943.

119 Ibid., 1943.

120 Ruth Andreas-Friedrich, "Reden wir doch mal darüber," *Kamerad Frau*, January 1944.

121 See Karl Christian Führer, "Pleasure, Practicality and Propaganda: Popular Magazines in Nazi Germany, 1933–1939," in *Pleasure and Power in Nazi Germany*, ed. Pamela E. Swett, Corey Ross, and Fabrice d'Almeida (Houndmills, UK: Palgrave Macmillan, 2011), 141.

122 That is not to say that men did not write advice columns. See, for instance, Lu Seegers, "Walther von Hollander as an Advice Columnist on Marriage and the Family in the Third Reich," in *Private Life and Privacy in Nazi Germany*, ed. Elizabeth Harvey, Johannes Hürter, Maiken Umbach, and Andreas Wirsching (Cambridge: Cambridge University Press, 2019), 206–30.

123 Ruth Andreas-Friedrich, "Es gab schon andere, bevor Du kamst," *Kamerad Frau*, June 1943.

124 Ruth Andreas-Friedrich, "Schreibt Du mir … Schreib ich Dir!" *Kamerad Frau*, January 1944.

125 Ruth Andreas-Friedrich, "Die goldene Brücke ins Leben," *Kamerad Frau*, August 1944.

126 Liesbet van Zoonen, "One of the Girls? The Changing Gender of Journalism," in *News, Gender and Power*, ed. Stuart Allan, Gill Branston, and Cynthia Carter (London: Routledge, 1998), 41.

127 Die Schriftleitung, "Liebe Leserinnen, liebe Kameradinnen," *Kamerad Frau*, April 1943.

128 Memo, DNB, 1943–1944, BArch-B, R34/457.

129 Ursula von Kardorff, "Helferin und nicht Soldat: Die Luftwaffe stellt Flakwaffenhelferinnen ein," *Deutsche Allgemeine Zeitung*, 6 June 1944; "Flakhelferinnen," *Deutsche Allgemeine Zeitung*, 25 November 1944.

130 Kardorff, "Helferin und nicht Soldat."

131 Ibid.

132 Memo, Dr. Schultz v. Dratzig to Reichspropagandaämter, betrifft: Einziehung der weiblichen Jahrgänge 20–24 als Flakwaffenhelferinnen, undated but likely 1944, BArch-B, R103/93.

133 See, for instance, Senta Ulitz, "Ein neuer Begriff: Flakwaffenhelferin," *Völkischer Beobachter*, 23 June 1944, Nr. 75, 3.

134 Ursula von Kardorff, "Die Frauen in Berlin: Brief an einen Neutralen," *Deutsche Allgemeine Zeitung*, 14 March 1944.
135 Ibid.
136 Ursula von Kardorff, "Die Frau von dreißig Jahren," *Deutsche Allgemeine Zeitung*, October 1944.
137 Ibid.
138 Christa Rotzoll, "Militante Frauen-Emanzipation," *Das Reich*, 4 April 1945, Nr. 14.
139 Ibid.
140 As quoted in Herf, *The Jewish Enemy*, 260.
141 Ibid., 181.
142 Ursula von Kardorff, *Berliner Aufzeichnungen aus den Jahren 1942 bis 1945* (Munich: Beck, 1992), 27 May 1943, 87.
143 "Koschere Kunst: So sahen die Juden die Frau," *Kamerad Frau*, February 1944.
144 Margret Boveri, "Landschaft mit doppeltem Boden: Einfluss und Tarnung des amerikanischen Judentums," *Frankfurter Zeitung*, 28 May 1943. See also Görtemaker, *Ein deutsches Leben*, 180–1. Görtemaker analyses a number of Boveri's articles about the war.
145 Görtemaker, *Ein deutsches Leben*, 180–1.
146 Thomas Pegelow Kaplan, *The Language of Nazi Genocide: Linguistic Violence and the Struggle of Germans of Jewish Ancestry* (Cambridge: Cambridge University Press, 2005), 9.
147 Görtemaker, *Ein deutsches Leben*, 182.
148 Ibid., 183–4.
149 Kallis, *Nazi Propaganda*, 86.
150 Letter, DNB to Margret Gröblinghoff, 30 March 1944, BArch-B, R34/471.
151 Elisabeth Noelle-Neumann, "Das Geschichtsbild der Amerikaner," *Das Reich*, 18 May 1941.
152 Ibid.
153 Elisabeth Noelle-Neumann, "Wer informiert Amerika? Journalisten, Radiosprecher, Filme," *Das Reich*, 8 June 1941.
154 Hannah Arendt, "Truth and Politics," in *Between Past and Future: Eight Exercises in Political Thought* (New York: Viking, 1968), 261.
155 Rahms, *Zwischen den Zeilen*, 113.

## 5 The Beautification of Total War and Occupation

1 As quoted in Niklas Frank, *Bruder Norman! "Mein Vater war ein Naziverbrecher, aber ich liebe ihn"* (Bonn: J.H.W. Dietz, 2013), 113.
2 Ibid.
3 This discourse was most closely associated with the work of Ernst Jünger, who wrote of the nobility of comradeship and personal sacrifice

that took place during the First World War and praised war for making ordinary soldiers into hardened men. See Ernst Jünger, *In Stahlgewitter: Ein Kriegstagebuch* (Berlin: Mittler & Sohn, 1934) and *Der Kampf als inneres Erlebnis* (Berlin: Mittler & Sohn, 1922).

4 Else Boger-Eichler, *Die Schriftleiterin* (Berlin: Akademisches Auskunftsamt der Deutschen Arbeitsfront, 1939), 8.

5 Candi S. Carter Olson, "'This Was No Place for a Woman': Gender Judo, Gender Stereotypes, and World War II Correspondent Ruth Cowan," *American Journalism* 34, no. 4 (2017): 428; see also Penny Coleman, *Where the Action Was: Women War Correspondents in World War II* (New York: Random House, 2002).

6 Deborah Chambers, Linda Steiner, and Carole Fleming, *Women and Journalism* (London: Routledge, 2004), 8.

7 See Claudia Koonz, *Mothers in the Fatherland: Women, the Family and Nazi Politics* (London: Jonathan Cape, 1987); Elizabeth Harvey, *Women and the Nazi East: Agents and Witnesses of Germanization* (New Haven, CT: Yale University Press, 2003); Wendy Lower, *Hitler's Furies: German Women in the Nazi Killing Fields* (London: Chatto and Windus, 2013); and Rachel Century, *Female Administrators of the Third Reich* (New York: Palgrave Macmillan, 2017).

8 In May 1943, she moved to Kyiv to write for the *Deutsche-Ukraine Zeitung*, Memo from the Reichsverband der Deutschen Presse (RDP), 1944, Bundesarchiv Berlin-Lichterfelde (BArch-B), R103/84.

9 Memo, RDP, 1944, BArch-B, R103/84.

10 Letter, Hella von Einsiedel to Einsatzstab Rosenberg, Kiev, 26 May 1943, Central State Archives of Ukraine (TsDAVO of Ukraine) file 61544651.

11 Memo, Einsatzstab Reichsleiter Rosenberg, Berlin, 10 June 1943, TsDAVO, file 61544651.

12 See Julia Torrie, *German Soldiers and the Occupation of France, 1940–1944* (Cambridge: Cambridge University Press, 2018).

13 Letter, Ilse Flach to Herr Oberregierungsrat, 24 July 1940, BArch-B, R103/44, and Memo, Reichsministerium für Volksaufklärung und Propaganda (RMVP), 22 June 1943, BArch-B, R103/44.

14 Der Mitgliederstand der Auslandsstelle Paris des RDP, 28 June 1944, BArch-B, R103/43.

15 Mitgliederstand der Auslandsstelle Paris des RDP, 25 June 1943, BArch-B, R103/43.

16 Liste der zurzeit in Paris und Vichy tätigen deutschen Auslandskorrespondenten, RDP, 29 January 1942, BArch-B, R103/43.

17 Ilse Urbach, "Sonntag an der Seine: Pariser Notizen," *Das Reich*, 12 April 1941.

18 Goebbels commissioned the film in 1940.

19 LA, "In der französischen Hauptstadt nach dem Einzug der Deutschen," *Frankfurter Zeitung*, 20 June 1940, Nr. 309. This was not the first time that Abegg had acted as a war reporter. She had also covered Japan's destruction of Nanking, China, in December 1937.

20 Ibid.

21 Correspondence, Hildegard Faber, 1942–43, BArch-B, R103/119.

22 Organization Todt was founded by Fritz Todt. After Todt's death in 1942, Minister of Armaments and War Production Albert Speer took over responsibility.

23 Inge Marszolek, "The Atlantic Wall: An Ambiguous Heritage," lecture, Amersfoort, Netherlands, 2 September 2010.

24 For instance, photojournalists Liselotte Purper and Usa Borchert published in the *Luftwaffenkurier* and *Signal*, respectively.

25 Other women journalists working on German papers in the East included, Ilse Schneider, *Litzmannstädter Zeitung*; Olga Selow, *Deutsche Tageszeitung*; Edith Stender, *Ostdeutscher Beobachter*; Maria Krüger, *Rigasche Rundschau*; Ruth Rosener, *Minsker Zeitung*; and Traudl Becker, *Bialystoker Zeitung*.

26 Harvey, *Women and the Nazi East*, 14–15.

27 After the 1939 Molotov-Ribbentrop pact, the National Socialist government arranged for ethnic Germans from the Baltic and Volhynian regions to resettle in the Wartheland.

28 Catherine Epstein, *Model Nazi: Arthur Greiser and the Occupation of Western Poland* (Oxford: Oxford University Press, 2010), 166. In 1941–42 Nazi leaders, believing that they were on their way to winning the war, expanded and solidified these goals under the General Plan East, a project that envisioned the expulsion and enslavement of Slavic peoples and the mass murder of Jews.

29 See Phillip T. Rutherford *Prelude to the Final Solution: The Nazi Program for Deporting Ethnic Poles, 1939–1941* (Lawrence: University Press of Kansas, 2007), 7.

30 Ilse Urbach, "Weibliche Hilfe im Wartheland," *Das Reich*, 29 December 1940.

31 Ibid.

32 Nancy Reagin, *Sweeping the German Nation. Domesticity and National Identity in Germany, 1870–1945* (Cambridge: Cambridge University Press, 2007), 13.

33 Doris Bergen, "The Nazi Concept of 'Volksdeutsche' and the Exacerbation of Anti-Semitism in Eastern Europe, 1939–45," *Journal of Contemporary History* 29, no. 4 (October 1994): 569. Bergen notes that *Volksdeutsche* also had connotations of blood and race, which the English term "ethnic Germans" does not capture.

34  Ibid., 573, 574.
35  Ibid.
36  Urbach, "Weibliche Hilfe im Wartheland." The Nazis decreed in November 1939 that Jews in Poland wear the Star of David.
37  Corey Ross, *Media and the Making of Modern Germany: Mass Communications, Society, and Politics from the Empire to the Third Reich* (Oxford: Oxford University Press, 2008), 362.
38  See "Die Presse und Propaganda-Arbeit der HJ. Tagung sämtlicher Stellenleiter des Gebietes Wartheland in Posen," *Ostdeutscher Beobachter*, 26 July 1941.
39  Melita Maschmann, *Account Rendered: A Dossier on My Former Self* (Lexington, MA: Plunkett Lake Press, 2016), 92.
40  Ibid., 112.
41  Miriam Z. Arani, *Fotografische Selbst- und Fremdbilder von Deutschen und Polen im Reichsgau Wartheland 1939–1945: Unter besonderer Berücksichtigung der Region Wielkopolska* (Hamburg: Verlag Dr. Kovač, 2008), 330.
42  Melita Maschmann, "BDM-Einsatz im Umsiedlerlagern," *Ostdeutscher Beobachter*, 12 July 1941.
43  Melita Maschmann, "1400 BDM-Führerinnen im Osteinsatz: Gauleiter-Stellvertreter Schmalz über den Ehrendienst der Jugend im Osten," *Ostdeutscher Beobachter*, 23 July 1941.
44  Karl Bayer, "Deutsche Kolonisten im Kaukasus unter Moskaus Würgegriff," n.d., BArch-B, R55/204.
45  Willy Stiewe, "Bildberichterstatter," *Handbuch der Zeitungswissenschaft, Band 1*, ed. Walter Heide (Karl W. Hiersemann: Leipzig, 1940), 625. See also Rolf Sachsse, *Die Erziehung zum Wegsehen: Fotografie im NS-Staat* (Dresden: Philo & Philo Fine Arts, 2003) and Jennifer Evans, Paul Betts, and Stefan-Ludwig Hoffmann, eds., *The Ethics of Seeing: Photography and Twentieth-Century German History* (New York: Berghahn, 2018).
46  Stiewe, "Bildberichterstatter," 625.
47  RMVP Memo, "Übernahme des Personals der Abt. Propaganda in den besetzten Ostgebieten," 4 July 1944, BArch-B, R55/184; Boger-Eichler, *Die Schriftleiterin*, 9.
48  Harriet Scharnberg, "Das A und P der Propaganda: Associated Press und die nationalsozialistische Bildpublizistik," *Zeithistorische Forschungen* 1 (2016): 11–37.
49  See Arani, *Fotografische Selbst- und Fremdbilder*, 339, and Elizabeth Harvey "Seeing the World: Photography, Photojournalism and Visual Pleasure in the Third Reich," in *Pleasure and Power in Nazi Germany*, ed. Pamela Swett, Corey Ross, and Fabrice d'Almeida (New York: Palgrave Macmillan, 2011), 177–204.

50  Women photojournalists who also worked in occupied Europe include Ilse Steinhoff, Ursula Roth, Elisabeth Hase, Olga Eichgrün, Roselotte Simon, Ursula Ostwald, Tita Binz, Hilde Zenker, Margot Monnier (pseudonym Hada), Elfriede Schaeder, Eleanor Saas, Inge Seeling, and Paula Lohr. See RDP files, BArch-B, R103.

51  Meldebogen, Ebba Feldweg, n.d., Staatsarchiv Ludwigsburg, EL 902/20.

52  Photograph, Ebba Feldweg "Das Wartheland dankt dem Altreich: Was alles an Schönem aus dem Altreich für unsere Umsiedler zu Weihnachten geschickt worden ist," *Ostdeutscher Beobachter*, 24 January 1941, 6.

53  Photograph, Ebba Feldweg "Die neue Geschäftsstelle des Deutschen Frauenwerks in Gostingen als Beispiel deutscher Heimgestaltung," *Ostdeutscher Beobachter*, 26 March 1941, 6. See also, photograph, Edda Feldweg "Ein Beispiel zur Erziehung zu deutscher Wohnkultur auf der Ausstellung Frau und Mutter: Lebensquell des Volkes," *Ostdeutscher Beobachter*, n.d.

54  Photograph, Ebba Feldweg "Das deutsche Gesicht," *Ostdeutscher Beobachter*, 18 March 1941.

55  Ibid.

56  Katja Protte, "Beruf: 'Bildberichterstatterin,'" *DHM-Magazin, Bildberichterstatterin im Dritten Reich. Fotografien aus den Jahren 1937 bis 1944 von Liselotte Purper*, Nr. 20, 1997, Deutsches Historisches Museum, 20.

57  Harvey, "Seeing the World," 194.

58  Protte, "Beruf: 'Bildberichterstatterin,'" 6.

59  Ibid.

60  Elizabeth Harvey, "'Ich war überall': Die NS-Propagandaphotographin Liselotte Purper," in *Volksgenossinnen: Frauen in der NS-Volksgemeinschaft*, ed. Sybille Steinbacher (Göttingen: Wallstein, 2007), 148.

61  Liselotte Orgel-Köhne, *Willst du meine Witwe werden? Eine deutsche Liebe im Krieg* (Berlin: Aufbau, 1995), 32.

62  Epstein, *Model Nazi*, 174.

63  Erika Groth-Schmachtenberger, *Meine liebsten Fotos: Erinnerungen einer Bildberichterin aus sechs Jahrzehnten* (Würzberg: Echter, 1984), 53, 54, 57.

64  Erika Groth-Schmachtenberger, "Deutschlands sechstgrößte Stadt: Litzmannstadt," *Münchner Illustrierte Presse*, 2 January 1941, 4–5. She also published in the *Ostdeutscher Beobachter*. See also Harvey, "Seeing the World," 187.

65  Groth-Schmachtenberger, "Deutschlands sechstgrößte Stadt," 5.

66  Ibid.

67  "Yugoslavia," Holocaust Encyclopedia, United States Holocaust Museum, https://encyclopedia.ushmm.org/content/en/article/yugoslavia. For more on the Holocaust in Croatia, see Alexander Korb, *Im Schatten*

*des Weltkriegs: Massengewalt der Ustaša gegen Serben, Juden und Roma in Kroatien, 1941–45* (Hamburg: Hamburger Edition, 2013).

68  Erika Groth-Schmachtenberger, "Ein Jahr freies Kroatien," *Berliner Illustrierte Zeitung*, Nr. 17, 240.

69  Arani, *Fotografische Selbst- und Fremdbilder*, 248.

70  Lars Jockheck, *Propaganda im Generalgouvernement: Die NS-Besatzungspresse für Deutsche und Polen 1939–1945* (Osnabrück: Fibre, 2006), 112. This achievement was due in part to the Wehrmacht, which purchased tens of thousands of copies.

71  Ibid., 139.

72  Emil Gassner, *Auf Vorposten: Drei Jahre Aufbau im Arbeitsbereich Generalgouvernement der NSDAP* (Krakow: Hauptarbeitsgebiet Presse im Arbeitsbereich Generalgouvernement der NSDAP, 1943).

73  Hedwig Franz, "Deutschland – Vaterland," *Krakauer Zeitung*, 14 July 1942.

74  Ibid.

75  Hedwig Franz, "Die Kinderlandverschickung rollt: Sammellager in Kobierzyn und Warschau – Jungen und Mädel neu eingekleidet," *Krakauer Zeitung*, 23 July 1942.

76  Ibid.

77  See Michelle Mouton, "The *Kinderlandverschickung*: Childhood Memories of War Re-Examined," *German History* 37, no. 2 (June 2019): 186.

78  Lisa Pine, *Education in Germany* (New York: Berg, 2010), 31.

79  Jost Hermand, *A Hitler Youth in Poland: The Nazi Children's Evacuation Program during the Second World War* (Evanston, IL: Northwestern University Press, 1998), 17.

80  Ibid.

81  Gerda Pelz, Personalbogen, 13 March 1941, BArch-B, R52-IV/72. Although not a member of the Nazi Party, Pelz had joined the German Air Defence Union (Reichsluftschutzbund, RLB) and the National Socialist People's Welfare Organization (Nationalsozialistische Volkswohlfahrt) in 1937.

82  Michael Burleigh, *Germany Turns Eastwards* (London: Pan Books, 1988), 230.

83  Ibid., 239. The IDO comprised eleven sections, which included agriculture, art history, economics, geology, history, law, linguistics, prehistory, and racial and ethnic research (*Rassen- und Volkstumsforschung*).

84  Jockheck, *Propaganda im Generalgouvernement*, 111.

85  Ibid.

86  Emil Gassner, *Auf Vorposten*.

87  Gerda Pelz, "Der Freischütz. Eröffnungsvorstellung des Staatstheaters," *Krakauer Zeitung*, 5 September 1941.

88  For more on German music and nationalism, see Celia Applegate and Pamela Potter, eds., *Music and German National Identity* (Chicago: University of Chicago Press, 2002).

89  Gerda Pelz, "Heilsame Wunderkraft der Musik: Frauen musizieren vor Verwundeten-Lazarettbaracke als Insel der Beglückung," *Krakauer Zeitung*, 14 December 1944.

90  Gerda Pelz, "Belohntes Schanzen," *Krakauer Zeitung*, 6 October 1944.

91  Gerda Pelz, "Das doppelte Leben: Betrachtung zu einer Burgmusik," *Krakauer Zeitung*, 22 October 1944.

92  Ibid.

93  Gerda Pelz, "Musik zum Jahresende: Ein philharmonisches und ein Wiener-Walzer-Konzert," *Krakauer Zeitung*, 2 January 1945.

94  Ibid.

95  Gerda Pelz, "Ehefrauen als Metallarbeiterinnen," *Krakauer Zeitung*, 8 October 1944.

96  Ibid.

97  Ibid.

98  Jockheck, *Propaganda im Generalgouvernement*, 104. Although men were drafted into the Wehrmacht, by the end of 1943 the paper still had seven full-time employees, one of whom was Gerda Pelz.

99  Maschmann, *Account Rendered*, 90.

100  Frank, *Bruder Norman*, 113.

101  Maschmann, *Account Rendered*, 104.

102  Ibid., 106.

103  Orgel-Köhne, *Willst du meine Witwe werden?* 29. Purper's pictures of the Lodz ghetto also included German guards and a sign that read "Wohngebiet der Juden. Betreten verboten" (Jewish residential area. Access forbidden). They remained unpublished until after the war.

104  Protte, *Bildberichterstatterin im Dritten Reich*, 11.

105  Orgel-Köhne, *Willst du meine Witwe werden?* 46.

106  Ibid., 65.

107  See Geoffrey P. Megargee, ed., *The United States Holocaust Memorial Museum Encyclopedia of Camps and Ghettos, 1933–1945* (Bloomington: Indiana University Press, 2009).

108  Harvey, *Seeing the World*, 198.

109  Orgel-Köhne, *Willst du meine Witwe werden?* 175.

110  Letter, J.E. Hoover to A.M. Thurston, American Embassy, London, 24 September 1943, British National Archives (BNA), KV 2/3711 C 589191.

111  Letter, Cowgill to Cimperman, 18 October 1943, BNA, KV 2/3711 C 589191. The response was from the head of MI6 Department V, who was responsible for counter-espionage outside of the territory of the British Empire.

112  Letter, Security Intelligence Far East to Head Office, 4 August 1956, BNA, KV 2/3711 C 589191. The report was a summary of a wartime report on Abegg.
113  Letter, Reichsleiter für die Presse der NSDAP to Wilhelm Weiß, 19 February 1945, BArch-B, R103/120.
114  Index of correspondents, journalists, publicists, sorted by country, undated, BArch-B, NS42/49.
115  Letter, Hildegard Faber to unnamed, 17 July 1944, BArch-B, R103/119.

## 6  New Patrons, New Entanglements

1  Ilse Urbach, "Garmischer Notizen," *Die Zeit*, 17 October 1946, 5.
2  Ibid.
3  Verband der Deutschen Presse (VDP), *Berliner Zeitung*, 21 October 1946, Bundesarchiv Berlin-Lichterfelde (BArch-B), DY10/354. By October 1946, the circulation had grown to 200,000.
4  See Robert Moeller, "The Elephant in the Living Room: Or Why the History of Twentieth Century Germany Should Be a Family Affair," in *Gendering Modern German History: Rewriting Historiography*, ed. Karen Hagemann and Jean Quataert (New York: Berghahn Books, 2010) and Elizabeth Heineman, *What Difference Does a Husband Make? Women and Marital Status in Nazi and Postwar Germany* (Berkeley and Los Angeles: University of California Press, 1999).
5  In reality, however, many women suffered under the triple burden of home, work, and the demands that they participate in East German social and political life. See Donna Harsch, "Sex, Divorce, and Women's Waged Work: Private Lives and State Policy in the Early German Democratic Republic," in *Gender and Everyday Life under State Socialism in East and Central Europe*, ed. Jill Massino and Shana Penn (Basingstoke, UK: Palgrave, 2010).
6  See Sigrun Schmid, *Journalisten der frühen Nachkriegszeit: Eine kollektive Biografie am Beispiel von Rheinland-Pfalz* (Cologne: Böhlau, 2000); Christina von Hodenberg, *Konsens und Krise: Eine Geschichte der westdeutschen Medienöffentlichkeit, 1945–1973* (Göttingen: Wallstein, 2006); Christian Sonntag, *Medienkarrieren: Biografische Studien über Hamburger Nachkriegsjournalisten 1946–1949* (Munich: Martin Meidenbauer, 2006); Jürgen Wilke, *Journalismus und Journalisten in der DDR: Berufsorganisation – Westkorrespondenten – "Der schwarze Kanal"* (Cologne: Böhlau, 2007); and René Möhrle, ed., *Umbrüche und Kontinuitäten in der deutschen Presse: Fallstudien zu Medienakteuren von 1945 bis heute* (Gutenberg: Computus Druck Satz & Verlag, 2020).
7  See Jennifer Lynn, *Contested Femininities: Representations of Modern Women in the German Illustrated Press, 1920–1960* (forthcoming) and Donna Harsch,

*Revenge of the Domestic: Women, the Family, and Communism in the German Democratic Republic* (Princeton, NJ: Princeton University Press, 2007).

 8 *The Fair Practice Guide for German Journalists: Wegweiser zum guten Journalismus* (Office of Military Government for Bavaria, Information Control Division / Press Control Branch, 1947), 10.

 9 Verband der Deutschen Presse, *Berliner Zeitungen*, 21 October 1946, BArch-B, DY10/354.

10 Max Keilson, "Strukturwandel im Journalistenberuf," *Neue Deutsche Presse*, October 1947, Nr. 6, 8–9.

11 Schmid, *Journalisten der frühen Nachkriegszeit*, 24.

12 Helene Rahms, *Die Clique: Journalistenleben in der Nachkriegszeit* (Bern: Scherz, 1999), 48.

13 Norbert Frei and Johannes Schmitz, *Journalismus im Dritten Reich* (Beck: Munich, 1989), 186–7. For more on denazification, see Alexander Perry Biddiscombe, *The Denazification of Germany: A History, 1945–1950* (Stroud, UK: Tempus, 2007).

14 Peter de Mendelssohn, *Zeitungsstadt Berlin: Menschen und Mächte in der Geschichte der deutschen Presse* (Berlin: Ullstein, 1959), 447.

15 Frei and Schmitz, *Journalismus im Dritten Reich*, 186–7.

16 Rahms, *Die Clique*, 63.

17 Axel Schildt, *Medien-Intellektuelle in der Bundesrepublik* (Göttingen: Wallstein Verlag, 2020), 65.

18 See Deborah Barton, "Rewriting the Reich: German Women Journalists as Transnational Mediators for Germany's Rehabilitation," *Central European History* 51 (2018): 563–84.

19 See Carmen Sitter, *"Die eine Hälfte vergisst man(n) leicht!" Zur Situation von Journalistinnen in Deutschland unter besonderer Berücksichtigung des 20. Jahrhunderts* (Pfaffenweiler: Centaurus, 1998), 264.

20 Verband der Deutschen Presse, Bericht über die 1. Mitglieder-Versammlung, 7 April 1946, BArch-B, DR2/1038. The VDP was founded in October 1945 and began operations in January 1946.

21 Ibid.

22 Ibid.

23 VDP, 16 April 1946, BArch-B, DY10/862.

24 VDP, Bericht über die 1. Mitgliederversammlung, 7 April 1946, BArch-B, DR2/1038.

25 Bundesstiftung Aufarbeitung, Biographische Datenbank https://www .bundesstiftung-aufarbeitung.de/de/recherche/kataloge-datenbanken /biographische-datenbanken/charlotte-hohmann?ID=1463.

26 de Mendelssohn, *Zeitungsstadt Berlin*, 274.

27 Case Report, Annedore Leber, Intelligence Section, ISC Berlin, 12 May 1947, BArch-B, Collection Former Berlin Document Center (BDC), Personenbezogene Unterlagen der Reichskulturkammer (RK), RK D43.

28  VDP, Statistik, 7 June 1946, BArch-B, DY10/354. Dr Brigitte Beer was co-editor of foreign politics, and Vilma Frielingsdorft was head of sports and fashion.
29  For more on Dönhoff, see Volker Berghahn, *Journalists between Hitler and Adenauer: From Inner Emigration to the Moral Reconstruction of West Germany* (Princeton, NJ: Princeton University Press, 2019).
30  Michael Jobbelson, US Civ. Chief of Research Section, Report, Office of Military Government, Information Control Branch, US Army, 2 June 1947, BArch-B, BDC, RK I7.
31  Among others, British-licensed publications included *Frauen-Telegraph* and *Constanze*; French, *Charme* and *Ihre Freundin*; American, *Frauenwelt*, *Der Regenbogen*, and *Lilith*; and Soviet, *Neues Frauenleben* and *Die Frau von Heute*.
32  Lissi Klaus, "Als Frau hatte man es natürlich leichter, natürlich schwerer," in *Medienfrauen der ersten Stunde: "Wir waren ja die Trümmerfrauen in diesem Beruf,"* ed. Angelika Engler and Lissi Klaus (Zurich: eFeF, 1993), 204; Sitter, *Die eine Hälfte*, 264, 284.
33  Sitter, *Die eine Hälfte*, 264.
34  Letter, Pelz to Herrn v. Niebelschütz, 17 May 1946, Deutsches Literaturarchiv Marbach (DLA),file 81,3411.
35  Christine Dippold, "Lebensstationen. Erika Groth-Schmachtenberger (1906–1992)," in *Im Fokus: Die Bildberichterstatterin Erika Groth-Schmachtenberger und ihr Werk*, ed. Christine Dippold and Monika Kania-Schütz (Grossweil: Echter, 2008), 38.
36  Letter, Kardorff to Frl. Rosenheim, 8 October 1946, Institute für Zeitgeschichte (IfZ) ED 348/6; letter, Kardorff to Peter Boyle, 20 September 1946, IfZ ED 348/5.
37  Alexa Godbersen, Felicitas Kapteina interview, in *Medienfrauen*, 59, 62.
38  Ibid., 62.
39  Gisela-Bonn-Preis, Deutsch-Indische Gesellschaft e.V., https://www .dig-ev.de/gisela-bonn-preis/. The Gisela Bonn Prize is awarded annually for special achievements by young scholars and journalists in the field of German-Indian relations.
40  Heike B. Görtemaker, *Ein deutsches Leben: Die Geschichte der Margret Boveri* (Beck: Munich, 2005), 229.
41  Boveri wrote for *Der Kurier*, the *Wirtschaftszeitung*, and the magazine *Merkur*.
42  Görtemaker, *Ein deutsches Leben*, 246–8. Former colleagues such as Paul Sethe had hoped to convince Boveri to write for the political section of the paper, an opportunity that she turned down in 1951.
43  Annamarie Doherr, Mitgliedsaufträge, Verband der Deutschen Presse, 28 December 1945, Landesarchiv Berlin (LAB), C Rep 060-26/126. She wrote

for *Die Frau* and the *Monatshefte für Auswärtige Politik* as well as acting as the East Asian specialist for publications such as *Deutsche Zukunft*. In June 1943, Dorherr became a reporter for the news agency Transocean-Europapress.

44 Uta Tellini, ed., *Frauenobjektiv: Fotografinnen 1940 bis 1950* (Cologne: Wienand, 2001), 139. The Kulturbund zur demokratischen Erneuerung Deutschlands was founded by the poet and politician Johannes R. Becher in Berlin in July 1945.

45 Elfriede Brüning, Fragebogen für Mitglieder, Die Reichsschrifttumskammer, 1 September 1937, BArch-B, BDC, RK9361-V/3909; Betrifft: Freistellung vom Arbeitseinsatz, 1943, BArch-B, BDC, RK 9361-V/3909; Elfriede Brüning, *Und außerdem war es mein Leben* (Munich: dtv, 1998), 294.

46 The four who had careers in Nazi Germany were Cläre Jung, Ilse Langer, Liselotte Thomas, and Hannelore Holz.

47 Hannelore Krollpfeiffer, *Wir lebten in Berlin: Eine Geschichte vom Ende des Krieges* (Berlin, 1947), 81.

48 Books by Gertrud Villforth include *Das große Lexikon der Hausfrau* (Munich: Südwest Verlag, 1966). Staatsarchiv Ludwigsburg, EL 902-20, BA 894119. The American Military Occupation had defined "follower" as "anyone who was not more than a nominal participant in, or a supporter of, the national socialistic tyranny." Control Council Directive No. 38, 12 October 1946, in Official Gazette of the Control Council for Germany, Nr. 11, 31 October 1946, 184, available at German History in Documents and Images, http://germanhistorydocs.ghi-dc.org/pdf/eng/Denazification%202%20ENG.pdf.

49 Letter, von Stieda to Ernst Jünger, 18 August 1962, DLA, file 6 BZ 94.9.

50 Melita Maschmann, *Account Rendered: A Dossier on My Former Self* (Lexington, MA: Plunkett Lake Press, 2016).

51 Lily Abegg file, BNA, KV 2/3711.

52 See Dagmar Herzog, *Sex after Fascism: Memory and Morality in Twentieth-Century Germany* (Princeton, NJ: Princeton University Press, 2007; Erica Carter, *How German Is She? Postwar West German Reconstruction and the Consuming Woman* (Ann Arbor: University of Michigan Press, 1997).

53 Denise Lynn, "Gendered Narratives in Anti-Stalinism and Anti-Communism during the Cold War: The Case of Juliet Pyontz," *Journal of Cold War Studies* 18, no. 1 (2016): 34.

54 Sitter, *Die eine Hälfte*, 251.

55 For instance, in January 1949, twenty-three male journalists were sent to the United States as part of this exchange program, but no women were included. See Memo, Press Branch, 18 January 1949, IfZ, OMGUS, 5/2360-2/10. In 1952, Liselotte Weisenheimer (Jokisch) became one of the

first women to take part in these programs. See letter, Weisenheimer to Schwiegermutter, 21 February 1952, Staatsarchiv Bremen (StAB), 7202-1 vol. 5.

56 Anja Meyer, Thea Fischer interview, in *Medienfrauen*, 108.

57 Constanze Gottschalk, Antje Huber interview, in *Medienfrauen*, 155.

58 Karin Friedrich, *Zeitfunken: Biographie einer Familie* (Munich: Beck, 2000), 274–5.

59 Rahms, *Die Clique*, 85.

60 Ibid., 86.

61 See Cynthia Carter, Linda Steiner, and Stuart Allan, eds., *Journalism, Gender and Power* (New York: Routledge, 2019); and Tracy Lucht and Kelsey Batschelet, "'That Was What I Had to Use': Social and Cultural Capital in the Careers of Women Broadcasters," *Journalism and Mass Communications Quarterly* 96, no. 1 (2019): 194–214.

62 Annette Lehmann, Helma Huffschmid interview, in *Medienfrauen*, 42–3.

63 Verband der Deutschen Presse, Mitgliederliste, 1 January 1951, BArch-B, DY10/862.

64 Schmid, *Journalisten der frühen Nachkriegszeit*, 208.

65 Brüning, *Und außerdem*, 331. See also BArch-B, DY10.

66 Görtemaker, *Ein deutsches Leben*, 222–3.

67 Abegg to Reifenberg, 22 June 1950, DLA, file 80.3.

68 Rahms, *Die Clique*, 48–9.

69 Ibid., 56.

70 Ibid., 66–7.

71 Ibid., 18.

72 Ibid.

73 For more on German-Jewish post-war relations, see Atina Grossmann, *Jews, Germans, and Allies: Close Encounters in Occupied Germany* (Princeton, NJ: Princeton University Press, 2007).

74 See, for instance, Marcus M. Payk, *Der Geist der Demokratie. Intellektuelle Orientierungsversuche im Feuilleton der frühen Bundesrepublik: Karl Korn und Peter de Mendelssohn* (Munich: Oldenbourg, 2008).

75 Rahms, *Die Clique*, 21.

76 Ibid.

77 Ursula von Kardorff, *Diary of a Nightmare: Berlin, 1942–1945* (New York: John Day, 1966), 228.

78 Ibid., 223–4.

79 Letter, Kardorff to Jürgen Schüddekopf, 7 November 1946, IfZ, ED348/6.

80 Kardorff, *Diary of a Nightmare*, 247.

81 Ursula von Kardorff, *Berliner Aufzeichnungen aus den Jahren 1942 bis 1945* (Munich: Beck, 1992), 361.

82 Margret Boveri, *Tage des Überlebens: Berlin 1945* (Berlin: WJS, 2004), 117.

83  Ibid., 214.
84  Ibid., 29.
85  Margret Boveri, *Amerikafibel für erwachsene Deutsche: Ein Versuch, Unverstandenes zu erklären* (Berlin: Landverlag, 1946). See also Michaela Hoenicke Moore, "Heimat und Fremde: Das Verhältnis im journalistischen Werk von Margret Boveri und Dolf Sternberger," in *Demokratiewunder: Transatlantische Mittler und die kulturelle Öffnung Westdeutschlands 1945–1970*, ed. Arnd Bauerkämper, Konrad Jarausch, and Marcus M. Payk (Göttingen: Vandenhoeck & Ruprecht, 2005). Hoenicke Moore focused on Boveri's *American Primer for Grown-Up Germans*. It charged the United States with hypocrisy, compared elements of US policy to that of the Nazis, including the euthanasia program in Germany (230), and argued that Germany was superior in terms of art and culture.
86  Görtemaker, *Ein deutsches Leben*, 224.
87  Ibid., 229.
88  Mendelssohn, *Zeitungsstadt Berlin*, 472, 480.
89  Ibid., 480.
90  Newspapers from each zone were distributed throughout the city, as confirmed by the Allied Control Council directive No. 55 from June 1947, which ordered the "free and unhindered exchange of newspapers, magazines and books between all four occupation zones of Germany and all four sectors of Berlin."
91  Boveri, *Tage des Überlebens*, 313.
92  de Mendelssohn, *Zeitungsstadt Berlin*, 445.
93  Ibid., 457.
94  Ibid., 478.
95  VDP Protokoll, n.d, but likely 1948, BArch-B, DY10/1.
96  The German Journalists Association soon moved its head office to Bonn, where it remained for decades. An earlier version of this section of the chapter was published in *Gendering Post-1945 German History: Entanglements*, edited by Karen Hagemann, Donna Harsch, and Friederike Bruenhoerener (New York: Berghahn, 2019).
97  von Hodenberg, *Konsens und Krise*, 23; see also Helene Rahms, *Die Clique*, 66.
98  Verband der Deutschen Presse – Bericht Mitgliederversammlung, 7 April 1946, BArch-B, DR2/1038.
99  Ibid.
100  Eva Siewert to Hans Leonard, 8 July 1947, Landesarchiv Berlin (LAB), E Rep. 200-63, Nr. 73.
101  Norman Naimark, *The Russians in Germany: A History of the Soviet Zone of Occupation, 1945–1949* (Cambridge, MA: Harvard University Press, 1997), 364.
102  See Berghahn, *Journalists between Hitler and Adenauer*, 67–73. Paul Sethe experienced tensions at the *Frankfurter Allgemeine Zeitung* before moving to *Die Welt*, *Der Stern*, and eventually *Die Zeit*.

103 Jürgen Wilke, *Presseanweisungen im zwanzigsten Jahrhundert: Erster Weltkrieg–Drittes Reich–DDR* (Cologne: Böhlau, 2007), 258.
104 Anke Fiedler, *Medienlenkung in der DDR* (Cologne: Böhlau, 2014), 149–50.
105 Ibid., 133.
106 Tellini, *Frauenobjektiv*, 139.
107 Erik Reger, "Editor's Letter," *Tagesspiegel*, 29 March 1951. Krollpfeiffer wrote under the name Hannelore Holtz.
108 Christa Rotzoll, *Frauen und Zeiten: Porträts* (Munich: Deutscher Tachenbuch Verlag (dtv), 1991), 145.
109 Ursula Rumin, Nachlass, BArch-B, NY4620.
110 Ursula Rumin, *Im Frauen-Gulag am Eismeer* (Munich: Herbig, 2005), 21.
111 Rumin Nachlass, BArch-B, NY4620/10.
112 Brigitte Gerland, *Die Hölle ist ganz anders* (Stuttgart: Steingrüben, 1954), 14.
113 Rumin Nachlass, BArch-B, NY4620/12; Gerland, *Die Hölle*, 14. The paper's full name was *Der Sozialdemokrat – Organ der Sozialdemokratie Groß-Berlin*.
114 Naimark, *The Russians in Germany*, 387.
115 Michael Lemke, "Foreign Influences on the Dictatorial Development of the GDR, 1949–1955" in *Dictatorship as Experience*, ed. Konrad H. Jarausch (Oxford: Oxford University Press, 2006), 96. See also Beatrix Bouvier, *Ausgeschaltet! Sozialdemokraten in der Sowjetischen Besatzungszone und in der DDR 1945–1953* (Bonn: Dietz, 1996).
116 Gordon E. Textor, Top Secret Memo, 15 June 1947, IfZ, Office of Military Government, OMGUS, 5/260–1/15.
117 Letter, Liselotte Weinsheimer to Schwiegermutter, 15 July 1953, Weinsheimer Nachlass, Staatsarchiv Bremen (StAB), 7202-1, vol. 5.
118 Letter, Liselotte Weinsheimer to "Mutti," 15 July 1953, Weinsheimer Nachlass, StAB, 7202-1, vol. 5.
119 Ibid., 247.
120 Gerda Zorn, *Wiederkehr des Verdrängten: Autobiographische Erinnerungen* (Berlin: Weist, 2008), 250.
121 Ibid., 251.
122 Michael Lemke, "Foreign Influences," 96.
123 Wilke, *Presseanweisungen*, 259.
124 Boveri, *Tage des Überlebens*, 283.
125 Görtemaker, *Ein deutsches Leben*, 232–3; Margret Boveri, "Niemandsland Europa. Ideologien–Machtstreben–Dollarpolitik," *Wirtschaftszeitung*, 8 August 1947.
126 Letter, Editor Weltbühne to Siewert, 31 October 1946; Eva Siewert, "Entgiftung der politischen Kämpfe," *Die Weltbühne*, LAB, E Rep 200-63, Nr. 671.

127 Görtemaker, *Ein deutsches Leben*, 251.

128 Berghahn, *Journalists between Hitler and Adenauer*, 98.

129 See Stephan Malinowski, *Vom König zum Führer: Der deutsche Adel und der Nationalsozialismus* (Frankfurt am Main: Fischer, 2004).

130 For more on Atlanticism, see Anne Zetsche, *The Atlantik-Brücke and the American Council on Germany, 1952–1974: The Quest for Atlanticism* (London: Palgrave Macmillan, 2021).

131 Sitter, *Die eine Hälfte*, 286.

132 Ibid. 286; *Der Regenbogen: Zeitschrift für die Frau*, January 1946.

133 "Für Dich fragte 31 Frauen: Welche Maßnahmen müssen Ihrer Meinung nach getroffen werden, um die Not dieses Winters zu steuern," *Für Dich*, 1946.

134 Emmi Klass, "Warme Sachen für die Frau, den Mann, das Kind," *Für Dich*, 1 Jahrgang, Nr. 6, 5.

135 Examples of Hillers's post-war articles include "Neue Berufe in Berlin: Die Unter-Vermieterin/Die Anschafferin," *Schweizer Illustrierte Zeitung*, February 1948; "Neue Berufe in Berlin: Der Trümmerverwerter," *Schweizer Illustrierte Zeitung*, February 1948; and "Frohe Jugend im Friedensland," *Ins neue Leben* 4, Nr. 17/18 (1949).

136 Marta Hillers, *Wir lernen Russisch: Eine Sprachfibel für Anfänger*, Heft 1 (Berlin: Herausgegeben im Auftrage der Deutschen Verwaltung für Volksbildung in der Sowjetischen Besatzungszone, 1945).

137 Ursula von Kardorff, "Gibt es noch Freude?" IfZ, ED348.0029, n.d.; Pauline Nardi, "Humor der Nachkriegszeit," *Die Weltbühne*, 31 October 1947, LAB, E REP 200-63, Nr. 671.

138 Memo, Frances McFadden to Bob Hatch, Questions for the Woman's Magazine, 26 July 1945, IfZ, OMGUS, 5/266-1/1.

139 Ibid.

140 "Ein neues Berlin! Wir schaffen es, wir kriegen es hin!" *Für Dich*, 1 Jahrgang (1946), Nr. 3, 3.

141 Erika Groth-Schmachtenberger, *Meine liebsten Fotos: Erinnerungen einer Bildberichterin aus sechs Jahrzehnten* (Würzberg: Echter, 1984), 84.

142 For more on post-war photography, see Donna West Brett, *Photography and Place: Seeing and Not Seeing Germany after 1945* (New York: Routledge, 2016).

143 Brüning, *Und außerdem*, 320.

144 Ibid.

145 Elfriede Brüning, "Gut aufgehoben, vorbildlich betreut," *Die neue Heimat*, 5 March 1948, 9.

146 Nadine Freund and Kerstin Wolff, "'Um harte Kerne gegen den Kommunismus zu bilden …' Die staatsbürgerliche Arbeit von Theanolte Bähnisch in der Zeitschrift 'Die Stimme der Frau,'" *Ariadne: Forum für Frauen- und Geschlechtergeschichte* 44 (November 2003): 67.

147  Ursula v. Kardorff, "Fragen an Heimkehrerinnen," *Süddeutsche Zeitung*, January. 1946, IfZ.
148  "Unheilige Ursula," *Die Weltbühne*, 1946, n.d., LAB, ED348/03105.
149  The Soviets abducted many Germans, women and men alike, and sent them to labour in the Soviet Union, regardless of their past.
150  "Im Westen geht der Hunger," *Für Dich*, 1 December 1946.
151  See also "Ernährungssorgen in Hamburg," *Für Dich*, 1 October 1946, and "Maria hungert," *Für Dich*, 7 November 1946.
152  "Im Westen geht der Hunger," *Für Dich*, 1 October 1946. Hans Schlange-Schöningen was a German politician and member of German aristocracy who fled East Pomerania in 1945.
153  Ursula von Kardorff, "Vom Reisen heutzutage," 1945/46, IfZ, ED348/15.
154  Ursula von Kardorff, "Im Kessel von Berlin: Aus dem Tagebuch von Ursula von Kardorff," 5 September 1948, IfZ, ED348/15.

## 7  Rewriting the Third Reich

1  Elisabeth Noelle-Neumann, *Die Erinnerungen* (Herbig: Munich, 2006).
2  In 1991, media expert Leo Bogart had published an article, "The Pollster and the Nazis," *Commentary*, August 1991, 47–9, about antisemitism in Noelle-Neumann's 1940 dissertation, "Opinion and Mass Research in the USA," which then led to dissention about her upcoming appointment as a visiting professor in political science at the University of Chicago.
3  William H. Honan, "U.S. Professor's Criticism of German Scholar's Work Stirs Controversy," *New York Times*, 27 August 1997, A13.
4  See Konrad Jarausch, *After Hitler: Recivilizing Germans, 1945–1995* (Oxford: Oxford University Press, 2006); Norbert Frei, *Adenauer's Germany and the Nazi Past: The Politics of Amnesty and Integration* (New York: Columbia University Press, 2002); and David A. Messenger and Katrin Paehler, eds., *A Nazi Past: Recasting German Identity in Post-war Europe* (Lexington: University Press of Kentucky, 2015).
5  For more on women journalists' presentation of their Third Reich experiences, see Christa Rotzoll, *Frauen und Zeiten: Porträts* (Berlin: Deutscher Taschenbuch Verlag (dtv), 1991); Marlen Sinjen, *"Du schaffst es": Erfahrungen eines ungewöhnlichen Lebens* (Frankfurt: Ullstein, 1993); Uta van Steen, *Macht war mir nie wichtig: Gespräche mit Journalistinnen* (Frankfurt: Fischer, 1988); Vilma Sturm, *Barfuß auf Asphalt* (Cologne: Kiepenheuer & Witsch, 1981); Karla Höcker, *Beschreibung eines Jahres: Berliner Notizen 1945* (Berlin: Arani, 1984); and Anonymous, *A Women in Berlin: Eight Weeks in a Conquered City* (London: Picador, 2006). The last book is by Marta Hillers.

6  For instance, Elfriede Brüning, who lived in the GDR, published her memoir, *Und außerdem war es mein Leben*, only in 2004. It was not translated into English, nor has it been republished.

7  Tony Judt, *Postwar: A History of Europe since 1945* (New York: Penguin, 2005), 829.

8  Volker Berghahn, *Journalists between Hitler and Adenauer: From Inner Emigration to the Moral Reconstruction of West Germany* (Princeton, NJ: Princeton University Press, 2019). While Paul Sethe and Hans Zehrer began their careers during the Weimar Republic, Marion von Dönhoff entered into journalism shortly after the collapse of Nazi Germany. See also Susan Neiman, *Learning from the Germans. Race and the Memory of Evil* (New York: Farrar, Straus and Giroux, 2019).

9  Ruth Andreas-Friedrich, *Berlin Underground, 1938–1945*, translated by Barrow Mussey (New York: Holt, 1947), xiii–xiv. An earlier version of this chapter's sections on Ruth Andreas-Friedrich and Ursula von Kardorff was published in an article for *Central European History* in December 2018: "Rewriting the Reich. Germen Women Journalists as Transnational Mediators for Germany's Rehabilitation."

10  Michael Jobbelson, US Civ. Chief of Research Section, report, Office of Military Government, Information Control Branch, US Army, 2 June 1947, Bundesarchiv Berlin-Lichterfelde (BArch-B), Berlin Document Collection (BDC), RK I7. The two books the report referred to were *Wir wollen heiraten* (1941) and *Glücklich verliebt: Glücklich verlobt* (1942). Both books were based on her advice column in *Die junge Dame*.

11  "Andreas Ruth (Friedrich)," Yad Vashem, The Righteous among the Nations Database, https://righteous.yadvashem.org/?search=Ruth%20Andreas-Friedrich&searchType=righteous_only&language=en&itemId=4065948&ind=0. Andreas-Friedrich was included in the Righteous among the Nations in 2002.

12  See Ruth Andreas-Friedrich file, Yad Vashem, Righteous among the Nations, M.31.2/9740 a. Letters written during and after the war by those Friedrich had aided repeatedly thank her for all that she had done.

13  See Jörg Drews, afterword in Ruth Andreas-Friedrich, *Der Schattenmann: Tagebuchaufzeichnungen 1938–1948* (Berlin: Suhrkamp, 2000), 570.

14  Karin Friedrich, *Zeitfunken: Biografie einer Familie* (Munich: Beck, 2000), 268, 276.

15  Ossietzky, the publisher of the leftist paper *Die Weltbühne* was arrested by the National Socialists in February 1933 and sent to Esterwegen concentration camp. He was awarded the Nobel Peace Prize two years later. He died in 1936.

16  Andreas-Friedrich, *Der Schattenmann*, 568–9.

17  Ruth Andreas-Friedrich, *Battleground Berlin: Diaries, 1945–1948*, translated by Anna Boerresen (New York: Paragon, 1962, 86).

18  Ibid.
19  Andreas-Friedrich, *Berlin Underground*, 70.
20  Ibid., 19.
21  Ibid., 191.
22  Ibid., 78.
23  Ibid., 118.
24  Richard Lutjens, "Vom Untertauchen: 'U-Boote' und der Berliner Alltag 1941–1945," in *Alltag im Holocaust, Jüdisches Leben im Großdeutschen Reich 1941–1945*, ed. Andrea Löw, Doris L. Bergen, and Anna Hájková (Munich: Oldenburg, 2013), 57.
25  Andreas-Friedrich, *Berlin Underground*, 134. See also Robert Gellately, *Backing Hitler: Consent and Coercion in Nazi Germany* (Oxford: Oxford University Press, 2001), 2.
26  Ibid., 1.
27  Andreas-Friedrich, *Berlin Underground*, 91.
28  Host Pöttker, *Abgewehrte Vergangenheit: Beiträge zur deutschen Erinnerung an den Nationalsozialismus* (Cologne: Herbet von Halem, 2005), 120–1.
29  *The Fair Practice Guide for German Journalists: Wegweiser zum guten Journalismus* (Office of Military Government for Bavaria, Information Control Division / Press Control Branch, 1947), 6.
30  For instance, see the report on German prisoners' reactions to the magazine HEUTE, n.d., Institut für Zeitgeschichte, Munich (IfZ), 5/265-1/11. The report discussed how they could make material appealing to Germans.
31  Friedrich claimed that she had "deliberately refrained from any subsequent emendations." See foreword, Andreas-Friedrich, *Berlin Underground*.
32  Ruth Andreas-Friedrich, *Berlin Underground, 1938–1945* (New York: Paragon House, 1989), 16. The correct spelling of the name of the shooter is (Herschel) Grynszpan.
33  See Ruth Andreas-Friedrich file, Yad Vashem, Righteous among the Nations, M.31.2/9740 a.
34  The German edition was titled *Der Schattenmann: Tagebuchaufzeichnungen 1938–1945*. It was republished several times throughout the 1970s, 1980s, and 1990s. See IfZ, ED348/9, letter from Max Tau, 9 August 1962.
35  Andreas-Friedrich, *Berlin Underground*, xii.
36  Hans Rothfels, *The German Opposition to Hitler: An Appraisal* (Hinsdale, IL: H. Regnery, 1948), 33.
37  See Petra Goedde, *GIs and Germans: Culture, Gender, and Foreign Relations, 1945–1949* (New Haven, CT: Yale University Press, 2003), xxi–xxii.
38  See Michaela Hoenicke Moore, *Know Your Enemy: The American Debate on Nazism, 1933–1945* (New York: Cambridge University Press, 2010), 10.
39  Ruth Andreas-Friedrich, *Berlin Underground* (London: Latimer House, 1948).
40  Letter from Manning Williams, Political Information Branch to Alfred M. Bingham, Chairman American Association for a Democratic Germany, 3 September 1948, IfZ, OMGUS, 5/2651/11.

41  Translation of Headlines and Captions of Illustrated Pamphlet "Berlin,"
    IfZ OMGUS, 5/265-1/11, 755039.
42  See Peter Hartl, foreword, in Ursula von Kardorff, *Berliner Aufzeichnungen
    1942 bis 1945* (Munich: Deutscher Taschenbuch Verlag, 1992),18.
43  Jürgen Wilke, *Presseanweisungen im zwanzigsten Jahrhundert: Erster
    Weltkrieg–Drittes Reich–DDR* (Cologne: Böhlau, 2007), 188.
44  See, for example, "Angst vor den Möbeln unserer Zeit," *Süddeutsche
    Zeitung*, 13 January 1953, IfZ, ED348/5.
45  See, for example, letter, Kardorff to Krellmann, 9 March, no year,
    but likely 1947, IfZ, ED348/5. In personal and professional
    correspondence, she discussed her distaste for what she described as
    "political women."
46  Ibid.
47  See Schöningh's post-war articles, such as Franz Joseph Schöningh,
    "Lohnt es sich noch zu leben?" *Süddeutsche Zeitung*, 6 October 1945.
48  Letter, Schöningh to Kardorff, 6 April 1946, IfZ, ED348/31.
49  Kardorff, "Schluss-Stimmung in Nürnberg," *Stuttgarter Zeitung*, n.d., IfZ,
    ED348/520.
50  Letter, Kardorff to Hans Wolfgang Schwerin, 12 November 1948, IfZ,
    ED348/6.
51  See the foreword by Peter Hartl to Ursula von Kardorff, *Diary of a
    Nightmare: Berlin 1942–1945*, translated by Ewan Butler (New York: John
    Day, 1966).
52  Letter, Kardorff to Charlotte von der Schulenburg, 20 August 1947, IfZ,
    ED 348/6.
53  Letter, Kardorff to Guy Wint, May 1946, IfZ, ED348/6.
54  Letter, Kardorff to Charlotte von der Schulenburg, 20 August 1947, IfZ,
    ED348/6.
55  Letter, Kardorff to Hans Wolfgang Schwerin, 12 April 1948, IfZ,
    ED348/6.
56  Letter from Deutsche Verlag, 19 November 1948, IfZ, ED348/7.
57  See Ursula von Kardorff's report on *Berliner Aufzeichnungen*, IfZ,
    ED348/7.
58  Letter, Kardorff to Peter Boyle, 29 September 1946, IfZ, ED348/5;
    Ursula von Kardorff, "Tagebuch: Auszüge aus Nürnberg," 8 July 1946,
    IfZ, ED348/13; see also Ursula von Kardorff, "Speer – ein Mann mit
    Verantwortung," *Wiesbadener Kurier*, 25 June 1946.
59  Report from the Office of Military Government for Bavaria, Press Control
    Section, 10 May 1946, IfZ, ED348/1.
60  Axel Schildt argues that von Kardorff wrote antisemitic articles during
    the Third Reich. Axel Schildt, *Medien-Intellektuelle in der Bundesrepublik*
    (Göttingen: Wallstein Verlag, 2020), 83.
61  Jack Fleischer, *Die Neue Zeitung*, to Kardorff, 20 March 1948, IfZ, ED348/7.
    Fleischer and *Die Weltbühne* were referring to Kardorff's articles on

*Flakhelferinnen.* Kardorff countered that *Die Weltbühne* had targeted her only because of her recent article about conditions in Russian prison camps. Kardorff to Fleischer, 20 March 1948, IfZ, ED348/7.

62  See, e.g., letter, Kardorff to Charlotte von der Schulenburg, 20 August 1947, IfZ, ED348/6, and letter, Kästner to Kardorff, 5 May 1957, IfZ, ED348/5.

63  Hartl, foreword, *Berliner Aufzeichnungen*, 29.

64  Kardorff, *Berliner Aufzeichnungen*, 37.

65  Ibid., 117.

66  Barbara Szerfozo, "Warring Narratives: The Diaries and Memoirs of Lore Walb, Ursula von Kardorff and Margret Boveri" (PhD diss., Georgetown University, 2002), 155.

67  Hartl, foreword, *Berliner Aufzeichnungen*, 29.

68  Kardorff, *Berliner Aufzeichnungen*, 31 October 1942, 40.

69  Schildt, *Medien-Intellektuelle*, 83.

70  Letter, Kardorff to Guy Wint, 13 November [no year], IfZ, ED 348/6.

71  Kardorff, *Diary of a Nightmare*, 193–4. In the post-war years, a number of women journalists claimed that their focus on soft news meant that they were uncompromised by Nazism.

72  Ibid., 46.

73  Letter, Goldmann to Kardorff, 12 December 1962, IfZ, ED348/9.

74  Letter, Kardorff to Goldmann, 13 December 1962, IfZ, ED348/9.

75  Ibid.

76  See Norbert Frei and Johannes Schmitz, *Journalismus im Dritten Reich* (Munich: Beck, 1989), 169.

77  Kardorff, *Diary of a Nightmare*, 91.

78  Ibid., 230.

79  Norman Naimark, *The Russians in Germany: A History of the Soviet Zone of Occupation, 1945–1949* (Cambridge, MA: Harvard University Press, 1997), 113–14.

80  See Elizabeth Heineman, "The Hour of the Woman: Memories of Germany's 'Crisis Years' and West German National Identity," *American Historical Review* 101, no. 2 (1996): 354–96.

81  Kardorff, *Diary of a Nightmare*, 246.

82  For more on German resistance to National Socialism, see Ian Kershaw, *The End: The Defiance and Destruction of Hitler's Germany, 1944–45* (New York: Penguin, 2011) and Nathan Stoltzfus, Mordecai Paldiel, Judith Tydor Baumel-Schwartz, eds., *Women Defying Hitler: Rescue and Resistance under the Nazis* (London: Bloomsbury Academic, 2021).

83  Letter, from Kardorff to unnamed, 5 August [no year], IfZ, ED348/6.

84  Kardorff, *Diary of a Nightmare*, 142. See also Frei and Schmitz, *Journalismus im Dritten Reich*, 152.

85  Letter, Kardorff to "H," 3 April 1933, IfZ, ED348/2.

86  Kardorff, *Berliner Aufzeichnungen*, 73. German painter Max Liebermann was a close colleague of von Kardorff's father. Liebermann died in 1935.

87  Kardorff, *Diary of a Nightmare*, 228.

88  Ibid., 229–30. For German views on Allied questionnaires and the experience of denazification, see Ernst von Salomon, *Der Fragebogen* (Hamburg: Rowohlt, 1951.)

89  See Robert Moeller, *War Stories: The Search for a Usable Past in the Federal Republic of Germany* (Berkeley and Los Angeles: University of California Press, 2001).

90  As quoted in Christopher R. Browning, "Spanning a Career: Three Editions of Raul Hilberg's Destruction of the European Jews," in *Lessons and Legacies*, vol. 8, *From Generation to Generation*, ed. Doris Bergen (Evanston, IL: Northwestern University Press), 191.

91  See Patrick Tobin, "No Time for 'Old Fighters': Postwar West Germany and the Origins of the 1958 Ulm Einsatzkommando Trial," *Central European History* 44, no. 4 (2011): 684–710.

92  See Rebecca Wittmann, *Beyond Justice: The Auschwitz Trial* (Cambridge, MA: Harvard University Press, 2005).

93  Letter, Max Tau, 9 August 1962, IfZ, ED348/9.

94  Josef Halperin, "Berliner Aufzeichnungen, 1942–1945," *Neue Zürcher Zeitung*, 12 September 1962, IfZ, ED348/31.

95  Letter, Karl Bergmann to *Die Welt*, 4 September 1962, IfZ, ED348/9.

96  Letter, unknown writer to Kardorff, 12 November 1961, IfZ, ED348/5.

97  *Saturday Review*, 21 May 1966.

98  *Kirkus Review*, 20 April 1966.

99  "Diary of a Nightmare: Berlin, 1942–1945," *New Yorker*, n.d., IfZ, ED348/31.

100  Bernardine Kielty, "Diary of a Nightmare: Berlin, 1942–1945," *Book of the Month Club News*, 1 September 1966, IfZ, ED348/31.

101  "Diary of a Nightmare by Ursula von Kardorff," *Booklist* 63, no. 91 (1966).

102  This generation was known as the 68ers.

103  The Sonderweg was an important step in this process. Although easily criticized, it did bring the exploration of the growth of Nazism to the forefront. Hans Ulrich Wehler and the Bielefeld School were proponents of Germany's "special path" to Nazism. See Wehler, *Das deutsche Kaiserreich, 1871–1918* (Göttingen: Vandenhoeck & Ruprecht, 1973). That is not to say that some academic work on the Third Reich had not begun earlier. See Karl Dietrich Bracher, *Die Auflösung der Weimarer Republik: Eine Studie zum Problem des Machtverfalls in der Demokratie* (Stuttgart: Ring-Verlag, 1955).

104  See Tim Mason, "Women in Germany," *History Workshop Journal*, no.17 (1976): 74–113; Jill Stephenson, *The Nazi Organisation of Women* (London: Croom Helm, 1981).

105  Heike B. Görtemaker, *Ein deutsches Leben: Die Geschichte der Margret Boveri, 1900–1975* (Munich: Beck, 2005), 285. The book was Boveri's response to various post-war criticisms levelled at journalists who had enjoyed successful careers in Nazi Germany and continued to hold esteemed positions in the post-war years.

106  Ibid., 293.

107  *Verzweigungen* appeared in 1977, two years after Boveri's death.

108  Margret Boveri, *Verzweigungen: Eine Autobiographie*, edited by Uwe Johnson (Munich: R. Piper, 1977), 214–15. Boveri clamied that she later rejected the notion of "inner emigration."

109  Ibid., 244.

110  Ibid., 268.

111  Görtemaker, *Ein deutsches Leben*, 73.

112  Ibid.

113  Ibid.

114  Boveri, *Verzweigungen*, 327.

115  Ibid., 298.

116  See Frei and Schmitz, *Journalismus im Dritten Reich*, 44.

117  The article was called "Rassenschande: Zwei Urteile in Hamburg."

118  See Patricia Szobar, "Telling Stories in the Nazi Courts of Law: Race Defilement in Germany, 1933–1945," *Journal of the History of Sexuality* 11, nos 1/2 (2002): 131–63.

119  Michael Wildt, *Hitler's Volksgemeinschaft and the Dynamics of Racial Exclusion* (New York: Berghahn, 2012), 275.

120  Boveri, *Verzweigungen*, 292.

121  Ibid.

122  Berghahn, *Journalists between Hitler and Adenauer*, 18.

123  Ibid., 227.

124  Margret Boveri, "Rudolph Sparing," *Frankfurter Allgemeine Zeitung*, 6 May 1955, 2.

125  Ibid.

126  Görtemaker, *Ein deutsches Leben*, 285.

127  Ibid.

128  Boveri, *Verzweigungen*, 363.

129  See Michaela Hoenicke Moore, "Heimat und Fremde: Das Verhältnis zu Amerika im journalistischen Werk von Margret Boveri und Dolf Sternberger," in *Demokratiewunder: Transatlantische Mittler und die kulturelle Öffnung Westdeutschlands 1945–1970*, ed. Arnd Bauerkämper, Konrad H. Jarausch, and Marcus M. Payk (Göttingen: Vandenhoeck & Ruprecht,

2005), 218–52. Hoenicke Moore demonstrates the ways in which Boveri's voice was also a force for democratic change in post-war Germany as she processed Germany's defeat and occupation.

130 Boveri's other post-war books include *16 Fenster und 8 Türen* (1953), *Die Deutschen und der Status Quo* (1974), and *Der Verrat im XX. Jahrhundert*, 4 vols (1956–60). The latter work was translated into English as *Treason in the Twentieth Century* (1961).

131 See the Nachlass der Journalistin Margret Boveri (1900–75), Staatsbibliothek Berlin, https://staatsbibliothek-berlin.de/die-staatsbibliothek/abteilungen /handschriften/nachlaesse-autographen/nachlaesse-a-z/boveri/

132 Titus Arnu, "'Wir lügen alle' – Serie über große Journalisten (XXV): Margret Boveri war klug, mutig, modern – und sie machte bei den Nazis Karriere," *Süddeutsche Zeitung*, 10 May 2010.

133 Ibid.

134 Foreword to Helene Rahms, *Zwischen den Zeilen: Mein Leben als Journalistin im Dritten Reich* (Bern: Scherz, 1997), 7.

135 Mechthild Küpper, "Ehrgeiz und Neugier: Helene Rahms erinnert sich an den Journalismus im Dritten Reich: Die Versuchung des schönen Schreibens," *Berliner Zeitung*, 26 April 1997.

136 Review, *Frankfurter Allgemeine Zeitung*, 5 April 1997, Nr. 79, B5; *Frankfurter Allgemeine Zeitung*, 25 September 1998, Nr. 223, 41.

137 Geoffrey H. Hartman, ed., *Bitburg in Moral and Political Perspective* (Bloomington: Indiana University Press, 1986), 263–5.

138 Ibid., 253–4.

139 See Charles S. Maier, *The Unmasterable Past: History, Holocaust, and German National Identity* (Cambridge, MA: Harvard University Press, 1997). See also Andreas Hillgruber, *Zweierlei Untergang: Die Zerschlagung des Deutschen Reiches und das Ende des europäischen Judentums* (Berlin: Siedler, 1986).

140 As quoted in Konrad H. Jarausch, "Removing the Nazi Stain? The Quarrel of the German Historians," *German Studies Review* 11, no. 2 (May 1988): 285–301.

141 The 1995 exhibition was called *Vernichtungskrieg: Verbrechen der Wehrmacht 1941 bis 1944*.

142 Rahms, *Zwischen den Zeilen*, 64.

143 Ibid., 12, 122. Rahms's title, *Zwischen den Zeilen*, invoked the notion that one could bypass Nazi censors and even critique the regime by "writing between the lines."

144 Ibid., 58.

145 Ibid., 51.

146 Ibid., 14.

147 Ibid., 13.

148  Ibid., 28–9.
149  Ibid., 35.
150  Ibid., 108–9.
151  Ibid., 166.
152  Ibid., 160–1
153  Ibid., 180, 184.
154  Ibid., 91.
155  Ibid., 31.
156  Ibid., 159.
157  Ibid., 161.
158  Robert Moeller, *Protecting Motherhood: Women and the Family in the Politics of Post-war West Germany* (Berkeley and Los Angeles: University of California Press, 1993), 12.
159  These dates were 1947, 1948, 1954, 1959, 1962, 1966, 1976, 1977, 1983, 1986, 1992, 1996, 1997, and 2000. See Norbert Frei and Johannes Schmitz, *Journalismus im Dritten Reich* (Munich: Beck, 1989).
160  See, for instance, Antony Beevor, *Berlin: The Downfall, 1945* (London: Viking, 2002) and Nicholas Stargardt, *The German War: A Nation under Arms, 1939–1945* (New York: Basic Books, 2015). Stargardt offers a thoughtful and balanced analysis of Ursula von Kardorff's wartime recollections.

**Conclusion**

1  Quoted in Elizabeth Gray, *Women in Journalism at the Fin de Siècle: Making a Name for Herself,* (London: Palgrave Macmillan, 2012), 1.
2  Liesbet van Zoonen, "One of the Girls? The Changing Gender of Journalism," in *News, Gender and Power,* ed. Stuart Allan, Gill Branston, and Cynthia Carter (London: Routledge, 1998), 34.
3  Quoted in Lutz Hachmeister, *Theoretische Publizistik: Studien zur Geschichte der Kommunikationswissenschaft in Deutschland* (Berlin: Volker Spiess, 1987), 49.

# Bibliography


### Archives

*Germany*

ARCHIV DER AKADEMIE DER KÜNSTE, BERLIN
Nachlass Annemarie Weber
Nachlass Hedwig Rhode

BUNDESARCHIV BERLIN-LICHTERFELDE (BARCH-B)
Former Collection Berlin Document Centre: Parteikorrespondenz, Personenbezogene
    Unterlagen der Reichskulturkammer
DR2 Ministerium für Volksbildung
DY10 Verband der Journalisten der DDR
DY27 Kulturbund der DDR
N/2079 Nachlass Grete Freund
N/2227 Nachlass Hermann Pörzgen
N/2346-1 Nachlass Milly Zirker
N/2346/5 *Pariser Tageblatt*
NS18 Reichspropagandaleiter der NSDAP
NS26 Hauptarchiv der NSDAP
NS42 Reichspressechef der NSDAP / Reichspressestelle
NS43 Außenpolitisches Amt der NSDAP
NS44 Reichsfrauenführung
NS45 Parteidienststellen der NSDAP außerhalb des Gebietes der
    nachmaligen BRD
NSD47 NS Frauenschaft Nachrichtendienst
NY4620 Nachlass Ursula Rumin
R34 Deutsches Nachrichtenbüro
R43 Reichskanzlei

R52-IV Institut für Deutsche Ostarbeit
R55 Reichsministerium für Volksaufklärung und Propaganda
R56-I Reichskulturkammer
R56-IV Reichspressekammer
R78 Reichsrundfunkgesellschaft
R103 Reichsverband der Deutschen Presse
R901 Auswärtiges Amt
Zsg117 Presseausschnittsammlung Hauptarchiv der NSDAP

BUNDESARCHIV FREIBURG
N979 Nachlass Paula von Reznicek

BUNDESARCHIV KOBLENZ
N1676 Nachlass Maria Reese
Z23 Presserat für die Britische Besatzungszone
Zsg116 Pressedienst-Sammlung Deutsches Nachrichtenbüro (DNB)
Zsg117 Zeitungsausschnittsammlung, Hauptarchiv der NSDAP

DEUTSCHES HISTORISCHES MUSEUM
Erika Groth-Schmachtenberger
Liselotte Purper
Ursula Litzmann

DEUTSCHES LITERATURARCHIV MARBACH (DLA)
73.2, 1–3 Ernst Jünger
79.12676 Benno Reifenberg
79.5287 Benno Reifenberg, *Frankfurter Allgemeine Zeitung*
Grimm H, Nachlass 832, Propaganda-Report, Maria de Smet
HS.1989.001.02621 Dolf Sternberger
HS.2002.0007 Luise Rinser
HS.2003.0061.00061 Ina Seidel
HS.2003.0061.00063 Ilse Urbach correspondence
HS.2005.0060 Ernst Jünger
HS.NZ68.0001 Gerhart Behl, Hauptmann-Archiv
HS.NZ84.0001 Marie Luise Kaschnitz
Manuskripte, Ursula Litzmann
SU.2010.002 SUA-Suhrkamp

LANDESARCHIV BERLIN
A Rep 243 Reichskulturkammer, Landeskulturwalter, Gau Groß-Berlin
A Rep 243-03 Reichspressekammer

A Rep 250-06-04 Zentralverlag der NSDAP Franz Eher Nachf. GmbH
B Rep 235-20 Zeitungsausschnittsammlung des Helene-Lang-Archiv
C Rep 118-01-14850 Hauptausschuss Opfer des Faschismus / Referat Verfolgte
  des Naziregimes
E Rep 200-30 Nachlass Otto Bach
E Rep 200-45 Nachlass Hans Habe E Rep 200-63, *Die Weltbühne*
E Rep 200-64 Nachlass Martha Stockfisch
E Rep 200-78 Nachlass Otto Eugen Hasso Becker
E Rep 200-79 Nachlass Hans Erman
F Rep 280 LAZ Sammlung 1945–1950
F Rep 290-1075 Allgemeine Fotosammlung, Annamarie Doherr

INSTITUT FÜR ZEITGESCHICHTE MUNICH (IFZ)
ED324 Nachlass Maria Gehrke
ED348 Nachlass Ursula v. Kardorff
ED364 Nachlass Marcia Kahn
ED374 Nachlass Edit von Coler
ED379 Nachlass Hildegard Hamm-Brücher
RC260 OMGUS files (Office of Military Government, United States)
Zs-1875 Nachlass Anna Steuerwald-Landmann
Zs-2031 Nachlass Hilde Walter

POLITISCHES ARCHIV DES AUSWÄRTIGEN AMTES (AA/PA)
NL136-1 Nachlass Richard Kempe
Presseabteilung
RZ 214/101184 Edit von Coler
RZ 701 Lily Abegg

STAATSBIBLIOTHEK BERLIN, PREUSSISCHER KULTURBESITZ
Handschriften – Nachlass Margret Boveri

STAATSARCHIV BREMEN (STAB)
7202-1 Nachlass Lilo Weinsheimer

STAATSARCHIV LUDWIGSBURG
EL902-20 Denazification files, Gertrud Villforth, Ebba Feldweg

*Israel*

Yad Vashem Righteous among the Nations – Ruth Andreas-Friedrich / Uncle
Emil

*Poland*

Biblioteka Jagiellońska
Institut für Deutsche Ostarbeit
Jagiellonian University Archives, Press clippings *Krakauer Zeitung*

*United Kingdom*

BRITISH NATIONAL ARCHIVES, LONDON (BNA)
KV 2/960 File Petra Vermehren
KV 2/1694 File Paul Scheffer
KV 2/3711 File Lily Abegg

*Ukraine*

Central State Archives of Supreme Bodies of Power and Government of
    Ukraine (TsDAVO of Ukraine), 61544651, File Hella von Einsiedel

*United States*

Library of Congress, Newspaper collection: *Deutsche Allgemeine Zeitung*,
    *Hamburger Fremdenblatt, Der Angriff*
United States Holocaust Memorial Museum, Newspaper collection:
    *Frankfurter Zeitung, Krakauer Zeitung*

*Online*

Internationales Biographisches Archiv, munziger.de. Elisabeth Noelle-Neumann,
    Lily Abegg
Universität Heidelberg, Bibliothek NS Frauen-Warte http://digi.ub.uni-heidelberg
    .de/diglit/frauenwarte1941?sid=f8600e13332f372363607d9e58686a28

## Newspapers and Periodicals

*Berliner Börsen-Courier*
*Berliner Börsen-Zeitung*
*Berliner Hausfrau*
*Berliner Illustrierte Zeitung*
*Berliner Lokal-Anzeiger*
*Berliner Tageblatt*
*Berliner Zeitung*
*Binghamton Press* (New York)
*Daily Express* (London)
*Das Reich*
*Das Schwarze Korps*

*Der Angriff*
*Der Angriff am Abend*
*Der Deutsche Student*
*Der Spiegel*
*Der Tag*
*Der Welt-Spiegel*
*Der Zeitschriften-Verleger*
*Deutsche Allgemeine Zeitung*
*Deutsche Flugillustrierte*
*Deutsche Presse*
*Deutsche Ukraine-Zeitung*
*Deutsche Zeitung für Canada*
*Deutsches Echo*
*Die Bewegung*
*Die Dame*
*Die junge Dame*
*Die neue Gartenlaube*
*Die neue Heimat*
*Die Neue Zeitung*
*Die Welt*
*Die Zeit*
*Düsseldorfer Nachrichten*
*Elegante Welt*
*Essener Nationalzeitung*
*Flensborg Avis*
*Frankfurter Allgemeine Zeitung*
*Frankfurter Hefte*
*Frankfurter Zeitung*
*Frauenkultur*
*Freie Presse für Texas*
*Frontarbeiter*
*Für Dich*
*Hamburger Fremdenblatt*
*Illustrierter Rundfunk*
*Ins neue Leben*
*Kamerud Frau*
*Kirkus Review*
*Krakauer Zeitung*
*Kurier*
*La Suisse*
*Leipziger Neueste Nachrichten*
*Luftwaffenkurier*
*Münchner Abendzeitung*

*Münchner Illustrierte Presse*

*Münchner Neueste Nachrichten*

*Nationalsozialistische Landpost*

*Neue Deutsche Presse*

*Neue Zeit*

*Neue Zürcher Zeitung*

*New York Times*

*New Yorker*

*Niederdeutscher Beobachter*

*NS Frauen-Warte*

*Ostdeutscher Beobachter*

*Saturday Review* (New York)

*Schlesische Sonntagspost*

*Schwäbische Zeitung*

*Schweizer Illustrierte Zeitung*

*Signal*

*Sonntag*

*Stuttgarter Zeitung*

*Süddeutsche Zeitung*

*Südharzer Kurier*

*Tagesspiegel*

*Völkischer Beobachter*

*Wall Street Journal*

*Weltbühne*

*Wiesbadener Kurier*

*Wirtschaftszeitung*

*World Press Review* (New York)

*Zeitschriften-Verleger*

*Zeitungs-Verlag*


## Published Primary Sources


Abegg, Lily. *Japans Traum vom Musterland: Der neue Nipponismus.* Munich: Kurt Desch, 1973.

– *Yamato: Der Sendungsglaube des japanischen Volkes.* Frankfurt: Societas Verlag, 1936.

Andreas-Friedrich, Ruth. *Battleground Berlin: Diaries, 1945–1948.* Translated by Anna Boerresen. New York: Paragon House, 1990.

– *Berlin Underground, 1938–1945.* New York: Holt, 1947; New York: Paragon House, 1989.

– *Der Schattenmann: Tagebuchaufzeichnungen 1938–1948.* Frankfurt: Suhrkamp, 2000.

Anonymous. *A Woman in Berlin: Diary, 20 April 1945 to 22 June 1945*. Translated by Philip Boehm. London: Picador, 2006.

Bluhm, Lothar. *Das Tagebuch zum Dritten Reich: Zeugnisse der inneren Emigration von Jochen Klepper bis Ernst Jünger*. Bonn: Bouvier, 1991.

Bogart, Leo. "The Pollster and the Nazis." *Commentary*, August 1991, 47–9.

Boger-Eichler, Else. *Die Schriftleiterin*. Berlin: Akademisches Auskunftsamt der Deutschen Arbeitsfront, 1939.

Boveri, Margret. *Amerikafibel für erwachsene Deutsche: Ein Versuch, Unverstandenes zu erklären*. Berlin: Landtverlag, 1946.

– *Tage des Überlebens: Berlin 1945*. Munich: R. Piper, 1968; Berlin: WJS, 2004.

– *Verzweigungen: Eine Autobiographie*. Edited by Uwe Johnson. Munich: R. Piper, 1977.

– *Wir lügen alle: Eine Hauptstadtzeitung unter Hitler*. Olten: Walter, 1965.

Breitenkamp, Edward Carlton. *The U.S. Information Control Division and Its Effect on German Publishers and Writers, 1945 to 1949*. Grand Forks, MI: University Station, 1953.

Brüning, Elfriede. *Und außerdem war es mein Leben*. Munich: dtv, 1998.

Döhrn, Gisela. *Das war Moskau: Vier Jahre als Berichterstatterin in der Sowjetunion*. Berlin: Albert Limberg Verland, 1941.

Dönhoff, Marion von. *Namen, die keiner mehr nennt: Ostpreußen – Menschen und Geschichte*. Düsseldorf: Diederichs, 1962.

Dresler, Adolf. *Die Frau im Journalismus*. Munich: Knorr & Hirth, 1936.

Dürkefälden, Karl, Herbert Obenaus, and Sibylle Obenaus. *"Schreiben, wie es wirklich war": Aufzeichnungen Karl Dürkefäldens aus den Jahren 1933–1945*. Hanover: Fackelträger, 1985.

Engler, Angelika, and Klaus Lissi, eds. *Medienfrauen der ersten Stunde:"Wir waren ja die Trümmerfrauen in diesem Beruf."* Zurich: eFeF, 1993.

*The Fair Practice Guide for German Journalists: Wegweiser zum guten Journalismus*. Office of Military Government for Bavaria, Information Control Division / Press Control Branch, 1947.

Frank, Niklas. *Bruder Norman! "Mein Vater war ein Naziverbrecher, aber ich liebe ihn."* Bonn: J.H.W. Dietz, 2013.

Friedrich, Karin. *Zeitfunken: Biographie einer Familie*. Munich: Beck, 2000.

Frobenius, Else. *Erinnerungen einer Journalistin: Zwischen Kaiserreich und Zweitem Weltkrieg*. Edited by Lora Wildenthal. Cologne: Böhlau, 2005.

Fröhlich, Elke. *Die Tagebücher von Joseph Goebbels*. Munich: K.G. Saur, 1998.

Fromm, Bella. *Blood and Banquets: A Berlin Social Diary*. New York: Harper, 1942.

Gassner, Emil. *Auf Vorposten: Drei Jahre Aufbau im Arbeitsbereich Generalgouvernement der NSDAP*. Krakow: Hauptarbeitsgebiet Presse im Arbeitsbereich Generalgouvernement der NSDAP, 1943.

Gellhorn, Martha. *Travels with Myself and Another*. London: Allen Lane, 1978.

Gerland, Brigitte. *Die Hölle ist ganz anders*. Stuttgart: Steingrüben, 1954.

Goebbels, Joseph. *Kampf um Berlin: Der Anfang*. Munich: Eher, 1937.

Groth-Schmachtenberger, Erika. *Meine liebsten Fotos: Erinnerungen einer Bildberichterin aus sechs Jahrzehnten*. Würzberg: Echter, 1984.

Habe, Hans. *Im Jahre Null: Ein Beitrag zur Geschichte der deutschen Presse*. Munich: K. Desch, 1966.

*Handbuch der deutschen Tagespresse*. Berlin: Duncker, 1934.

Heide, Walter. *Handbuch der deutschsprachigen Zeitungen im Ausland*. Berlin: Walter de Gruyter, 1935.

–, ed. *Handbuch der Zeitungswissenschaft*. Leipzig: Karl W. Hiersemann, 1940.

Hermand, Jost. *A Hitler Youth in Poland: The Nazi Children's Evacuation Program during the Second World War*. Evanston, IL: Northwestern University Press, 1998.

Heuss, Theodor. *Preludes to Life: Early Memoirs*. Translated by Michael Bullock. New York: Citadel Press, 1955.

Hillers, Marta. *Wir lernen Russisch: Eine Sprachfibel für Anfänger*. Vol. 1. Berlin: Herausgegeben im Auftrage der Deutschen Verwaltung für Volksbildung in der Sowjetischen Besatzungszone, 1945.

Hitler, Adolf. *Mein Kampf*. Translated by Ralph Manheim. Boston: Houghton Mifflin, 1943.

Höcker, Karla. *Beschreibung eines Jahres: Berliner Notizen 1945*. Berlin: Arani, 1984.

Hofmann, Josef. *Journalist in Republik, Diktatur und Besatzungszeit: Erinnerungen, 1916–1947*. Edited by Rudolf Morsey. Mainz: Matthias-Grünewald, 1977.

Hummerich, Helga. *Wahrheit zwischen den Zeilen: Erinnerungen an Benno Reifenberg und die Frankfurter Zeitung*. Freiburg: Herder, 1984.

Jacobi, Lucy von. *Journalistin: Mit Aufsätzen und Kritiken von Lucy von Jacobi*. Munich: ET+K, 2009.

Jünger, Ernst. *Der Kampf als inneres* Erlebnis. Berlin: Mittler & Sohn, 1922.

– *Stahlgewittern: Ein Kriegstagebuch*. Berlin: Mittler & Sohn, 1934.

Kardorff, Ursula von. *Berliner Aufzeichnungen aus den Jahren 1942 bis 1945*. Munich: Beck, 1992.

– *Diary of a Nightmare: Berlin, 1942–1945*. Translated by Ewan Butler. New York: John Day Co., 1966.

Kirkpatrick, Clifford. *Women in Nazi Germany*. London: Jarrolds, 1939.

Kirmsse, Erika. *Deutsches Frauenschaffen: Jahrbuch der Reichsfrauenführung*. Berlin: Reichsfrauenführung, 1937.

Klemperer, Victor. *I Will Bear Witness: A Diary of the Nazi Years, 1933–1941*. Translated by Martin Chalmers. New York: Modern Library, 1999.

– *I Will Bear Witness: A Diary of the Nazi Years, 1942–1945*. Translated by Martin Chalmers. New York: Random House, 1999.

– *The Language of the Third Reich: LTI, Lingua Terti Imperii – A Philologist's Notebook*. Translated by Martin Brady. London: Continuum, 2002.

Korn, Karl. *Lange Lehrzeit: Ein deutsches Leben*. Frankfurt: Societäts-Verlag, 1975.

Krempel, Lore. *Die deutsche Modezeitschrift: Ihre Geschichte und Entwicklung nebst einer Bibliographie der deutschen, englischen und französischen Modezeitschriften*. Coburg: Tageb.-Haus, 1935.

Krollpfeiffer, Hannelore. *Wir lebten in Berlin: Eine Geschichte vom Ende des Krieges*. Berlin, 1947.

Länderrat des Amerikanischen Besatzungsgebiets. *Statistisches Handbuch von Deutschland 1928–1944*. Munich: Ehrenwirth, 1949.

Leonhard, Susanne. *Gestohlenes Leben: Schicksal einer politischen Emigration in der Sowjetunion*. Stuttgart: Steingrüben, 1956.

Maschmann, Melita. *Account Rendered: A Dossier on My Former Self*. Lexington, MA: Plunkett Lake Press, 2016.

Matthies, Marie. *Journalisten in eigener Sache: Zur Geschichte des Reichsverbandes der deutschen Presse*. Berlin: Journalisten-Verband, 1969.

Noakes, Jeremy, and Geoffrey Pridham. *Nazism, 1919–1945*. Vol. 2. *State, Economy and Society 1933–1939*. Exeter: University of Exeter Press, 1984.

–, eds. *Nazism, 1919–1945*. Vol. 3. *Foreign Policy and Racial Extermination*. Exeter: University of Exeter Press, 1997.

Noelle-Neumann, Elisabeth. *Die Erinnerungen*. Munich: Herbig, 2006.

Oebsger-Röder, Rolf. *Vom Zeitungsschreiber zum Schriftleiter: Untersuchung über den Bildungsstand der deutschen Journalisten*. Leipzig: Noske, 1936.

Orgel-Köhne, Liselotte. *Willst du meine Witwe werden? Eine deutsche Liebe im Krieg*. Berlin: Aufbau, 1995.

Peterson, Jürgen. "Journalist im Dritten Reich: I. Lehrjahre in Darmstadt und Berlin." *Frankfurter Hefte*, 3 March 1981.

Rahms, Helene, *Auf dünnem Eis: Meine Kindheit in den zwanziger Jahren*. Bern: Scherz, 1992.

– *Die Clique: Journalistenleben in der Nachkriegszeit*. Bern: Scherz, 1999.

– *Zwischen den Zeilen: Mein Leben als Journalistin im Dritten Reich*. Bern: Scherz, 1997.

Rotzoll, Christa. *Frauen und Zeiten: Porträts*. Berlin: Deutscher Taschenbuch Verlag (dtv), 1991.

Rumin, Ursula. *Im Frauen-Gulag am Eismeer*. Munich: Herbig, 2005.

Salomon, Ernst von. *Der Fragebogen*. Hamburg: Rowohlt, 1951.

Sänger, Fritz. *Verborgene Fäden: Erinnerungen und Bemerkungen eines Journalisten*. Bonn: Neue Gesellschaft, 1978.

Schieder, Theodor, ed. *Documents on the Expulsion of the Germans from Eastern and Central Europe*. Bonn: Federal Ministry for Expellees, Refugees and War Victims, 1956–61.

Schmidt, Alfred. *Publizistik im Dorf*. Dresden: M. Dittert, 1939.

Schulz, Günter. *Der Schriftleiter: Das Schriftleitergesetz vom 4. Oktober 1933 als richtungweisendes Gesetz im neuen Deutschland*. Greifswald: Alder, 1935.

Sebastian, Mihail. *Journal, 1935–1944*. Translated by Patrick Camiller. Chicago: Ivan R. Dee, 2000.

Silex, Karl. *Mit Kommentar: Lebensbericht eines Journalisten*. Frankfurt: Fischer, 1968.

Sinjen, Marlen. *"Du schaffst es": Erfahrungen eines ungewöhnlichen Lebens*. Frankfurt: Ullstein, 1993.

*Statistisches Handbuch von Deutschland, 1928–1944*. Munich: Franz Ehrenwirth, 1949.

Steen, Uta van. *Macht war mir nie wichtig: Gespräche mit Journalistinnen*. Frankfurt: Fischer, 1988.

Stiewe, Dr Willy. *Das Pressefoto als publizistisches Mittel*. Leipzig, 1936.

Stiewe, Willy. "Bildberichterstatter." In Heide, *Handbuch der Zeitungswissenschaft*. Vol. 1, 615–29.

Sturm, Vilma. *Barfuß auf Asphalt*. Cologne: Kiepenheuer & Witsch, 1981.

Sündermann, Helmut. *Der Weg zum deutschen Journalismus: Hinweise für die Berufswahl junger Nationalsozialisten*. Berlin: Franz Eher, 1938.

Toepser-Ziegert, Gabriele, Hans Bohrmann, and Fritz Sänger. *NS-Presseanweisungen der Vorkriegszeit: Edition und Dokumentation*. Munich: Sauer, 1984.

Trampler-Steiner, Josephine. "Die Frau als Publizistin und Leserin: Deutsche Zeitschriften von und für Frauen." PhD diss., University of Munich, 1938.

Vrba, Rudolf, and Alan Bestic. *Escape from Auschwitz: I Cannot Forgive*. 1964; New York: Grove Press, 1986.

Walb, Lore. *Ich, die Alte – ich, die Junge: Konfrontation mit meinen Tagebüchern 1933–1945*. Berlin: Aufbau, 1998.

Waldeck, R.G. *Athene Palace. Hitler's "New Order" Comes to Romania*. Chicago: University of Chicago Press, 1942.

Wetzler, Alfred. *Escape from Hell: The True Story of the Auschwitz Protocol*. Edited by Péter Várnai, translated by Ewald Osers. New York: Berghahn Books, 2007.

Zander-Mika, Anneliese. "Frau und Presse." In Heide, *Handbuch der Zeitungswissenschaft*, 1159–76.

Zorn, Gerda. *Wiederkehr des Verdrängten: Autobiographische Erinnerungen*. Berlin: Weist, 2008.

**Selected Secondary Sources**

Aly, Götz. *Hitler's Beneficiaries: Plunder, Racial War, and the Nazi Welfare State*. Translated by Jefferson Chase. New York: Metropolitan Books / Henry Holt, 2007.

Applegate, Celia, and Pamela Potter, eds. *Music and German National Identity*. Chicago: University of Chicago Press, 2002.

Arendt, Hannah. "Truth and Politics." In *Between Past and Future: Eight Exercises in Political Thought*. New York: Viking, 1968.

Arani, Miriam Z. *Fotografische Selbst- und Fremdbilder von Deutschen und Polen im Reichsgau Wartheland, 1939–1945: Unter besonderer Berücksichtigung der Region Wielkopolska*. Hamburg: Verlag Dr. Kovač, 2008.

Averbeck, Stefanie, and Arnulf Kutsch. "Thesen zur Geschichte der Zeitungs- und Publizistikwissenschaft, 1900–1960." In *Die Spirale des Schweigens: Zum Umgang mit der nationalsozialistischen Zeitungswissenschaft*, edited by Wolfgang Duchkowitsch, Fritz Hausjell, and Bernd Semrad, 55–66. Vienna: Lit Verlag, 2004.

Bajohr, Frank. *"Aryanisation" in Hamburg: The Economic Exclusion of Jews and the Confiscation of Property in Nazi Germany*. New York: Berghahn, 2002.

– *Parvenüs und Profiteure: Korruption in der NS-Zeit*. Frankfurt: S. Fischer, 2001.

Balfour, M.L.G. "Reforming the German Press, 1945–1949." *Journal of European Studies* 3 (1973): 268–73.

Bankier, David. *The Germans and the Final Solution: Public Opinion under Nazism*. Oxford: Blackwell, 1992.

–, ed. *The Jews Are Coming Back. The Return of the Jews to Their Countries of Origin after World War II*. Jerusalem: Yad Vashem, 2005.

Baranowski, Shelley. *Nazi Empire: German Colonialism and Imperialism from Bismarck to Hitler*. Cambridge: Cambridge University Press, 2011.

– *Strength through Joy: Consumerism and Mass Tourism in the Third Reich*. Cambridge: Cambridge University Press, 2004.

Barton, Deborah. "Rewriting the Reich: German Women Journalists as Transnational Mediators for Germany's Rehabilitation," *Central European History* 51 (2018): 563–84.

Bartov, Omer. *Hitler's Army: Soldiers, Nazis, and War in the Third Reich*. New York: Oxford University Press, 1992.

Beevor, Antony. *Berlin: The Downfall, 1945*. London: Viking, 2002.

Below, Irene, and Ruth Oelze. *Lucy von Jacobi: Journalistin*. Munich: Richard Boorberg, 2009.

Beorn, Waitman Wade. *Marching into Darkness: The Wehrmacht and the Holocaust in Belarus*. Cambridge, MA: Harvard University Press, 2014.

Bergen, Doris. "The Nazi Concept of 'Volksdeutsche' and the Exacerbation of Anti-Semitism in Eastern Europe, 1939–45." *Journal of Contemporary History* 29, no. 4 (October 1994): 569–82.

– "Social Death and International Isolation: Jews in Nazi Germany, 1933–1939." In *Nazi Germany, Canadian Responses: Confronting Antisemitism in the Shadow of War*, edited by Ruth L. Klein. Montreal and Kingston: McGill-Queen's University Press, 2012.

– *Twisted Cross: The German Christian Movement in the Third Reich*. Chapel Hill: University of North Carolina Press, 1996.

Bergerson, Andrew Stuart. "Integrating in the Accusative: The Daily Papers of Interwar Hildesheim." *Issues in Integrative Studies* 15 (1997): 49–76.

– "Listening to Radio in Hildesheim, 1923–1953." *German Studies Review* 24, no. 1 (February 2001): 83–113.

Berghahn, Volker. *Industriegesellschaft und Kulturtransfer: Die deutsch-amerikanischen Beziehungen im 20. Jahrhundert*. Göttingen: Vandenhoeck & Ruprecht, 2010.

– *Journalists between Hitler and Adenauer: From Inner Emigration to the Moral Reconstruction of West Germany*. Princeton, NJ: Princeton University Press, 2019.

– *Otto A. Friedrich, ein politischer Unternehmer. Sein Leben und seine Zeit, 1902–1975*. New York: Campus Verlag, 1993.

Bering, Dietz. *The Stigma of Names: Antisemitism in German Daily Life, 1812–1933*. Cambridge: Polity Press, 1992.

Berkhoff, Karel C. *Motherland in Danger: Soviet Propaganda during World War II*. Cambridge, MA: Harvard University Press, 2012.

Bessel, Richard, and Dirk Schumann, eds. *Life after Death: Approaches to a Cultural and Social History of Europe during the 1940s and 1950s*. Cambridge: Cambridge University Press, 2003.

Betts, Paul. *Within Walls: Private Life in the German Democratic Republic*. Oxford: Oxford University Press, 2010.

Bialas, Wolfgang, and Anson Rabinbach, eds. *Nazi Germany and the Humanities*. Oxford: Oneworld, 2007.

Biddiscombe, Alexander Perry. *The Denazification of Germany: A History, 1945–1950*. Stroud, UK: Tempus, 2007.

*Bildberichterstatterin im Dritten Reich: Fotografien aus den Jahren 1937 bis 1944 von Liselotte Purper*. Deutsches Historisches Museum, Heft 20, Jahrgang Sommer 1997, 19.

Bloch, Ernst. *Der unbemerkte Augenblick: Feuilletons für die Frankfurter Zeitung, 1916–1934*. Frankfurt: Suhrkamp, 2007.

Bock, Gisela. *Zwangssterilisation im Nationalsozialismus: Studien zur Rassenpolitik und Frauenpolitik*. Opladen: Westdeutscher Verlag, 1986.

Bödeker, Birgit. *Amerikanische Zeitschriften in deutscher Sprache, 1945–1952: Ein Beitrag zur Literatur und Publizistik im Nachkriegsdeutschland*. Frankfurt: P. Lang, 1993.

Bösch Frank. *Mass Media and Historical Change: Germany in International Perspective, 1400 to the Present*. New York: Berghahn Books, 2017.

Bösch, Frank, and Dominik Geppert, eds. *Journalists as Political Actors: Transfers and Interactions between Britain and Germany since the Late 19th Century*. Augsburg: Wissner, 2008.

Bourdieu, Pierre. "The Forms of Capital." In *Handbook for Theory and Research for the Sociology of Education*, edited by J.G. Richardson, 241–58. Westport, CT: Greenwood Press, 1986.

Bouvier, Beatrix, *Ausgeschaltet! Sozialdemokraten in der Sowjetischen Besatzungszone und in der DDR, 1945–1953*. Bonn: Dietz, 1996.

Bracher, Karl Dietrich. *Die Auflösung der Weimarer Republik: Eine Studie zum Problem des Machtverfalls in der Demokratie*. Stuttgart: Ring-Verlag, 1955.

Brett, Donna West. *Photography and Place: Seeing and Not Seeing Germany after 1945*. New York: Routledge, 2016.

Bronnen, Barbara, ed. *Geschichten vom Überleben: Frauentagebücher aus der NS-Zeit.* Munich: Beck, 1998.

Broszat, Martin, Elke Fröhlich, and Falk Wiesemann. *Bayern in der NS-Zeit.* Munich: Oldenbourg, 1977–83.

Browning, Christopher. *Ordinary Men: Reserve Police Battalion 101 and the Final Solution in Poland.* New York: HarperCollins, 1992.

– "Spanning a Career: Three Editions of Raul Hilberg's Destruction of the European Jews." In *Lessons and Legacies.* Vol. 8. *From Generation to Generation,* edited by Doris Bergen, 191–202. Evanston, IL: Northwestern University Press.

Bruns, Jana F. *Nazi Cinema's New Women.* New York: Cambridge University Press, 2009.

Brysac, Shareen Blair. *Resisting Hitler: Mildred Harnack and the Red Orchestra.* Oxford: Oxford University Press, 2000.

Burleigh, Michael, *Germany Turns Eastwards.* London: Pan Books, 1988.

Burleigh, Michael, and Wolfgang Wippermann. *The Racial State: Germany, 1933–1945.* Cambridge: Cambridge University Press, 1991.

Butler, Judith. *Excitable Speech: A Politics of the Performative.* New York: Routledge, 2021.

– *Gender Trouble: Feminism and the Subversion of Identity.* New York: Routledge, 2006.

Bytwerk, Randall L. *Bending Spines: The Propagandas of Nazi Germany and the German Democratic Republic.* East Lansing: Michigan State University Press, 2004.

– *Julius Streicher: Nazi Editor of the Notorious Anti-Semitic Newspaper Der Stürmer.* New York: Cooper Square Press, 2001.

Caplan, Jane. "The Administration of Gender Identity in Nazi Germany." *History Workshop Journal* 72 (23 August 2011): 171–80.

– "'Jetzt judenfrei': Writing Tourism in Nazi-Occupied Poland." Annual lecture, German Historical Institute, London, 2012.

Carter, Cynthia, Linda Steiner, and Stuart Allan, eds. *Journalism, Gender and Power.* New York: Routledge, 2019.

Carter, Erica. *How German Is She? Postwar West German Reconstruction and the Consuming Woman.* Ann Arbor: University of Michigan Press, 1997.

Carter, Erica, Ian Palmowski, and Katrin Schreiter. *German Division as Shared Experience: Interdisciplinary Perspectives on the Postwar Everyday.* New York: Berghahn Books, 2019.

Century, Rachel. *Female Administrators of the Third Reich.* New York: Palgrave Macmillan, 2017.

Chambers, Deborah, Linda Steiner, and Carole Fleming. *Women and Journalism.* London: Routledge, 2004.

Chu, Winson. "The 'Lodzermensch': From Cultural Contamination to Marketable Multiculturalism." In *Germany, Poland and Postmemorial*

*Relations: In Search of a Livable Past*, edited by Kristin Kopp and Joanna Niżyńska, 239–58. New York: Palgrave Macmillan, 2012.

Coleman, Penny. *Where the Action Was: Women War Correspondents in World War II*. New York: Random House, 2002.

Confino, Alon. "Traveling as a Culture of Remembrance: Traces of National Socialism in West Germany, 1945–1960." *History and Memory* 12, no. 2 (Fall/Winter 2000): 92–121.

Corner, Paul, ed., *Popular Opinion in Totalitarian Regimes: Fascism, Nazism, Communism*. Oxford: Oxford University Press, 2017.

Cox, John M. *Circles of Resistance: Jewish, Leftist, and Youth Dissidence in Nazi Germany*. New York: Peter Lang, 2009.

Crew, David, ed. *Nazism and German Society, 1993–1945*. New York: Routledge, 1995.

Dahrendorf, Ralf. *Society and Democracy in Germany*. Westport, CT: Greenwood, 1979.

Daniel, Ute. *Beziehungsgeschichten: Politik und Medien im 20. Jahrhundert*. Hamburg: Verlag des Hamburger Institutes für Sozialforschung, 2018.

Davis, Belinda. *Home Fires Burning: Food, Politics, and Everyday Life in World War I Berlin*. Chapel Hill: University of North Carolina Press, 2000.

de Beauvoir, Simone. *The Second Sex*. New York, Knopf, 1953.

de Mendelssohn, Peter. *Zeitungsstadt Berlin: Menschen und Mächte in der Geschichte der deutschen Presse*. Berlin: Ullstein, 1959.

Dippold, Christine. "Lebensstationen. Erika Groth-Schmachtenberger (1906–1992)." In Dippold and Kania-Schütz, *Im Fokus*, 33–46.

Dippold, Christine, and Monika Kania-Schütz, eds. *Im Fokus: Die Bildberichterstatterin Erika Groth-Schmachtenberger und ihr Werk*. Grosweil: Echter, 2008.

Döhring, Kirsten, and Renate Feldmann. *Von "N.S. Frauen-Warte" bis "Victory": Konstruktionen von Weiblichkeit in nationalsozialistischen und rechtsextremen Frauenzeitschriften*. Berlin: Logos, 2004.

Domeier, Norman. *Weltöffentlichkeit und Diktatur. Die amerikanischen Auslandskorrespondenten im "Dritten Reich."* Göttingen: Wallstein, 2021.

Doob, Leondard W. "Goebbels' Principles of Propaganda." *Public Opinion Quarterly* 14, no. 3 (1950): 419–42.

Ebbinghaus, Angelika, ed. *Opfer und Täterinnen: Frauenbiographien des Nationalsozialismus*. Nördlingen: Delphi Politik, 1987.

Eckert, Astrid M. *West Germany and the Iron Curtain: Economy, Culture and Environment in the Borderlands*. Oxford: Oxford University Press, 2019.

Eder, Jacob. *Holocaust Angst: The Federal Republic of Germany and American Holocaust Memory since the 1970s*. New York: Oxford University Press, 2016.

Edwards, Julia. *Women of the World: The Great Foreign Correspondents*. Boston: Houghton Mifflin, 1988.

Eksteins, Modris. *The Limits of Reason: The German Democratic Press and the Collapse of Weimar Democracy*. London: Oxford University Press, 1975.

Engstron, Erika, Tracy Lucht, Jane Marcellus, and Kimberly Wilmot Moss. *Mad Men and Working Women: Feminist Perspectives on Historical Power, Resistance, and Otherness*. New York: Peter Lang, 2014.

Epstein, Catherine. *Model Nazi: Arthur Greiser and the Occupation of Western Poland*. Oxford: Oxford University Press, 2010.

Ericksen, Robert P. *Complicity in the Holocaust: Churches and Universities in Nazi Germany*. Cambridge: Cambridge University Press, 2012.

Evans, Jennifer, Paul Betts, and Stefan-Ludwig Hoffmann, eds. *The Ethics of Seeing: Photography and Twentieth-Century German History*. New York: Berghahn, 2018.

Evans, Richard J. *The Third Reich in Power*. New York: Penguin Books, 2006.

– *The Third Reich at War*. New York: Penguin, 2009.

Fahs, Alice. *Out on Assignment: Newspaper Women and the Making of Modern Public Space*. Chapel Hill: University of North Carolina Press, 2014.

Fay, Brendan. "The Nazi Conspiracy Theory: German Fantasies and Jewish Power in the Third Reich," *Library and Information History* 35, no. 2 (2019): 75–97.

Fehrenbach, Heide. *Cinema in Democratizing Germany: Reconstructing National Identity after Hitler*. Chapel Hill: University of North Carolina Press, 1995.

Fiedler, Anke. *Medienlenkung in der DDR*. Cologne: Böhlau, 2014.

Fink, Carole. *Defending the Rights of Others: The Great Powers, the Jews, and International Minority Protection, 1878–1938*. Cambridge: Cambridge University Press, 2004.

Fischer, Peter. *Die deutsche Publizistik als Faktor der deutsch-polnischen Beziehungen, 1919–1939*. Wiesbaden: O. Harrassowitz, 1991.

Föllmer Moritz. *Culture in the Third Reich*. Oxford: Oxford University Press, 2016.

Frederiksen, Elke, and Martha Kaarsberg Wallach, eds. *Facing Fascism and Confronting the Past: German Women Writers from Weimar to the Present*. Albany: State University of New York Press, 2000.

Frei, Norbert. *Adenauer's Germany and the Nazi Past: The Politics of Amnesty and Integration*. New York: Columbia University Press, 2002.

– *Und Wir: Das Dritte Reich im Bewusstsein der Deutschen*. Munich: Beck, 2005.

Frei, Norbert, and Johannes Schmitz. *Journalismus im Dritten Reich*. Munich: Beck, 1989.

Frevert, Ute. *Women in German History: From Bourgeois Emancipation to Sexual Liberation*, translated by Stuart McKinnon-Evans in association with Terry Bond and Barbara Norden. Oxford: Berg, 1990.

Friedlander, Henry. *The Origins of Nazi Genocide: From Euthanasia to the Final Solution*. Chapel Hill: University of North Carolina Press, 1995.

Friedländer, Saul. *Nazi Germany and the Jews, 1933–1939: The Years of Persecution*. London: Phoenix, Orion Books, 1997.

– *Nazi Germany and the Jews, 1939–1945: The Years of Extermination*. New York: HarperCollins, 2007.

Fritzsche, Peter. *Germans into Nazis*. Cambridge, MA: Harvard University Press, 1998.

– *Life and Death in the Third Reich*. Cambridge, MA: Harvard University Press, 2008.

– *Reading Berlin, 1900*. Cambridge, MA: Harvard University Press, 1998.

Fritzsche, Peter, and Alon Confino, eds. *The Work of Memory: New Directions in the Study of German Society and Culture*. Urbana: University of Illinois Press, 2002.

Führer, Karl Christian. *Medienmetropole Hamburg: Mediale Öffentlichkeiten, 1930–1960*. Munich: Dölling und Galitz, 2008.

– "Pleasure, Practicality and Propaganda: Popular Magazines in Nazi Germany, 1933–1939." In Swett, Ross, and d'Almeida, *Pleasure and Power in Nazi Germany*, 132–53.

Führer, Karl Christian, and Corey Ross, eds. *Mass Media, Culture and Society in Twentieth-Century Germany*. New York: Palgrave Macmillan, 2006.

Fulbrook, Mary. *The People's State: East German Society from Hitler to Honecker*. New Haven, CT: Yale University Press, 2005.

– *A Small Town Near Auschwitz: Ordinary Nazis and the Holocaust*. Oxford: Oxford University Press, 2012.

Fulda, Bernhard. *Press and Politics in the Weimar Republic*. Oxford: Oxford University Press, 2009.

Gailus, Manfred. *Protestantismus und Nationalsozialismus: Studien zur nationalsozialistischen Durchdringung des protestantischen Sozialmilieus in Berlin*. Cologne: Böhlau, 2001.

Ganeva, Mila. "Fashion amidst the Ruins: Revisiting the Early Rubble Films *The Heavens Above* (1947) and *The Murderers Are among Us* (1946)." *German Studies Review* 37, no. 1 (February 2014): 62–85.

Gebhardt, Miriam. *Crimes Unspoken: The Rape of German Women at the End of the Second World War*. Cambridge: Polity Press, 2017.

Gellately, Robert. *Backing Hitler: Consent and Coercion in Nazi Germany*. Oxford: Oxford University Press, 2001.

Gellately, Robert, and Nathan Stoltzfus, eds. *Social Outsiders in Nazi Germany*. Princeton, NJ: Princeton University Press, 2001.

Gerhard, Gesine. *Nazi Hunger Politics: A History of Food in the Third Reich*. Washington DC: Rowman & Littlefield, 2015.

Gerlach, Christian. *Kalkulierte Morde: Die deutsche Wirtschafts- und Vernichtungspolitik in Weißrußland, 1941–1944*. Hamburg: Hamburger Edition, 1999.

Gienow-Hecht, Jessica C.E. *Transmission Impossible: American Journalism as Cultural Diplomacy in Postwar Germany, 1945–1955*. Baton Rouge: Louisiana State University Press, 1999.

Gillessen, Günther. *Auf verlorenem Posten: Die Frankfurter Zeitung im Dritten Reich*. Munich: Siedler, 1992.

Goedde, Petra. *GIs and Germans: Culture, Gender and Foreign Relations, 1945–1949*. New Haven, CT: Yale University Press, 2003.

Goldstein, Cora Sol. *Capturing the German Eye: American Visual Propaganda in Occupied Germany*. Chicago: University of Chicago Press, 2009.

Goodpaster Strebe, Amy. *Flying for Her Country: The American and Soviet Women Military Pilots of World War II*. Westport, CT: Praeger Security International, 2007.

Görtemaker, Heike B. *Ein deutsches Leben: Die Geschichte der Margret Boveri*. Munich: Beck, 2005.

Gottschalk, Maren. *Der geschärfte Blick: Sieben Journalistinnen und ihre Lebensgeschichte*. Weinheim: Beltz, 2001.

Götz, Norbert. "German-Speaking People Fand Germany Heritage: Nazi Germany and the Problem of Volksgemeinschaft." In *The Heimat Abroad: The Boundaries of Germanness*, edited by Krista O'Donnell, Renate Bridenthal, and Nancy Reagin, 58–82. Ann Arbor: University of Michigan Press, 2005.

Grabowski, Jan. "German Anti-Jewish Propaganda in the General Government, 1939–1945: Inciting Hate through Posters, Films, and Exhibitions." *Holocaust and Genocide Studies* 23, no. 3 (Winter 2009): 381–412.

Gray, Elizabeth, ed. *Women in Journalism at the Fin de Siècle: Making a Name for Herself*. New York: Palgrave Macmillan, 2012.

Greffrath, Bettina. *Gesellschaftsbilder der Nachkriegszeit: Deutsche Spielfilme 1945–1949*. Pfaffenweiler: Centaurus, 1995.

Grossmann, Atina. "Feminist Debates about Women and National Socialism." *Gender and History* 3, no. 3 (1991): 350–8.

– "Gendered Defeat: Rape and Fraternization after the 'Zusammenbruch.'" Paper presented at the Theorizing German Suffering: Bombing, Rapes and Expulsions conference, University of Toronto, 2007.

– *Jews, Germans, and Allies: Close Encounters in Occupied Germany*. Princeton, NJ: Princeton University Press, 2007.

– "A Question of Silence: The Rape of German Women by Occupation Soldiers." *October* 72 (Spring 1995): 42–63.

Groth, Michael. *The Road to New York: The Emigration of Berlin Journalists, 1933–1945*. Munich: Minerva, 1984.

Guenther, Irene. *Nazi Chic? Fashioning Women in the Third Reich*. Oxford: Berg, 2004.

Haar, Ingo, and Michael Fahlbusch, eds. *German Scholars and Ethnic Cleansing, 1919–1945*. New York: Berghahn, 2005.

Habermas, Jürgen. *The Structural Transformation of the Public Sphere: An Inquiry into a Category of Bourgeois Society*. Cambridge, MA: MIT Press, 1989.

Hachmeister, Lutz. *Theoretische Publizistik: Studien zur Geschichte der Kommunikationswissenschaft in Deutschland*. Berlin: Volker Spiess, 1987.

Hagemann, Jürgen. *Die Pressenlenkung im Dritten Reich*. Bonn: Bouvier, 1970.

Hagemann, Karen, Donna Harsch, and Friederike Brühöfener. *Gendering Post-1945 German History: Entanglements*. New York: Berghahn Books, 2019.

Hagemann, Karen, and Jean H. Quataert, eds. *Gendering Modern German History: Rewriting Historiography*. New York: Berghahn Books, 2007.

Hale, Oron J. 1964. *The Captive Press in the Third Reich*. Princeton, NJ: University Press, 1964.

Hallet, Theo. *Umstrittene Versöhnung: Reagan und Kohl in Bitburg, 1985*. Erfurt: Sutton, 2005.

Hamilton, John Maxwell. *Journalism's Roving Eye: A History of American Foreign Reporting*. Baton Rouge: Louisiana State University Press, 2009.

Hardy, Alexander G. *Hitler's Secret Weapon: The "Managed" Press and Propaganda Machine of Nazi Germany*. New York: Vantage, 1968.

Harsch, Donna. *Revenge of the Domestic: Women, the Family, and Communism in the German Democratic Republic*. Princeton, NJ: Princeton University Press, 2007.

– "Sex, Divorce, and Women's Waged Work: Private Lives and State Policy in the Early German Democratic Republic." In *Gender and Everyday Life under State Socialism in East and Central Europe*, edited by Jill Massino and Shana Penn, 97–113. Basingstoke, UK: Palgrave, 2010.

Hartman, Geoffrey H., ed. *Bitburg in Moral and Political Perspective*. Bloomington: Indiana University Press, 1986.

Harvey, Elizabeth. "'Ich war überall': Die NS-Propagandaphotographin Liselotte Purper." In *Volksgenossinnen: Frauen in der NS-Volksgemeinschaft*, edited by Sybille Steinbacher, 138–53. Göttingen: Wallstein, 2007.

– "Seeing the World: Photography, Photojournalism and Visual Pleasure in the Third Reich." In Swett, Ross, and d'Almeida, *Pleasure and Power in Nazi Germany*, 177–204.

– *Women and the Nazi East: Agents and Witnesses of Germanization*. New Haven, CT: Yale University Press, 2003.

Harvey, Elizabeth, Johannes Hürter, Maiken Umbach, and Andreas Wirsching, eds. *Private Life and Privacy in Nazi Germany*. Cambridge: Cambridge University Press, 2019.

Heineman, Elizabeth. *Before Porn Was Legal: The Erotica Empire of Beate Uhse*. Chicago: University of Chicago Press, 2011.

– "The Hour of the Woman: Memories of Germany's 'Crisis Years' and West German National Identity." *American Historical Review* 101, no. 2 (1996): 354–96.

– *What Difference Does a Husband Make? Women and Marital Status in Nazi and Postwar Germany*. Berkeley and Los Angeles: University of California Press, 1999.

Heinsohn, Kirsten, Barbara Vogel, and Ulrike Weckel, eds. *Zwischen Karriere und Verfolgung: Handlungsräume von Frauen im nationalsozialistischen Deutschland*. New York: Campus, 1997.

Herbert, Ulrich. *Hitler's Foreign Workers: Enforced Foreign Labor in Germany under the Third Reich*. New York: Cambridge University Press, 1997.

Herf, Jeffrey. *Divided Memory: The Nazi Past in the Two Germanys*. Cambridge, MA: Harvard University Press, 1997.

– *The Jewish Enemy: Nazi Propaganda During World War II and the Holocaust*. Cambridge: Harvard University Press, 2006.

Herwig, Holger. *The Demon of Geopolitics: How Karl Haushofer "Educated" Hitler and Hess*. Lanham, MD: Rowman & Littlefield, 2016.

Herzer, Martin. *Auslandskorrespondenten und auswärtige Pressepolitik im Dritten Reich* Vienna: Böhlau, 2012.

Herzog, Dagmar. *Sex after Fascism: Memory and Morality in Twentieth-Century Germany*. Princeton, NJ: Princeton University Press, 2007.

Higonnet, Margaret R., Jane Jenson, Sonya Michel, and Margaret Weitz Collins, eds. *Behind the Lines: Gender and the Two World Wars*. New Haven, CT: Yale University Press, 1987.

Hilberg, Raul. *The Destruction of the European Jews*. Chicago: Quadrangle Books, 1961.

Hillgruber, Andreas. *Zweierlei Untergag: Die Zerschlagung des Deutschen Reiches und das Ende des europäischen Judentums*. Berlin: Siedler, 1986.

Hirsch, Marianne. *Family Frames: Photography, Narrative, and Postmemory*. Cambridge, MA: Harvard University Press, 1997.

Höck, Alfred. "Bilder aus dem Salzburger Land." In Dippold and Kania-Schütz, *Im Fokus*, 133–64.

Hodenberg, Christina von. *Konsens und Krise: Eine Geschichte der westdeutschen Medienöffentlichkeit, 1945–1973*. Göttingen: Wallstein, 2006.

– "Mass Media and the Generation of Conflict: West Germany's Long Sixties and the Formation of a Critical Public Sphere." *Contemporary European History* 15, no. 3 (August 2006): 367–95.

Hodorowicz, Sophie. *Wearing the Letter "P": Polish Women as Forced Laborers in Nazi Germany, 1939–1945*. New York: Hippcrene Books, 2016.

Hoenicke Moore, Michaela. "Heimat und Fremde: Das Verhältnis zu Amerika im journalistischen Werk von Margret Boveri und Dolf Sternberger." In *Demokratiewunder: Transatlantische Mittler und die kulturelle Öffnung Westdeutschlands, 1945–1970*, edited by Arnd Bauerkämper, Konrad Jarausch, and Marcus M. Payk, 218–52. Göttingen: Vandenhoeck & Ruprecht, 2005.

– *Know Your Enemy: The American Debate on Nazism, 1933–1945*. New York: Cambridge University Press, 2010.

Hoffmann, Hilmar. *The Triumph of Propaganda: Film and National Socialism, 1933–1945*. Translated by John A. Broadwin and V.R. Berghahn. Providence, RI: Berghahn Books, 1996.

Hoffmann, Peter. *The History of German Resistance, 1933–1945*. Translated by Richard Barry. Montreal and Kingston: McGill-Queen's University Press, 1996.

Höhn, Maria. *GIs and Fräuleins: The German-American Encounter in 1950s West Germany*. Chapel Hill: University of North Carolina Press, 2002.

Hurwitz, Harold, J. *Die Stunde Null der deutschen Presse: Die amerikanische Pressepolitik in Deutschland, 1945–1949*. Cologne: Wissenschaft und Politik Verlag, 1972.

Ioanid, Radu. *The Holocaust in Romania: The Destruction of Jews and Gypsies under the Antonescu Regime, 1940–1944*. Chicago: Ivan R. Dee, 2000.

Jahn, Bruno, ed. *Die deutschsprachige Presse: Ein biographisch-bibliographisches Handbuch*. Munich: K.G. Sauer, 2005.

Jarausch, Konrad H. *After Hitler: Recivilizing Germans, 1945–1995*. Oxford: Oxford University Press, 2006.

– *The Conundrum of Complicity: German Professionals and the Final Solution*. Washington, DC: United States Holocaust Memorial Museum, 2001.

–, ed. *Dictatorship as Experience*. New York: Berghahn Books, 1999.

– "Removing the Nazi Stain? The Quarrel of the German Historians." *German Studies Review* 11, no. 2 (May 1988): 285–301.

– *The Unfree Professions: German Lawyers, Teachers, and Engineers, 1900–1950*. New York: Oxford University Press, 1990.

Jarausch, Konrad H., and Michael Geyer. *Shattered Past: Reconstructing German Histories*. Princeton, NJ: Princeton University Press, 2003.

Jaskot, Paul B. *The Architecture of Oppression: The SS, Forced Labor and the Nazi Monumental Building Economy*. New York: Routledge, 2000.

Jenkins, Jennifer. *Provincial Modernity: Local Culture and Liberal Politics in Fin-de-Siècle Hamburg*. Ithaca, NY: Cornell University Press, 2003.

Jockheck, Lars. *Propaganda im Generalgouvernement: Die NS-Besatzungspresse für Deutsche und Polen 1939–1945*. Osnabrück: Fibre, 2006.

Johnston, Donald H., ed. *Encyclopedia of International Media and Communications*. Vol. 2. San Diego: Academic Press, 2003.

Judt, Tony. *Postwar: A History of Europe since 1945*. New York: Penguin, 2005.

Kaiser, Rolf, and Hermann Loddenkemper. *Nationalsozialismus: Totale Manipulation in der beruflichen Bildung?* Frankfurt: Lang, 1980.

Kallis, Aristotle A. *Nazi Propaganda and the Second World War*. New York: Palgrave Macmillan, 2005.

Kaplan, Marion. *Between Dignity and Despair: Jewish Life in Nazi Germany*. Oxford: Oxford University Press, 1999.Kater, Michael H. *Doctors under Hitler*. Chapel Hill: University of North Carolina Press, 1989.

Kay, Alex J., Jeff Rutherford, and David Stahel, eds. *Nazi Policy on the Eastern Front, 1941: Total War, Genocide, and Radicalization*. Rochester, NY: University of Rochester Press, 2012.

Kershaw, Ian. *The End: The Defiance and Destruction of Hitler's Germany, 1944–45*. New York: Penguin, 2011.

– "How Effective Was Nazi Propaganda?" In *Nazi Propaganda: The Power and the Limitations*, edited by David Welch, 180–205. Oxford: Routledge, 2015.

– *Popular Opinion and Political Dissent in the Third Reich, Bavaria, 1933–1945*. Oxford: Oxford University Press, 1983.

– "'Working toward the Führer': Reflections on the Nature of the Hitler Dictatorship." *Contemporary European History* 2, no. 2 (1993): 103–18.

Klaus, Lissi. "Als Frau hatte man es natürlich leichter, natürlich schwerer." In Engler and Klaus, *Medienfrauen der ersten Stunde*, 191–218.

Knoch, Habbo. *Die Tat als Bild: Fotografien des Holocaust in der deutschen Erinnerungskultur*. Hamburg: Hamburger Edition, 2001.

Köhler, Otto, and Monika Köhler, eds. *Wir Schreibmaschinentäter: Journalisten unter Hitler und danach*. Cologne: Pahl-Rugenstein, 1989.

Koonz, Claudia. *Mothers in the Fatherland: Women, the Family and Nazi Politics*. London: Jonathan Cape, 1987.

– *The Nazi Conscience*. Cambridge, MA: Belknap Press, 2003.

Kopp, Kristen. *Germany's Wild East: Constructing Poland as Colonial Space*. Ann Arbor: University of Michigan Press, 2012.

Korb, Alexander. *Im Schatten des Weltkriegs: Massengewalt der Ustaša gegen Serben, Juden und Roma in Kroatien, 1941–45*. Hamburg: Hamburger Edition, 2013.

Kramer, Nicole. *Volksgenossinnen an der Heimatfront: Mobilisierung, Verhalten, Erinnerung*. Göttingen: Vandenhoeck & Ruprecht, 2011.

Kravetz, Melissa. *Women Doctors in Weimar and Nazi Germany: Materialism, Eugenics and Professional Identity*. Toronto: University of Toronto Press, 2019.

Krimmer, Elizabeth. *German Women's Life Writing and the Holocaust: Complicity and Gender in the Second World War*. Cambridge: Cambridge University Press, 2018.

Kudlien, Fridolf. *Ärzte im Nationalsozialismus*. Cologne: Kiepenheuer & Witsch, 1985.

Kühne, Thomas. *Belonging and Genocide: Hitler's Community, 1918–1945*. New Haven, CT: Yale University Press, 2010.

– "Introduction: Masculinity and the Third Reich." *Central European History* 51, no. 3 (2018): 354–66.

– *Kameradschaft: Die Soldaten des nationalsozialistischen Krieges und das 20. Jahrhundert*. Göttingen: Vandenhoeck & Ruprecht, 2006.

Künheim, Haug von. *Marion Dönhoff*. Reinbek: Rowohlt, 2000.

Lacey, Kate. *Feminine Frequencies: Gender, German Radio, and the Public Sphere, 1923–1945*. Ann Arbor: University of Michigan Press, 1996.

Lansing, Charles B. *From Nazism to Communism: German Schoolteachers under Two Dictatorships*. Cambridge, MA: Harvard University Press, 2010.

Large, David Clay, ed. *Contending with Hitler: Varieties of German Resistance in the Third Reich*. Cambridge: Cambridge University Press, 1991.

Laurien, Ingrid. *Politisch-kulturelle Zeitschriften in den Westzonen, 1945–1949: Ein Beitrag zur politischen Kultur der Nachkriegzeit.* New York: Lang, 1991.

Law, Ricky W. *Transnational Nazism: Ideology and Culture in German-Japanese Relations, 1919–1936.* Cambridge: Cambridge University Press, 2019.

Leff, Laurel. *Buried by the Times: The Holocaust and America's Most Important Newspaper.* Cambridge: Cambridge University Press, 2005.

Lemmes, Fabian. "Arbeiten für das Reich: Die Organisation Todt in Frankreich und Italien, 1940–1945." PhD diss., European University Institute, 2009.

Lemke, Michael. "Foreign Influences on the Dictatorial Development of the GDR, 1949–1955." In *Dictatorship as Experience,* edited by Konrad H. Jarausch, 91–108. Oxford: Oxford University Press, 2006.

Lemmons, Russel. *Goebbels and Der Angriff.* Lexington: University Press of Kentucky, 1994.

Lindemann, Albert S., and Richard S. Levy eds. *Antisemitism: A History.* Oxford: Oxford University Press, 2010.

Lipstadt, Deborah. *Beyond Belief: The American Press and the Coming of the Holocaust, 1933–1945.* New York: Free Press; London: Collier Macmillan, 1986.

Liss, Andrea. *Trespassing through Shadows: Memory, Photography, and the Holocaust.* Minneapolis: University of Minnesota Press. 1998.

Lonsdale, Sarah. "The 'Awkward' Squad: British Women Foreign Correspondents during the Interwar Years." *Women's History Review,* 23 May 2021, 1–21.

Lott, Sylvia. *Die Frauenzeitschriften von Hans Huffzky und John Jahr: Zur Geschichte der deutschen Frauenzeitschrift zwischen 1933–1970.* Berlin: Wissenschaftsverlag Volker Spiess, 1985.

Löw, Andrea, and Markus Roth. *Juden in Krakau unter deutscher Besatzung, 1939–1945.* Göttingen: Wallstein, 2001.

Lower, Wendy. *Hitler's Furies: German Women in the Nazi Killing Fields.* London: Chatto and Windus, 2013.

Lucht, Tracy, and Kate Batschelet. "'That Was What I Had to Use': Social and Cultural Capital in the Careers of Women Broadcasters." *Journalism and Mass Communications Quarterly* 96 (2019): 194–214.

Lüdtke, Alf, ed. *Alltagsgeschichte: Zur Rekonstruktion historischer Erfahrungen und Lebensweisen.* Frankfurt: Campus, 1989.

Lutjens, Richard. "Vom Untertauchen: 'U-Boote' und der Berliner Alltag 1941–1945." In *Alltag im Holocaust: Jüdisches Leben im Großdeutschen Reich, 1941–1945,* edited by Andrea Löw, Doris L. Bergen, and Anna Hájková, 49–64. Munich: Oldenburg, 2013.

Lynn, Denise. "Gendered Narratives in Anti-Stalinism and Anti-Communism during the Cold War: The Case of Juliet Pyontz." *Journal of Cold War Studies* 18, no. 1 (2016): 31–59.

Lynn, Jennifer. *Contested Femininities: Representations of Modern Women in the German Illustrated Press, 1920–1960.* Forthcoming.

Maier, Charles S. *The Unmasterable Past: History, Holocaust, and German National Identity*. Cambridge, MA: Harvard University Press, 1997.

Mailänder, Elissa. *Gewalt im Dienstalltag: Die SS-Aufseherinnen des Konzentrations- und Vernichtungslagers Majdanek*. Hamburg: Hamburger Edition, 2009.

Malinowski, Stephan. *Vom König zum Führer: Der deutsche Adel und der Nationalsozialismus*. Frankfurt am Main: Fischer, 2004.

Marhoefer, Laurie. *Sex and the Weimar Republic: German Homosexual Emancipation and the Rise of the Nazis*. Toronto: University of Toronto Press, 2015.

Marrus, Michael R. *The Nuremberg War Crimes Trial, 1945–46: A Documentary History*. Boston: Bedford Books, 1997.

Marszolek, Inge. "The Atlantic Wall: An Ambiguous Heritage." Lecture at Redefining the Atlantic Wall conference, Amersfoort, Netherlands, 2 September 2010, http://congres2010.atlantikwallplatform.eu.

Martin, Benjamin G. *The Nazi-Fascist New Order for European Culture*. Cambridge, MA: Harvard University Press, 2016.

Mason, Tim. "Women in Germany." *History Workshop Journal*, no. 17 (1976): 74–113.

Maubach, Franka. *Die Stellung halten: Kriegserfahrungen und Lebensgeschichten von Wehrmachthelferinnen*. Göttingen: Vandenhoeck & Ruprecht, 2009.

Maza, Sarah. *Private Lives and Public Affairs: The Causes Célèbres of Prerevolutionary France*. Berkeley and Los Angeles: University of California Press, 1993.

Mazower, Mark. *Hitler's Empire: Nazi Rule in Occupied Europe*. London: Allen Lane, 2008.

McFarland-Icke, Bronwyn Rebekah. *Nurses in Nazi Germany: Moral Choice in History*. Princeton, NJ: Princeton University Press, 1999.

Megargee, Geoffrey P., ed. *The United States Holocaust Memorial Museum Encyclopedia of Camps and Ghettos, 1933–1945*. Vol. 1. Bloomington: Indiana University Press, 2009.

Merziger, Patrick. "'German Humour' in Books: The Attractiveness and Political Significance of Laughter during the Nazi Era." In Swett, Ross, and d'Almeida, *Pleasure and Power in Nazi Germany*, 107–31.

Messenger, David A., and Katrin Paehler, eds. *A Nazi Past: Recasting German Identity in Postwar Europe*. Lexington: University Press of Kentucky, 2015.

Meyen Michael, and Anka Fiedler. "Journalisten in der DDR: Eine Kollektivbiografie." *Medien und Kommunikationswissenschaft* 59 (2011): 23–39.

Mills, Kay. *A Place in the News: From the Women's Pages to the Front Page*. New York: Columbia University Press, 1990.

Moderegger, Johannes Christoph. *Modefotografie in Deutschland*. Norderstedt: Libri Books, 2000.

Moeller, Robert. "The Elephant in the Living Room: Or Why the History of Twentieth Century Germany Should Be a Family Affair." In Hagemann and Quataert, *Gendering Modern German History*, 228–50.

– *Protecting Motherhood: Women and the Family in the Politics of Postwar West Germany*. Berkeley and Los Angeles: University of California Press, 1993.

– *War Stories: The Search for a Usable Past in the Federal Republic of Germany*. Berkeley and Los Angeles: University of California Press, 2001.

–, ed. *West Germany under Construction: Politics, Society, and Culture in the Adenauer Era*. Ann Arbor: University of Michigan Press, 1997.

Möhrle, René ed. *Umbrüche und Kontinuitäten in der deutschen Presse: Fallstudien zu Medienakteuren von 1945 bis heute*. Gutenberg: Computus Druck Satz & Verlag, 2020.

Mommsen, Hans. *Alternatives to Hitler: German Resistance under the Third Reich*. Translated and annotated by Angus McGeoch. Princeton, NJ: Princeton University Press, 2003.

Mosberg, Helmuth, *Reeducation: Umerziehung und Lizenzpresse im Nachkriegsdeutschland*. Munich: Universitas, 1991.

Mouton, Michelle. "From Adventure and Advancement to Derailment and Demotion: Effects of Nazi Gender Policy on Women's Careers and Lives." *Journal of Social History* 43, no. 4 (Summer 2010): 945–71.

– *From Nurturing the Nation to Purifying the Volk: Weimar and Nazi Family Policy, 1918–1945*. Cambridge: Cambridge University Press, 2007.

– "The *Kinderlandverschickung*: Childhood Memories of War Re-Examined." *German History* 37, no. 2 (June 2019): 186–204.

Mühlenberg, Jutta. *Das SS-Helferinnenkorps: Ausbildung, Einsatz und Entnazifizierung der weiblichen Angehörigen der Waffen-SS, 1942–1949*. Hamburg: Hamburger Edition, 2010.

Müller, Ingo. *Hitler's Justice: The Courts of the Third Reich*. Cambridge, MA: Harvard University Press, 1991.

Müsse, Wolfgang. *Die Reichspresseschule: Journalisten für die Diktatur? Ein Beitrag zur Geschichte des Journalismus im Dritten Reich*. Munich: Saur, 1995.

Naimark, Norman. *The Russians in Germany: A History of the Soviet Zone of Occupation, 1945–1949*. Cambridge, MA: Harvard University Press, 1997.

Neiman, Susan. *Learning from the Germans Race and the Memory of Evil*. New York: Farrar, Straus and Giroux, 2019.

Neitzel, Sönke, and Bernd Heidenreich, eds. *Medien im Nationalsozialismus*. Paderborn: Fink, 2010.

Nye, Joseph S. *Soft Power: The Means to Success in World Politics*. New York: Public Affairs, 2004.

Olson, Candi S. Carter. "'This Was No Place for a Woman': Gender Judo, Gender Stereotypes, and World War II Correspondent Ruth Cowan." *American Journalism* 34, no. 4 (2017): 427–47.

Ortmeyer, Benjamin. *Indoktrination: Rassismus und Antisemitismus in der Nazi-Schülerzeitschrift "Hilf mit!" (1933–1944): Analyse und Dokumente*. Weinheim: Juventa, 2013.

Owings, Alison. *Frauen: German Women Recall the Third Reich*. New Brunswick, NJ: Rutgers University Press, 1993.

Paperno, Irina. "Personal Accounts of the Soviet Experience." *Kritika: Explorations in Russian and Eurasian History* 3, no. 4 (2002): 577–610.

Pauwels, Jacques R. *Women, Nazis, and Universities: Female University Students in the Third Reich, 1933–1945*. Westport, CT: Greenwood, 1984.

Payk, Marcus M. *Der Geist der Demokratie. Intellektuelle Orientierungsversuche im Feuilleton der frühen Bundesrepublik: Karl Korn und Peter de Mendelssohn*. Munich: Oldenbourg, 2008.

Pegelow Kaplan, Thomas. "'German Jews,' 'National Jews,' 'Jewish Volk' or 'Racial Jews'? The Constitution and Contestation of 'Jewishness' in Newspapers of Nazi Germany, 1933–1938." *Central European History* 35, no. 2 (2002): 195–221.

– *The Language of Nazi Genocide: Linguistic Violence and the Struggle of Germans of Jewish Ancestry*. Cambridge: Cambridge University Press, 2009.

Peiffer, Jürgen. *Menschenverachtung und Opportunismus: Zur Medizin im Dritten Reich*. Tübingen: Attempto, 1992.

Pendas, Devin O. *The Frankfurt Auschwitz Trial, 1963–1965: Genocide, History, and the Limits of the Law*. Cambridge: Cambridge University Press, 2006.

Peukert, Detlev. *Inside Nazi Germany: Conformity, Opposition and Racism in Everyday Life*. London: Batsford, 1987.

Picard, Jacques. *Edit von Coler: Als Nazi-Agentin in Bukarest*. Bonn: Schiller, 2010.

Pine, Lisa. *Education in Germany*. New York: Berg, 2010.

Plato, Alexander von, Almut Leh, and Christoph Tonfeld, eds. *Hitler's Slaves: Life Stories of Forced Labourers in Nazi-Occupied Europe*. New York: Berghahn, 2010.

Poiger, Uta. *Jazz, Rock and Rebels: Cold War Politics and American Culture in a Divided Germany*. Berkeley and Los Angeles: University of California Press, 2000.

Port, Andrew. *Conflict and Stability in the German Democratic Republic*. Cambridge: Cambridge University Press, 2007.

Pöttker, Host. *Abgewehrte Vergangenheit: Beiträge zur deutschen Erinnerung an den Nationalsozialismus*. Cologne: Herbet von Halem, 2005.

Preston, Paul. *We Saw Spain Die: Foreign Correspondents in the Spanish Civil War*. London: Constable, 2008.

Prokasky, Judith, ed. *Zwischen den Zeilen? Zeitungspresse als NS-Machtinstrument*. Berlin: Stiftung Topographie des Terrors, 2013.

Protte, Katja. "Beruf: 'Bildberichterstatterin,' in 'Bildberichterstatterin im Dritten Reich': Fotografien aus den Jahren 1937 bis 1944 von Liselotte Purper." *Deutsches Historisches Museum Magazine*, no. 20 (Summer 1997): 1–60.

Przyrembel, Alexandra. "Transfixed by an Image: Ilse Koch the 'Kommandeuse of Buchenwald'." *Germany History* 19, no. 3 (2001): 369–99.

Raack, R.C. "Stalin Plans His Post-War Germany." *Journal of Contemporary History* 28, no. 1 (January 1993): 53–73.

Reagin, Nancy. *Sweeping the German Nation: Domesticity and National Identity in Germany, 1870–1945*. Cambridge: Cambridge University Press, 2007.

Reese, Dagmar, ed. *Die BDM-Generation: Weibliche Jugendliche in Deutschland und Österreich im Nationalsozialismus*. Berlin: Verlag für Berlin-Brandenburg, 2007.

Rein, Leonid. "Local Collaboration in the Execution of the 'Final Solution' in Nazi-Occupied Belorussia." *Holocaust and Genocide Studies* 20, no. 3 (Winter 2006): 381–409.

Rentschler, Eric. *The Ministry of Illusion: Nazi Cinema and Its Afterlife*. Cambridge, MA: Harvard University Press, 1996

Requate, Jorg. *Journalismus als Beruf. Entstehung und Entwicklung des Journalistenberufs im 19. Jahrhundert. Deutschland im internationalen Vergleich*. Göttingen: Vandenhoeck und Ruprecht, 1995.

Roberts, Marie Louise. *Disruptive Acts: The New Woman in Fin-de-Siècle France*. Chicago: University of Chicago Press, 2002.

Roseman, Mark. *A Past in Hiding: Memory and Survival in Nazi Germany*. New York: Metropolitan Books, 2001.

Röser, Jutta. *Frauenzeitschriften und weiblicher Lebenszusammenhang: Themen, Konzepte und Leitbilder im sozialen Wandel*. Opladen: Westdeutscher, 1992.

Ross, Corey. *Media and the Making of Modern Germany: Mass Communications, Society, and Politics from the Empire to the Third Reich*. Oxford: Oxford University Press, 2008.

Rothberg, Michael. *The Implicated Subject: Beyond Victims and Perpetrators*. Stanford, CA: Stanford University Press, 2019.

Rothfels, Hans. *The German Opposition to Hitler: An Appraisal*. Hinsdale, IL: H. Regnery, 1948.

Ruault, Franco. *Neuschöpfer des deutschen Volkes: Julius Streicher im Kampf gegen "Rassenschande."* Frankfurt: Lang, 2006.

Rutherford, Jeff. *Combat and Genocide on the Eastern Front: The German Infantry's War, 1941–1944*. New York: Cambridge University Press, 2014.

Rutherford, Phillip T. *Prelude to the Final Solution: The Nazi Program for Deporting Ethnic Poles, 1939–1941*. Lawrence: University Press of Kansas, 2007.

Sachsse, Rolf. *Die Erziehung zum Wegsehen: Fotografie im NS-Staat*. Dresden: Philo & Philo Fine Arts, 2003.

– "Im Schatten der Männer: Deutsche Fotografinnen 1940 bis 1950." In *Frauenobjectiv: Fotografinnen 1940 bis 1950*, 12–25. Cologne: Wienand, 2001.

Sandler, Willeke. *Empire in the Heimat: Colonialism and Public Culture in the Third Reich*. New York: Oxford University Press, 2018.

Scharnberg, Harriet. "Das A und P der Propaganda: Associated Press und die nationalsozialistische Bildpublizistik." *Zeithistorische Forschungen* 1 (2016): 11–37.

Schildt, Axel. *Medien-Intellektuelle in der Bundesrepublik*. Göttingen: Wallstein Verlag, 2020.

Schmid, Sigrun. *Journalisten der frühen Nachkriegszeit: Eine kollektive Biographie am Beispiel von Rheinland-Pfalz*. Cologne: Böhlau, 2000.

Schmoeckel, Mathias. *Die Juristen der Universität Bonn im "Dritten Reich."* Cologne: Böhlau, 2004.

Schoenbaum, David. *Hitler's Social Revolution: Class and Status in Nazi Germany, 1933–1939*. New York: W.W. Norton, 1997.

Schroeder, Steven M. *To Forget It All and Begin Anew: Reconciliation in Occupied Germany, 1944–1954*. Toronto: University of Toronto Press, 2013.

Schwarz, Gudrun. *Eine Frau an seiner Seite: Ehefrauen in der "SS-Sippengemeinschaft."* Hamburg: Hamburger Edition, 1997.

Schwarzer, Alice. *Marion Dönhoff: Ein widerständiges Leben*. Cologne: Kiepenheuer & Witsch, 1996.

Scott, Joan. *Gender and the Politics of History*. New York: Columbia University Press, 1988.

Seegers, Lu. "Walther von Hollander as an Advice Columnist on Marriage and the Family in the Third Reich." In Harvey et al., *Private Life and Privacy in Nazi Germany*, 206–30.

Seidler, Franz W. *Die Organisation Todt: Bauen für Staat und Wehrmacht, 1938–1945*. Koblenz: Bernard & Graefe, 1998.

Semmens, Kristin. *Seeing Hitler's Germany: Tourism in the Third Reich*. New York: Palgrave Macmillan, 2005.

Sereny, Gitta. *Albert Speer: His Battle with Truth*. New York: Vintage, 1995.

– *The German Trauma: Experiences and Reflections, 1938–1999*. London: Allen Lane, 2000.

Seul, Stephanie. "A Female War Correspondent on the Italian Front, 1915–1917: The Austrian Travel Journalist and Photographer Alice Schalek." *Journal of Modern Italian Studies* 21, no. 2 (2016): 220–51.

Shandley, Robert R. *German Cinema in the Shadow of the Third Reich*. Philadelphia: Temple University Press, 2001.

Sheffer, Edith. *Burned Bridge: How East and West Germans Made the Iron Curtain*. New York: Oxford University Press, 2014.

Shephard, Ben. "The Clean Wehrmacht, the War of Extermination, and Beyond." *Historical Journal* (May 2009): 455–73.

– *The Long Road Home: The Aftermath of the Second World War*. New York: Anchor Books, 2010.

Shneer, David. *Through Soviet Jewish Eyes: Photography, War, and the Holocaust*. New Brunswick, NJ: Rutgers University Press, 2011.

Shtyrkina, Olga. *Mediale Schlachtfelder: Die NS-Propaganda gegen die Sowjetunion (1939–1945)*. Frankfurt: Campus Verlag, 2017.

Sitter, Carmen. *"Die eine Hälfte vergisst man(n) leicht!" Zur Situation von Journalistinnen in Deutschland unter besonderer Berücksichtigung des 20. Jahrhunderts*. Pfaffenweiler: Centaurus, 1998.

Smelser, Ronald, and Edward J. Davies II. *The Myth of the Eastern Front: The Nazi-Soviet War in American Popular Culture*. Cambridge: Cambridge University Press, 2008.

Snyder, Timothy. *Bloodlands: Europe between Hitler and Stalin*. New York: Basic Books, 2010.

Sonntag, Christian. *Medienkarrieren: Biografische Studien über Hamburger Nachkriegsjournalisten, 1946–1949*. Munich: Martin Meidenbauer, 2006.

Sösemann, Bernd, and Marius Lange. *Propaganda, Medien und Öffentlichkeit in der NS- Diktatur: Eine Dokumentation und Edition von Gesetzen, Führerbefehlen und sonstigen Anordnungen sowie propagandistischen Bild- und Textüberlieferungen im kommunikatorischen Kontext und in der Wahrnehmung des Publikums*. Stuttgart: Steiner, 2011.

Ständecke, Monika. "Idylle und Wirklichkeit: Landleben im Sucher." In Dippold and Kania-Schütz, *Im Fokus*, 79–106.

Stargardt, Nicholas. *The German War: A Nation under Arms, 1939–1945*. New York: Basic Books, 2015.

Stark, Tricia. *The Body Soviet: Propaganda, Hygiene, and the Revolutionary State*. Madison: University of Wisconsin Press, 2008.

Steber, Martina, and Bernhard Gotto, eds. *Visions of Community in Nazi Germany: Social Engineering and Private Lives*. Oxford: Oxford University Press, 2014.

– *Wie der Sex nach Deutschland kam: Der Kampf um Sittlichkeit und Anstand in der frühen Bundesrepublik*. Munich: Siedler, 2011.

Steiner, Linda. "Failed Theories: Explaining Gender Differences in Journalism." *Review of Communication* 12, no. 3 (2012): 201–23.

Steinweis, Alan E., and Daniel E. Rogers, eds. *The Impact of Nazism: New Perspectives on the Third Reich and Its Legacy*. Lincoln: University of Nebraska Press, 2003.

Stephenson, Jill. *The Nazi Organisation of Women*. London: Croom Helm, 1981.

– *Women in Nazi Germany*. Toronto: Longman, 2001.

– "Women and the Professions in Germany, 1900–1945." In *German Professions, 1800–1950*, edited by Geoffrey Cocks and Konrad Jarausch, 270–88. New York: Oxford University Press, 1990.

Stewart, Mary Lynne. *Gender, Generation, and Journalism in France, 1910–1940*. Montreal and Kingston: McGill-Queen's University Press, 2018.

Stibbe, Matthew. *Women in the Third Reich*. New York: Oxford University Press, 2003.

Stoltzfus, Nathan. *Resistance of the Heart: Intermarriage and the Rosenstrasse Protest in Nazi Germany*. New York: Rutgers University Press, 2001.

Stoltzfus, Nathan, Mordecai Paldiel, and Judith Tydor Baumel-Schwartz, eds. *Women Defying Hitler: Rescue and Resistance under the Nazis*. London: Bloomsbury Academic, 2021.

Stone, Dan. "Genocide as Transgression." *European Journal of Social Theory* 7, no. 1 (2004): 45–65.

Struk, Janina. *Private Pictures: Soldiers' Inside View of War*. London: I.B. Tauris, 2011.

Swett, Pamela E. "Private Life in the People's Economy: Spending and Saving in Nazi Germany." In Harvey, Hürter, and Umbach, *Private Life and Privacy in Nazi Germany*, 135–55.

– *Selling under the Swastika: Advertising and Commercial Culture in Nazi Germany*. Stanford, CA: Stanford University Press, 2014.

Swett, Pamela E., Corey Ross, and Fabrice d'Almeida, eds. *Pleasure and Power in Nazi Germany*. Houndmills, UK: Palgrave Macmillan, 2011.

Szerfozo, Barbara. "Warring Narratives: The Diaries and Memoirs of Lore Walb, Ursula von Kardorff and Margret Boveri." PhD diss., Georgetown University, 2002.

Szobar, Patricia. "Telling Stories in the Nazi Courts of Law: Race Defilement in Germany, 1933–1945." *Journal of the History of Sexuality* 11, nos 1/2 (2002): 131–63.

Tegel, Susan. *Nazis and the Cinema*. London: Continuum Books, 2007.

Tellini, Uta, ed. *Frauenobjektiv: Fotografinnen, 1940 bis 1950*. Cologne: Wienand, 2001.

Thacker, Toby. *The End of the Third Reich: Defeat, Denazification and Nuremberg, January 1944–November 1946*. Stroud, UK: Tempus, 2006.

Thiel, Shayla. "Shifting Identities, Creating New Paradigms." *Feminist Media Studies* 4, no. 1 (2007): 21–36.

Timm, Annette. *The Politics of Fertility in Twentieth-Century Berlin*. New York: Cambridge University Press, 2010.

Timpe, Julia. *Nazi-Organized Recreation and Entertainment in the Third Reich*. London: Palgrave Macmillan, 2017.

Tobin, Patrick. "No Time for 'Old Fighters': Postwar West Germany and the Origins of the 1958 Ulm Einsatzkommando Trial." *Central European History* 44, no. 4 (2011): 684–710.

Tomasevich, Jozo. *War and Revolution in Yugoslavia, 1941–1945*. Stanford, CA: Stanford University Press, 2010.

Tooze, Adam. *The Wages of Destruction: The Making and Breaking of the Nazi Economy*. New York: Penguin, 2007.

Torrie, Julia. *German Soldiers and the Occupation of France, 1940–1944*. Cambridge: Cambridge University Press, 2018.

Turner, Henry Ashby. "Two Dubious Third Reich Diaries." *Central European History* 33, no. 3 (2000): 415–22.

Tworek, Heidi J.S. *News from Germany: The Competition to Control World Communications, 1900–1945*. Cambridge, MA: Harvard University Press, 2019.

Uzulis, André. "'Darf nichts bringen': Eine Nachrichtenagentur im Dritten Reich." In *"Diener des Staates" oder "Widerstand zwischen den Zeilen"? Die Rolle der Presse im Dritten Reich*, edited by Christoph Studt, 107–14. Berlin: Lit, 2007.

– *Nachrichtenagenturen im Nationalsozialismus: Propagandainstrumente und Mittel der Presselenkung*. New York: Lang, 1995.

Viola, Lynne. "Bab'i Bunty and Peasant Women's Protest during Collectivization." *Russian Review* 45, no. 1 (January 1986): 23–42.

Waddington, Lorna. *Hitler's Crusade: Bolshevism and the Myth of the International Jewish Conspiracy*. London: I.B. Tauris, 2007.

Wagner, Johnathan F. "The *Deutsche Zeitung für Canada*: A Nazi Newspaper in Winnipeg." *MHS Transactions*, series 3, no. 33 (1976), http://www.mhs.mb.ca/docs/transactions/3/deutschezeitung.shtml#59.

Wehler, Hans Ulrich. *Das deutsche Kaiserreich, 1871–1918*. Göttingen: Vandenhoeck & Ruprecht, 1973.

Wehr, Laura. *Kamerad Frau? Eine Frauenzeitschrift im Nationalsozialismus*. Regensburg: Roderer, 2002.

Weinberg, Gerhard L. *Hitler's Foreign Policy, 1933–1939: The Road to World War II*. New York: Enigma Books, 2010.

Weinreb, Alice. *Modern Hungers: Food, War, and Germany in the Twentieth Century*. Oxford: Oxford University Press, 2017.

Weiss-Wendt, Anton, and Rory Yeomans, eds. *Racial Science in Hitler's New Europe, 1938–1945*. Lincoln: University of Nebraska Press, 2013.

Welch, David. "Nazi Propaganda and the Volksgemeinschaft: Constructing a People's Community." *Journal of Contemporary History* 29, no. 2 (April 2004): 213–38.

– *Propaganda and the German Cinema, 1933–1945*. London: I.B. Tauris, 2001.

– *The Third Reich: Politics and Propaganda*. London: Routledge, 2002.

Whitaker, Elizabeth Dixon. *Measuring Mamma's Milk: Fascism and the Medicalization of Maternity in Italy*. Ann Arbor: University of Michigan Press, 2009.

Wiesen, Jonathan S. *Creating the Nazi Marketplace: Commerce and Consumption in the Third Reich*. Cambridge: Cambridge University Press, 2011.

Wilcox, Larry D. "Hitler and the Nazi Concept of the Press in the Weimar Republic." *Journal of Newspaper and Periodical History* 2, no. 1 (January 1985): 17–29.

Wildenthal, Lora. *German Women for Empire, 1840–1945*. Durham, NC: Duke University Press, 2001.

Wildt, Michael. *Hitler's Volksgemeinschaft and the Dynamics of Racial Exclusion*. New York: Berghahn, 2012.

–*Volksgemeinschaft als Selbstermächtigung: Gewalt gegen Juden in der deutschen Provinz, 1919 bis 1939*. Hamburg: Hamburger Edition, 2007.

Wilke, Jürgen. *Journalisten und Journalismus in der DDR: Berufsorganisation, Westkorrespondenten,"Der schwarze Kanal."* Cologne: Böhlau, 2007.

– *Presseanweisungen im zwanzigsten Jahrhundert: Erster Weltkrieg–Drittes Reich– DDR*. Cologne: Böhlau, 2007.

Winter, Sebastian. *Geschlechter- und Sexualitätsentwürfe in der SS-Zeitung "Das schwarze Korps": Eine psychoanalytisch-sozialpsychologische Studie*. Gießen: Psychosozial-Verlag, 2013.

Wistrich, Robert S., ed. *Routledge Who's Who in Nazi Germany*. New York: Routledge, 1995.

Wittmann, Rebecca. *Beyond Justice: The Auschwitz Trial*. Cambridge, MA: Harvard University Press, 2005.

Wright, Karin, Martin Scott, and Mel Bunce. "Soft Power, Hard News: How Journalists at State-Funded Transnational Media Legitimize Their Work." *International Journal of Press Politics* 25, no. 4 (2020): 607–31.

Wulf, Joseph. *Presse und Funk im Dritten Reich: Eine Dokumentation*. Gütersloh: S. Mohn, 1964.

Zelizer, Barbie. *Remembering to Forget: Holocaust Memory through the Camera's Eye*. Chicago: University of Chicago Press, 1998.

Zetsche, Anne. *The Atlantik-Brücke and the American Council on Germany, 1952–1974: The Quest for Atlanticism*. London: Palgrave Macmillan, 2021.

Zoonen, Liesbet van. "One of the Girls? The Changing Gender of Journalism." In *News, Gender and Power*, edited by Stuart Allan, Gill Branston, and Cynthia Carter, 33–46. London: Routledge, 1998.

# Index

Page numbers with (f) refer to illustrations

Milton Keynes UK
Ingram Content Group UK Ltd.
UKHW010812150624
444077UK00004B/35/J